Kliman, Bernice W.

Hamlet

$45.00

DATE			

Hamlet

Hamlet

Film, Television, and Audio Performance

Bernice W. Kliman

Rutherford ● Madison ● Teaneck
Fairleigh Dickinson University Press
London and Toronto: Associated University Presses

Associated University Presses
440 Forsgate Drive
Cranbury, NJ 08512

Associated University Presses
25 Sicilian Avenue
London WC1A 2QH, England

Associated University Presses
P.O. Box 488, Port Credit
Mississauga, Ontario
Canada L5G 4M2

Roobol58689

Library of Congress Cataloging-in-Publication Data

Kliman, Bernice W.
    Hamlet : film, television, and audio performance.

    Bibliography: p.
    Includes index.
    1. Shakespeare, William, 1564-1616. Hamlet.
2. Shakespeare, William, 1564–1616—Film and video
adaptations. 3. Shakespeare, William, 1564–1616—Audio
adaptations. I. Title.
PR2807.K57   1988   822.3′3   85-46000
ISBN 0-8386-3290-4 (alk. paper)

Printed in the United States of America

Contents

Part IV: The Spiral of Influence

Preface

This book is for Shakespeare fans, people who not only go to every stage performance they can find but who also stay up until 4:00 A.M. to see even a cut version of Olivier's *Hamlet* on television, and who would be willing to walk any number of miles to see Kozintsev's *Hamlet*—people who love to talk and think about Shakespeare. I would also like to woo Shakespeareans who perhaps feel standoffish toward moving images (film, television, videotape) and sound recordings: the literary scholars who prefer close readings of the text to any production; performance critics who do not value nonstage versions; and media critics who do not consider Shakespeare on film worthy of serious concern as film. To the first, I would like to say that media performances can be a way to get into the text; to the second that these performances share many qualities with stage presentations and often are the only record we have of some very great stage productions; to the third that the best Shakespeare media versions have been notable for their form as well as for their matter, and that the others can nevertheless yield much of interest about form as well as matter. Since, however, I am more likely to be addressing fans, it is to them that I principally speak.

A Note on the Illustrations

I shot all the stills with a Nikon FG directly from television, film, or Steenbeck screens. They illustrate particular moments in the productions better than do publicity stills, which most often are not taken from films but are shot separately by still cameras for publicity purposes. Often, such stills bear only a family resemblance to shots from the film. The quality of stills taken from productions varies considerably because some of the works have already deteriorated significantly, particularly the silent films, but also some of the videotapes and sound films. My stills capture these fragile works at a particular moment in time. I appreciate the advice of Jack J. Jorgens, who also used stills taken from films rather than publicity stills in his book *Shakespeare on Film*.

7

To my family

Acknowledgments

This work builds on the work of many others—scholars and teachers in Shakespeare, film, and theater studies. I am grateful to those who produced the body of work on Shakespeare films that has preceded mine, to Robert Hamilton Ball, who brought filmed Shakespeare into the mainstream of modern scholarship with his monumental history of *Shakespeare on Silent Film* (1968), to Roger Manvell, who in *Shakespeare and the Film* (1971) showed that discussions of films could usefully combine insightful description with revelations from behind the scenes and who produced a most readable general history, and to Jack J. Jorgens, whose dictum in *Shakespeare on Film* (1977) I have tried to follow: "We ought," he says, "to remain open to as many different kinds of excellence in Shakespeare films as possible" (15). My work differs from theirs both in narrowing the focus to one play and in broadening the scope to more than one medium, including television and audio recordings as well as both silent and sound films. Moreover, my purpose—to demonstrate the connectedness among theater, moving image, and sound recordings—led me to select for examination details somewhat different from theirs and to use those details in different ways.

"Shakespeare on film" is a discipline not only because of the efforts of Ball, Manvell, and Jorgens but also because of other scholars such as Thomas L. Erskine and James M. Welsh, whose *Literature/Film Quarterly* encouraged many to turn to the scholarly examination of Shakespeare on film; Harry M. Geduld, whose *Filmguide to Henry V* (1973) first demonstrated what could be accomplished by meticulous attention to a film's details; and others, such as Lillian Wilds and Jay Halio, who wrote important early articles.

Like so many, I am grateful to Charles Shattuck for his *The Shakespeare Promptbooks*, which led me to the riches at the Folger and other libraries. I appreciate the libraries where I read promptbooks and scripts as well as screened films on Steenbeck editors and listened to sound recordings:

9

first in fact and affection, the Folger Shakespeare Library, whose Shakespeare Collection and Film Archives are unmatched; also the Library of Congress Moving Picture and Recorded Sound Division, the UCLA Theater Collection and the UCLA/ATAS Film Archives, the Huntington Library, the Library of the British Film Institute, the film archives at The Museum of Modern Art, The Museum of Broadcasting, the Furness Library at the University of Pennsylvania, the Library of the Performing Arts at Lincoln Center, and the Library at Nassau Community College, which supplied me with all the secondary sources I needed. Candace Bothwell, the film archivist at the Folger, and Sam Brylawski, the audio archivist at the Library of Congress, deserve special mention among the many helpful professionals who assisted me.

My personal thanks to Coleman O. Parsons, who several years ago guided my doctoral dissertation and who kindly read and commented on an early manuscript of the present work, and to Marion Perret, whose comments and suggestions at various stages have been unfailingly helpful. I wish also to thank my colleagues in the writing group at Nassau Community College who have listened and responded to various parts of this work.

I am grateful also for the friendship of Kenneth S. Rothwell whose early articles on Shakespeare films in the *Literature/Film Quarterly* inspired our collaboration on the *Shakespeare on Film Newsletter*, which we co-founded in 1976 and continue to co-edit. I wish also to thank Michael Mullin, who nurtured my fledgling effort in the field, for the seminar at MLA he chaired in December 1976; and Davenport College, Yale University, for opportunities to teach "Film from Fiction" and "Shakespeare on Film" in the college seminar program.

I also thank the State University of New York for a summer research grant that enabled me to visit libraries and archives in Washington and California and the National Endowment for the Humanities for the summer fellowship to attend the Institute on Shakespeare in Performance at the Folger Library, led by Bernard Beckerman. My thanks also to Nassau Community College for the sabbatical leave that allowed me to begin the manuscript.

Though I have used many texts in conjunction with my examination of the various productions—generally for each production a different pocket text on which I could indicate cuts, tone, business, and from which I quote for those films, I am especially indebted to Vietor's *Hamlet Parallel Texts*, whose version of F1 I have quoted wherever convenient, and several helpful editions, such as *The Riverside Shakespeare*, the Norton *Hamlet*, and the Craig/Bevington *Shakespeare*.

I have, in the notes, indicated my indebtedness to the many works to which I refer. Still I know that many people who have influenced my thinking over the last ten years are omitted because their work has so become part of the fabric of my mind that I cannot recollect the particular debts I owe them; I am certain that works I have not cited were nevertheless models for my efforts. One I can mention here with appreciation is Maynard Mack's essay "The World of Hamlet," which helpd form my perceptions of the play. I regret any omissions.

Harry Keyishian of Fairleigh Dickinson Press, the kindest and most patient of editors, helped me sort out many tangles; the text is clearer than it would have been without him. All remaining muddles are my own. Film study is particularly chastening because one has memory and notes but often not the artifact itself. I know that at times I have recollected details that are not there. I hope I have caught most of these.

Finally I come to my husband, Merwin, who did not type the manuscript but who helped me choose a word processor on which I could type it, who was willing to read bits and pieces of the work in progress and provide his refreshing layman's view, and whose support and love encourages me always.

Portions of chapters have previously been published in different forms:

"The BBC *Hamlet*, a Television Production," *Hamlet Studies* 4 (1982): 99–105.
"Kozintsev's *Hamlet*, A Flawed Masterpiece," *Hamlet Studies* 1.2 (1979): 117–28.
"Olivier's *Hamlet*: A Film Infused Play," *Literature/Film Quarterly* 5.4 (1977): 305–14.
"The Setting in Early Television: Maurice Evans' Shakespeare Productions." In *Shakespeare and the Arts: A Collection of Essays from the Ohio Shakespeare Conference, 1981 Wright State University*, edited by Cecile Williamson Cary and Henry S. Limouze. Washington, D.C.: University Press of America, 1982.
"The Spiral of Influence: One Defect in *Hamlet*," *Literature/Film Quarterly* 11:3 (1983): 159–66.

I wish to thank the editors of *Literature/Film Quarterly* and *Hamlet Studies* and the University Press of America for permission to use this material.

Introduction

The first *Hamlet* I saw was Olivier's on film when I was fifteen years old. I went to see it four or five times. It descended to subliminal levels, and when I studied *Hamlet* later, I "knew" certain truths about it deep in my being. I knew that "To be" had to precede the players' arrival; it made sense only that way, because how could Hamlet move from the exuberant joy of "The play's the thing / Wherein I'll catch the conscience of the king" to the despair of "To be, or not to be"? I also "knew" that Hamlet loved Ophelia but that she, weak and immature, disappointed him; that a queer sort of relationship between Hamlet and his mother was at the root of Hamlet's problem; that Horatio was a noble fellow, fit to be king after Hamlet; that Polonius was awfully silly, a little senile, in fact; that the ghost was to be pitied.

I no longer "know" these things in the same way. I see all of Olivier's interpretations as choices, not textual givens. Now I realize, for example, that exuberant joy is just one of Hamlet's possible reactions to "The Mousetrap" idea. On the contrary, Hamlet could be aware that Claudius, perceiving him to know of the poisoning, might kill him before he can avenge his father. Hamlet's awareness could evoke not despair but a reasoned philosophical meditation on death—such as some find in the "To be" soliloquy. Though I recognize many more choices than I did when I was fifteen, fondness for Olivier's work inspires this study of performances of *Hamlet*, which will examine the texts for the choices they afford in production and media performances for those they have made. By "texts," singular or plural, I mean those printed versions that performances use as scripts.

Hamlet is an ideal focus for a study of media performances, both because what is true for this play will apply to others as well and because *Hamlet* presents deliciously knotty puzzles—to which there can be no final solutions but to which each production offers its own temporary answers. Since so many productions have been mounted in the last eighty years, including many moving-image productions since 1948, *Hamlet* offers a complex and varied body of performance samples. All its fabricators—on stage, on screen, on radio, and on recordings—make choices. But no set of choices can reconcile all inconsistencies. Such a proliferation of explanations as has grown up for *Hamlet* suggests there is no tidy explanation. By making choices possible for readers, playgoers, viewers and listeners, *Hamlet*'s open-endedness inspires the collaborative imagination and stimulates investigation.

I choose to study media productions of *Hamlet* not only because of their inherent appeal to one who teethed on them but also because film and television, that is, moving images, more and more are the media of presentation for Shakespeare's plays. While theatrical performances are also alive and well, more people will see a particular audio-visual production than will attend a whole run of a theatrical production—in which one may often detect influences from film and television. People raised in our milieu of audio-visual media have been influenced by that contact, and this includes stage directors.

Significantly, it is also true that most moving-image directors of Shakespeare plays have had stage experience, sometimes extensive and primary experience. While modern stage productions make allusions to moving images as well as to previous stage productions, the converse is also true: audio-visual media depend on stage as well as on previous audio-visual productions. Audio-visual performances, as well as modern stage performances, can connect us to the stage tradition that has nurtured both. This is true regardless of the differences among the performance vehicles: stage, moving image, and sound recording. Productions of Shakespeare's texts in all media demonstrate conventional cuts, business, and characterizations; theatrical conventions, for good and ill, inform media productions. Though each performance, with its many unique elements, has autonomy, just as each human being is unique in spite of genetic resemblances to forebears, it is illuminating to explore the links among these performance forms. Since Professor Arthur Colby Sprague has already detailed much of traditional stage business up to the early twentieth century, I will limit my references to stage productions contemporaneous with the twentieth-century media that have been and remain viable.

While productions can be studied, of course, independently of tradition and independently of the texts, they yield more when studied in conjunction with both. The makers (actors, directors, and set designers) interpret the texts by choosing some of the text's possibilities and rejecting others. Examining many different performances, I can see many more of the choices that the texts offer than I would see if I were to examine the texts alone. Even when a performance reshapes a text— perhaps distorting it, perhaps delving for an essential "truth" in the text—it can lead me to question why Shakespeare did not make that choice and thus to approach Shakespeare's intention or meaning. Whatever a production does, Shakespeare remains inviolable; the texts are there for anyone to read and interpret.

But to look at performances only to see what they tell us about Shakespeare would be unfair to the artistic integrity of the makers. They create works that have value in themselves, as is evident from the fact that audiences that have had no contact with Shakespeare's text go to see productions, such as Olivier's *Hamlet*, and respond to them as independent works of art. Just as it would be limiting to read *Hamlet* only as a tool for clarifying its source *Amleth*, so too it would be limiting to use modern productions only to look backwards. While no Shakespeare users have transcended their source as he transcended *his* sources, respect must be paid. Every change that directors make from the text helps to clarify their intentions.

Texts, moreover, being blueprints for performance, are, of course, in themselves incomplete. Performance choices point up that incompleteness, which otherwise might be unnoticed as readers unconsciously fill in the gaps without realizing that they are doing so. The texts, for example, determine that Ophelia is distracted, but directors and actors can choose just how this madness will be expressed. Her clothes may be in disarray or inappropriate, echoing Hamlet's method of show-

The Olivier *Hamlet*. Ophelia says, "Pray you, love, remember" as she places an herb on Hamlet's chair. *(Still courtesy Janus Films.)*

ing his pretended or real madness, or they may be ripped, presaging violence, as in the 1982 Papp production. She may be strident or sweetly pathetic or matter-of-fact, wispy or harsh, sad or happy, openly sexual or demure. She may have flashes of sanity or be totally insane. We have only Laertes's clue that she makes madness pretty—in the second mad scene, not the first. Her action in this scene should, most feel, correlate with her demeanor in other scenes. The shot that has Jean Simmons, for example, say "Pray you, love, remember" (4.5.175) most touchingly as she places a dried weed on the arm of Hamlet's chair—clear-minded for a brief moment—establishes, in Olivier's *Hamlet*, Ophelia's love for Hamlet as the probable cause of her madness, softens our perception of her earlier betrayal of him, and deepens the irony of Hamlet's emotional display at the graveside scene.

Performances offer possibilities for closure, completeness, and definiteness as the texts cannot. They *anchor* the text. Performances seldom obfuscate because the velocity of concomitant forces blurs the many choices into singleness—like twenty-four frames per second coalescing into one vision. But no performance is an archetype of the *Hamlet* Shakespeare intended, any more than a performance can be the embodiment of the conception in the director's mind: too many factors fall out of control. Only in broad outline can a performance be deemed an incarnation of an ideal. Performance-centered criticism helps us avoid arbitrarily freezing an indeterminate text by reminding us that the texts contain an infinity of performances.

Not all interpretations can coexist, but if the director-juggler can keep several balls in the air at once, we feel he or she reflects something close to the complexity of the texts. The reader has little difficulty doing this juggling act; this is one of the factors that, for some, makes the theater of the mind more satisfying than live performances. In its relation to the texts, a fully saturated performance, one that reveals a plenitude of possible interpretations, can compete with this mental theater. A production can, for example, suggest that Hamlet and Ophelia are lovers and yet withhold final confirmation.

In the performance of the mind, one almost always shapes a unified work of art by subordinating recalcitrant aspects, for *Hamlet* is, in truth, not a unified work. The eighteenth-century resurgence of classicism gave rise to a desire for unity that still exists today. Much of what is in *Hamlet*, however, has little to do with the tragic action, but is an amplification to demonstrate "the atmosphere, the situation, and the prehistory of the characters" (Auerbach, 281). When seeing a performance, I hope for unity and yet recognize that there are irreconcilable discrepancies in the play. The great thing is seeing how many facets of the text performances can sandblast into clarity. What a performance chooses to clarify is in itself significant.

Performances tell us something about the time they were conceived, about social beliefs and conventions—anachronistically displaying conventions of the 1950s, for example, in the 1980s and 1990s. Often, the conventions of our own time are transparent to us. Unlike stage productions, which, except for some promptbooks and the occasional book-length study, remain limited to their own time (unless indeed they are filmed or taped), film and television productions—and potentially radio productions and audio recordings—can be brought back again and again for study and comparison in a way that stage productions can not.

Performances can also tell us about the limits of their medium. Comparisons of stage, screen (film and television) and audio productions reveal that the medium dictates some choices, while other choices may have little or nothing to do with the medium, resulting instead from the director's interpretation. Understanding the difference helps one to see what is unique about each medium. The medium determines set design, for example, but not costume.

Comparative studies are absolutely essential. The historical constraints of time, place and condition on the perceived and the perceiver limit what is knowable. Those choices which seem time-bound and those which seem to some extent time-free stand out from each other when we put the 1913 Forbes Robertson film, for example, next to the Olivier *Hamlet*. Diachronic realizations, performances from different time periods, bring *Hamlet*'s multiplicity into focus. The only hope we have to know anything about Shakespeare's text or a performance of that text is to compare two or more of these ungraspable artifacts (because we cannot notice everything about them) and by their differences and similarities come upon something we can accept as true. This is something like what the nuclear physicist does, studying in cloud chambers the nature of almost incomprehensible particles by the tracks left of their collision with other incomprehensible particles.

Each performance isolates a set of choices, but there are so many variables within each performance, each with its larger or smaller effect, that no one would or could explicate, that is, codify the performance object. (Perhaps only Barthes had the standing to explicate a work line by line as he did in *S/Z*, and even so, he left much out.) Instead, the critic must make a flying leap into generalization, based on selected examples. Interpretation, fortunately, is not only a cognitive activity. The plunge beyond cognition towards an intuitive or gestalt grasp of the whole—either as it passes in the stream of time or afterwards—depends on the critic's felt and remembered response. A performance unfolds in time but then is recalled as a whole or as a set of parts: emotion recollected in tranquility and recreated. I am as interested in the recollection as I am in the actual production because a performance, even one captured on tape or film, is ephemeral.

Hamlet

Part I

Hamlet on Stage, Page, and Screen

Though Olivier's *Hamlet* is indeed a film, it attempts to capture the atmosphere of the stage; therefore, it is a good place to begin a discussion of the links among the media and particularly the close connections of moving images and sound recordings to the theater. The first chapter looks through the film to find the play within it. The second chapter examines a particular feature of the texts—exits and entrances—to explore the performance possibilities. The third chapter considers cuts, especially those in a version of the play that was cut relatively little, the BBC-TV production, not only to determine the effect of cuts on character interpretation in a specific production but also to speculate about the opportunities those lines afforded Shakespeare; thus again, this is a study of text, as well as of a media production. The fact that almost all the cuts in the television *Hamlet* follow traditional patterns of stage and film cuts demonstrates at the same time the connections of tradition and convention among the media. The fourth chapter turns to the most filmic of all *Hamlet* adaptations, Kozintsev's *Hamlet*, to note how visualizations convert the play into a moving image.

1

Laurence Olivier's *Hamlet*

Since Laurence Olivier brought Shakespeare into the modern era with *Henry V* in 1944, he has explored the relationship between theater and film in all his Shakespeare films. For *Henry V* he devised the Globe prologue, the fiction that the film was a re-creation of a staging of the play in 1600. As the scene widened out, he retained reminders of the stage setting in virtually every scene by relying on flat, obviously painted scenery, with roly-poly tree tops and settings based on the *Hours* of the Duc de Berry. At the end he returned to the Globe. For *Richard III* (1955), he built a large unit setting, which placed each scene within a few steps of every other scene, creating theatrical rather than filmic verisimilitude. *Othello* (1965), not directed by Olivier but certainly influenced by him, seemed an actual stage performance, though the setting was specially built for the film. In *Hamlet* (1948), the relationship between stage and film was somewhat more complicated; the film is a hybrid form, not a filmed play, not precisely a film, but a film-infused play or a play-infused film, a form Olivier conceived as being the best possible for presenting the heightened language of Shakespeare. Thoroughly and consciously in every detail he applies his first purpose: to use film both to suggest and to transcend the modern stage, through setting, acting, and lighting.[1] At the same time his second purpose is to express, through additions and transpositions, his own substantive interpretation of plot and character, an interpretation which could have been managed on stage, but which is clarified by the possibilities of film.

Film to Suggest and Transcend the Stage

Olivier announces his first purpose near the start of the film by a visual inventory, repeated near the end, of the important symbols and locations of the play, with appropriate musical themes. Even more, the very beginning of the film, with a sound of the orchestra warming up, suggests a play more than a film. In a third framing device, an overhead shot of a jarringly unrealistic model of Elsinore dissolves to a closeup of the topmost platform of the castle, with a tableau of Horatio and the four soldiers bearing Hamlet's body on a pallet, his sword making a cross on his body, a shot held for a few moments before dissolving to show only the empty platform. At the film's end, Olivier shows Horatio in silhouette with the others bearing "Hamlet like a soldier to the stage," almost, but not quite, returning to the earlier shot on the platform. However cinematic in actual execution, these self-conscious elements warn the audience to modify its expectations, to accept the work as a blend of film and play.

Why then did not Olivier simply film a play? Obviously he wanted to free himself from two of the restrictions of stage: space and perspective. His sets, for example, can be explained by the fact that he sees film as Shaw did—as a way to expand theater. Olivier is like Eisenstein, who, in those last efforts before he finally turned to films altogether, staged plays in giant warehouses or factories, moving audiences around on stairways and catwalks to avoid the static perspective of the fixed seat. With film,

The Olivier *Hamlet*. The large, empty set for the nunnery scene. (*Still courtesy Janus Films.*)

Olivier opens up space and moves the audience without losing the theatrical essence of nonrealistic space.

Setting

First he expands theater by creating a set too mammoth to fit any known theater. But it is still very much a stage set, with movable stairways and pillars and halls paced out exactly to match each character's lines. Carmen Dillon, who built the sets, says that they leaned on theatrical tradition for set design: "sets soar into the sky without any attempt at persuading the audience that they do, in fact, support a roof or that they have any geographical relationship with one another" (Cross, 44). Sets change dramatically to fit the mood even in the same location: the walls of the room where Hamlet sits on his chair are dispensed with for the scene when the players arrive; curtains suddenly appear on arches so that Polonius and Claudius may hide behind them. Extremely abstract, suggestive, and symbolic sets are not of course totally foreign to film— from *The Cabinet of Dr. Caligari* to Welles's *Macbeth*—but such sets are not in the mainstream of film art.[2] Olivier's setting provides the connected space of a stage set, rather than the disjunctive space of film. Even in

The Olivier *Hamlet*. Gertrude looks at the poisoned cup. *(Still courtesy Janus Films.)*

Caligari and *Macbeth*, space is discontinuous, made so by crosscuts in parallel time from one space to another. But Olivier's spaces all flow into each other. Even when he crosscuts (for example, from Polonius, Claudius and Gertrude plotting the "unloosing" to Hamlet overhearing; or from Horatio reading Hamlet's letter to Laertes arguing with Claudius; or from Claudius plotting with Laertes to the very different communication of Hamlet and Horatio), Olivier is careful to keep the spaces between the crosscuts unified. He connects the spaces with his moving camera and through deep-focus photography.

The emptiness of these sets (and the absence of the amenities of daily life) certainly runs counter to cinematic convention. Elaborate realistic sets are possible in the theater, just as bare or symbolic sets are possible on film, but verisimilitude, details, artifacts of daily life seem to provide the most satisfying background for film. On the other hand, largely empty or suggestive and symbolic sets have seemed best for Shakespearean plays, at least since William Poel (1852–1934) and Gordon Craig (1872–1966). Following theatrical style, and contrary to film realism, Olivier chose an empty set—though with architectural elements decorated and deeply textured.

Second, he expands theater with his traveling, tracking camera. Olivier can move his audience anywhere he wants them in this immense set, near or far from his action. Deep focus seems to allow us to see all the actions and reactions in a shot, not merely those of the major figures, just as we view blocking on a stage set.[3] In reality, however, the director guides the viewer's attention in both media. The camera movements, for which he has sometimes been criticized according to Jorgens (211), can be understood as a device to push against theatrical constraint and also to push against the naturalism of the film medium.[4] With every obvious camera movement or cut or dissolve or unfocusing of the lens, Olivier reminds us of artifice, working against the inherent naturalism of film with film's own techniques. Thus he has overcome two limits of theater— the limits of space and of the fixed point of view—without sacrificing the feeling of theater.

Discontinuous space in film has a good deal to do with conveying time and rhythm. Both stage time, which is close to real time, and film time may convey realism. But when in a film we see a character walking in a city, next a plane taking off, next the character arriving in another city, then driving a car through some rural landscape—when we see all these in less time than it takes to read these words, something has happened not only to space but also to time. Perhaps that is why the images on film seem always to be timeless or in the immediate present tense. In a stage set, on the other hand, continuous space usually corresponds to continuous time. On stage, in each scene, there is a flow of time. Time can move either slowly or quickly, but there is a sense of time passing. When the scene changes, there can be a gap of time or not, but *within* each scene there is flow. With aural and visual transitions, Olivier rushes events along in a continual flow. At the end of the disclosure scene in which Horatio and the others tell Hamlet about the ghost, music begins, a relentless driving sound interspersed with bells. A fade ends the scene, but the music continues, and as the next scene (1.4) begins, ascending music sweeps us to the top of the set. The bells give point to the lines: "I think it lacks of twelve." "No, it is struck" (1.4.4–5). We have heard it strike. Thus the two scenes are linked in spite of the fade. Often the music used at the very end of one scene continues into the next scene and then stops. There are musical accompaniments during scenes, as with the "too, too solid flesh" soliloquy, and there is music as an intrinsic part of the play, as in "The Mousetrap" and at Claudius's and Gertrude's processionals. But most often, Olivier uses music to link scenes. Altogether, the 155-minute film contains fifty minutes of William Walton's music. Although today music is no longer a customary part of stage performance, it does provide in Olivier's film the sense of flow normally associated with the theater.

Visual connections reinforce this sense of continuity in time and space. Ophelia, for example, puts the herb on the arm of Hamlet's chair in her second mad scene, and when Claudius and Laertes return inside after the funeral, the herb is still there. Without calling undue attention to this, the camera brings us close enough to notice it, and we realize that only a short time has passed. Thus, the sequences are made to flow together as they might on stage, through aural, visual, and spatial devices intrinsic to film.[5]

Acting

The stylized sets form a suitably nonrealistic background for the flow that Olivier creates, and they also provide a setting appropriate for stage acting. Roger Manvell has pointed out the stagelike blocking of characters (41). In a film the camera will usually focus attention naturally, through closeups, two-shots, three-shots, and their variants. On stage, of course, blocking and acting will focus attention. In the film, Olivier consistently uses both techniques. First the characters move together or apart as on stage; then the camera will close in or move away as on film. In the play-within-the-play scene a camera mounted on a circular track behind "The Mousetrap" audience gives us continual groupings of Claudius and Gertrude, of Horatio and others watching Claudius, of Hamlet with Ophelia, of the players. The music keeps up a complicated harmony with the various groupings as each reacts overtly and obviously—one is tempted to say excessively—to the unfolding of the play and its aftermath. Stage acting, along with medium shots and closeups, provides us with clues like the heaving of Gertrude's bosom in the last scene when she eyes first the cup of wine, then Claudius, and then the cup of wine again. In the expanse and distance of the theater, the audience might not notice her silent ratiocination and determination, particularly while an exciting duel is in progress. Through the film device of the medium shot, Olivier forces us to notice. Yet his means for giving us the information is not the film means of juxtaposition. Eisenstein, for example, would probably have had an extreme closeup of wide eyes, then a closeup of the cup.[6] Olivier has a medium shot with the cup held by a courtier in left foreground and Gertrude just beyond. Through shots that require acting, Olivier reminds us of the stage.

The film has a feeling of emptiness in most scenes not only because of the sparse sets but also because of the few supporting actors, who, when present, seem to lack a life of their own. Their whole attention is absorbed by the main characters. In most films, Kozintsev's *Hamlet* being a case in point, such figures seem to lead their own lives. However appropriate—because they are courtiers and Claudius is king—that the extras pay attention to Claudius, their poses come from the stage, rather than the cinema.

Lighting

Film generally relies on natural light or the illusion of natural light. Olivier's lighting recalls the theater, particularly the spotlights on certain actions. During Ophelia's reverie about Hamlet's visit to her chamber (the second tableau, 2.1.76–100), after beginning with a full light on Ophelia, who faces the camera, sewing, a tight spot centers on her face, leaving all else in darkness. The spot opens slightly to include Hamlet as he enters, finally spreading out to full frame again. The sequence ends in the same way, first a spot and then a fully lit view of Ophelia as at the beginning. The portion within the framing device of the spotlight, Olivier suggests, is Ophelia's mental, subjective recollection of Hamlet's visit. In another sequence, a spotlight catches Hamlet when he leaps to the stage, flinging his arms wide and crying out: "The play's the thing / Wherein I'll catch the conscience of the king." Elsewhere, as in the arrival of the players, Claudius at prayer, and Hamlet and Horatio waiting for the fencing match to begin, spotlights illuminate the hair, face, or body of the actors in an otherwise darkened setting. The spots, while certainly effective, remind us of the theatricality of the film. Thus setting (space and time), acting, and lighting consistently come from a theatrical tradition.

Interpretation

Film devices also make a significant contribution to Olivier's interpretation of plot and characters. But his interpretation has little to do with the tragic flaw concept taken from the second ghost vigil and inserted at the beginning as a prologue: "So oft it chances in particular men, / That for some vicious mole of nature in them, / . . . His virtues else, be they as pure as grace / . . . Shall in the general censure take corruption / From that particular fault" (1.4.23–36), and ending with the statement of theme: "This is the tragedy of a man who could not make up his mind."[7] Rather, Hamlet's feelings about Gertrude and Ophelia are the centers of his motivation.[8] The notorious Freudian interpretation, carried over from the 1937 Old Vic production, is muted because Ophelia in the film has become as important to Hamlet as is his mother. Olivier's Hamlet is a man made sick with disgust by his mother's lustful insensitivity in her "o'er hasty" marriage to the inferior Claudius. When Ophelia, whom he has loved, disappoints him, his rage extends to her also. Helpless to obey the ghost's command for revenge, sunk in melancholy, he plays at madness until he chances on the stratagem of "The Mousetrap." With his melancholia transformed into action, the turning point takes place in his mother's closet, when he can at last unburden himself of his revulsion and loathing for her sensuality. (No wonder he is so easily distracted from killing Claudius; his wish to confront his mother, and not cowardice or excessive thinking, motivates him.) From the moment he plunges the sword into Polonius until after the graveyard scene, he behaves impulsively, actively.[9] But when we see him again with Horatio, he has changed. He is, like Horatio, a man who will not be Fortune's fool. Though for Ophelia it is too late, he can at the grave openly admit his love for her because he has resolved his feelings about his mother. At the fencing match he seems serene, ready to accept his fate, whatever it is. Through omissions, additions and transpositions, Olivier molds the play to serve his purpose of smoothing out Hamlet's progression toward serenity.

Omissions

Olivier's cuts serve his design. In fact, there is nothing left out that would have benefited his plans, though a few details remain—like the advice to the players, with the camera's loving perusal of the props—that are only incidental. Olivier's omission of Rosencrantz and Guildenstern reduces the constraints on Hamlet's behavior. He does not seem to be hemmed in by spies or even by casual courtiers, as he is in the Kozintsev film. The absence of Fortinbras eliminates an important parallel to

Hamlet, a son who turns from revenge but who could represent military valor and, at the end, political stability. All these omissions serve Olivier well because these characters do little to intensify the woman-centered motivation. In fact, they would detract from his interpretation. Although he says he had to eliminate them simply to shorten the film, their absence serves him. The preproduction script, though cutting Fortinbras, did nevertheless plan a fourteen-shot sequence for scene 4.4. Its subsequent elimination forced the removal of "How all occasions do inform against me," a soliloquy Olivier says he tried to keep but cut in the end when "it just would not play." One reason it no longer "played" is that it would have broken the smooth curve of Hamlet's development in Olivier's conception. Hamlet is on an upward course leading to his quiet apotheosis just before the fencing match. Olivier also omits the earlier "O what a rogue and peasant slave am I," ostensibly because the player's speech about Hecuba is gone. But again, it does not fit Olivier's Hamlet, who comes out of a morass of inaction after Polonius announces the players' arrival and Hamlet sees how he can use them. His immediate response is a clipped and pointed "He that plays the king shall be welcome." This line, which in the text is buried within a whole passage (2.2.306–12) but which in the film is spoken by itself, indicates that, as soon as the players are announced, Hamlet thinks of "The Mousetrap." Because he instantly translates his idea into action (in the next scene in the film he advises the players, 3.2), there is no need to berate himself for inaction.

Additions

Since Olivier felt he had to make a film less than three hours long, the viewer might not expect additions. Most of them indeed operate concurrently with the other aspects and take up little time. The additions at the opening of the film and the music have already been discussed. The most provocative additions are the living tableaux. Unnaturalistic and stagy, with their softened outlines and disembodied voices, Olivier's tableaux can be produced very easily on film. One can imagine an ingenious nineteenth-century stage director trying his hand at the stream for Ophelia (a technical problem not unlike that posed by Little Liza and the ice floes), and though it might be difficult to produce the pirate ships, it could be done, as it was in Joseph Papp's production of *The Pirates of Penzance.* But if Olivier adds them to provide yet another element to remind us of the stage—while furthering his plot—he is out of date, such tableaux having gone out of style after Sir Herbert Beer-bohm Tree abandoned His Majesty's Theatre before World War I.[10]

A further problem with the tableaux is a blurring of point of view, particularly in the last one. Olivier attempts to express the tableaux as mental pictures in the first three scenes but not in the fourth. In the first instance, the ghost tells Hamlet about the murder, Hamlet closes his eyes, and then we see the tableau. At the end there is a dissolve to Hamlet's face, his eyes still closed, the implication being that the tableau is his mental picture. The use of spotlights as a framing device in the second tableau, Hamlet's visit to Ophelia's closet, has already been discussed. In the third, Hamlet's voice covers both the scene of Horatio reading Hamlet's letter and the dissolve into the tableau, the pirate adventure. Since no closeup of Horatio's forehead signals the point of view clearly as in the first tableau, the images we are seeing in the tableau might be Horatio's or Hamlet's mental projection. The tableau of Ophelia's drowning, however, is not clearly an imaginative construction by any character. When we see the screen exactly mirroring the words we hear, we accept what we see as objective reality. What we see on the screen, in other words, we tend to accept as absolute and nonsubjective truth—not reality as filtered through the consciousness or psychology of a particular character, unless film techniques press a point of view. The fourth tableau, with narration by Gertrude, has no frame of reference, no view of the person whose perceptions we are seeing; Ophelia sings from within the tableau and Laertes responds to Gertrude. More importantly, the tableaux pose a problem because, unlike Kozintsev's interpolations, which are mostly mimed, the tableaux include the text. The images

The Olivier *Hamlet*. Hamlet overhears the plot to use Ophelia to spy on him. *(Still courtesy Janus Films.)*

merely reflect the words, making them redundant. They may also be objected to on grounds of sheer lack of artistry and tact. Do we really want to see that funny looking King Hamlet (possibly Olivier himself)? In my opinion, of all the effects that Olivier tried, they alone can be judged as failures.

Transpositions

Even more revealing of Olivier's interpretation than the omissions and additions are the transpositions. Olivier creates flow and clarity by grouping scenes that are separated in Shakespeare, scenes that unwind a single narrative thread. Alan Dent in the published text of the film points out that the transpositions are "deeply and carefully considered experiments." The first occurs when, after the "too, too solid flesh" soliloquy (1.2.129–59), Hamlet sinks into his chair. The camera, which had been tracking him throughout, comes around, revealing the passage to Ophelia's chamber behind him. The camera moves down this corridor, taking us to her bright apartment as we hear Ophelia's music. The scene of Laertes advising Ophelia follows (1.3), partly in the chamber, partly on a balcony beyond the apartment, and finishing at the end of the same corridor. When Polonius forbids her to speak to Hamlet, he has

The Olivier *Hamlet*. Hamlet sees Ophelia before the nunnery scene. (*Still courtesy Janus Films.*)

noticed Hamlet sitting far down the long hall, but Polonius enters the apartment before Hamlet has noticed him. Ophelia remains immediately outside, looking down the long hall towards the darkened area where Hamlet sits. Hamlet raises his head, looks to his right, and sees her. She looks yearningly towards him, but when her father sharply calls her in, she enters the apartment. Hamlet's arms, which had been slightly lifted, fall. He does not see Polonius, only Ophelia's rejection of him. Then Horatio, Marcellus, and Bernardo arrive to tell him of the ghost (1.2.160–end); immediately afterwards they meet to confront the spirit (1.4).

Robert Duffy points out that by this transposition, placing Ophelia's scene before Horatio comes to tell Hamlet about the ghost, Olivier can establish a contrast between the symbolic darkness surrounding Hamlet and the airy lightness associated with Ophelia (147–48). More importantly perhaps, Olivier connects her with his dejection over his mother's betrayal of both him and his father by the placement of Ophelia's scene right after Hamlet's dismal acknowledgment, "It is not, nor it cannot come to good. / But break my heart, for I must hold my tongue," and by the extreme long shot from Ophelia's apartment back to Hamlet at the end of the scene, and from his point of view back to her. An ordinary stage could not convey the distance and yet the attraction between them. Olivier proudly calls it "the longest distance love scene on record."

In Shakespeare there is nothing to connect Hamlet with Ophelia from his point of view, only from hers. Because Olivier sees the problems with women at the heart of Hamlet's tragedy, he wants to make clear that Hamlet loves her and that she does not respond to him, though she wants to. Also, in the play, since time must pass between the disclosure about the ghost and the vigil and since the characters on stage for both are the same, Shakespeare inserts the Ophelia scene. With film, there is no problem indicating the passage of time, because a dissolve or fade and a change of light can accomplish it. These are standard conventions of film. More importantly, by placing Horatio's information about the ghost before Ophelia's scene, Shakespeare gives Hamlet something to do, thus dissipating for a time Hamlet's depressed mood. Shakespeare's Hamlet is altogether more complex than Olivier's. Olivier does not change Hamlet's moods as much as Shakespeare does, nor does he have as many. The transposition, in other words, is motivated by Olivier's interpretation. Film merely helps him to make connections between Hamlet and Ophelia that are not in the text.

Another transposition shows how Olivier smooths out Shakespeare's plot. In the film, after the fishmonger segment (2.2.170–213), Ophelia is "unloosed" to encounter Hamlet.[11] Olivier chooses J. Dover Wilson's interpretation (106), having Hamlet overhear Polonius talking to Claudius and Gertrude, something very easy to do in film with a crosscut from Hamlet's point of view and then another cut back to the plotters. On stage we would have to accept (and of course we would) the convention of a Hamlet that the audience can see, but who is unnoticed by the other characters—though the device seems more appropriate to comedy than to tragedy, as in *Twelfth Night*, when Malvolio finds his letter while others watch. Even Othello's pain when he eavesdrops on Iago and Cassio does not prevent the scene on stage from having comic overtones. After the confrontation between Hamlet and Ophelia, Olivier omits her soliloquy, "O what a noble mind is here o'erthrown," perhaps as too rational for a girl on the edge of madness.[12] This declaration, which provides us with yet another picture of Shakespeare's many-faceted Hamlet, also may be too detached to express a great deal of passionate love. After this tumultuous scene, understandably in Olivier's version, comes the often troublesome "To be, or not to be" soliloquy. In its Q2 and F1 placement the soliloquy could show Hamlet's mercurial moodiness, or, as in Kozintsev, it could reveal Hamlet's despair about the death likely to result after Claudius realizes his crime has been discovered. In Olivier's film the soliloquy does neither. It comes not after the idea for "The Mousetrap," a high point for this Hamlet, but right after his lowest point, after Ophelia's betrayal of him and before the players arrive to give him a plan and an opportunity for his continuous upward rise. Then, while still imbued with a sense of woman's perfidy, he no longer is overcome by the melancholia that an absence of a plan had induced in him.[13] Olivier's transposition, which serves his interpretation, could be done on stage as well as on film, but film supplies the transition between Polonius's plot and the actual unloosing of Ophelia in an easy, natural way.

Another transposition—one that connects the scene of Ophelia's madness to the scene of her drowning—clarifies Laertes's motivation. Before Laertes enters (4.5.110), sailors greet Horatio with news of Hamlet (4.6). Horatio has been put in charge of Ophelia, now mad, whom we hear singing and see picking herbs outside, but he leaves her to go to Hamlet. The camera follows as she moves into a courtyard where Claudius and Laertes are arguing, beginning with 4.5.130. Ophelia's entrance distracts Laertes. Before she leaves, a closeup tells us that she has thought of suicide, a thought that might be difficult for an actress to convey on stage. As she leaves, the camera follows, belatedly, so that, by the time it gets to her apartment, she is no longer there; she has gone through the opposite door leading outside. Then there is a dissolve to the willow tableau. With music providing the transition, we hear the disembodied voice of Gertrude telling about her death, as it is enacted. Only after the graveyard scene do Laertes and Claudius finish their plot against Hamlet (4.7.2–160), the camera emphasizing each aspect by cutting to a medium two-shot and then moving from them three times in rhythm with the triple plot. By transposing and cutting part of Laertes's argument with Claudius in 4.5, Olivier avoids two knotty problems: one is Laertes's motivation in turning so swiftly from rebel to accomplice of Claudius. Of course, this problem is caused by the usual practice of severely cutting Claudius's manipulative and flattering persuasion of Laertes in 4.7.[14] By placing part of the plot after Ophelia's death, Olivier provides motivation enough.

Also, because he has Horatio reading Hamlet's letter to substitute for the first thirty lines of Laertes's entrance—both taking place at the same time in Olivier's film—he can omit Gertrude's defense of Claudius ("But not by him," line 128). In Olivier's interpretation, Gertrude breaks decisively with Claudius during the closet scene, a fact sharply emphasized visually when she and Claudius go up separate stairs when they next part. This break from him gives her the detachment to realize at the fencing match that the cup of wine is poisoned and the resolve to drink it in a futile effort to save her son. Thus Hamlet's upward path parallels Gertrude's acceptance of Hamlet's view of Claudius and of her sensuality.

Olivier's final transposition places Hamlet's praise of Horatio's constancy before the fencing match, rather than, as in Shakespeare, before "The Mousetrap" (3.2.46–66); thus, Olivier underscores Hamlet's smooth progression towards serenity.

How can one, finally, evaluate the film? Olivier's *Hamlet* is not Shakespeare's. It fails then to be a substitute for or even an illustration of Shakespeare's text. But since that is not the purpose of the film (or of any performance), this failure need not enter into our evaluation. Fortunately, we are not forced to make a choice between Olivier and Shakespeare. We have both. One can always return to the font of inspiration. This is not to say that there is an ultimate, essential *Hamlet* that we can discover by reading the Riverside or the Arden text or even the First Folio or Second Quarto. Not only does every text carry its own interpretation through choices of punctuation and spelling, omissions and additions, but also readers of a text superimpose on it their own interpretation, as often as not based on performances they have seen, which, for this generation of critics, would include Olivier's. Because Olivier uses every means at his disposal to create a meaningful, coherent, and unified work, because he clarifies with his rigorously applied conception much of the nature of film and theater, his work is, in spite of its few flaws, outstanding. The scenes one remembers—the soliloquies using voiceover; the closeups of the two foils, the one bated and the other unbated; the semi-transparent ghost with the unforgettable voice; the moving torch filling the frame before Hamlet thrusts it into Claudius's face—all these could be expressed only on film. But more important are those aspects that film and stage can share: the clear interpretation and the magnificent acting of all, but especially of Olivier himself. As director, he fruitfully plays one medium against the other, producing a film that makes a significant comment on the nature of each medium.

Notes

1. Jack Jorgens's persuasive and beautifully written *Shakespeare on Film* includes essays on Olivier and Kozintsev. While Jorgens recognizes that Olivier's theatricality is purposeful (211), he damns Olivier with faint praise by listing purported criticisms and then halfheartedly defending Olivier. He much prefers Kozintsev's *Hamlet.*

2. For the most insightful discussion of the relation of film and theater, see Bazin 1: 76–124. On *Caligari,* see Bazin 1: 108–109.

3. Olivier certainly learned this from Welles's films in which Greg Toland's deep focus was a special feature. See Kael's book on Welles. See also Gross, especially 65–66.

4. See Clay and Krempel, 251: "It is important to see that this use of the camera derives from the production concept and not just from any strong desire to remake the play in purely film terms."

5. Olivier, in joining such scenes, works against what Bernard Beckerman refers to as Shakespeare's episodic plan in *Hamlet.* He says, in *Shakespeare at the Globe* (54–55), that Shakespeare's scenes tend to be self-contained, ending on a low, rather than a high key, avoiding onward impulse. See also Hirsh, 29.

6. See Lev Kuleshov's experiments in juxtaposition, described in Mast (191). Josef von Sternberg, the American director, felt that the actor could contribute little to the emotional effect of a film compared to the effect achieved by lighting, framing, and editing (Brownlow, 203). Not every director would agree; nevertheless, there is more than a modicum of truth in such assertions.

7. Since the preproduction script mentions only that some explanatory statement of the "one defect speech" will be added, we may surmise that the idea of the tragic flaw superseded the explanation, which trivializes it. See Kliman, "Palimpsest." Jorgens says that "without the opening quotations, which obscure more than they reveal, Olivier's becomes a more complex performance, and the work a more interesting one" (209).

8. Duffy (148) speaks of the link between Gertrude and Ophelia created by circle patterns associated with their surroundings.

9. For a different view, see Jorgens, 215.

10. His inspiration for the tableaux may not have been the stage but the illustrations that accompany many nineteenth-century editions of *Hamlet,* where scenes of Claudius poisoning King Hamlet and Ophelia drowning were particularly popular (the subjects of two of Olivier's insets). See, for example, the line drawings of Moritz Retzsch, 1902.

11. I suppose we might say that he follows Q1 order, but that's true only in so far as the nunnery scene follows the unloosing plot. Q1 puts "to be" *before* the nunnery scene and the fishmonger scene *after.*

12. Jean Simmons (56) says that Olivier wanted to plant the idea of her madness here.

13. This does not mean that he loses the melancholy completely, but melancholia is not necessarily a bar to action, as Bevington notes: "Elizabethan theories of melancholy did not suppose the sufferer to be made necessarily inactive" (5).

14. See, for example, the difficulties of the actor playing Laertes in Guthrie's production, in Rossi, 55. Guthrie, by the way, had worked with Olivier on the 1937 Old Vic *Hamlet.*

2

Exits and Entrances: Texts and Productions

Exits and entrances are sensitive points separating a play from the world surrounding it and thus are mediating points between artifice and reality. On open stages, exits and entrances are accomplished in full view of the audience. At the end of scenes the stage empties; new characters emerge from the tiring house. Within scenes, characters enter or leave, creating new configurations of interactions. On film, characters enter and exit through the narrow or wide aperture of the frame. Though theater and moving images generally treat their opportunities differently, with conventions suited to each medium, each may also use the conventions of the other—awakening, paradoxically, one's sense of the distinctions between the media. Verges between scenes and restructurings of dynamics within scenes can tell us not only about the similarities and differences between theater and moving images but also about the choices that the texts—Q1, Q2, and F1—support in both media.[1] Further, the director's management of exits and entrances helps the audience to shape its judgment of characters. They are, then, worth looking at in detail.

Artifice and Realism

Since the absence of lighting and curtain forced Shakespeare to show exits and entrances, he wove them into his art; they became part of his resources. He worked his craft with a small number of points of entry/exit, probably two on platform level. Characters needed time to move from the upstage area where they entered to the downstage area where they were apt to play (Styan 1967, 72–76 and passim). At the Globe Theatre or similar open, thrust stages, if characters were to enter up-stage, talking as they move to the downstage playing area, their first lines might be sacrificed. Similarly, and perhaps more importantly, if they have a few lines to effect their move from the downstage area back towards the tiring doors, the specific meaning, certainly the impact, of those final lines may be obscured by the actor's exit, with back to the audience.[2] Undoubtedly, because of our tradition of a strong curtain-closer, the impact is stronger when a character stands downstage and says his or her last words just before the curtain falls or the lights dim. On thrust stages today, characters can say their lines downstage, then run off quickly, with something of the same effect. Burton, for example, says his last lines of the soliloquy in act 2 downstage, then runs to the upstage exit, and says his final lines quickly: "The Play's the thing, / Wherein Ile catch the Conscience of the King." But we cannot know if that was Shakespeare's style. Quick exits are like a camera coming in for a closeup of the character saying the last few lines to the camera/audience.

Shakespeare may have had actors enter the playing area as actors, who would become characters only after they arrived downstage, speaking only then. Olivier, playfully demonstrating the illusionary limitations of theater, does this for the mid-conversation beginning of the second scene of *Henry V* (1944), where we see first in the backstage area actors as themselves preparing to go on, then the actors as actors entering the playing area and accepting the cheers of the crowd, and finally the actors as characters settling into a conversation-in-progress (see Geduld). The scene ends with the process in reverse. And of course, the film actors who impersonate these sixteenth-century actors add yet another layer or two. Managed thus, no lines would be lost at all, but upon the actors' entrance and exit, the audience would be aware of the stage's artifice.[3] Possibly at these points of entrance and exit Shakespeare did not attempt to be natural.[4]

Perhaps to suggest the artifice many producers see in Shakespeare, the edges of scenes in some film and stage productions suggest artifice also, though in different ways. On stage, dissolves can lend a stylized, almost surreal, effect—as in The Boston Shakespeare Company production (1981) where those entering interacted with those exiting (Kliman 1986). Dissolves, in the forties the usual film transition, though they are return-ing, are seldom used in moving images of the seventies and eighties because they are considered mannered. Thus, when they are used, they are artificial. (As in *The Big Chill*, 1983, and *Prizzi's Honor*, 1985.) Wipes are now almost exclusively the property of farce, but directors can introduce jump cuts and odd juxtapositions (as in Peter Hall's *A Midsummer Night's Dream*), white-outs and freeze frames to pull viewers out of a film and make them aware of artifice. More usually, however, film technique embraces its inherent naturalness and realism, its capacity for engendering audience belief.

A study of the texts shows that Shakespeare probably used both natural and artificial entrances and exits. Two exit signals allow a character to exit naturally: The first starts him on his move towards the tiring doors. Then he can stop and listen or say a few words more until after another exit line he moves offstage. Shakespeare frequently provides two exit signals, probably to effect this pacing. If Q1 is an inferential text, that is, the result, at least partly, of someone's perception of what a performance of *Hamlet* in Shakespeare's own time conveyed to him or her, then such exits in the early performance remembered therein were so natural that the second signal went unnoticed, for Q1 seldom provides both signals. If Q1 is an early draft, on the other hand, Shakespeare revised toward more complex and perhaps more natural exits. A character's rhymed couplet, which because of its strength almost demands to be said downstage, is artificial. Claudius and Hamlet have all these rhymed couplets except one, Polonius's to Ophelia, which is not likely to be heard by American audiences, because "move" and "love" do not rhyme for us:

> This must be knowne, which being kept close might move
> More greefe to hide, then hate to utter love.
>
> $(2.1.119–20)^5$

This couplet ends the scene in F1 and, in slightly different form, in Q1.

When a final couplet is followed by another line, the actor can begin to move offstage while still in character. Thus a static rhymed couplet can turn, with an additional line, into a paced ending. Q2 and BBC follow Polonius's couplet with another "Come." So also Hamlet's concluding couplet of act 1 in all texts:

> The time is out of joint: Oh cursed spight,
> That ever I was borne to set it right.
> Nay, come let's goe together.
>
> (1.5.189–91)

Just as speech can continue to the exit door, so it can also begin at the entrance door. When characters enter in the midst of conversation, the action seems realistic—though certainly there is nothing inherently unrealistic about processionals (natural in a court seting) or encounters. When characters enter speaking, however, Shakespeare implies action that takes place between the scenes. Anything that suggests that the action on stage is not all the action we could know makes the presentation seem more realistic. Shakespeare's work is compatible with film and television where mid-conversation openings are frequent. Of the twenty scenes found in modern texts (see Hirsh), fifteen call for a mid-conversation beginning; only three clearly begin with the onset of dialogue (1.1, 1.2, 2.2), while two others could begin either way (1.3, 4.4). The sense we have that the action is real enhances our identification with the characters, and this identification is central to the moving-image experience.

Character-Disclosing Multiple-Signal Exits

Whether realistic or artificial, Shakespeare makes some exits disclose character and motivations by marking them with multiple signals, conveying much more than exit information. The king at the end of the first court scene has two exit signals: his exit phrases, "Madame come" and "come away," bracket the high declamatory style of

> No jocond health that Denmarke drinkes to day,
> But the great Cannon to the Clowds shall tell,
> And the Kings Rouce, the Heavens shall bruite againe,
> Respeaking earthly Thunder.
>
> (1.2.125–28)

The high style obscures the fact that Claudius, as someone has said, celebrates the reconciliation with Hamlet by exiting with everyone except Hamlet. Claudius's second exit request, however, could be addressed to Hamlet too, and Hamlet could purposely ignore it to stay behind alone. Most productions choose to have Claudius exclude Hamlet, giving control to the king.

Using the exit to display the king's character, Olivier has Claudius, with a short, peremptory command ("Madam come"), jealously draw Gertrude away from Hamlet, whom she is caressing and kissing. Claudius's high rhetorical style, then, masks his displeasure. Quickly, while he speaks, he sweeps Gertrude to the head of the councillors' table again, from which he directs his "Come away" only to her, the shot expanding from medium closeup into long shot to encompass the whole set. As on stage, they leave through an exit, upstage, in a procession defined by Walton's music, while most of the courtiers exit through the "wings," except Hamlet, who remains there for his soliloquy.

Polonius's exit signals in the nunnery scene (3.1) provide the opportunity for the king's first disclosure of guilt. Polonius calls for his and the king's seclusion with two lines: "Gracious so please ye / We will bestow our selves" (3.1.44–45) and "I heare him comming, let's withdraw my Lord" (3.1.55). Again, as is usual with more than one exit signal, there is time to say a few lines, here about deceit and guilt, before they actually

The Olivier *Hamlet*. Claudius looks at Ophelia before retiring behind the arras. *(Still courtesy Janus Films.)*

leave the stage. Though Olivier retains both exit lines, he omits the intermediate lines, suggesting, however, a sense of the king's hesitancy by having him pause and look at Ophelia, thus occasioning Polonius's second exit line.

In the exit marked by his couplet, Polonius says "come" three times to Ophelia after she tells him about Hamlet's visit to her closet (Q2, BBC, once in F1), as well as "Goe with me, I will goe secke the King" and "Come, go we to the King"—multiple signals, in addition to the couplet. The signals may be used to cover the exit, but they may also indicate Ophelia's reluctance, for indeed there is no sign, except in Q1, that she does join Polonius in seeking the king. Some productions (CBS, McCarter, American Shakespeare Theatre), though they follow Q2 or F1, have Ophelia remain with Polonius for the next scene (2.2). The Boston Shakespeare Company *Hamlet*, on the other hand, dramatized her resistance by having her run away from Polonius, shaking her head "no" to show she was opposed to having her private pains exposed to the king. When productions do have her enter 2.2 with Polonius, either following Q1 or assuming her presence because of the ending of 2.1, she is usually embarrassed to be there (as in the CBS production).

After the scene with Hamlet in her closet, Gertrude may be showing the same kind of silent resistance to Claudius as Ophelia to Polonius, for the king says "come" three times to her after she tells him that Hamlet has murdered Polonius (4.1.28, 38, 40). Later, Claudius twice says "Let's follow" (4.7.193, 196) after Laertes dashes out, giving the king and queen time to get from downstage to upstage and out or providing Gertrude with yet another opportunity to resist going with Claudius. With the absence of any verbal response on Ophelia's or Gertrude's part, Shakespeare could be signaling their opposition or even defiance. This would be a matter of directorial choice. The option for Gertrude's resistance is taken up, for example, in the Evans *Hamlet.*

The several exit signals after Hamlet's last speech of the ghost scene (1.5) attest to Hamlet's ingratiating charm. "With all my love I doe commend me to you" is the first (184) in the last speech. Then "Let us goe in together" (187) describes how he, Marcellus, and Horatio are to leave, that is, side by side, and finally "Nay, come let's goe together" (191) would seem to be a response to their hanging back to let Hamlet go first and his refusal to accept this mark of deference. In some productions he says his final couplet directly to both or to Horatio alone, in others to himself; he either embraces others or excludes them.

More than one or two exit announcements may also imply a kind of distraction on the part of the speaker. This may be true of Polonius and Claudius in the scenes already cited, and it undoubtedly is true when Hamlet says farewell to Ophelia three times before he exits the nunnery scene (Q2, F1, BBC: 139, 144, 148; Q1 has none of them). Many productions have him leave and return, but other possibilities are more dramatic. The three signals may denote Ophelia's resistance to his departure—she may even be holding him back—or his agitation, the latter very likely since he says eight more lines after his third "farewell." Because of mental anguish, Hamlet constantly thinks of something else to say. This seems to be so when he four times says good night to his mother in her closet, the first time at line 159, the fourth at 217, fifty-nine lines later. When, however, within fifteen lines, Hamlet gives three exit signals for the players, then detains the First Player, he indicates not so much distraction as intention: he is trying to hurry the others off precisely because he wants the First Player to remain behind.

Multiple signals may also express urgency as, for example, when the king commands the others present to

> Follow [Hamlet] at foote,
> Tempt him with speed aboord:
> Delay it not, Ile have him hence to night.
> Away, for every thing is Seal'd and done
> That else leanes on th'Affaire pray you make hast.
>
>   (4.3.55–59)

These five lines, the first two short, show Claudius's fevered determination and allow ample time for the swift exit of all so that he can be alone for his soliloquy. Q2 and F1 do not mark an exit but it is unlikely they would stay for the king's final lines, an apostrophe to England calling for Hamlet's death. But were Rosencrantz and Guildenstern to remain, their presence would corroborate Hamlet's line, "Why man, they did make love to this imployment" (F1 only, 5.2.57).

Claudius, on the other hand, announces his precipitous exit from the play scene with only one signal, rushing out with one "Away" (3.2.250). Still, there are three signals, two by other characters. During the play, Ophelia notices the king's move ("The King rises") before the king calls (in Q1 it is Polonius who has the line after the king calls); then either Polonius (Q2, Q1, BBC) or all (F1) second his call for lights. All exit except Hamlet and Horatio. Olivier speeds Claudius's exit through the self-consciously employed cinematic technique of montage, with rapid intercutting of images. Following Dover Wilson's view (196), Olivier shows the court in a panic, but since Olivier does not dramatize Wilson's notion that the attendants view *Gonzago* as a threat by a nephew to kill his uncle the king, the montage of shots showing screaming, fainting ladies and distraught gentlemen seems gratuitous.[6] Nevertheless, many productions have copied Olivier's business. Shakespeare could if he wished have achieved the same effect through many short speeches and exclamations, and perhaps he does this by having the whole court, not Polonius, say "Lights, lights, lights" in F1, assuming this to be a revision. The scattering of cries effectively mirrors Claudius's discomposure.

Character-Disclosing Points of Exit

Where there is only one signal—or even none—the specific line chosen to effect an exit sometimes has a powerful effect on characterization and therefore on meaning. Q1 marks Laertes's exit after the king grants his suit in the first court scene, and the stage direction is preceded by a "fare thee well" from the king and a leavetaking by Laertes. Q2, F1 and BBC show no exit for Laertes and there is no farewell or formal leavetaking. Nevertheless, Laertes does exit at this point in many productions that follow these texts, including the BBC-TV production; as he exits, some show interplay between Laertes and Ophelia, if she is present (F1 names Ophelia as one of those in the scene), or between Laertes and Hamlet (as in the BBC production). The CBS production with John Neville has both: Polonius, Laertes and Ophelia cross the frame behind Hamlet, she says his name, tries to get his attention, but Laertes insists she come with him. Laertes in Olivier's film does not exit, but the camera avoids showing his reaction because the frame excludes him once he seats himself near the foot of the table—in effect an exit. If Q1 is based on someone's recollection of the text plus the inference he or she drew when viewing the performance, we can say that Q1's author had the impression that Laertes took no further part in this scene. Several productions take the Q1 tack, though following the Q2 text. When Laertes does not leave, directors have an opportunity to show his reaction to Hamlet and to Hamlet's words; as in the Chamberlain version (1970), it can be warm, thus making Laertes himself a more sympathetic figure.

Laertes's exit from 1.3 also has an impact on characterization. When Laertes takes leave of his father and bids Ophelia a second farewell, in the theater we are willing to accept the stage convention that Laertes, having turned away to exit, wil not hear Polonius's question to Ophelia: "What ist Ophelia he hath said to you?" though indeed the director might have him hear, or Polonius's question might not come until after his exit. Film ordinarily can simply cut away from that departing character; out of sight, out of mind. We would have to see the character's reaction to what is said to realize that he has heard. Or the camera can even show that the character has *not* heard. In the Christopher Plummer production (1964) Laertes is in a boat some distance offshore unable to hear as Polonius speaks to Ophelia. In the CBS version, Ophelia and Polonius watch Laertes go through a corridor and doorway. Also in that version, Laertes did not want his last words to be audible to his father; he whispers to her and she to him. If a Laertes were to hear his father's question, he might show satisfaction that the matter of Hamlet will receive attention or chagrin that he has gotten Ophelia into trouble. Excluding Laertes concentrates attention on Ophelia and emphasizes her innocence: if Laertes can hear her, she is forced to be honest; without Laertes, her honesty is her own decision. The style of Laertes's exit affects our perception of Ophelia.

The exit of Polonius and Ophelia at the end of their conversation about Hamlet (1.3) is another instance of an exit that yields more than one interpretation. In the text, "come your wayes" could be an exit line for Ophelia, meaning roughly "come in," which is, in fact, what Q1 has. Most often, when Shakespeare uses the phrase, it means "come along; don't hang back." Or it could mean: "Do what is wanted." An Elizabethan quotation cited by Elizabeth Jenkins (171) seems to have the latter meaning. If the former, they exit together, and her agreement to obey could refer mainly to her coming in (as in Q1 where her "I will my lord" can apply *only* to his words "Come in"); if the latter, they might exit together, which could imply her ready agreement, or separately, which could imply her reluctance or unhappiness. In most productions she acquiesces to Polonius's demands about Hamlet, but Shakespeare could intend a less complete assent on her part. The difference is crucial for responding to Ophelia's character. Each choice about Ophelia in her

The Olivier *Hamlet*. Polonius scurries round to speak to the king and queen during the fishmonger scene. *(Still courtesy Janus Films.)*

several scenes may seem insignificant, but together they contribute to portrayals different from, even opposite to the usual. The problem is that most of us have been conditioned by instructors and performances to see her as a pathetically weak character, but if a director would take advantage of each choice that puts her in the most positive light we would see a modestly assertive young woman.

In Q2, F1, BBC, Polonius officiously asks both king and queen to withdraw while he "boards" Hamlet. In Olivier's film, they do not exit entirely but retire behind a pillar so that Polonius can run over to them to say:

> How say you by that? Still harping on my daughter: yet he knew me not at first; he said I was a Fishmonger: he is farre gone, farre gone. . . . Ile speake to him againe. (2.2.189–93)

Presumably Hamlet does not hear this. Their continued presence exposes not only Polonius's character but also Gertrude's as well as Claudius's willingness to spy on Hamlet.

With no stage direction giving Polonius's specific exit line, it is not clear whether he is on to hear "These tedious old fooles" (2.2.224). The choice of exit line for Polonius affects Hamlet's characterization. The productions that conceive of Hamlet as ever the gracious gentleman choose of course to have Polonius not hear; their Hamlet would not be so cruel.

Booth, for example, has Polonius exit before the offending line to maintain Hamlet's gentlemanly character. Burton, on the other hand, wanted Polonius to hear.

In Olivier's film, Polonius leaves the frame, but since the camera shows only Hamlet's exit from the lobby, we are not sure that Polonius exits; he could be returning to the pillar where the king and queen are waiting. For the juncture of the fishmonger and nunnery scene, Olivier invented a film equivalent for "double time," that perception we have in Shakespeare's plays that only a few days have gone by and yet that enough time has passed, for example, for Desdemona to have lain with Cassio a thousand times. Or, to use an example from *Hamlet*, that sense we have that Ophelia's mad scene follows her father's death by only a day or two but that Hamlet has had time to come close to the shores of England, be captured by pirates and return to Elsinore (at least four to five days). Olivier creates his double-time effect through exits and entrances.

Hamlet exits; the camera looks towards Ophelia's corridor. After a dissolve she appears, walking into the lobby where Polonius's hand reaches into the frame with the book she is to read. The dissolve has traditionally signified the passage of time. Still we are not sure whether time has passed or not because Polonius and the king are still in the lobby. The queen is nowhere in sight, but used as we are to the camera's exclusions, we may not note that. Ophelia presumably knows about the unloosing plot, which would mean time has passed, yet we had seen Hamlet exit with his book out of the portal into the sunshine, and a few minutes after Claudius and Polonius hide, we see him entering from that same portal, with a book and in the same clothes. This suggests that little time has passed. Like Shakespeare, Olivier has it both ways. Olivier used the same technique in the transition from Hamlet's "too, too solid flesh" soliloquy to the first Polonius family scene (1.3). After Hamlet expresses, mostly in voiceover, his despairing thoughts about his mother, the camera moves from Hamlet's face to peer down the corridor we will associate with Ophelia, a connection reinforced by Walton's Ophelia theme. A dissolve as the camera tracks down the corridor suggests that time has passed; this suggestion is strengthened when we see Laertes, now with his cloak on. Yet, when next we see Hamlet, he is sitting in the same chair in the same posture, implying that this is happening close to the time of the previous scene. Moving images can create these ambiguities of time more easily than can stage productions.

In the nunnery scene, the three basic texts offer different exit possibilities for Ophelia from which productions can choose. Q1 and Q2 have her exit after her woe-begone speech, but this seems to be a mistake in Q2, since in that version (and in F1 and BBC) Polonius addresses her after he and the king re-enter and speak. The king's couplet signals his exit with Polonius. If Ophelia does not exit earlier, then she might overhear the king's and her father's plan to entrap and dispose of Hamlet. Some productions get around this by having her leave before her father says "My Lord, do as you please" (Burton *Hamlet*) or by having her crying distractedly so that she cannot comprehend what they are saying (Olivier). In the Boston Shakespeare Company production, in contrast, that she does hear and is helpless to oppose them drives her into madness. When in a production she listens to them unmoved, as in BBC, she manifests naiveté or worse. Olivier increases Ophelia's importance by her "exit." Her last speech cut, she remains in the scene after Polonius and Claudius walk out of the frame. The camera draws away from her sprawled on the steps where Hamlet has thrown her, her head tilted upwards pleadingly, and in a surrealistic montage, the camera ascends. Through an arch, far below, we see her figure, still posed as if pleading, then three more stairways and music speed us to the top of High Tor, where Hamlet considers killing himself. Olivier's visual connection between Ophelia's "exit" and Hamlet's next "entrance" signals a cause and effect relationship between the two segments, a signal that might have been missed had the two scenes simply been juxtaposed and that indeed none of the texts provides. Shakespeare, then, did not make Ophelia the necessary cause of Hamlet's emotion in "To be." The American Shakespeare Theatre's 1982 production, which follows Olivier's at several points, goes even further by having Hamlet return and say the "To be" speech *to* Ophelia. His "Soft you now" warns her to leave as Polonius enters for the fishmonger scene.

Absence of Exit Signals

Shakespeare fairly consistently provides exit signals, but tradition has added several exits where no signal occurs in the dialogue or in stage directions. Laertes's exit in 1.2 has already been mentioned. Another is an exit for Gertrude at the end of 3.4: many productions end with a fade or curtain, leaving her in place, but putting a cap on the segment. Other productions have her exit before or after Hamlet. Several productions cut the next scene (4.1) entirely (Wirth and American Shakespeare Theatre, for example). In contrast, Q1, Q2, and F1 show no exit for Gertrude, making it probable that what has been called a new scene since Rowe's 1709 edition is actually a continuation of the closet scene.[7] By the continuous action of what has been called 3.4 and 4.1, Shakespeare speeds events, making Claudius's reaction more immediate and therefore more threatening than it seems when the scenes are separated. Q1 and F1 call for the entrance of the king (with Lords and alone, respectively) but not for the entrance of the queen. Q2 and BBC call for the entrance of king, queen, Rosencrantz and Guildenstern. Shakespeare, however, seldom has a character leave at the end of one scene and enter again at the first line of the next scene. (An exception is Gaunt's exit at the end of the first scene in *Richard II* and then his re-entrance for the next scene, but the time and place of the second scene are so obviously different that the exit-entrance would not be confusing.) Films, however, can accomplish sequential exits and entrances by the same person easily, with a dissolve or a fade-in. But technical possibility does not mean dramatic excellence. Especially in a localized setting, as is usual in moving images, the more powerful actualization has Claudius enter Gertrude's bedroom immediately after Hamlet exits, as in the McKellen TV version. The Evans version comes close by connecting the two scenes with a dissolve showing that only enough time has passed for Claudius to enter. The king is saying "Oh heavy deed" (4.1.13) to Gertrude, who is still sitting on the bed.

Significantly, the final scene has no exit signals (except for Osric's exit and return) until the very end. Shakespeare choreographs the catastrophe and resolution with four bodies remaining in full view. Fortinbras's speech gives an illusion of rest (in a musical sense) that is contradicted by the sight of all those bodies sprawled in the grotesque postures of sudden death. Both the beginning and end of Fortinbras's speech force the audience to remember those bodies:

> Where is this sight?

> His quarry cries on havocke. Oh proud death,
> What feast is toward in thine eternall Cell.
> That thou so many Princes, at a shoote,
> So bloodily hast strooke.

> Take up the body; Such a sight as this
> Becomes the Field, but heere shewes much amis.

Those bodies make the end of *Hamlet* untidier than the intimations of an ongoing society promise. Moving images resolve the ending decisively, usually ending with the moving-camera image of a final procession that takes us away from the scene of carnage, or at least that closes in on Hamlet. Many stage productions, too, like Forbes Robertson's, have the bodies carried off. While the Chamberlain TV version ends with a shot of the four bodies, they are so symmetrically arranged, as seen in an overhead shot, that they suggest artifice more than violent reality. With Fortinbras removed from Olivier's film, Horatio commands that Hamlet be taken to the stage. This exit affords Olivier the opportunity to track with the bearers past all the scenes of the drama—Hamlet's chair,

Chamberlain's *Hamlet*. **The arrangement in death is symmetrical.** *(Still courtesy Chamberlain-LeMaire Ltd.)*

A Russian stage version of the ending of *Hamlet* **(ca. 1900) with all the dead bodies on view.** *(Photograph courtesy the Folger Shakespeare Library.)*

Ophelia's corridor, the queen's bed, the chapel—and up to the High Tor where it began, ending as an almost perfect match of the film's early high overhead shot above High Tor of dead Hamlet.[8] While this ending is beautifully symmetrical and concentrates attention on Hamlet, it, like the last notes of Walton's music, leaves us with a much more settled feeling than might the text realized on stage. Yet, the very symmetry of the arrangement at the end also smacks much more of stage than it does of life, as we expect from cinema. Kozintsev accomplishes a similar effect more naturalistically by following Hamlet out of the dueling chamber and then having him borne from the castle over the drawbridge that first admitted him.

Multiple Entrance Signals

Like exits, entrances can also be effected in a variety of ways with a variety of results: a multiply-announced entrance heightens audience anticipation, a processional suggests pomp and majesty, a sudden entrance can surprise or frighten. One of the most elaborately treated entrances is the players'. Rosencrantz and Guildenstern prepare us for their arrival, which is then announced by a flourish and Guildenstern's response to it: "There are the Players." Polonius returns to announce them yet again, and Hamlet signals their entrance with "looke where my Abridgements come." Typically, Q1 shortens this somewhat and also omits Guildenstern's response to the flourish, but in the other texts, the preparation of some hundred lines denotes the players' importance to the play.

The Olivier *Hamlet.* Hamlet, sitting in darkness, before the entrance of the players. *(Still courtesy Janus Films.)*

With Rosencrantz and Guildenstern cut, Olivier gives Polonius the lines announcing the players. The film lacks the *dramatis personae* necessary for the text's elaborate introduction of the players. Olivier, however, emphasizes it structurally not only by making it the turning point in Hamlet's psychological state, but also by the setting and lighting. The scene opens in blackness on a fade after "To be"; Hamlet is revealed sitting lost in thought as light flickers on his face and music faintly sounds, the players' music. Following the direction of Hamlet's gaze, a cut shows Polonius entering with the torch, coming toward the camera. The music becomes louder. Polonius looks to his right, which allows for the expected cut to a shot of what he sees—in long shot, the arrival of the players, spilling down steps, holding torches that light the space. Then a cut shows Hamlet in medium closeup, smiling at them. Most productions follow Olivier in the elaborateness of the players' entrance.

The point of entrance may also be significant. Horatio's entrance before the play scene in the texts follows the players' exit, after Hamlet has hurried Rosencrantz and Guildenstern and Polonius off to "hasten the players." The stage direction for Horatio's entrance in F1 precedes Hamlet's call (Hamlet calls to Horatio *as* he sees him), in Q2 is printed just right of the call and in the BBC text follows the call (Horatio enters in response to Hamlet's call). This latter choice suggests that Horatio is constantly in attendance on Hamlet, discreetly out of view but close enough for Hamlet to call upon at any time. Olivier, by putting Horatio at Hamlet's side throughout the whole scene of advice to the players, implies that they have indeed become comrades. Olivier responds here to the subtext as he understands it. The Boston Shakespeare Company production also strengthens the notion of Horatio as constant companion by having him present for the advice to the players, though not at Hamlet's side. The BBC production produces the opposite effect by having Hamlet walk to Horatio, who is reading at a table and who is hardly to be dislodged from his book. The choices affect both Hamlet's and Horatio's characters.

The first public scene after "The Mousetrap" (4.3) opens in Q2, F1 and BBC with the king in the midst of conversation with his councillors. Several signals indicate that Hamlet's arrival is expected: "I have sent to seeke him [Hamlet], and to find the bodie." Claudius has, clearly, already told them about Polonius's death. Rosencrantz, who now enters, is greeted by the king: "How now? What has befalne?" Hamlet and the others enter only after the king asks where Hamlet is, is told he is outside, and commands that he be brought in. Rosencrantz gives the actual command: "Hoa, Guildensterne? Bring in my Lord." The repeated signals prepare the audience for the sight of the prince under custody; Shakespeare could count on his audience to feel the strangeness of this: Hamlet, the heir to the throne, and in fact perhaps the rightful

The Neville *Hamlet*. Hamlet closed in by sword points.

king, treated like a criminal. Equivalently, moving images can startle the audience with a view of Hamlet at the hub of sword spokes—as is John Neville.

Processional Entrances

The first court scene (1.2), the second court scene, the play-within-a-play, Ophelia's funeral and the duel all call for processionals, an opportunity for an elaborate entrance. The pomp of such scenes lends Claudius an air of stability and authenticity. If Shakespeare had the processional coincide with the end of the previous scene or segment, equivalent to a dissolve, the play would speed along. Certainly on a modern stage such overlap is likely.

In the list of those entering in the first processional, Q2 and BBC label Polonius and Laertes as "Counsaile." This makes sense, for it would explain why Laertes needs to ask so earnestly to return to France. (Only with the Quarto of 1676, according to Harold Jenkins, is Polonius labelled as Chamberlain; he has been so designated since in most texts and productions, including Rowe, 1709.) In both F1 and Q1 the list names Hamlet right after the king and queen; Q2 mentions Hamlet last of the named figures, just before the "Cum Aliis," the unnamed atten-

The Olivier *Hamlet.* **First court scene, no view of Hamlet.** *(Still courtesy Janus Films.)*

dants. The BBC names him last of all. Every director has to decide where to place him, following the king and queen, as is appropriate to his rank, or hanging back. Burton came late to the court, a sign of his disrespect. In contrast, Forbes Robertson, though the last to enter, comes right after the king and queen, a sign of his respect.

Films, since they usually show the scene *in medias res,* have other decisions to make about Hamlet's position on the set. Several moving-image productions begin the first court scene with the stagelike "discovery" of all in place; through camera framing, however, only gradually do we see all who are present. When the moment comes for Laertes's appearance, for example, the camera eases back to reveal him. Joseph Papp, though using a processional entrance, chose just such a delayed discovery for his 1982 stage *Hamlet,* where Diane Venora as Hamlet, leaning negligently against a doorpost, all but hidden behind some pillars, remains unnoticed until she steps forward (Kliman 1984). Kozintsev combines the best features of both modes: the processional's pomp (conveyed by the herald and the courtiers for the opening of 1.2) coupled with the discovery's intimacy and ability to surprise (conveyed by the cut to the council room for the continuation of 1.2).

In the texts, the second court scene also begins with a procession, and not in mid-conversation, for the welcome to Rosencrantz and Guildenstern certainly is Claudius's first speech to them. As for the first court scene, Q2 calls for a flourish. In films, however, Claudius and Gertrude might be discovered on the set when Rosencrantz and Guildenstern enter, thus undercutting the effect the procession would certainly convey, making Claudius seem more accessible, perhaps, or more affable and homely than he otherwise would.

In the texts, the entrance of the king and queen for the play-within-a-play calls for the most elaborate entrance—at the very center of the play. The funeral procession is certainly more quiet, occasioning Hamlet's expression about "maimed rites." For the duel scene's procession (5.2.236), Q2 calls for "A table prepared, Trumpets, Drums and officers with Cushion,. King, Queen and all the state, Foiles, daggers, and Laertes." Although neither Q1 nor F1 mentions the trumpets and drums, the entrance of the "Lords" with the rest suggests a formal occasion, as befits the duel. Moving images sometimes forgo the entrance itself, eliminating this opportunity for contrasting the beginning and end of this scene. In the texts, the other major entrance in this scene, of Fortinbras and the English Ambassadors, is also colorful and noisy, with flags and drums, an ironic contrast to the silence of death hanging on the scene. Fortinbras's entrance can also jolt our preconceptions about the Hamlet/Fortinbras parallels. If we had thought that Fortinbras as avenging son was deflected by his uncle, Norway, from Denmark to an "eggshell," his aggressive entrance at the end can stagger us with its implications for revenge—Hamlet's as well as his own—accomplished by indirection, culminating in violence. Papp's *Hamlet* with Sam Waterston (1975) electrified the audience with its resolute Fortinbras, rushing in to take over, an interpretation that, in retrospect, changed the meaning of the whole play. Earlier, John Gilbert, the illustrator, in 1864 had depicted just such a Fortinbras, entering ready to attack, not yet noticing the bodies that make his menace pointless. Bernard Shaw speaks of this illustration as determining his own interpretation of the play and of his shock and dismay to discover Fortinbras cut from contemporary stage productions. No moving image production that I have seen has dared such a strong Fortinbras.

The processionals of Olivier and Kozintsev especially serve useful purposes in developing character interrelations. Hamlet's loving bound up the stairs to greet his mother and lead her to her place for the play (Olivier) and Ophelia's rigid conformity in the procession preceding the play-within-a-play (Kozintsev) are telling moments of characterization.

Sudden Entrances

No less than processions, sudden entrances can startle the audience into special alertness—particularly those that interrupt a scene in pro-

The W. G. Simmonds ghost. *(Photograph courtesy the Furness Memorial Library, University of Pennsylvania.)*

gress. The sudden entrance/exit we expect movies to do best is the ghost's. Since Georges Méliès before 1900 discovered that the camera could be stopped while a character left the scene and then started again, producing what appears to be the instant disappearance of the character, this technique has been used often for ghosts. Superimpositions of a transparent image on another image was another technique early developed, also perfect for showing ghosts. Both techniques can be seen, for example, in the Forbes Robertson film (1913). Film may have borrowed from illustrations where transparent, luminous, and disappearing ghosts abound—for example, W. G. Simmonds's work ca. 1910. Problems in matching the action on the main film with that on the superimposed film may arise, as they do in the early CINES film and the earliest television production (1953, Maurice Evans), but when the matching is done well, it can be very convincing.

Having established within a few lines a mood of dread and foreboding to prepare us for the entrance of the ghost, Shakespeare has it enter at the exact moment that Bernardo narrates the circumstances of his previous appearances. Bernardo's reference to the "same Starre," and his pointing towards it, must draw the audience's attention from the ghost's entrance so that, with Bernardo and Horatio, we notice it suddenly. Olivier uses music, heartbeats and camera focusing-unfocusing to create the illusion of the ghost's presence, the illusion of danger. The look on Marcellus's face in closeup as he stares straight ahead teaches the audience what its reaction should be—fear and dread. A sudden movement of his head to his right, the quick words "breake thee of; look where it comes again," and a zip pan in the opposite direction onto the spectral transparency—all these conspire to make the audience feel the horror of it. We see no "entrance"; the ghost is simply *there*. The interesting thing is that Olivier has a strongly reacting character, one the audience is sure to focus on, stare in a direction different from where the ghost is. On stage, this would be a technique to effect the surprising entrance of the ghost, for, while the audience's attention is caught by Marcellus's reaction, they would not see the ghost. As soon as he whips his head toward the ghost, they would see it as if it had suddenly materialized. On film Olivier does not need to use this technique of having Marcellus stare in a different direction because the closeup already directs the audience's attention. But he does it anyway, and he does it for each of the ghost's appearances, when Hamlet sees it later in act 1 and also in act 3. It is yet another link that Olivier forges between film and stage.

Shakespeare makes the ghost's entrances and exits reveal something of its nature. In the text, a few lines after the ghost comes, it leaves, in Q1 right after Horatio charges it to speak, but in Q2 and F1 not until just before "'Tis gone." The dialogue marks its gradual disappearance:

Hor. By Heaven I charge thee speake.
Mar. It is offended.
Bar. See, it stalkes away.
Hor. Stay: speake; speake: I Charge thee, speake.
                    Exit the Ghost.
Mar. 'Tis gone, and will not answer.

It is offended, perhaps by Horatio's command that it speak, perhaps by the word "Heaven," either because it wants to retain its earthly pre-rogatives or because it is demonic.[9] Shakespeare's clues serve as warnings about trusting it. In all versions, Horatio sees the ghost and announces its return to the others. The ghost re-enters, depending on the text, as Horatio tells of the "sheeted dead" who "Did squeake and gibber" (Q2, BBC) or as Horatio tells about young Fortinbras's vengeance (Q1, F1). Q2's ghost may be drawn back by Horatio's credulity, while the ghost of Q1 and F1 may be drawn back by the model of young Fortinbras as avenger.

For the ghost's next appearance Hamlet enters with Horatio and Marcellus in mid-conversation—small talk to pass the time (1.4): "What hower now" suggests Hamlet has asked this question before. Their realistic entrance heightens the power of the ghost's supernatural entrance. The text delays the exit of Marcellus and Horatio to allow time for Hamlet and the ghost to exit and re-enter. Marcellus says, "Let's follow; 'tis not fit thus to obey him." Horatio's answer "Have after" seems to mean "I'm with you" (*Variorum* 1.4.89), but he retards their exit by asking "to what issue will this come?" until Marcellus finally puts a stop to chat with "Nay, let's follow him" (Q2, F1, BBC). Papp's 1982 *Hamlet* screwed an interesting twist on this conversation by showing Horatio reluctant to follow. His "Have after" clearly meant "You go after if you want; I'm not budging." Horatio's cowardice made petite Diane Venora's Hamlet seem more brave.

Film can easily move *with* Hamlet and the ghost to a new space, but even on nonillusionistic stages, we cannot accept that Hamlet and the ghost are in a more removed part of the castle unless we see them leave and re-enter. In the text, when the ghost and Hamlet enter again (1.5), Hamlet's first words imply he has been following the ghost for some time: "Where wilt thou lead me? speak; Ile go no further" (Q1, Q2, F1, BBC).[10] Olivier conveys the effect of time passing, in spite of the fact that we remain with Hamlet and the ghost, by a montage of shots that show first one, then the other, moving into new spaces, climbing stairs (feet only), entering mists. Stage can achieve the same effect by using mists and perhaps two levels; more frequently, however, when Hamlet and the ghost re-enter, Hamlet immediately speaks, implying that he has followed the ghost between the scenes.

For the ghost's final appearance, in the closet scene, Q1 has the ghost enter in his nightgown when Hamlet tells his mother to "throw away the worser part" of her heart; Q2, F1 and BBC do not have this line until long after the ghost has left (157). In these three, the ghost's entrance (dress not specified) follows Hamlet's diatribe against Claudius—not for murder but for stealing the kingdom from her son—and her plea "No more," the fourth time she has said "No more." Traditionally, critics

The Olivier *Hamlet*. Hamlet follows the ghost. *(Still courtesy Janus Films.)*

think that the ghost enters to protect Gertrude, but it is just as possible, as seems clear in Q1, that it enters after Hamlet has effected a change of heart in Gertrude. The ghost's entrance comes with no warning, making Hamlet break off and exclaim: "Save me; and hover o're me with your wings / You heavenly Guards." This is strange if Hamlet has indeed proven to his own satisfaction that the ghost is *not* evil. He can, however, say it not out of terror but as a kind of ejaculation, which would negate the force of the words.

Other characters aside from the ghost enter unexpectedly or suddenly. Because Horatio's, Bernardo's, and Marcellus's entrance after Hamlet's first soliloquy comes without any preparation such as "But soft, what noise is that," we can infer that their entrance is sudden, with Horatio's "Haile to your Lordship" to get Hamlet's attention. Many productions show that Hamlet hardly pays attention to his greeter until he realizes, belatedly, with a double-take, that the speaker is Horatio. The Boston Shakespeare Company production, however, had a tearful Hamlet apply the words "I do forget my selfe" to himself; he leaves out the word "or." Yet another possibility is that Hamlet actually does not recognize Horatio; he could be saying, "Aren't you Horatio? If my memory doesn't deceive me, you are." This is the question one would ask of someone he does not know well, and of course this makes sense, since Horatio does not approach Hamlet until he has something specific to tell him. The friendship grows during the course of the play.

Olivier and Wirth employ the film technique of the reverse shot from Hamlet's point of view to show Hamlet's sudden entrance, unseen by the others, in the midst of the plot by Polonius to loose his daughter to Hamlet (and on stage, Gielgud, in 1936, tried this, according to Mills, 219). Polonius prepares us for Hamlet's entrance by saying "You know sometimes / He walkes foure houres together, heere / In the Lobby." Dover Wilson used Polonius's announcement to build his case that Hamlet enters in time to hear the spying plan that Polonius develops, though none of the texts shows an early entrance. All have Hamlet enter just before or after the queen's announcement: "But looke where sadly the poore wretch / Comes reading." (The king says this in Q1.) Olivier, in fact, fashions two entrances for Hamlet, the one that only the audience is aware of and then the one that Hamlet contrives for the benefit of the spies. For the latter one, we see him, in long shot, as on stage, enter through one of the gallery entrances. As usual, Olivier combines film and stage techniques.

Shakespeare, at least in F1, provides for another surprise entrance— that of Gertrude into the midst of Laertes's and Claudius's plot to kill her son. Q1, Q2, and BBC prepare for the queen's entrance (Q1: *Laertes*: "Here comes the Queene"; Q2 and BBC: *Claudius*: "but stay, what noyse?"); but F1 has her enter with no signal: *Claudius:* "Our purpose may hold there; how sweet Queene." Steven Urkowitz maintains with considerable force that F1 may represent a revision of the text, for the queen's entrance here without warning must startle the men who are plotting her beloved son's death—a highly dramatic and ironic twist.

Connected to surprise entrances is the stage convention of the character who enters but remains unseen for a time. The play begins with the entrance of two sentinels, probably from separate doors (Q1, Q2, F1). The BBC's stage direction, following a long stage tradition (found in Edwin Booth's promptbook of 1878, for example), has: "*Francisco at his post. Enter to him Bernardo.*"[11] Their lines attest to the abruptness of their encounter: "Who's there?"; "Nay answer me: Stand & unfold your selfe." They are obviously not in the midst of conversation. On film, Bernardo and Francisco must be unable to see each other clearly for their lines to be effective. Even on stage, producers find it necessary to create a contrived separation to account for their inability to recognize each other: perhaps Bernardo offstage for his first "Who's there?" (as in Booth), or scaffolds (as in McCarter). On Shakespeare's sunlit Globe stage, paradoxically, the inability to see might have been more persuasive because it would have had to be acted, just as the nighttime setting would have had to be acted.

A few lines after Bernardo's entrance, Shakespeare emphasizes the entrance of Horatio and Marcellus by having Bernardo tell Francisco to "bid them make hast" should he, see them on the way out and also by having Francisco say "I thinke I heare them," followed by his challenge to them. On film or television and even on stage, Francisco has somehow to be close enough to Horatio and Marcellus to speak to them without their being able to perceive Bernardo. Those high scaffolds accomplished the illusion for the McCarter stage production, while the Papp *Hamlet* with Diane Venora went back to an earlier tradition, found in Forbes Robertson's 1913 film derived from the 1897 production, of having Bernardo leave the stage, as if looking for his fellow watchers somewhere in the off-stage area. Thus Francisco is alone on stage when Marcellus and Horatio arrive. These manipulations show that even stage productions attempt to avoid straining an audience's willingness to suspend disbelief overmuch.

To summarize: Shakespeare's two or more exit signals allow for a natural, in-character move from downstage to upstage and out—an exit, then, that is compatible with film realism, which can achieve the same effect without the two signals. The multiple exit signals, as well as choice of exit line may also, however, reveal something of character and motivation, as we have seen with examples of Claudius's, Polonius's, Ophelia's, Gertrude's, Laertes's, the ghost's, and Hamlet's exits. These character-revealing exits are also possible to convey on film, either by following the text or with film equivalents, for example, a closeup on Claudius's troubled face instead of his guilty admission between the exit lines just before the nunnery scene. Signaled, processional, and sudden entrances also affect the audience's perception of character and motives. Since Shakespeare communicates so much through his exits and entrances, it is not surprising that, in changing some, either through film techniques or through transpositions of the text, through ignoring or adding to signals in the text, filmmakers create new meanings (some would say by distorting Shakespeare's meaning). The two moving images at either end of the scale—Olivier's as the most theatrical, Kozintsev's as most cinematic—and the many between the two are witness to the fact that *Hamlet* affords an explosion of possibilities. The strong affinity that Shakespeare's method has to moving-image style can obscure the substantial differences in effect that varying choices have on the audience's perception of the drama's meaning.

Notes

1. The texts of Q1 (First Quarto, 1603), Q2 (Second Quarto, 1604–5), and F1 (First Folio, 1623) are conveniently arranged for collation in Vietor. For comparison purposes, I also refer to the modern text edited by Peter Alexander in the version published by the BBC for their series "The Shakespeare Plays" (BBC). Unless otherwise noted, quoted lines are from F1 in Vietor (letters modernized, i.e., short "s," "u" for "v," etc.).

2. Such for example is the effect of exit lines recited on the way to the tiring doors in a

televised *Romeo and Juliet*, performed on the Globe-reminiscent stage at St Georges Theatre in London, directed by Paul Bosner, 1976. See [Rothwell] 1977.

For an illuminating discussion of exits and entrances in *Coriolanus*, see John Ripley, 6–12. Styan (1967) has detailed analyses of the dramatic possibilities of exits and entrances.

3. No *Hamlet* media production attempts to duplicate this effect, except an experimental piece written by Joe Chang shown at the Northeast Modern Language Association in 1982 (reviewed by Berringer) and possibly the Coronado *Hamlet*, made for TV, with Helen Mirren as both Gertrude and Ophelia.

4. This is not to say that the acting within each scene could not be natural, no matter how unillusionistic the entrance or exit. Remarks critical of a ham actor by John Stephens (1615) indeed suggest that the ideal actor was natural: "When he doth hold conference upon the stage; and should looke directly in his fellows face; hee turnes about his voice into the assembly for applause-sake, like a Trumpeter in the fields, that shifts places to get an echo" (198).

5. It's interesting to note that the same rhyme on "move" and "love" occurs in Hamlet's poem to Ophelia.

6. Wilson's description of the court's exit was part of his theory that the king does not respond to the dumb show because he does not see it. For an important discussion of Wilson's theory, see Hawkes, 11–30. See also Silviria, 44.

7. Hirsh, in an appendix, lists 4.1 as a separate scene, though his definition of a scene is a unit marked by the exit of all living characters (15).

8. In his 1936 production of *Hamlet*, John Gielgud ended with a similar tableau (Mills, 225).

9. Slater (23), in her important and germinal study of stage directions in Shakespeare's plays, says the ghost is offended because of that unfortunate word "usurp'st" to a usurped king, but since Horatio speaks three and one-half lines after the word "usurp'st," it seems more likely that the words "I charge thee" in his last line cause the ghost's hasty withdrawal.

10. When the versions are reasonably close, I do not distinguish; here, for example, Q1 reverses the two phrases and omits "speak."

11. Harold Jenkins in the Arden text says that Q1 has this same stage direction, but I do not see it in the Q1 facsimiles I have. Nor does Vietor show the direction in his parallel texts of Q1, Q2 and F1. Furness uses the direction, following the Globe Edition and early editors, such as Rowe and Dyce.

3

Cuts: BBC-TV *Hamlet*
"Here's Snip and Nip and Cut and Slish and Slash"

If indeed Q1 is an acting version of *Hamlet*, then cutting, transposing, interpreting began almost immediately after *Hamlet* was first staged. However it was performed during Shakespeare's time, we know for a certainty that from Davenant on, it, like all the plays, was cut and pasted. We should expect no different from media versions. Conventional stage cuts appear in all moving image productions. William P. Halstead's monumental multivolumed text, *Shakespeare As Spoken: A Collation of 5000 Acting Editions and Promptbooks,* is an immeasurable aid in comparing the media productions to stage tradition—though he includes only those two moving picture productions of *Hamlet* that have published texts (the Olivier and the Old Vic television *Hamlet*s, the latter designated as CBS).[1] I am concerned here not only to show how moving images compensate or substitute for missing lines with visual effects and to consider what interpretive purpose may have been served by the omission but also to investigate how those lines may have functioned in the original text. As Alan Dessen has demonstrated for cuts in stage versions, concentrating on omitted lines can fix one's attention on passages that might otherwise be glossed over. Speaking of Delacroix, Grigori Kozintsev demonstrates how "A concept of a certain role can be understood by what cuts were made in the character's lines. . . . Delacroix," he says, "cut passion, sarcasm, coarseness, and even wit" from Hamlet's role to achieve his "young, delicate, beautiful," pale and impractical hero (128–29). Because producers may unquestioningly accept conventional cuts, sometimes their interpretation actually runs counter to the cuts— has to fight the cuts, as it were. More often, productions accept the conventional cuts because they suit the interpretation.

Beginning with the 1980 BBC *Hamlet* seems appropriate when talking about cuts because originally the producers announced that although they would have to pare other plays down to two or three hours, they would have as much time as they wanted for *Hamlet* (Wilders). Theirs is one of the longer media productions. Originally, to judge by the published BBC text, few cuts were planned (more was cut from the United States broadcast, but that's another story). Though some of what the text indicates as cut was restored and some additional lines were cut, overall the text (from which all quotations are cited in this chapter) can serve as an adequate guide. We may assume that the producers cut nothing, however reluctantly, merely to save time; therefore, every cut had its communicative purpose. It is not so much that cuts promote an overall directorial design as that they chip at facets of characters.[2]

Most of the cuts eliminate difficult words or phrases, especially in discourse that has "repetition with variation," a frequent Shakespearean method of amplification. All productions cut for this reason—though producers may differ about what they think is difficult. But, of course, even those lines omitted simply to avoid difficulties affect meaning. Other omissions cannot be accounted for that way; one of the more important reasons for the BBC's cuts is that they are *usual*: as with almost all productions, conventional cuts from stage influence cuts in the media.

Ophelia

Characters with few lines like Ophelia, Gertrude, and Horatio are especially vulnerable to distortion by cuts because there is no place for the actor to make up for what is missing.[3] The BBC's Ophelia, played by a lackluster Lalla Ward, tries to show some mettle but has hard going against the tide of cuts, both in others' lines to her and in her own lines. Irene Dash in *Wooing, Wedding, and Power* has alerted us to the pernicious effects of traditional cuts on women's roles. She has amply supported her thesis that Shakespeare creates strong, resourceful, intelligent women, but that his creations are undermined by directors' cuts. Though she does not discuss *Hamlet*, we can readily see that effect in the BBC performance. In the scene in which first Laertes and then Polonius attempt to persuade Ophelia to discourage Hamlet (1.3), deletions in others' speech to her diminish her character. Some of Laertes's lines to her are probably cut to eliminate difficult words and phrases, such as

> For nature crescent does not grow alone
> In thews and bulk, but as this temple waxes,
> The inward service of the mind and soul
> Grows wide withal.
>
> (11–14)

But difficulty is no excuse for eliminating "I stay too long" (52) after her advice to him. These four words suggest she has hit the mark with her request that he follow his advice to her (also cut in Q1 and CBS). There is something tart and knowing about her, which is emphasized by his desire to escape. Other productions, keeping the words, make them a response to seeing his father again, Olivier's going so far as to reverse the line: "But here my father comes. I stay too long."

The BBC omissions of part of Laertes's argument against Hamlet (36–44), especially of those battle images that could frighten her, and of fifteen lines of Polonius's argument (94–97, 120–26, 127–31) make this too easily swayed Ophelia much weaker than Shakespeare's character. With Polonius's first strong demand ("From this time / Be something scanter of your maiden presence") eliminated, Polonius's second command does not come at the top of a crescendo:

> This is for all—
> I would not, in plain terms, from this time forth
> Have you so slander any moment leisure
> As to give words or talk with the Lord Hamlet.
> Look to't, I charge you. Come your ways.
>
> (131–35)[4]

The BBC production makes this command so abrupt that she is given no time to mobilize her energies. She does attempt to show her resistance by turning her back to him while he is speaking and to look impatient, but the speed of his attack—without all those wordy images—does not give her room to maneuver. Her next line is "I shall obey, my lord."

These cuts in Ophelia's first scene are typical, following a pattern set by stage productions and continuing in film and television. In *Shakespeare As Spoken*, Halstead lists dozens of productions that omit Polonius's lines:

> If it be so—as so 'tis put on me,
> And that in way of caution—I must tell you
> You do not understand yourself so clearly
> As it behoves my daughter and your honour.
>
> (94–97)

> These blazes, daughter,
> Giving more light than heat—extinct in both,
> Even in their promise, as it is a-making—
> You must not take for fire.
>
> (117–19)

> From this time
> Be something scanter of your maiden presence;
> Set your entreatments at a higher rate
> Than a command to parle. For Lord Hamlet,
> Believe so much in him, that he is young,
> And with a larger tether may he walk
> Than may be given you.
>
>   (120–26)

> For they [his vows] are brokers,
> Not of that dye which their investments show,
> But mere implorators of unholy suits,
> Breathing like sanctified and pious bonds,
> The better to beguile.
>
>   (127–31)

While the BBC retains the second of these speeches, it omits the others. In fact, so many productions omit these sentences that Halstead must continue the listing at the bottom of the page and at the end of the play.

If a production is satisfied with a submissive Ophelia, there is no problem with these omissions—except of course that Polonius loses the first chance to show what he is like, for this scene affords him his first opportunity to speak at length. Even if the producers want a malleable Ophelia, they also lose a chance to give her some substance through her interaction with Polonius. After all, we should have some notion why Hamlet would be interested in her, and how can we, if she is given no opportunity to be interesting? If a more spunky Ophelia is wanted, cuts make this difficult, if not impossible. Obviously, most productions are happy with a shallow Ophelia. Thus, producers distort Ophelia's character by omitting lines said to her.

Jean Simmons's Ophelia in Olivier's *Hamlet* is even less spunky, even more submissive than the BBC's. In her first scene, the film cuts almost all her lines, almost all her father's lines to her. Only fourteen of the fifty lines of dialogue remain, compared to twenty-five even in Q1. All she can show is yearning, effected by the long gaze she bestows on Hamlet at the end of her conversation with her father. Though this version cuts even "I shall obey, my lord," her demeanor makes amply clear that she will obey.

The Chamberlain 1970 *Hamlet* has a similar pattern of cuts in the scene but makes one cut that strengthens her. She does not say "I do not know, my lord, what I should think" (not in Q1). Though Shakespeare presumably includes the line to show the limits of her independence, productions that use it (such as Olivier and BBC), and yet exclude other lines that can allow her to exhibit some force, distort the portrait. The problem for productions, like the Evans and Chamberlain, that want to show a somewhat spirited Ophelia and still keep the traditional cuts is always what to do about that last line. The Boston Shakespeare Company production (1981) resolved the problem of an independent Ophelia by having her say the words but obviously without any intention of obeying. With no cuts, there is time for Polonius to persuade her, to bring her from resistance to submission. This is what happened in the uncut McCarter production (Princeton, 1982), which began with a strong Ophelia but had her nodding in agreement as Polonius brings the strength of his personality and his logic to bear on the issue. But if the lines are not there and Ophelia begins strong, what is to make her cave in? This is true particularly in Chamberlain's version, where Polonius (Michael Redgrave) remains gentle throughout and where she begins as one who knows her view of Hamlet to be correct; there is just no accounting for her passive, "I shall obey, my lord."

Naturally, cuts in her own lines also affect our perception of her character. The most telling omissions occur as Ophelia and Hamlet watch *The Murder of Gonzago.* In the text, she keeps up her end of the small talk, responding to Hamlet's double entendre—"Be not you asham'd to show, he'll not shame to tell you what it means"—with, "You are naught, you are naught. I'll mark the play" (3.2.140–43). Her line could call for a playful tone. The BBC production omits their dialogue and also the repartee that follows Hamlet's line, "This is one Lucianus, nephew to the King," including her line, "Still better, and worse"—her recognition again of Hamlet's double meaning, which she both admires and reproves. Her tone in the latter line would seem to be lightly sardonic, making more probable a light reading for the previous response to his puns. This line is a favorite omission because, though it can be played madly or sadly—aspects of Ophelia most directors prefer—it does not easily lend itself to that interpretation. Again, Halstead shows dozens of productions omitting her repartee. Even productions that prefer the spunky Ophelia sometimes omit the lines either because they suggest a more sexually knowing Ophelia than wanted or because, like the Boston Shakespeare Company production and the CBS production, they want to begin to indicate her descent into madness here, and her lines show too much self-possession to do this. The American Shakespeare Repertory Company (ASR) exploited fully the sexual subtext of the dialogue by transposing it to the scene of Laertes's advice. As he begins speaking to her, she relives an encounter with Hamlet, a flirtatious interlude, obviously customary, obviously sexual. Hearing the lines this way demonstrated how comfortably they yield a buoyant sexuality. Though her lines can be said madly, it is easier to omit them than to try to extract a meaning from them that they do not easily surrender.

Perhaps because many productions use the mad scenes to show pathos, a comfortable interpretation of Ophelia, few full productions cut her lines; the BBC not at all. Only by exploring the subtext can a performance make the lines admit more interesting possibilities such as anger or terror. With the cooperation of Patrick Stewart's Claudius, whose reaction showed that she moved him, Lalla Ward's Ophelia was a sensuous, seductive woman. One of the most successful mad scenes, however, is Barbara Jefford's in the CBS production, believable but immensely varied, in spite of cuts.

Gertrude

Ophelia is present in five scenes (six if she enters with Polonius to show the king and queen Hamlet's letter as in Q1, seven if we count her as present in the graveyard scene when she is buried). Gertrude is in ten, yet Gertrude has about the same number of lines. In any production, the queen's presence is more telling than her words, and yet her few words are among the most enduring in social memory: "The lady doth protest too much," "There is a willow grows aslant the brook," "Sweets to the sweet." Their music is conventional, regular, and unsurprising, but pure and sweet. Rarely speaking more than four lines at a time, she responds more frequently than she initiates conversation and then often with a half line. In her most important scenes, the closet scene and Ophelia's mad scenes, not she but the person to whom she responds takes stage center.

The BBC production omits only a few of her speeches, but does cut one of the longest, her political remark to Rosencrantz and Guildenstern promising rewards for doing the king's will, lines that indicate her power over the king and her awareness of political reality:

> If it will please you
> To show us so much gentry and good will
> As to expend your time with us awhile
> For the supply and profit of our hope,
> Your visitation shall receive such thanks
> As fits a king's remembrance.
>
> (2.2.21–26)

Of course, productions, like Olivier's, that eliminate Rosencrantz and Guildenstern altogether perforce omit these lines too; however, Halstead lists dozens of productions that eliminate her speech, not all of which cut Rosencrantz and Guildenstern. Q1 is perhaps the model here as in so many other places.

The BBC in the same scene cuts her command that "some of you" escort Rosencrantz and Guildenstern to "where Hamlet is" (36b–37b).

This is Shakespeare's stage direction calling for several supernumeraries; without it the stage can be more bare, the court more stripped down. Perhaps that is why so many productions cut the lines. But cutting them eliminates Gertrude's only opportunity to give a command, to show herself as queenly. The command, "Go, some of you" also calls for Gertrude to raise her voice above the intimate tones reserved for "Thanks, Guildenstern and gentle Rosencrantz," calls for opening up the frame of audience attention. Of course, a production can avoid this opening and still keep the line. In Evans's *Hamlet,* for example, a groom bends into the tight frame to do something at the moment Gertrude needs someone to escort Rosencrantz and Guildenstern to Hamlet. Later in the scene, the BBC, by omitting the line "So he does, indeed" (160), avoids the opportunity that Shakespeare provides for Gertrude to show by her enthusiasm or lack of it her complicity in the spying or her reluctance to be part of the plot that Claudius initiates and Polonius executes. "So he does, indeed" may, however, merely denote Gertrude's sympathetic pain for Hamlet, as it does in the McKellen production (1971). Halstead lists only three productions, including Q1, that cut it. In her closet, the BBC cuts her second image describing Hamlet's demeanor after he has seen the ghost (3.4.119–22); the text editor may have been troubled by the word "excrements." In the same speech, however, he also cuts

> O gentle son,
> Upon the heat and flame of thy distemper
> Sprinkle cool patience!
>
> (122–24)

—an interesting irony if, as her preceding lines demand, her words to Hamlet have shown her own disquiet and anguish. (Halstead shows that many productions, following Q1, cut these same lines.)

The BBC keeps one of her most knotty lines, "But not by him" (4.5.125b). Olivier, as we have seen, avoids the line by beginning the second mad scene later, but Halstead lists only three other (nineteenth-century) productions that cut the line. Evans, eliminating Laertes's entrance and the whole second mad scene, of course cuts the line. The problem is, if Gertrude truly sees into her soul, recognizes what Claudius represents ("the rank sweat of an enseamed bed"), knows also what Claudius has done (at the very least stolen the crown from Hamlet)—if she understands all this, how can she not only deny Claudius's guilt a short time later but also in doing so endanger her son? For "If not Claudius, then who?" must be Laertes's next question. She, in fact, with her exclamation prepares the way for Claudius's persuasion of Laertes.

Perhaps Q1, which has her reveal in a discussion with Horatio that she understands what Claudius is and is determined to side with Hamlet and which also has the line "But not by him," can help us. In Q1, the two attitudes—understanding and denial of Claudius's guilt—do not conflict. After making her rejection of Claudius explicit with the added Horatio-Gertrude scene, Q1 did not make Gertrude's exclamation a defense of Claudius per se. Since Q1 may represent someone's inferences drawn from seeing a performance of *Hamlet*, the Globe performance through acting and stage business may have made clear that Gertrude distances herself from Claudius after the closet scene in spite of "But not by him." The cry has dramatic value, for it gives Gertrude an opportunity to exhibit her bravery, her indomitable spirit and fearlessness. The line is a fascinating one because it can be used in so many ways: the Boston Shakespeare Company *Hamlet* had Gertrude say it to protect not Claudius but Laertes, who, powerless and alone, self-destructively throws himself at Claudius as one would splat a tomato against a wall. The Circle Repertory Company production had Gertrude say it out of a natural abhorrence for violence, but as soon as her words leave her mouth, with horror she realizes the implications for Hamlet's safety of what she has said. Perhaps only an actress of the calibre of Jacqueline Brookes, who played the role, could evoke so much from so few words.[5] On the other hand, Wirth (1960) has his Gertrude frankly cleave to Claudius.

As the BBC's Claire Bloom interprets the role, Gertrude in the closet scene believes that she will avoid Claudius from then on, and in fact, does not follow Claudius when he says "Come" to her in 4.1. But when Hamlet speaks about the lascivious bed, we see her guilty embarrassment telling us she is all too drawn to that bed. Thus, after Hamlet leaves and Claudius approaches her for sympathy ("O Gertrude, Gertrude! /When sorrows come, they come not single spies, / But in battalions!" 4.5.74–76), she responds to her husband. Bloom plays a woman who needs a man's support and who needs to support a man. Had Hamlet remained, one feels her allegiance would have been to him. "But not by him" denotes her forthright protection of Claudius.

Horatio and the Political World

At first glance, Horatio may seem to offer fewer interpretative possibilities than either Gertrude or Ophelia; however, with no cuts he has more lines than either, making him an important character. Horatio functions as an audience surrogate when his skepticism about the ghost and then his conversion affect audience belief. The BBC production keeps all of his exchanges with Marcellus and Bernardo that are specifically about the ghost, but many other productions eliminate some of these. He can also function as expositor, as in the first scene, which contains his most expansive speeches, those about Old Fortinbras and King Hamlet (1.1.79–107, from which BBC cuts six lines) and about Rome (112–25). The BBC, following Q1 and F1, and indeed most productions, omits the latter fourteen lines in which he expostulates on the significance of ghosts in Rome before Julius Caesar died. Since Horatio says little to Hamlet, and since many of his lines must disappear when Fortinbras is eliminated (Globe text: 1.1.79–107; 5.2.373–74, 383–97, 402–6), as he commonly is—though not in the BBC—Horatio's lines on Rome give us the opportunity to hear him at his most voluble, when he is with those of equal or perhaps inferior status. Possibly also the credulity, the belief in ghosts, expressed in these lines brings the ghost on again, for it immediately reappears. These lines start us on what seems to be a false trail that ironically proves to be true because, though the ghost does not come about wars, the result is the death of kings and the transfer of control over Denmark to foreigners. In spite of the use Shakespeare makes of these lines, they are omitted not only by BBC, but also by a very large number of stage productions listed by Halstead.

A side of Hamlet's relationship with Horatio disappears with the omission of their playful banter after the play scene. The BBC cuts:

> *Ham.* Would not this, sir, and a forest of feathers—if the rest of my fortunes turn Turk with me—with two Provincial roses on my raz'd shoes, get me a fellowship in a cry of players, sir?
> *Hor.* Half a share.
> *Ham.* A whole one, I.
> For thou dost know, O Damon dear,
>   This realm dismantled was
> Of Jove himself; and now reigns here
>   A very, very—peacock.
> *Hor.* You might have rhym'd.

$$(3.2.269–79)$$

The Boston Shakespeare Company production also cuts these lines, as do a large number in Halstead. Shakespeare's Horatio is no "yes" man, the kind Hamlet deplores in several of his speeches, including the dialogue about clouds with Polonius in this same scene. When Hamlet exults, "Would not this . . . get me a fellowship in a cry of players, sir?", Horatio possibly teases with his response, "Half a share." Responding in kind, Hamlet extravagantly claims a whole one. After Hamlet sings the song denigrating Claudius, Horatio approves Hamlet's unexpressed thought with the line "You might have rhym'd," meaning you might have called Claudius an ass. The BBC's Horatio could not have been so daring, Olivier's so ungentlemanly, Kozinstev's so lighthearted; thus these productions all omit the lines.

Olivier, in spite of cuts, raises Horatio's stature when Hamlet dismisses Bernardo and Marcellus and reserves "come, let's go together" for Horatio alone (1.5.191). The cut of the first "Let us go in together" (1.5.187) emphasizes the subtext, Hamlet's feelings for Horatio, by showing that Hamlet's relationship with Horatio differs in kind from his relationship with the sentries. Olivier's film, in fact, makes the most of Horatio's character, because, in the absence of Fortinbras, Horatio will assume authority at the end. This is in spite of cutting his lines explaining the reasons for the warlike preparations (mostly retained in the BBC version) as well as his lines about Rome—for, since the ghost appears only once in Olivier's first scene, he needs no chat to separate the two appearances. Closeups, a magnificent costume, and a strong, handsome physical presence, give Olivier's Horatio, played by Norman Wooland, the importance that even his missing lines alone could not have supplied. So too the Boston Shakespeare Company production increases Horatio's importance in spite of cuts by keeping him on stage almost all the time, throughout most of 2.2, for example, and during Hamlet's advice to the players. In contrast, the BBC production shifts Horatio into nonentity status not only by eliminating his longest speeches but also by casting Robert Swann, a sweet-faced but pallid actor, in the role.

The BBC does not cut very much more from Horatio's lines; only the opening of the scene when the sailors come with their message from Hamlet (4.6.1–5), and a couple of bits from the graveyard scene. This production allows him his full scope in the last scene, giving him the memorable lines upon Hamlet's death ("Good night, sweet prince, / And flights of angels sing thee to thy rest!") and also his longest speech since the first scene, fifteen lines addressed to Fortinbras. The fact that a Horatio with lines cut (Olivier's) can still appear to be magnificent and that a Horatio with most of his lines can sink in importance (BBC) demonstrates that visual business can conquer the force of the words.

When we add up the significance of the cut political lines, such as Horatio's on the king, we begin to realize that Jan Kott may have been correct about *Hamlet*. That is, it takes quite a few deletions to strip the play of its political sinews, as does the BBC production.[6] Some of these political lines give a sense of action that takes place between the scenes, a sense that what we see enacted on stage is only a portion of the life at Elsinore. The attendants that give the sense of a whole political world are missing in the BBC version.[7] Though very often cut in productions, no doubt for very good, practical reasons—not necessarily to vitiate the political aspect—the attendants serve important functions. Their presence implies that one cannot easily gain access to the nobles at court, particularly to the king or queen, as we see from Hamlet's request that Horatio intercede to get the pirates' letters through to the king (4.6.11–12). Attendants isolate the king and queen.

One of the BBC's most interesting political omissions comes from the first scene, after the ghost's second appearance. Horatio has just said "Let us impart what we have seen tonight / Unto young Hamlet; for, upon my life, / This spirit, dumb to us, will speak to him." Horatio's next two lines ("Do you consent we shall acquaint him with it, / As needful in our loves, fitting our duty?"), which may be taken as an example of repetition with variation, can say much more, depending on their tone. Horatio's suggestion ("Let us impart"), followed by the question ("Do you consent . . .?"), especially as the second is worded, make it possible for a question to rise in our minds about what their duty *is.* Why not *King* Hamlet in this first mention of the dead king's son? If *he* is not the king, why not tell the king? Horatio seems to be trying to persuade Marcellus and Bernardo when he refers to "loves" and "duty." If Horatio says "Do you consent" blandly, no significance would attach to the lines, and they might as well be cut. But if they are spoken conspiratorially, followed by an earnest, pleading tone and then a gesture of relief upon their agreement, the political significance would be clear.[8] In describing how this might be played, I am probably overstating it somewhat, but actors could convey the political undertones much more subtly. In spite of these cuts, the BBC does in a muted way offer a somewhat political view of the play through retention of the ambassadors and Fortinbras.

In contrast, one of the more apolitical *Hamlet*s, Olivier's, eliminates virtually every political line. With Cornelius, Voltemand, Fortinbras, and even Rosencrantz and Guildenstern gone, with all those extra attendants missing, the film submerges almost every political point. Yet the court scenes communicate something of a political element. In the first we see aged councillors nodding sagely, listening with convinced faces to Claudius's advice to Hamlet on mourning. One telling moment comes at the end of the film when in an overhead shot we see a ring of guards point their long halberds at Claudius; they have accepted Laertes's explanation and have chosen sides. The film, having cut so many lines and characters, makes its few political points visually. On the other hand, Kozintsev cuts to emphasize the political *Hamlet*, while his visualizations support the text he has carved from Shakespeare's.

Laertes, Claudius, Polonius

Other cuts affect the characterization of Hamlet's opponents. The BBC cuts fifteen lines from Laertes's forty lines of warning to Ophelia about Hamlet, as I have already mentioned when discussing her. Looking at his speech in this scene, we can see that Shakespeare makes him speak sententiously, with a good deal of repetition with variation. Before we ever hear this kind of speech from Polonius, we hear it from his son. Shakespeare wants us to perceive the similarity.

Both Claudius's and Laertes's characters are affected by the BBC's omission of much of Claudius's flattery of Laertes for his skill in fencing (4.7.73–81; 83–94; 100–102). Without these lines, Claudius is less manipulative; Laertes capitulates too easily. When no lines are removed from 4.7, we may excuse Laertes to some extent because of Claudius's skill; without some of the lines, Laertes becomes more culpable because too eager. On the other hand, with the scene eliminated altogether, as it is in the Boston Shakespeare Company production and in two other productions mentioned in Halstead, we must withhold judgment about Laertes and postpone consideration of Laertes's rash revenge compared to Hamlet's deliberate or delayed revenge until the encounters at the graveside and at the duel. Cutting part of the scene, as the BBC production does, puts him in the most negative light.

The BBC production also cuts Claudius's lines to Laertes that seem to some to be a key to the play but which are found only in Q2 and are cut in many productions:

> That we would do,
> We should do when we would; for this 'would' changes,
> And hath abatements and delays as many
> As there are tongues, are hands, are accidents;
> And then this 'should' is like a spendthrift's sigh
> That hurts by easing.
>
> (4.7.118–23)

The Olivier *Hamlet*. Claudius looks at Hamlet's chair as he speaks, "That we would do, We should do when we would." (*Still courtesy Janus Films.*)

The actor could show—or not—that the words might apply to Hamlet, as in Olivier's version, where Claudius says them while looking at and touching Hamlet's chair, almost forgetting about Laertes in his recollection of Hamlet. There is no way that the BBC actor, Patrick Stewart, could compensate for these cut lines.

Polonius's excised lines, on the other hand, are perhaps compensated for by other lines. The BBC Polonius is the literary critic, the rememberer of his youth, the prideful spy, the source of humor and sometimes of wisdom in spite of omitted lines here and there that express these characteristics.[9] But cuts in other characters' lines can affect Polonius's characterization, though theoretical considerations will not suffice always to tell us precisely how. Since, for example, the BBC omits much of the First Player's declamation on Pyrrhus (2.2.471–91), Polonius's line "This is too long" (2.2.492) describes a mere nine lines instead of thirty, making him even more foolishly impatient and making Hamlet's rejoinder even more appropriate: "He's for a jig, or a tale of bawdry, or he sleeps." But perhaps Shakespeare intended Polonius's criticism of the First Player's lengthy speech to receive a sympathetic response from at least some in the audience and perhaps not just from those for whom caviar would be a waste. Perhaps the audience too would be impatient with this seemingly digressive display, which brings all action to a standstill and which seems to have nothing to do with Hamlet's task. Eliciting a sympathetic response for Polonius here could be part of Shakespeare's plan to make him a positive as well as negative character. On the other hand, perhaps Shakespeare counted on his audience to be fascinated by the First Player's declamatory skill or even to understand the relevance of a speech about Pyrrhus, the seeker of revenge, told from the point of view of the victim; in that case, by today's standards, which incline towards impatience with long speeches, perhaps nine lines are enough to make us agree with Hamlet—any more and we would tend to agree with Polonius. Everything depends on the First Player: if he mesmerizes us, then Polonius is wrong, whether he allows the First Player nine lines or thirty lines; if he bores us, then Polonius is as right after nine lines as after thirty.

Of course, cuts in Polonius's lines also affect others, just as cuts in Ophelia's lines do. One of the BBC's omissions, after "How pregnant sometimes his replies are," for example, removes a clue about Hamlet's reason for pretending madness, if indeed he does pretend:

a happiness that often madness hits upon, which reason and sanity could not so prosperously be delivered of.

(2.2.207–9)

Hamlet's madness allows him to say what he could not were he deemed sane. And of course, these lines are more evidence of Polonius's humor or wisdom, depending on how they are acted. (Hume Cronyn in the Burton *Hamlet* certainly raises a laugh with them, as he does from almost all his lines.)

The BBC version, unlike most productions, retains almost the entire Reynaldo scene. Directors who cut it lose an opportunity Shakespeare provided to show Polonius's suspiciousness, his underhandedness, his proclivities for spying—even on his own son. Perhaps more importantly, the Reynaldo scene also reveals that some time has passed, enough for Polonius to send money after Laertes, enough to make one wonder what Hamlet has been doing all this time. Since, however, skipping Reynaldo has been more the rule than not even in productions that present a dilatory Hamlet, a performance can certainly communicate a sense of Hamlet as unequal to his task without such hints as the lapse of time, without "How all occasions," often without "O what a rogue and peasant slave am I!" and even without his refusal to kill the praying Claudius. Acting alone can show Hamlet's unwillingness or inability. As Pasternak says in the context of his textual omissions:

> As soon as a theatre has penetrated [Shakespeare's] artistic intention and mastered it, one can and should sacrifice the most vivid and profound lines (not to mention the pale and indifferent ones), provided that the actors have achieved an equally talented performance of an acted, mimed, silent, or laconic equivalent. . . . (Kozintsev, 215)

The BBC also keeps most of Polonius's exchange with Ophelia in her closet scene (2.1), unlike Olivier, who disengages Ophelia altogether from Polonius, choosing instead a voiceover of Ophelia speaking in a bemused tone as if to herself. The film does not provide the lines through which Shakespeare gave opportunities (accepted or not) to show Polonius as solicitous (or not) of Ophelia or sorry about his misjudgment of Hamlet.

Shakespeare also gives Polonius ample opportunity to express his self-satisfaction through such lines as

Hath there been such a time—I would fain know that—
That I have positively said "Tis so',
When it prov'd otherwise?

(2.2.152–54)

If circumstances lead me, I will find
Where truth is hid, though it were hid indeed
Within the centre.

(2.2.156–58)

These lines are found in all three basic texts, but omitted by BBC and several other productions, including CBS. Olivier omits the second set. Nevertheless, actors such as Eric Porter (BBC) and Felix Aylmer (Olivier) effectively express Polonius's self-satisfaction: this is a generalized character trait that an actor's demeanor can signify. But an actor cannot, without the lines, give the information, which the version broadcast in the United States and Olivier's film cut:

> And truly in my youth I suff'red much extremity for love. Very near this.
>
> (2.2.187–88)

There is something endearing about these lines, found in Q1, Q2, and F1, even though we sense the ludicrousness of his comparison of himself to Hamlet.[10]

At the end of the nunnery scene, the BBC retains two important lines, cut by the Boston Shakespeare Company production, Richardson, Olivier, CBS, and some ten others, as listed by Halstead. Polonius understands the tenor of Claudius's determination to send Hamlet to England, for he says, "To England send him; *or confine him where / Your wisdom best shall think*" (italics mine; 3.1.186–87). Polonius in the Plummer version (1964) says the lines carelessly, distractedly, concerned more with Ophelia's pain than with Claudius. But these lines, said differently, could be very chilling. While most productions that retain the lines hurry Ophelia off so that she will not hear, the BBC shows a three-shot of Ophelia, Polonius, and Claudius; it is almost as if neither Polonius nor Ophelia recognizes the import of these lines. But another production choice would allow for Polonius to understand fully what he is saying and for Ophelia to show some reaction to this intelligence.

Ghost

While one cannot include the ghost among the opponents, Horatio's question to the ghost about extorted treasure could have shed a negative light on the ghost (1.1.136–39—found in Q1, Q2 and F1, but cut in BBC, Olivier, Chamberlain, and many stage productions listed in Halstead). This omission, coupled with the BBC's omission of Hamlet's lines (in Q1, Q2, and F1, but cut in many productions,[11] including several that cut the whole prayer scene), suggests a conscious effort on the script writer's part not to denigrate the ghost:

> And how his [Hamlet's father] audit stands who knows save heaven?
> But in our circumstance and course of thought
> 'Tis heavy with him. . . .
>
> (3.3.82–84)

It is true the BBC retains the lines about the crowing of the cock and the ghost's swift departure; when these are cut, as they are in the Chamberlain version, no ambiguity about the ghost remains, no reason for Hamlet's testing of the ghost's word, for the more credible the ghost, the less justification there is in Hamlet's delay; his reason for delay, "The spirit I have seen / May be a devil . . ." (2.2.594–95), becomes rationalization. Still, Shakespeare's whole fabric is subtle. The question is, would any audience be able to catch the doubts about the ghost's nature that Shakespeare builds into the scene if any of the relevant lines are cut, especially if the production retains all the lines suggesting the ghost's riveting presence and credibility. The BBC does not cut a single line of the ghost's, so this production gives him his full dignity, his full opportunity to be convincing.

Olivier's *Hamlet*, with only one visitation by the ghost, cuts Horatio's initial challenge, kept in BBC:

> *Hor.* What are thou that usurp'st the time of night
>   Together with that fair and warlike form
>   In which the majesty of buried Denmark
>   Did sometimes march? By heaven I charge thee, speak!
> *Mar.* It is offended.
> *Ber.*   See, it stalks away.
> *Hor.* Stay! Speak, speak! I charge thee, speak!
>
>   [*Exit Ghost*]
>   (1.1.46–51)

These lines present us at the outset with suspicion about the ghost's nature. Horatio assumes that some being has usurped the form of King Hamlet. His skepticism and suspicion, even his awe, increase the audience's doubts. Omitting these lines eliminates the doubt, and indeed Olivier cuts Hamlet's expression of doubt with the omission of his "O, what a rogue and peasant slave am I" soliloquy (2.2.594–601).

Olivier's film also cuts lines that refer to the ghost's warlike nature or to its feats of arms, about its being privy to its country's fate, about its treasure. The film also cuts Hamlet's early lines about the ghost that reflect doubt about the ghost's nature:

>   If it assume my noble father's person,
>   I'll speak to it, though hell itself should gape
>   And bid me hold my peace. . . .
>
>   (1.2.243–45)

These lines, found in all three primary texts and in most productions, including BBC, weave the tissue of doubt in the audience's mind. The Boston Shakespeare Company production also cuts many of these lines, and surely for the same purpose: to eliminate any lines that cast doubt on the ghost. This purification of the ghost affects the audience's perception of Hamlet.

Hamlet

The BBC production does not cut very many of Hamlet's lines. Still, changes in other characters affect Hamlet's depiction. If Ophelia is even weaker than the text's Ophelia, then Hamlet is more cruel to castigate her, less admirable in loving her. The BBC, for example, cuts none of Hamlet's lines to her in the nunnery scene but earlier cut some of her opportunities to show strength, as we have seen. The BBC makes up for this imbalance by cutting some of Hamlet's cruelest lines to her during "The Mousetrap," making him a less brutal Hamlet. But when Ophelia's responses to his double entendres are cut, so too are the double entendres, with their effect on an audience's perception of Hamlet's character (negative in the nineteenth century, more positive in our own sexually open age). If Horatio, given fewer words to say, is more vapid, then Hamlet's reliance on him seems misplaced, and thus reflects back on Hamlet, making him appear pathetic to lean on such a slender pillar. If Claudius is less clever because his manipulative speeches are cut, then he is a less formidable foe and Hamlet becomes weaker too. All these effects appear without cutting many lines of Hamlet's. Thus, all the excisions in the BBC's other characters have an effect on Hamlet.

The BBC does leave intact many passages that other media productions eliminate. When Hamlet's greetings to Marcellus and Bernardo are cut, as Chamberlain and Kozintsev cut them (1.2.173–77), his affability is diminished. (Q1 has "good even sir*s*" rather than "sir"; Halstead lists only four stage productions that cut the greetings, and only one additional media production, CBS, that cuts "good even, sir," traditionally addressed to Bernardo.) Similarly, when the stage directions in "Let us go in together" and "Nay, come, let's go together" are ignored, as they are in so many productions (the Boston Shakespeare Company production, Kozintsev), an important aspect of Hamlet's character, his civility and graciousness, his princely condescension, disappears. The BBC text does allow Hamlet his full scope for princeliness by retaining these lines.

As usual for cut lines, the majority of Hamlet's cuts in the BBC version contain either a difficult word or a repetition with variation or both. Whatever the purpose of the BBC cuts, they nevertheless weaken the portrait Shakespeare builds through line after line of characterization. Some, however, are more expendable than others. It omits, for example, the difficult "dram of eale" lines (1.4.36–38); Hamlet has already imparted their sense. (Only Q2 contains the whole passage, on one defect, in which the "dram of eale" lines appear; Halstead lists many productions that omit the whole passage, but several others omit only these same lines.) The BBC cuts other difficult passages or repetitions with variation in the closet scene, where, since Hamlet has so many lines, they can perhaps be sacrificed. The first, 3.4.45–51, constitutes about half the lines that Hamlet says to express his disgust at Gertrude's remarriage. The BBC keeps the first five lines:

> Such an act
> That blurs the grace and blush of modesty;
> Calls virtue hypocrite; takes off the rose
> From the fair forehead of an innocent love,
> And sets a blister there; makes marriage-vows
> As false as dicers' oaths.

However, it cuts the last six, more impassioned, but more difficult, lines:

> O, such a deed
> As from the body of contraction plucks
> The very soul, and sweet religion makes
> A rhapsody of words. Heaven's face does glow
> O'er this solidity and compound mass
> With heated visage, as against the doom—
> Is thought-sick at the act.

Many productions, including the BBC, omit lines such as these that refer to religion, God or heaven.

The second BBC cut in this scene contains only one difficulty, the word "mope":

> Eyes without feeling, feeling without sight,
> Ears without hands or eyes, smelling sans all,
> Or but a sickly part of one true sense
> Could not so mope.
>
> (3.4.78–81)

This passage, found only in Q2, is omitted by a large number of productions, according to Halstead. Steevens, in Furness's *Variorum*, explains "mope" as meaning "exhibit such marks of stupidity," and the glossary in the BBC text follows suit, but since "mope" means something so different today, the passage's whole meaning might be lost. Hamlet says that even one with impairments of the senses would not have chosen as Gertrude has.

The BBC cuts another image that uses religion in this scene, right after "Assume a virtue, if you have it not":

That monster custom, who all sense doth eat,
Of habits devil, is angel yet in this,
That to the use of actions fair and good
He likewise gives a *frock* [emphasis mine] or livery
That aptly is put on.

(3.4.161–65)

These lines are explained in those that follow: "Refrain to-night; / And that shall lend a kind of easiness / To the next abstinence." The production then omits the next, further amplification: "For use almost can change the stamp of nature, / And either curb the devil, or throw him out, / With wondrous potency" (3.4.168–70). These lines are found in Q2 only, and there in corrupt form; therefore, it is not surprising that many productions omit them.

Many productions listed by Halstead end the scene with the couplet "I must be cruel only to be kind; / Thus bad begins and worse remains behind" or with the first line of the couplet (3.4.178–79). The BBC, however, does continue the scene to the end. Its final cut in this scene (occurring right after the sarcastic " 'Twere good you let him know") contains an image that would probably be unclear to a modern audience:

For who that's but a queen, fair, sober, wise,
Would from a paddock, from a bat, a gib,
Such dear concernings hide? Who would do so?
No, in despite of sense and secrecy,
Unpeg the basket on the house's top,
Let the birds fly, and, like the famous ape,
To try conclusions, in the basket creep
And break your own neck down.

(3.4.189–96)

Halstead lists another large block of productions that omit this passage, though found in both Q2 and F1, probably because the fable Shakespeare alludes to is lost. Such lines are understandably excised; to omit so many, however, is to vitiate Hamlet's portrait. These lines, with their difficult diction and imagery, reveal that quirky turn of mind that so characterizes the prince.

Some cuts in the BBC production do not fall into the category of these examples, however. Other excisions have a more direct effect on the audience's perception of Hamlet's character. Hamlet's parting words to the ghost watchers, for example, contain neither difficulty nor redundancy. I have already mentioned the absence of lines that promise rewards:

And what so poor a man as Hamlet is

May do t'express his love and friending to you,
God willing, shall not lack.

(1.5.185–87)

In addition to a political thought, these lines tell us that Hamlet inspires a selfless loyalty, that Horatio, Marcellus, and Bernardo have brought the news of the ghost to Hamlet in spite of the expectation of a more certain reward from the king. The lines can betray also, depending on intonation, wit, a gentlemanly humility, or self-pity in the words "so poor a man as Hamlet," a suitable prologue to his reluctance: "O cursed spite, / That ever I was born to set it right!"

The dozens of cuts in the BBC version affect all facets of the character Shakespeare creates. The BBC's omission of "Then are our beggars bodies, and our monarchs and outstretch'd heroes the beggars' shadows" (2.2.263–64), a traditional cut according to Halstead, affects our perception of Hamlet as philosophical. Here, the script not only cuts most of Hamlet's attempt to parry wits with Rosencrantz and Guildenstern but also Hamlet's first allusion to beggars and kings, which will be amplified in Hamlet's last interview with Claudius (4.3.21–24).

With cuts of two of Hamlet's three conjurations of his schoolfellows to be honest with him (2.2.283–86, all three also cut in Olivier and CBS), we lose the excess that smacks of the sort of teasing Hamlet engages in with Osric. The lines could indicate, in fact, that they have already lost his confidence; a sarcastic tone could make up to some extent for their omission, as it does in the BBC production. On the other hand, depending on the actor and the director's interpretation, the lines could also allow Hamlet to express his sincere hope that his schoolfellows can be, will be honest with him.

The lines showing Hamlet's awareness that his demeanor to Rosencrantz and Guildenstern has not been what it could have been do contain some slight difficulties that may have occasioned their excision—many productions do eliminate them. In these lines, having asked for their hands again, Hamlet explains why:

. . . lest my extent to the players, which, I tell you, must show fairly outwards, should more appear like entertainments than yours.

(2.2.368–70)

But the lines also reveal important information about Hamlet's character. We may assume from these lines either that his warmth to the players is put on, if he is speaking sincerely to Rosencrantz and Guildenstern (which he may not be), or that he has not so far shown much warmth to his school friends.

In the BBC production, all the comments about the players—the knight, the lover, the wit, the clown, the lady—are gone (2.2.318–22), leaving a stark "He that plays the king shall be welcome—his Majesty shall have tribute from me" (317–18). Hamlet's tone suggests that he is thinking of Claudius and that he has already had a glimmer of an idea about using a play to trap Claudius. This would be difficult to underline in the rush of the succeeding lines; thus, many productions, including Olivier and CBS, eliminate the rest. But again, loss of these lines removes an opportunity for Hamlet to display his wit, attractive energy, and broad interests.

Hamlet's words to Polonius, immediately before the players arrive, being unclear, indicate that Hamlet is again playing at being mad:

> and then, you know,
> 'It came to pass, as most like it was.'
> The first row of the pious chanson will show you more. . . .
>
> (411–14)

But his demeanor could do this also. Perhaps that is why so many productions, including the BBC, cut them (Halstead lists thirty-five that do). Productions that cut the lines, however, diminish Hamlet's verbal high spirits.

The BBC cuts much of Hamlet's advice to the players at the beginning of 3.2, especially about overacting and overstepping the bonds of nature, from "O, it offends me to the soul" to "Pray you avoid it" (six lines) and from "O, there be players that I have seen" to "pitiful ambition in the fool that uses it" (thirteen lines). Even Q1 has a version of these lines, but a large number of productions do cut them. Inherently fascinating as an expression of Shakespeare's ideas about acting, useful as an indication of Hamlet's interests and knowledge, the lines may also be relevant to how *The Murder of Gonzago* is played. In the BBC production particularly, Hamlet's evident impatience with the acting troupe's dramatic efforts would have been better prepared for if the advice about naturalness had been left in. Of course, the barely muted disdain with which the First Player listens to Hamlet's advice would have made the longer version painful to watch.

The BBC cuts part of Hamlet's directions to Horatio just before *Gonzago* is to begin:

> Give him heedful note;
> For I mine eyes will rivet to his face;
> And, after, we will both our judgments join
> In censure of his seeming.
>
> (3.2.82–85)

Halstead lists fewer than a dozen productions that cut these lines, including Olivier and CBS. These lines are important because they tell us that

Hamlet has no intention of acting against Claudius during the play; without these lines we might, with some critics, consider his failure to act directly upon Claudius's reaction yet another piece of evidence for Hamlet's weakness.

Unlike many productions, the BBC retains the scene where Hamlet plays cat and mouse with Rosencrantz and Guildenstern after he has hidden Polonius's body (4.2, omitted in Q1) and the scene with Fortinbras's captain as Hamlet is leaving for England (4.4, only Q2 has the full scene; both Q1 and F1 stop after the dialogue between Fortinbras and the captain). In the latter scene the BBC's only serious omission is from the soliloquy, after "Now, whether it be / Bestial oblivion, or some craven scruple / Of thinking too precisely on th' event":

> A thought which, quarter'd, hath but one part wisdom
> And ever three parts coward. . . .
>
> (42–43)

Though the word "craven" in line 40, which is kept, does reflect the same idea as the word "coward" in line 43, the repetition here emphasizes Hamlet's self-criticism and thus could, depending on tone, make it seem excessive, a self-criticism that the audience could not agree with (Bevington, 6). As Kozintsev says, "It is not always necessary to believe what people say about themselves" (223). Or the repetition could underline Hamlet's opinion about cowardice. Halstead lists among those that retain the scene no production that cuts these lines.

Like many productions, the BBC cuts some of Hamlet's musing on death and skulls. Several of these, but not all, seem to be cut for the usual reasons, difficulty or repetition with variation. The usual reasons for excision, do not apply to the long *ubi sunt* declamation on the bones of the lawyer (96–97; 99–112). Shakespeare through these lines provides insights into Hamlet's character, especially important at this late point in the play. The prince accepts wryly the transience of the world, the limited meaning of life in the flesh. The BBC omits other lines because of difficulty or because they could make Hamlet sound like a snob: "By the Lord, Horatio, this three years I have took note of it: the age is grown so picked that the toe of the peasant comes so near the heel of the courtier, he galls his kibe" (133–36). But such smoothings of his character ultimately make him less interesting.

Later in the scene, the BBC cuts Hamlet's important self-assessment:

> For, though I am not splenitive and rash,
> Yet have I in me something dangerous,
> Which let thy wiseness far. Hold off thy hand.
>
> (255–57)

Q1 does not have the first of these lines; Halstead lists twenty-three productions, including CBS, that cut these lines. In the last scene, the BBC cuts two lines that express Hamlet's opinion that his enemies moved much faster than he, faster than he could have been expected to, perhaps: "Ere I could make a prologue to my brains, / They had begun the play" (30–31, found in Q2 and F1; Q1 does not have the first part of the scene corresponding to the first 75 lines in F1, and many productions cut in accordance with Q1). Shakespeare gives Hamlet the opportunity to state the case against those who criticize him for delay.

BBC also cuts five lines that contain no difficulty, lines that describe Hamlet's hoisting of Rosencrantz and Guildenstern with their own petard:

> Folded the writ up in the form of th' other;
> Subscrib'd it, gave't th' impression, plac'd it safely,
> The changeling never known. Now, the next day
> Was our sea-fight; and what to this was sequent
> Thou knowest already.
>
> (5.2.51–55)

Found in both Q2 and F1, these lines are cut by many productions. With their short, parallel phrases and short words, the lines give the utterance a breathlessness and excitement that express Hamlet's feelings about his coup, a feeling to which Shakespeare expected the audience to respond.

The BBC cuts some sixteen lines of Hamlet's to or about Osric, none containing any great difficulty; most could be clarified by gestures. On the other hand, the BBC cuts none of Hamlet's apology to Laertes, nor Laertes's answer to Hamlet. In fact, in the duel and its aftermath there is only one small cut:

> I'll ha't.
> . . . what a wounded name,
> Things standing thus unknown, shall live behind me!
>
> (335–37)

This omission leaves a sentence that begs Horatio to act on his behalf: "O, God! Horatio, If thou didst ever hold me in thy heart, Absent thee from felicity awhile. . . ," yet Shakespeare's line makes the "O, God! Horatio" part of Hamlet's expression of dismay: "O, God! Horatio, what a wounded name, / Things standing thus unknown, shall live behind me!" His request to Horatio is couched not in such pleading language as the BBC makes it, but simply: "If thou didst ever hold me in thy heart, / Absent thee from felicity awhile . . . ." Shakespeare's version is quieter and more compelling, because Hamlet demands less.

Though the BBC cuts few of Hamlet's lines relative to other productions, the effect is nevertheless to produce a simplified, smoothed out and less interesting character than Shakespeare provides a blueprint for in his script. In chapter 12 I discuss the concept that informs the director's cuts and other choices and the brilliant acting that can compensate for some of the cuts. Here, the important point to note is that many of the BBC cuts are traditional, often deriving from long stage practice. Looking carefully at the cut lines—even lines innocently cut to remove difficulties or to avoid repetitions—reveals that they contribute either to the characterization of the person whose lines they are or to that of other characters. The omissions of lines can also affect the whole ambience of the play, de-emphasizing the political element, changing the ghost from problematic to unquestionably sympathetic. Examining the function of the cut lines helps to discover their use by Shakespeare; the omissions of lines distorts or weakens such characters as Ophelia, Gertrude and Horatio, Hamlet's enemies and Hamlet himself—sometimes in ways that contradict what the production is trying to do. That happens because directors accept the traditional cuts instead of rethinking the entire text. This is true although directors do not turn to an acting text, with passages already excised, but use instead a conflated text, such as the Signet edition, as the script for the production.

Since many successful productions do cut lines, often more than the BBC, with stunning effect, it would be foolish to say that productions should not cut any of Shakespeare's lines. All sorts of reasons make this true: for one, visual effects and interpretative acting obviate the need for some lines; for another, Shakespeare has given us almost too much to grasp within the play's two-hour (actually closer to four-hour) passage on the stage. Sometimes cuts reshape the text to fit the director's concept, a procedure to which I do not automatically object. At other times, visual substitutions make the lines redundant. Kozintsev's *Hamlet* both cuts to reshape and substitutes visual effects to compensate for lines.

Notes

1. In this chapter I use Halstead's abbreviation for the *Hamlet* with John Neville (CBS). Referring to *Hamlet*, Jay Halio (324) says that "the richer the play, the more it may respond to pruning and reshaping"; this may partially explain the number of cuts in *Hamlet* productions. For a detailed account of the cuts in Richardson's *Hamlet*, see Mullin.

2. If there is a directorial design, it is that Hamlet stands alone, virtually friendless in a not unfriendly world. I discuss the concept in chapter 12.

3. For Van Dam's summary of speeches, in verse and in prose, taken from the Globe edition (derived from Q2), see Appendix 3.

4. Harley Granville-Barker (1.181–82) notes the pauses that mark the crescendo: "How," he asks about the words after the second pause, "can any sensitive speaker miss the increased emphasis, the 'No nonsense now!' of the three monosyllables, 'From this time . . .'?"

5. Beatrice Straight originated the role in this production, which played during the winter of 1979–80.

6. Other lines in this category, all omitted in the BBC production: Hamlet's promise of a reward to those who serve him (1.5.185–87—also omitted by the Boston Shakespeare Company production and CBS but found in Q1, Q2, and F1, and most productions, though some change it to eliminate the mention of God); Gertrude's promise, already mentioned, of a reward to Rosencrantz and Guildenstern (2.2.21–26); Claudius's lines, about attending to diplomatic matters, that give us a sense of a political Claudius who works at being king (2.2.81–83—found in Q1, Q2, and F1, but not often said on stage, since so many productions cut the ambassadors to whom these lines are addressed); one of Rosencrantz's repetitions of the word "ambition" in the first confrontation of the two spies with Hamlet (2.2.260–61—Q1 and F1 cut the whole section on ambition); Hamlet's cynical lines to Horatio about courtiers' flattery (3.2.58–60—found in all three basic texts, but cut by many productions); Claudius to Gertrude about consulting with "our wisest friends" (4.1.37–44—not in Q1 and many productions); Claudius to Laertes about consulting with "your wisest friends" (4.5.200—in Q2 and F1, but cut by many productions).

7. Missing attendants include the one who tells Horatio that sailors are seeking him (4.6.1–5, in Q2 and F1) and the Lord who repeats Osric's message (5.2.189–200, found only in Q2). The BBC *Hamlet* even cuts the lines, found in Q1, Q2, and F1 but cut in many productions, indicating that Laertes has followers: "Sirs, stand you all without. . . . Keep the door" (4.5.109–12). Many productions eliminate not only these but others as well: the gentleman with Horatio (only in Q2) in Ophelia's first mad scene and the reference to one Claudio who receives Hamlet's letters from the sailors (4.7.40, in Q2 and F1).

8. The lines are also omitted in the Boston Shakespeare Company production, Olivier, Richardson, Burton, and many productions listed by Halstead, but are found in all three basic texts.

9. See especially these omissions: 2.1.103–6, 113–17; 2.2.125–27, 152–54, 156–58.

10. Halstead erroneously says that Q1 omits these lines; actually they are transposed to follow the nunnery scene.

11. Halstead sometimes, as in this instance, says that Q1 cuts a line that is included in essence; that is, Q1 contains the *idea* of the line or lines, perhaps in fewer lines than Q2 or F1.

4

Kozintsev's Visual Mastery

Though Kozintsev, like virtually every other media producer of *Hamlet*, has a theatrical background, having directed *Hamlet* on stage long before attempting film, he perhaps more than anyone directing *Hamlet* before Ragnar Lyth saw that the visual medium has to be different from the stage. In his response to Pasternak on the "rightness" of radical excisions, Kozintsev says that on the screen one could use equivalents but "on the stage, the spoken word is king . . ." (215).[1] He asserts in an excerpt derived from his director's diary, "Film rhythm [must] replace the verse harmony with a new fabric as rich in its way as the verbal one was." To do this is to create "not a 'movie version,' but cinematographic poetry" (234–35). Through both extratextual and textual visualizations, both enhanced by emblems, Kozintsev indeed created cinematographic poetry.

Extratextual Elements: Setting

By "extratextual" I mean all those visualizations not specifically called for in Shakespeare's text. According to this definition, setting is not usually extratextual, for even if a production were to provide the barest of sets, the words and gestures of the actors would call forth the idea of setting:

> 'Tis bitter cold. . . .
>
> (1.1.8)

> But look, the morn in russet mantle clad
> Walks o'er the dew of yon high eastward hill.
>
> (1.1.166–67)

What if it tempt you toward the flood, my lord,
Or to the dreadful summit of the cliff
That beetles o'er his base into the sea. . . .
The very place puts toys of desperation,
Without more motive, into every brain
That looks so many fathoms to the sea
And hears it roar beneath.[2]

(1.4.69–78)

These textual examples are obvious, but even for scenes where the text does not explicitly note the setting, such as the first court scene, the audience will recognize and shape a setting appropriate to the occasion, however bare the actual set. Kozintsev includes none of these lines, but instead creates his own setting that has little to do with what Shakespeare suggests in the text. For that reason, we may call his use of setting "extratextual." Kozintsev separates viewers from the everyday and plunges them into a highly charged Elsinore in a Denmark with Russian overtones. As Kozintsev says in his diary: "However much we might try to reproduce the English or the Danish world, the film . . . will be Russian" (243). However carefully, one might add, the film reproduces Renaissance costumes and medieval settings, the film will be contemporary.

Kozintsev highlights the political *Hamlet,* a treatment that invites the viewer to make comparisons with modern political regimes, particularly with Stalin's dictatorship. Arthur P. Mendel (746, quoted in Rowe, viii) speaks of "the Aesopian language of literary criticism, traditional among the Russian intelligentsia, that ostensibly talks about other places and other times when the subject is here and now." Kozintsev offers an Aesopian interpretation of *Hamlet.* But he is not much interested in interpretations that can be reduced to one sentence. He strives to make each moment vibrant through film's visual means.

Extremely important for grounding the mood of the whole, the first moments of the film (I note four segments) introduce us most forcefully to the world of the film. Kozintsev omits the first ghost scene (and thus takes no opportunity to individualize the guards). Instead, a prologue (segment one) introduces the first archetypal images of sea, earth, stone, iron and fire—as Jack Jorgens observes (223). Sea sounds give way to those first riveting notes of Shostakovich's startling music, which leads to the drama of the death of King Hamlet (segment two): the camera pans past the edge of the stone wall to reveal beyond it the back of a man holding a black flag ready. Two horsemen give a signal from below for the flag signifying the death of the king to be flown, and in a reverse shot we see flag after flag unfurled from the wooden veranda overlooking the courtyard of the castle. A cut to the beach shows Hamlet's arrival (segment three): we hear the pounding of hooves on rocky ground and water sounds telling us that surf is near. Hamlet on a white horse, his posture intense, his cape, flaglike, flying out behind him, plunges toward the castle. When he is completely out of the frame, we see others following him and bystanders watching him. He pounds across the drawbridge. On foot now, he runs up stone outer stairs to find his mother. Inside, they run into each other's arms. All in black, she is noticeably well turned-out, with jewels adorning her fingers. A closeup two-shot shows their faces buried in each other's shoulders. Finally, Hamlet is closed in (segment four): a cut to a black-caped figure shows his signal for cannons to go off. A wheel fills the screen, its spokes manned by workers straining to turn the wheel that lifts the drawbridge, enclosing Hamlet. We see the bridge from a low angle going up; beyond it, a soldier stands in the sunny courtyard. As the shot holds, the edge of the bridge fills more and more of the screen, closing off the sunlight within as the teeth of the portcullis go down. After a closeup of these cruel teeth, a cut frames the castle wall in a doorway through an aperture. The camera tracks back making this aperture smaller and smaller. A high-angle shot of the circular moat shows the last moment of the drawbridge-closing, the moat reflecting the castle. The four segments of the first sequence are aural-visual, not verbal. The visual images do not require verbal reinforcement, nor is there any great movement of actors until Hamlet's forceful entry. All his first gestures suggest great energy, but the atmosphere of the castle enervates him.

The effect of these approximately three minutes of film time is, first, to stop time, because their pace is extremely slow for the most part. Through the long minutes of the first segments, Kozintsev forces us to give in to his time scheme. This technique is reminiscent of Kurosawa's in *Throne of Blood*, in which shot after shot of Washizu (Macbeth) and Miki (Banquo) lost in the forest force us to accede to the slow pace. The plot will unfold as he wishes. At the same time, in both films, we get an impression that what we are seeing is happening in the present. While the text withholds information about time, providing it (when it does) so incidentally that many will miss the references, Kozintsev's film tells us that the death is very recent. Indeed we virtually see it happen when we watch the guard waiting for the signal to unfurl the black flag. The windows are being swathed in mourning cloth even at Hamlet's arrival. The third segment provides an image of the rider's intense feeling for the person who has died. By his concentration, his negligence of those around him, the young man establishes himself both as bereaved and kingly. The last, slow shots of the drawbridge and moat enclosing Hamlet effectively image Denmark as a prison. We see this again when Hamlet, after the graveyard scene, enters the castle. To complete this image of Denmark as a prison, Kozintsev has Hamlet after his death carried to freedom, beyond the drawbridge.

Film settings, more than stage settings, more than television settings, can be expansive in both time and space. While viewers expect film to provide a satisfying illusion of temporal and spatial reality, stage and even television are free from this demand. But movies sometimes upset that expectation or at least manipulate it. While Kozintsev's setting seems real, an actual visitable space rather than a studio creation, he manipulates it in such a way that we see exactly what he wants us to see, not what we would see were we to go to the location site. He withholds or emphasizes setting information to establish the special ground of the play—mirroring the romantic sensibility of Hamlet with symbolic, emblematic elements. The visual expansiveness of frames filled with sea provide little means to grasp the extent of the image. The shadow on the sea, Kozintsev says, is of a merchant's *dacha*, a famous sight (268). But to Western viewers, this, the one view we have of Elsinore, is a mystery. Of Elsinore Kozintsev says, "The boundaries should not be distinct, nor forms complete" and "The general view of the castle must not be filmed" (266, 267). For this is poetry, meant to suggest more than the literal. Almost never showing a long shot of the whole, no establishing shot like Olivier's at the beginning, repeating a few familiar locales but occasionally showing a few unfamiliar ones to suggest that there is much more that we could be shown, Kozintsev provides the comfort of familiarity but withholds a completeness that would relieve us entirely of anxiety.

From the beginning, with the mysterious shots of slow-motion waves

The Kozintsev *Hamlet*. The last black flag being withdrawn. *(Still Courtesy Corinth Films.)*

that seem to draw us into another world, the shots are always connected by straight cuts, an editing choice that provides no clue about the passage of time. There is not one fade, not one dissolve in the entire film. Though familiar enough now, to use straight cuts alone was a relatively unusual technique in 1964. After the sequence of shots showing the enclosing of Hamlet within the castle, the camera cuts to a drummer on horseback for the scene of Claudius's proclamation (1.2). Does this happen immediately? The straight cut implies so, but it cannot be. Yet as the proclamation begins we see that the first black flag is still flying from the tower. Within a few seconds, someone draws it in: mourning is officially over. After the ghost leaves Hamlet, a straight cut reveals Hamlet leaning against a rock. Is this the next morning? Kozintsev has not "completed" the ghost scene as Shakespeare has; there is no reunion of Hamlet with Horatio and Marcellus, no declaration of intent to put a seal of completion on the scene.

Does the next scene, with Ophelia, take place the morning after Hamlet has spoken with his father's ghost? She would not yet have had the opportunity to reject Hamlet. If so, this timing implies that Hamlet cuts himself off from her, rather than she from him, because his life has no room for two great emotional demands. That would justify her implied complaint to him that she has not seen him: "How does your honor for this many a day? . . . I have remembrances of yours / That I have longed long to re-deliver." The implication that Hamlet has avoided her would hardly be appropriate if she had been the one who had repulsed him. Of course, that inconsistency might be precisely what arouses Hamlet's suspicions. But in Kozintsev's version, it seems that her words, which he retains, are accurate.[3] Hamlet must realize that she is too weak to join with him as she cringes from his keen stare. His rejection of Ophelia thus does not imply a revulsion against women in general because of his mother, as in Olivier's film.

Kozintsev retains the lines from the play mentioning time: "But two months dead" (1.2.139) and " 'Tis twice two months, my lord" (3.2.116). The straight cuts, however, provide no visual correlative for the passing of time. Kozintsev says, for example, of the time of "To be": "How long has he thought—an hour, a day, a week?" (253). What are we to make, then, of the question of Hamlet's delay? Editing which obscures the passing of time suggests that Kozintsev de-emphasizes the question, an interpretation corroborated by his not having Hamlet come upon Claudius alone at prayer; we cannot accuse Hamlet of missing any opportunity. Because we are unaware of objective time and also because Claudius seems so well shielded, Kozintsev never allows us to feel impatient with Hamlet. Kozintsev does retain some notion of Hamlet's lassitude by repeated images of Hamlet leaning against a rock, much as Olivier suggested Hamlet's melancholy by repeated images of Hamlet sitting in his chair. Still, though Hamlet suggests that he delays, Kozintsev does not encourage the audience to concur. As he says, "It is not always necessary to believe what people say about themselves" (223). Only Hamlet accuses himself of delay, a sense not based on any external reality but on the fact that he cannot keep his hatred white hot, he cannot cease loving his mother—he uses an affectionate diminutive for "mother" even as he enters her bedroom—and he feels more pity than disgust for Polonius. He is, in short, a moderate man caught in an extreme situation.

Both Kozintsev and Pasternak, the text translator, saw Hamlet as a hero, not as a vacillating weakling and not as an Aristotelian tragic figure with a fatal flaw (France, 201). Merely to resist a tyrant like Claudius, even passively, if only by allowing scepticism to show, is heroic. He gives up his own brilliant political prospects, quietly promised by Claudius (1.2.109; 115–17), for the higher aim of resisting evil by not agreeing with it. *"Hamlet,"* says Pasternak, "is not a drama of weakness, but of duty and self-denial" (Rowe, 148). Kozintsev, in a letter to Pasternak, reveals he wanted to end not with Fortinbras (as he finally did in the film) but with Sonnet 74, which he asks Pasternak to translate. He wanted the poem to express, he says, "the force of noble human aspirations, the force of poetry which refuses to make peace with the baseness and degradation of the era" (Rowe, 152–53). In *Time and Conscience,* Kozintsev says that Hamlet has nobility of soul along with the inability to act, but productions must stress one or the other of these. Choosing the former (116), he distinguishes between hamletism and Hamlet: hamletism is melancholia, weakness of will, inability to act. It is a generic name derived from *an* interpretation of *Hamlet* (127). By removing the flow of time, Kozintsev dodges hamletism. Something as simple, then, as editing style, the straight cuts, conveys Kozintsev's meaning.

Kozintsev represents not so much the *passing* of time as the *meaning* of time: its connection to mortality, its inexorableness. A repeated image forces awareness of time without signifying a specific time: the clock with the figures of bishop, king, queen, soldier, and death. We see this just before Hamlet and the others await the ghost, again faintly through an arch when Polonius seeks Hamlet out for the fishmonger scene, and again after the graveyard scene. The bells, sounding during the titles and between many scenes, remind one of the source of bells: the clock, the church, the churchyard, the graves, death. In his "Director's Diary" (211–76), Kozintsev speaks of this association of bells and death: " 'To be or not to be.' A dull northern day. A church in the distance, the leisurely tolling of a bell. The poor are buried. Hamlet envies the lowliest of the dead" (221).

Other sounds permeate the film, contributing not only to setting but also to meaning. Or rather setting *is* meaning. Sea sounds are never long absent, reminding us of timelessness, ceaseless change yet permanence. The murmur of voices is another constant. Wind is yet another. Shostakovich's romantic music, portentous and powerful, dominates the film, its purpose connected as much to interpretation as to setting. Most often reinforcing the visual image, as for example the music that matches Ophelia's puppetlike dance, sometimes it operates at cross purposes to what we see, offering an ironic contrast, as when the mad Ball music jars in the early part of the ghost scene. At times also the music is the primary conveyer of an idea. For example, when Hamlet finally kills Claudius, the ghost music tells us that Hamlet's father has triumphed. Once during the scene Hamlet fingers his father's portrait on the chain around his neck, but that is a momentary gesture not as potent as the music, which lasts throughout the scene.

More importantly, the music most clearly associated with Hamlet is that played during his declaration "What a piece of work is a man, how noble in reason, how infinite in faculties . . ." (2.2.292–95). Through this musical theme, Kozintsev is able to suggest that Hamlet epitomizes the nobility he describes. But he.is the only one. Music, a traditional extratextual part of stage and screen productions, contributes forcefully to Kozintsev's interpretation by associating sound to meaning, rather than to spaces, as in Olivier's film.

Kozintsev also treats his spaces to some extent differently from Olivier. One setting recurs—the stairway set with warm wood balustrade and turned uprights standing near a corner of the lobby: on the right wall, a giant fireplace and tapestries; beyond the stairway, on the facing wall, large stained-glass windows; under the stairs, a doorway leading to Gertrude's room. Hamlet is walking up these stairs when he sees Horatio and the two honest soldiers. As they walk into the lobby, the fireplace becomes more prominent. It becomes an emblem as it objectifies Hamlet's state of mind, high with flames at moments of passionate resolve, banked or stone cold at other times. Unable to fire his anger, damped as it is with melancholia engendered by being unable, alone, to change society, Hamlet subsides into inaction. Ophelia is unloosed here, the windows streaming with light so that she is all backlit innocence. She returns to this scene again when she is mad, seeming to relive the only precious moment she can remember, when Hamlet put his cheek against hers, a painful pleasure at the time but now her only joy. Guards pace here, waiting for the inevitable entrance of Laertes. The setting realistically is not the property of any one character or one mood, but paradoxically has sufficient associations with Hamlet and Ophelia to make it seem a special sign.

The courtyard, another recurring setting, dark and windswept for the first ghost scene (1.4), is wonderfully frightening in high angles, with huge creaky gate and stables with agitated horses. But later when the players come through this same gate, it will be filled with sunshine, will contain chickens and dogs and even children, the only time they are evident in this castle. Again, the setting does not reflect one mood—as a setting frequently does in Olivier.

But for another recurring setting, the stone by the sea carved with primitive religious symbols against which Hamlet appears, Kozintsev does adopt the association of a particular space to a person. As Olivier's Hamlet in his chair broods in the council chamber, so Kozintsev's Hamlet against the stone broods by the sea—after the ghost's visitation, before the fishmonger scene, at "To be," after the nunnery scene, and finally at the end when Hamlet chooses to die outside where he was most drawn throughout the action. In Pasternak's view, Hamlet is the Christlike sacrificial figure, assigned a "task" by his father. Of "To be" Pasternak says, "These are the most heartfelt and frenzied lines ever written on the anguish of the unknown at the gates of death, in strength of feeling they rise to the bitterness of Gethsemane" (Rowe, 161). By suffering, Hamlet reaches more than heroism. Kozintsev, in having Hamlet's posture at death mimic the broken cross of the graveyard scene (Jorgens, 233), indeed by having his posture reminiscent (in retrospect) of the broken cross in several scenes, may be hinting at the same identity between Hamlet and Christ.

Aside from these and other settings that we see at least twice (the queen's bedroom, Ophelia's bedroom, the lion lobby, councillors' chamber, the mirror room where Claudius prays and plots), Kozintsev also provides a number of settings used only once: Hamlet's room is an example. Hamlet takes Rosencrantz and Guildenstern there for private disclosures that prove to him that they are not his friends. The room of a scholar, with cluttered desk, maps, and globe, its tapestry with a scene from *Metamorphoses* of a nymph turning into a tree as a young man grasps her, signifies that change destroys but that change is necessary for escape. Other settings used once: the ship, the well-traveled road along which Hamlet, a survivor, walks with determination towards the castle again; the graveyard. Since one-time settings imply that more could be seen, they are a device of verisimilitude.

Kozintsev's camera movement and distance, obviously linked to spatial representation, enhance his interpretation. With long shots and either high- or low-angle shots, the camera establishes in the first scene a mood of cool objectivity. We are watching from the vantage point of the ubiquitous peasants—concerned but helpless to affect events—or of the depersonalized guards on the cliffs and ramparts.[4] Often, when there is a medium closeup, it captures an unimportant person, a courtier perhaps. Closeups and even extreme closeups (eyes only) do occur but only after the long shots have already established the audience's relation to the events.

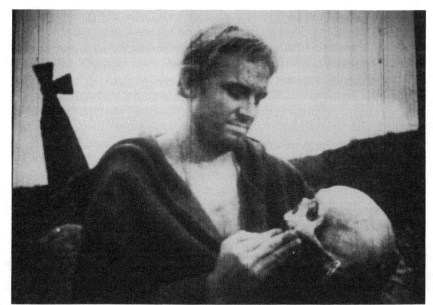

The Kozintsev *Hamlet.* **The graveyard scene; the broken cross.** *(Still courtesy Corinth Films.)*

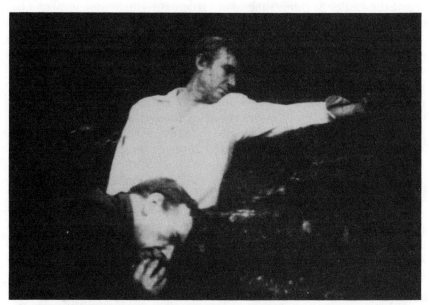

The Kozintsev *Hamlet.* **Hamlet's death.** *(Still courtesy Corinth Films.)*

Camera movement, as in the panning that follows the flame or in the tracking that keeps Hamlet-on-horseback in the right portion of the frame for a time, is extremely natural. That is, the camera movment in general follows the direction of the dominant screen image. Editing too is natural; for example, the straight cut from the wheel to the draw-bridge, that is, from cause to effect; and from elderly courtiers backing away to an unbuttoned Hamlet sitting on the floor in the lobby, that is, from reaction shot to cause of reaction. Tracking is pervasive, but there is no abrupt zooming. The camera is thus conservatively handled, allowing the viewer to accept the reality of the world within the film. It does not encourage audience detachment as do the films of Peter Hall (*Midsummer Night's Dream*, with its cuts according to verse lines) and Peter Brook (*King Lear*, with white-outs). That is, while the long shots and high and low angles keep us in the role of observer, we are never encouraged to remember that what we are seeing is a film, an artifact that we should view as an object. Rather, we are meant to believe that what is happening is real but that we are as powerless to change events as are the observers within the film.

The frame is sometimes pictorially static, as when the bridge goes up, with the soldier beyond it seen standing in the sunlight. "All," says the frame, "is within the narrow confines of the castle." The masking effect of shots into the drawbridge-opening intensifies the claustrophobic men-ace of the castle. At other times, very frequently, the frame implies a life beyond its limits by cutting people in half, showing, say, a shoulder or an arm in left foreground, cutting off a character whose speech we can hear, or revealing only the hands of the serving woman holding up a mirror for Gertrude to look into while she asks Hamlet why death is so particular to him. To the vain Gertrude, people are unimportant; appro-priately, then, the frame catches only the mirror. Later, Hamlet, stalking back and forth in the crowded chamber room, walks in and out of the frame, sometimes coming so close to the camera that the shot goes out of focus. The frame's inability to hold him mirrors Hamlet's turbulent mood.

These two styles of framing—the static and dynamic—are very dif-ferent from each other and stake out the limits of *Hamlet* interpretation. The pictorially static implies artifice, a measured selection complete and perfect in itself. The dynamic implies life, untidy, ragged-edged, an imperfect and arbitrary choice from the richness available. The first also suggests that the whole of *Hamlet*, or a whole, can be grasped, the second that we can only be aware of part of the whole. Kozintsev's framing style corresponds to his spatial setting, the contrivance of not letting us see all or of letting us catch a glimpse of a new setting. It gives us the sense that there could be more beyond the limits of the film image. Shakespeare creates the same effect when he alludes to happenings between the

The Kozintsev *Hamlet*. The first soliloquy; a glimpse of Osric. *(Still courtesy Corinth Films.)*

scenes, as for example, Hamlet's revelation to Horatio of the ghost's message sometime between the friends' two meetings in the plot.

> There is a play to-night before the king.
> One scene of it comes near the circumstance
> Which I have told thee of my father's death.
>
> (3.2.67–69)

In addition to settings—an extratextual element enhanced by icons and sound and revealed and concealed by editing, camera movement, and framing—Kozintsev offers two kinds of discrete extratextual units: first, visualizations of scenes summarized in the text; second, visualizations of scenes outside the range of the text (part of the story rather than the plot; see Bernard Beckerman's distinction [1971, 170–174]), including visualizations of scenes leading into scenes found in the text.

To the extent that Kozintsev depends on extratextual scenes outside the text, even scenes leading into textual scenes, his work is non-Shakespearean, for, though Shakespeare offers tantalizing little glimpses of a life before the events paraded on stage and also of offstage occurrences between those events, most of the dramatic energy, as Beckerman asserts, centers on the plot, the sequence of incidents in the play itself (174). Unlike setting and sound, which co-occur with the plot, the extratextual story units must push aside plot elements: there simply is not time for both. Through these additions and the subsequent deletions, Kozintsev molds his political interpretation of the play.

Scenes completely outside the text, such as the opening sequence, are rare in Kozintsev's film. Most extratextual scenes either present what in the text is summary or provide lead-ins to textual scenes. Filmmakers early on, even in the earliest *Hamlet* films, recognized that films could include actions virtually forced off stage. Two examples are Hamlet's struggle with the pirates and Ophelia's death. Though both are possible onstage, they would strain credibility—not to say the unities—a bit too far. Olivier includes both in living tableaux, that highly artificial means made famous by D. W. Griffith in *The Birth of a Nation.* Kozintsev skips the first opportunity for filmic flamboyance and minimizes the second. Other scenes that Shakespeare summarizes rather than shows, presumably for his own good reasons (because they could indeed be staged)—such as support for Hamlet's disdainful description of Claudius's drinking (1.4.7–23), the scene in Ophelia's closet (2.1), and Hamlet's exchange of the letter calling for his death (5.2)—are natural film moments, especially as each can be largely mimed rather than spoken. Cutting all of these verbal summaries from the text, Kozintsev treats them visually with consummate skill.

Summary into Scene

Kozintsev intercuts the scene of Danish revels with the ghost vigil (1.4). As Hamlet and the others walk against the wind in the dark courtyard, the faint sound of music reaches them and us. A quick cut and the camera brings us indoors where the music loudly sounds out its message of debauchery. The wild music contrasts with the dignified face of an old courtier, who is bowing to king and queen, both off frame. First, panning left in a candlelit room crowded with courtiers, the camera picks up and tracks rapidly with a broadly smiling Claudius and Gertrude, now not in the sedate black gown with white ruff we had seen her wearing earlier that day when Claudius announced the marriage but in light-colored finery. They move off frame to reveal a satyrlike dance: bare legs, a bull head on a dirt-covered body, a man carrying a girl, figures throwing grotesque shadows. A cut shows a closeup of Claudius moving swiftly, Gertrude, looking at him, fanning herself rapidly (as she will later when "The Mousetrap" agitates her). As he turns towards the camera, his smile fades: he looks at Gertrude and then at the bedroom meaningfully, signaling his intention. She continues to smile, but her fanning slows as he draws her through an arch. His guard with torch remains at the doorway through which the camera reveals the satyrs and women dancing in a ring, a whirling scene. Framing in this segment frequently shows faces only, sometimes with a principal partly off frame. Inside, the queen is off frame but Claudius turns toward her, his lust evident. The scene contrasts dramatically with the two segments of the ghost vigil that surround it: silence versus noise, aloneness versus crowdedness. In telling us about Claudius and Gertrude, it also provides as it were an objective correlative of Hamlet's words:

> The king doth wake to-night and takes his rouse,
> Keeps wassail, and the swagg'ring up-spring reels,
> And as he drains his draughts of Rhenish down,
> The kettledrum and trumpet thus bray out
> The triumph of his pledge.
>
> (1.4.8–12)

> This heavy-headed revel east and west
> Maks us traduced and taxed of other nations.
> They clepe us drunkards, and with swinish phrase
> Soil our addition. . . .
>
> (1.4.17–20)

In another of Kozintsev's visualizations of summarized scenes, we see a mimed interpretation of Ophelia's encounter with Hamlet in her closet. In her room with its casement window and flower-patterned walls bathed with light, Ophelia, dressed simply, sits at her easel with a box— of remembrances? Her head is lovely with its long neck. She moves to her bed to remove a four-inch-round picture of Hamlet from beneath her pillow. On its obverse his words to her are written. Her lips quivering, she says them:

> Doubt thou the stars are fire,
>   Doubt that the sun doth move;
> Doubt truth to be a liar;
>   But never doubt I love.
>
> (2.2.115–18)

Hearing a noise, she looks up. Hamlet enters, disheveled, his cloak over his arm, as if he has come directly from outside where we had seen him a few moments before. Grabbing her arm, he frightens her; she draws as far away as possible. Quite mad, it seems, shading his eyes with his free hand, he looks at her with an intense question. He releases her hand as if with difficulty, and moves out, leaving his shadow for a moment. The segment tells us quite clearly that they love each other but are drawn apart by forces they cannot control. She has been warned about Hamlet but yearns for him; he questions her ability to be a confidant. Unlike Shakespeare's text and Olivier's film version, which give us the scene as filtered through Ophelia's perception and speech, Kozintsev offers us an objective view: what we see is what happened—without, it seems, the mediation of anyone's sensibility.

In another example of a visualization of a summarized scene, immediately after Hamlet's soliloquy in 4.4 we see a montage of shots: men climb the rigging of a ship. A low angle shot of Hamlet shows sails behind him being raised. While film comfortably handles this outdoor, large-action scene, the next segment could easily be staged. Rosencrantz and Guildenstern are in a ship's cabin, a chest prominently in view, undressing. We see water, a lowering sky. Hamlet sits up, yawns; we hear sounds of ship's gear creaking, perhaps also sounds of Rosencrantz and Guildenstern preparing to retire. Again, a shot of water, tilted as if seen from the ship. The voice of the ghost whispers, "Adieu, adieu. Remember me," with the sound of rigging in counterpoint. As if in response, Hamlet gets up and goes with a torch to the little chest, Shostakovich's Hamlet music now announcing hope. Moving the sleeping Guildenstern's hand from the chest, Hamlet with his dagger unlatches it. "There's a divinity that shapes our ends, / Rough-hew them how we will," the music says (5.2.10–11). Taking the document to the shifting light of the swinging lantern, he reads it, voiceover. Then he burns it in the lantern but saves the seal. Rosencrantz and Guildenstern sleep restlessly, Rosencrantz turning over. Hamlet thinks, ". . . 'tis the sport to have the engineer / Hoist with his own petar . . ." (3.4.210–11). His music continuing, Hamlet writes a new letter that demands the death of Rosencrantz and Guildenstern. Kozintsev, presenting the scene Hamlet summarizes to Horatio (5.2.4–62), uses it to show the resolution Hamlet expresses in the concluding couplet of his last soliloquy (in the text but not the film): "O, from this time forth, / My thoughts be bloody, or be nothing worth" (4.4.65–66). Of course, Kozintsev thus loses the voice of Horatio: "So Guildenstern and Rosencrantz go to't"; "Why, what a king is this!" The latter comment Kozintsev does not need, because he shows so clearly what a king Claudius is; the former suggests a repugnance in Horatio for Hamlet's act that the music does not allow us to feel. Again, Kozintsev presents what appears to be an objective view of the scene, while Shakespeare in this case filters the event through the consciousness of both Hamlet and Horatio. Also, rather than burn the document, Hamlet shows it to Horatio to "read it at more leisure" (5.2.26). Easy to gloss over without Kozintsev's change to jog one's mind, the line contains perhaps the germ of a plan: Hamlet can use this document to defeat Claudius somehow, and, of course, Horatio will have this piece of paper as proof for his strange revelations after Hamlet's death.

For the scene of Ophelia's drowning, Kozintsev employs the most restrained of images. We see only Ophelia's bedroom, her tapestry with innocent animals reclining in a bed of flowers. We hear her song, but see as the camera pans that the room is empty. A cut shows the willow growing aslant a brook, the sky reflected in the water. The camera pans, revealing Ophelia under the water, her hair floating, flowers moving on the surface of the water. The shot holds for an instant only. The camera pans away from her to the open sea. When a bird, representing her release from the repressive Elsinore, flies out over a rock, a bell tolls. The music, rising to a full symphonic sound, speaks of exaltation. Recognizing that Kozintsev ignores Shakespeare's purpose for the summaries—the one of Ophelia's death perhaps to tell something about Gertrude and to force us to pity Laertes at the same moment we deplore his eagerness to enter into Claudius's duplicitous plot—we can admire the purely visual beauty and centeredness of these sequences. Kozintsev uses them to provide the illusion that he is giving an objective view of events.

Lead-In Scenes

By far the largest number of Kozintsev's visual additions to the text lead into textual scenes. Since the camera may move anywhere, it need not wait passively for characters to enter the textual playing space. Instead, it may search out the actor.

The Kozintsev *Hamlet*. Ophelia robed in mourning clothes, caged in steel. *(Still courtesy Corinth Films.)*

The lead-ins to Ophelia's scenes enlarge her role. In the medieval room that is Polonius's chamber, we see her before the beginning of the advice scene being led in a highly structured puppetlike dance by an old duenna in black farthingale playing a celesta. When the advice scene ends, she returns to this dance and music. The lead-in, then, is an emblem of her powerlessnes, her manageability. The lead-in to her madness scene shows first her shadow at her window when Hamlet looks up on his way to England, then Ophelia being dressed by several old women for the funeral of her father. Where we had seen her in the first scenes in a loose simple gown, now she is corseted in steel and covered in black.

An extratextual visualization that connects revenge and religion leads into Laertes's entrance, showing his arrival and readiness. Though Hamlet is gone, the castle stirs uneasily in the night. A shot of an empty room reveals a statue of Claudius with his false smile. Soldiers in armor guard the stairway room where Ophelia was unloosed. As usual, a bell tolls. A high-angle closeup of a great dane, the fireplace behind him, yields to another high-angle scene of guards by Gertrude's bedroom. All eye each other suspiciously. They hear sounds. Inside, Gertrude in bed, that same four poster we had seen her in before, draws away from Claudius, pulling the covers with her, when he extends his hand to her as if he wants to join her. The text begins at 4.5.76–80, Claudius's lament to Gertrude: "When sorrows come, they come not single spies, / But in battalions. . . ." A cut to the outside reveals different guards. To the accompaniment of sea sounds, a man runs to a door in a rock, from which Laertes darts. He and the man cross the frame from right to left and appear inside Polonius's apartment. Laertes walks deliberately in. A servant opens a chest in which lies a sword on damask. Laertes lifts it. With four others, still in his cloak and hood, Laertes strides with the family sword away from the camera towards the chapel and to the altar, the camera tracking with him. He kneels. In a reverse shot, face on, he lifts the sword horizontally with two hands towards a picture of Christ and then kisses the sword in a solemn pledge. In most productions, Hamlet is the one who kisses his sword in a solemn pledge to his father's spirit. Kozintsev omits that pledge but includes this one, surely for ironic purpose. Hamlet need not make a pledge to effect the required revenge, but Laertes's promise here seems to point at Hamlet's deficiency: at this moment, Laertes appears to be the "better" son. Later, however, their positions will be reversed, when Laertes falls prey to Claudius's manipulations and Hamlet reveals that he is capable of action, that he does not need to swear in order to do. The suspense and ritual of the drama with the family sword express theme and characterization visually, especially to those familiar with the conventional staging.

The tendency of film is to segment scenes, to divide them into smaller units than usual on stage and to intercut two scenes that might be presented sequentially on stage: both segmenting and intercutting have to do with film's spatial freedom. Shakespeare's scene divisions (as defined by Hirsh) tend in that direction in any case. In the film, Laertes's entrance is spread over three segments, intercut with other segments: first, there is the one I have just described; next, Laertes rushes in with others to threaten the king; finally, Laertes approaches Ophelia after she distributes her "flowers," here, appropriately for the connection with Hamlet, twigs from the fireplace, that emblem of his psychic state. Because a camera is not restricted to a specific space, we can see not only the result of an action like Laertes's entrance into the king's presence in 4.5 but also the preparation for the action. That is why Kozintsev so easily can add lead-in scenes.

Textual Elements: The First Court Scene

From this discussion of extratextual segments, it may seem that Kozintsev's creativity can flower only when he is unrestrained by the text. Certainly, when he is shaping something outside the text, Kozintsev can be purely visual and filmic. Close attention to his free shaping of the text, however, shows that his creative energy is not diminished by the text; scenes he takes from Shakespeare as well as those he imagines freshly can be equally successful on film. While all of the extratextual additions accomplish much for Kozintsev, his achievement can perhaps be best analyzed in actualizations of the text, including not only interpretation of text but also casting: the actor's physical presence, voice, and interior life.

The first court scene, which introduces the main characters, demonstrates Kozintsev's methods and interpretation. In the courtyard a drummer, a drum on either side, beats a message. Peasants have gathered, interested in a suspicious and worried way. The camera first focuses on an old man and woman, then, in a long shot, on the whole group, panning as the first words begin. A soldier, perhaps the same who signaled for the cannon to be shot off, reads Claudius's proclamation while walking on a platform above the people. The low-angle shot holds; we are among those assembled. The peasants' faces are impassive. "Taken to wife" are the last words in this segment.

Inside now, we see ministers coming down stairs, others walking in a crowded room, the room with the crouching lions near the rear doors and stairs at the front. (It is deceptive to speak of stairs at the front or doors at the rear because at any moment Kozintsev's camera can turn around and reorient the landmarks.) We track with two, quite closely, then cut to others, women who are hemmed in by their Renaissance farthingales. The effect is nervous, excited, as if we are trying to take in all this complicated scene. Diplomats from various courts (we hear Russian, then German, then French), are all talking about the proclamation, repeating its words: "in equal scale"; "With an auspicious and a drooping eye." All seem content. The segment ends with a long shot of the crowded room.

A cut takes us to an inner council chamber, to a table, where Claudius continues to a select dozen or so, his queen by his side: ". . . nor have we herein barred / Your better wisdoms, which have freely gone / With this affair along." There is something insinuating about the way he says "which have freely gone / With this affair along." "Freely," indeed, is said with a threat in his voice, the slightly low-angle shot forcing us to look up to him. His councillors glance at each other; they do not appear to be any too happy, except Polonius, who looks towards Claudius. Gertrude is quite stiff in her dignity. The old men stand at his thanks, but look cowed. Though Claudius makes a gesture as if to hold them in their seats, they continue standing, the camera showing a closeup of worried ministers bowing. Panning down the table, the camera reveals Hamlet sitting in a classic pose, one that seems familiar from many *Hamlet* productions: in profile, one arm on the arm of the chair, another in his lap, turned away from the table. The shot is held for less time than it takes to describe it. Then the camera shows a medium shot of Claudius, who speaks of the Norwegian threat. When he mentions Fortinbras, Claudius smiles at Fortinbras's daring, in medium closeup. The queen smiles serenely, with self-satisfaction. Claudius hears sounds of music, which draw his attention. Motioning for shutters to be opened, he walks to the window and looks down. A high-angle shot of the courtyard reveals preparations for war. We see below, accompanied by the warlike music, soldiers on horse, cannons on wagons, and soldiers on foot, marching from right to left off frame. This is no Claudius who depends on diplomacy. "[We ask him] to suppress / His further gait herein," said oilily, is ironic in view of the war machine we have just seen operating. As Claudius speaks of Polonius, we see in this five-shot Gertrude with a smug smile too. The camera pans to include Laertes and then back to exclude him, forcing Laertes to move closer to be included. When Claudius turns to Hamlet, the camera pans to the chair for the expected reaction shot, but Hamlet has gone.

The camera shows him descending the stairs into the lobby where many people walk. Gertrude enters from the left, from around or below the stairs, and speaking to him, walks towards him; he turns towards her as she speaks, coming closer, until finally they are in a two-shot. No fire at all is visible in the fireplace when Gertrude speaks to Hamlet. A large wall painting behind them depicts a martial subject. Then the hand with the mirror comes into the frame. She smiles in the mirror as she speaks of the inevitability of death, patting her high collar. Claudius approaches between them, coming into the frame with a quiet promise of heirship. This is not an announcement. They both touch Hamlet, lead him off right. A shot shows bowing ladies, who by their demeanor indicate that they admire Hamlet. The camera tracks with the king, queen, and prince as they walk right, Hamlet closest to the camera, Gertrude in the middle, Claudius backframe, a little right. Polonius and the ministers are there too. Gertrude and Claudius do not concentrate their attention exclusively on Hamlet but notice the crowd walking along with them and between the camera and them. The camera follows them, cutting Hamlet off so that as he promises to obey he is not in the frame. Gertrude, jolly, moves to Claudius, who also appears joyful; Gertrude, Polonius, and the ministers look pleased also. We must infer that Hamlet had been the bar to Claudius's succession; it is Hamlet's just claim to the throne that had worried the councillors (except Polonius, who was on Claudius's side from the beginning—as Claudius implies in his lines, "The head is not more native to the heart . . . Than is the throne of Denmark to thy father" 1.2.47, 49). Once Hamlet seems to accept the situation, they are certainly free to accept it also—and they know they had better. As Claudius talks about drinking, a scribe, who bends into the frame, writes about "jocund health," a low-angle shot making Claudius look important and big. Gertrude keeps that same broad smile on her face. Claudius kisses Gertrude's hand after "the great cannon to the clouds shall tell." All clap and shout, "Long live the King." The two exit.

Busy, busy music marks the hustle, bustle of the scene. Most of the councillors are now smiling. They walk in Claudius's direction. We have seen the last sign of any breath of dissent from them. Hamlet soliloquizes, voiceover, the camera concentrating on his face, tracking with him. Still, we see courtiers on both sides of him, that is, between the camera and him, milling. Osric is one of them, we may recall later. Hamlet's lips open as if he is about to speak. We see a tear at his eye when he says "within a month." He stops when he says, "a little month." Some people bow to him; others watch him, but he pays little attention. Candles are becoming more dominant. We see their flames in closeup as he passes. He enters the first area of this large room, the stairway section.

For the disclosure, the camera shows three men, who seem to be waiting for Hamlet, who is off frame. By their clothes, by their demeanor, they are of a different class from the people we have just been seeing. Horatio, who wears a flat hat with earmuffs, looks different from the soldiers and different from Hamlet.[5] There is now a fire in the fireplace behind them. Hamlet walks towards the stairs again and up without looking at them. He turns, saying "Horatio?" with real pleasure in his voice. They shake hands over the banister. Just as he does with Rosencrantz and Guildenstern, Hamlet asks what he is doing there. After he greets the two soldiers, he and Horatio walk together to the fireplace. Over Hamlet's shoulder flames are barely there. But more and more the flames dominate as the camera tilts upward. As the scene proceeds, the fire fills the frame. Hamlet's reaction to the news of the ghost is disbelief. One of the soldiers pushes the other out of the distracted Hamlet's way, but he pays no attention to them. When Hamlet decides he will "watch tonight," a low-angle shot of him accents his intensity. The music in this section is ghostly and threatening. After Bernardo and Marcellus both say "Our duty to your honour," Hamlet replies, "Your loves, as mine to you" to them. They nod, leave. He does not say farewell to Horatio, but just puts his hand on his chest and shoulder. Horatio stays for a moment longer, then exits.

Turning away from the fire, Hamlet walks off the frame. A cut shows the flame, then Hamlet walking off, the fireplace visible through an arch. He closes the door on the stairway room with the fireplace, having entered the council room. In front of the two chairs he says the concluding couplet.

In this sequence, scene 1.2, we can analyze Kozintsev's method. In describing these segments, the smooth flow of subordination, with events happening concurrently (as in participial phrases), belies the structure of film. Film's method is paratactic, shot added to shot added to shot, often without any subordination at all. Even within a shot, the elements are not connected to each other in any easy way. To say that as Hamlet speaks we see the fire rising is to connect with the subordinate conjunction "as" what in the shot merely exists together. In film, without the transitional, bridging devices as in Olivier's *Hamlet,* the only connection is juxtaposition.

Marcellus and Bernardo are without personality, with no way to differentiate them because Kozintsev eliminates "their" scene, the first ghost scene, beginning instead with his visual prologue and then the court scene. Besides saving his harrowing ghost scene, Kozintsev gains political points: the underclass is anonymous. However class-structured Shakespeare's England may have been, Shakespeare saw each character as an individual. In Stalinist Russia, a few rule; the rest are the masses. Kozintsev's only individualized commoner is the phlegmatic and crude gravedigger, whose personality depends on his ability to ignore his "betters." After the broil between Laertes and Hamlet, we see him, quite unconcerned, nails in his mouth like any honest carpenter, hammering shut the coffin. Kozintsev frequently fills the first scenes with incidental people. Hamlet, though he pays scant attention, is accompanied in his determined ride toward the castle. People are everywhere. Mother and son, in that first intimate family moment, are surrounded by others exhibiting various states of concern. People from all over the civilized world, it seems, exult with Claudius at his coronation and wedding. The presence of all the people is a vital aspect of Kozintsev's interpretation. They not only carry great political weight, but also show how insulated Claudius can be, always surrounded by guards, retainers, and syc-ophants. How difficult it will be, we feel, for Hamlet to get *at* Claudius. It is a matter of one good man (or two counting the impotent Horatio) against a whole corrupt world. This is clear later, after Hamlet kills Polonius, when he surveys the circle of councillors assembled to do "justice," flunkies all, who paste on smiles or frowns in concert with Claudius.

In film's best manner, Kozintsev divides scene 1.2 into seven segments, each with its setting: the courtyard for the proclamation, the lion lobby for the view of the diplomats, the council room (intercut with the courtyard below), the stair set leading into the lobby, then again the stair set and finally the council chamber. He molds space, conveying the expansiveness and variability possible on film without losing the flow of the scene, which Shakespeare too divides into at least three distinct parts: one dominated by Claudius's agenda (itself divided into four parts—the marriage, Fortinbras, Laertes, and Hamlet), a second by the soliloquy, and a third by the disclosure. Within these parts, actors may be speaking or silent, in motion or still, revealing inner feelings or not, alone or with others in the frame.

Character and Casting

We see, too, how Kozintsev uses casting. Voices contribute another aural effect, from the bass of Claudius, the rich baritone of Polonius, the tenors of Laertes and Hamlet, the mellow contralto of the sensuous Gertrude, the bell-toned soprano of the delicate, innocent Ophelia. The firmness of all the male voices denotes their strength, their formidable power as adversaries. We note the tones especially of Polonius, an auto-crat in his own home whose voice expresses his absolute certainty he will not be gainsaid, a despot among the servants and lower courtiers as we see when he disregards them in entering the queen's chamber (2.2), and a subservient sycophant with Claudius. Claudius (Mikhail Nazvanov) is burly, younger than Gertrude, wearing the little smile that Jan Kott says was a Stalin hallmark (1979, 387). He has an outward affability of sorts but is steely within. Kozintsev conveys his ruthlessness partly from the subservient behavior of the others to him. Claudius has his own moment of humanity in the prayer scene, but significantly, it takes place after he has determined that Hamlet is to die (so how can his sin be past?), and his open shirt revealing a hairy chest indicates moral disintegration. The scene is played not at an altar but before the mirror, with two images, Claudius and reflection, aptly denoting duplicity. Later, when Claudius persuades Laertes to help murder Hamlet, he dashes a cup of wine at his reflection upon catching a glimpse of himself in this same mirror.

Gertrude, played by Elsa Radzin, is the older woman flattered by the attention of the younger man who holds power partly through her. A shallow woman, her nature is fully revealed by a few visual images, several of which appear in this first court scene: the smug smile, the self-loving gaze into the mirror, the failure to understand Hamlet's pain. In her closet, the falling arras reveals the manikins that hold her sumptuous garments. Like them, she is an empty shell covered with worldly vanity. Only when she pulls away from Claudius (4.5) and when she worries about Hamlet (5.2) does she redeem herself.

Polonius (Yuri Tolubeev) does not have a great opportunity to expose his character in the first court scene, but Kozintsev provides in germ what further scenes will make clearer. It takes the omission of many lines to make Polonius into a sober if pompous statesman rather than the garrulous butt of Hamlet's wit. Generally, Kozintsev's choice, with respect to the text, is the opposite of Olivier's—to shorten each scene rather than omit any characters. Thus we have Fortinbras, Rosencrantz and Guildenstern, even Reynaldo—just about everyone. His goal, however, is still to manipulate the text to reinforce his interpretation. All of Polonius's speeches are cut substantially. In this first scene, his four lines (in Q2) to say, "yes, Laertes has my permission to leave" (1.2.58–61) are gone. Later, twenty-six lines of precepts to his son become three complete lines and parts of seven (1.3.55–81). His conversation with Reynaldo about Laertes is compressed from seventy-five to about seven lines, almost half of them Reynaldo's (2.1.1–74). In Shakespeare, these lines make Polonius not only comically verbose but suspicious, intrigue-loving, and untrusting—to mention only the surface implications. In his conversation with Gertrude and Claudius about Hamlet's love for Ophelia, all the elements of unintended humor, all the rhetorical flourishes are gone. Through the segment, he says only:

> [My] daughter hath given me this. . . "To the celestial, and my soul's idol, Ophelia" . . . [I said to her] "Lord Hamlet is a prince out of thy star." She took the fruits of my advice; And he [repulsed] fell into a fast, thence to a watch, thence into a weakness. . . . Take this from this, if this be otherwise. . . . I'll loose my daughter to him. Be you and I behind an arras. (From 2.2.86–166)

These few words, together with his dignified, concerned demeanor, negate any humor in the portrayal.

Although he does say "This is too long" (2.2.469), Polonius no longer plays the literary critic (see, for example, 2.2.110–11; 475, which are cut), no longer is tedious—and Hamlet cannot say "These tedious old fools" (2.2.215), no longer is ridiculous in announcing the players because he does not announce them (2.2.373–78). His full humanity is also eliminated—for example, when he seems to be sorry for suspecting Hamlet's motives with Ophelia (2.1.110–17) and when he says of the player, "Look whe'r he has not turned his color, and has tears in's eyes. Prithee no more" (2.2.490–91). Also gone is all his sentimentality about being a lover: "And truly in my youth I suffered much extremity for love. Very near this" (2.2.187–88).

Minute by minute, the filmgoer, even one familiar with Shakespeare, is not aware, perhaps, of the extent or the tendency of the textual omissions. Much of what does or does not happen in the film may be ascribed to the translator, but Kozintsev, it seems, fully concurred, since he knew English well and could easily compare Pasternak's version with Shakespeare's. For example, Kozintsev notes that "Metaphors concerning gangrene, putrefaction, and decomposition fill the tragedy" (138), yet evidently he did not object to Pasternak's omissions of these metaphors. There is no better place to determine intent than here, placing the two texts (Shakespeare's and Pasternak's for Kozintsev) together to see the effect of the differences. As Kozintsev says of others' versions, "A concept of a certain role can be understood by what cuts were made in the character's lines" (129). Kozintsev uses his characterizations to suggest the political climate of Russia under Stalin.

The effect of the cuts in Polonius's lines is that the play's atmosphere is considerably darkened and simplified. Polonius is a calculating courtier who has cast his lot with Claudius. The king is all the more dangerous because he is not surrounded by fools (neither Polonius nor Osric is a fool). Polonius's attitude toward Ophelia in Kozintsev's version goes a long way towards explaining her madness. Significantly, she does not appear until the scene of Laertes's and Polonius's advice. She is not one of the ladies promenading in the lobby, nor, of course, is she a member of the inner council. Pasternak and Kozintsev, in the Russian tradition, make Ophelia totally pure and naive (Rowe, 150). Nothing could be farther from, say, the performance of Marianne Faithfull in Richardson's *Hamlet* than Anastasia Vertinskaya's Ophelia. She is an innocent flower, blasted by the rot in Claudius's kingdom. As Kozintsev says in his diary, "They force her to renounce love and to look for a dirty trick in everything. This, essentially, is the cause of her madness. . . ." (256). Polonius is the one who teaches her. Interestingly enough, he does not even demand that she repulse Hamlet; he simply belittles her for dreaming that Hamlet could be honest. She tries her best, in her trusting innocence, to defend Hamlet, but Kozintsev effectively demontrates her inability to withstand the force of Polonius's cynical yet not cold-hearted argument. Earlier, we had seen both Laertes and Ophelia listening to Polonius's advice as if it were pure gold. In the next segment, blocking places her much below Polonius, as he sits with a book in a high chair, wearing a huge, fur-trimmed robe. Her open-necked gown makes her seem from a different, warmer world. Kozintsev not only omits Polonius's lines after the nunnery scene that offer her perhaps perfunctory comfort; he also has Polonius push her aside then and again when she needs him after "The Mousetrap" scene. Her madness begins early. In this portrayal, all her spunk is eliminated. She does not playfully ask her brother to reck "his own rede" (1.2.51). Nor does she answer Hamlet's barbed wit with gentle ripostes of her own, as in "Still better and worse" (3.2.232). Kozintsev thus sharply etches the contrast between Ophelia and Polonius/Claudius, who represent Stalinist repression.

Hamlet, played by Innokenti Smakhtunovski, his supple body a contrast to the prosperous portliness of Claudius and Polonius, has a face wonderfully revealing of depths of pain, of despair. Barely mobile, as if any slackening of tension would allow him to disintegrate into tears, his face seems to melt towards the bottom, his short upper lip suggesting weakness, in spite of the full lower lip and cleft chin. During the first soliloquy, he flashes also with barely restrained anger. His silence is sardonic, his disappearance from the council room daringly disrespectful. Throughout, he moves with grace and power.

In this first scene there is only a hint of the impatience with himself he expresses later by his distracted look and drumming of his fingers during the player's Hecuba speech.[6] Kozintsev transposes the internal monologue "O, what a rogue and peasant slave am I" (2.2.516–72) to precede the exit of the players. The uninterested guards, the bewildered players, and the domesticity of the courtyard scene contrast ironically with Hamlet's agitation, his near madness, until he breaks out with a roar, not of exultation, but of despair. He reveals his impatience more often in gestures and guttural groans and sighs than in speech. Hamlet, grasping the opportunity offered by the players to set his "Mousetrap," recognizes that in entrapping Claudius he will be hastening his own death—and perhaps to no effect. Thus, his mood is despairing. Kozintsev need not transpose the speech to precede the players' arrival as does Olivier because the text's order fully sustains the Russian's interpretation. Shots of sea pounding, then subsiding to a murmuring swell, are metaphors for Hamlet's mood as he sinks from turmoil to the dejection of "To be, or not to be" (3.1.56–88).

To create an intensely righteous, heroic Hamlet, Pasternak and Kozintsev had to eliminate or play down most of the aspects of Hamlet's characterization that make him the controversial, endlessly fascinating, mercurial character he is. Almost all his playfulness is cut out. This includes his biting wit, love of language—especially rich metaphors and

similes—manic glee, and joy in the theatrical. Kozintsev loses few opportunities to eliminate exemplification and metaphor. For example, lines
expressing Hamlet's determination to follow the ghost (1.4.82–85) are
cut, leaving a very Dostoevskian-sounding "My fate cries out" to stand
alone.

Even in the first court scene we see the beginnings of the tendency to
eliminate Hamlet's playfulness. Kozintsev's Hamlet does not pun acidly
on "kin" and "kind," does not say "I am too much in the sun." Even the
sardonic humor of "Thrift, thrift, Horatio. The funeral baked-meats /
Did coldly furnish forth the marriage tables" is underplayed, with parts
of the interchange cut (for example, "I prithee do not mock me, fellow-
student"). In a later scene he does tease Rosencrantz and Guildenstern
by stopping to take a pebble out of his shoe in a scene that does provoke
a mild smile (4.2), but this hardly balances all that is gone. The manic
humor Hamlet displays in his conversation with Horatio and Marcellus
after the ghost scene is lost because the sequence is omitted (1.5.116–89).
His witty baiting of Polonius is left out, of course, because it would not fit
this Polonius (2.2.171–213; 366–95; 498–501; 3.2.346–51). Gone too are
almost all his comments about the theater (2.2.407–35; much of 3.2.1–
38). The suggestion that his mind may be unhinged remains (Hamlet
sitting on the floor in the lobby; shading his eyes in Ophelia's closet)
without the wit and humor Shakespeare associates with Hamlet's real or
pretended madness. There is no conversation with Horatio and Marcellus in which he says he plans to put on an antic disposition. Most of his
playfulness with Osric is cut, as is his verbal irony with Rosencrantz and
Guildenstern.

If these witty and playful aspects of Shakespeare's Hamlet are what
charm and delight us, the contemplative and speculative elements in
Hamlet's character deepen our appreciation for his growth as a tragic
figure. But in Kozintsev, except for "too, too solid flesh" and "To be, or
not to be," almost all of Hamlet's soliloquies and other speeches revealing the philosophic man are eliminated or severely truncated. Gone is
Hamlet's discussion of the one defect (1.4.23–48), as well as almost all his
self-criticism (as in 2.2.533–55). From "To be, or not to be" Kozintsev
leaves out "Thus conscience does make cowards of us all." "How all
occasions do inform against me" is entirely missing (4.4.32–66). Instead,
after seeing the soldiers and asking Rosencrantz and Guildenstern to go
"a little before," he says only:

> Two thousand souls and twenty thousand ducats
> Will not debate the question of this straw.
> This is th' imposthume of much wealth and peace,
> That inward breaks, and shows no cause without
> Why the man dies—
>
> (4.4.25–29)

as if the proposed battle were yet another manifestation of a tyrant's arbitrary exercise of power. Most of the speeches having to do with religion are gone (at the same time that Kozintsev adds some powerful visual images, such as the broken cross). But perhaps most important is Kozintsev's elimination of the reason for Hamlet's praise of Horatio, which Kozintsev moves to their meeting after Hamlet's return:

> thou hast been
> As one in suff'ring all that suffers nothing,
> A man that Fortune's buffets and rewards
> Hast ta'en with equal thanks; and blest are those
> Whose blood and judgment are so well comeddled
> That they are not a pipe for Fortune's finger
> To sound what stop she pleases. Give me that man
> That is not passion's slave, and I will wear him
> In my heart's core, ay, in my heart of heart,
> As I do thee.
>
> (3.2.57–66)

By cutting these lines, Kozintsev does not allow Hamlet to recognize the value of accepting Fortune's blows patiently. Kozintsev also eliminates Hamlet's reference to the "divinity that shapes our ends, / Rough-hew them how we will" (5.2.8–11), which for many indicates a turning point in Hamlet toward serene acceptance of his own fate and of the part he is forced to play. A hero cannot refer to "acceptance" and "divinity" in the face of the megalomanic evil of a Stalin-like Claudius.

The obvious allusions to Stalin (statues of Claudius all over, the actor himself, the court and the sad-eyed commoners; see Kott, 1979) amply explain all the omissions. Stalin disliked *Hamlet*. Thus it was not often played until after his death in 1953. Kozintsev's stage version of 1954 marks, Rowe states, a turn towards "*Hamlet* fever" (135), a turn that can be seen as a political statement. Kozintsev proceeds towards his goal of showing the political side of *Hamlet* with unrelenting vigor. From the beginning, Hamlet's cause is doomed. The evil of this Russian Elsinore is so deeply embedded that no one can excise it. Not even death will purify this world. No wonder Hamlet despairs. No wonder there is no growth of awareness. He sees it all from the beginning and hopelessly plays the role meted out to him.

If the film disappoints, it is because those early shots raise expectations that Kozintsev will encompass the whole complex *Hamlet*. He creates this expectation by the forcefulness with which he makes manifest the concrete worlds of court and peasant from the beginning and by the camera techniques that promise realistic ambiguity. Moreover, his film techniques make the audience more aware of the characters' inner life and their relationship to their surroundings than do most productions. But

Kozintsev's Hamlet, a narrower creature than Shakespeare's, remains the same, does not grow or develop. Olivier's simpler version benefits from its structure; it gains in momentum. His Hamlet descends downward into deep depression, then ascends upward into action culminating in a serene compliance with destiny and death. Kozintsev's, however, loses momentum because there is nowhere to go; his *Hamlet* begins and ends on the same note of political hopelessness. Thus, to a viewer dependent on the well-made plot, Olivier's film may seem preferable, while to a viewer attuned to shapeless plots, Kozintsev's will seem more modern and finally more accessible.

Whatever the shortcomings in plot and characterization, the visual images transcend the limits of the film's thesis. The film succeeds on many levels in spite of the pruning of characters forced by the interpretation. We remember the film's dynamic use of space—beach, sky, sea, castle; its Hamlet at once desperate and altruistic; its terrible, awe-inspiring ghost scenes with the slow-motion silhouettes, the haunted, very human eyes of the ghost; its evil player queen in a massive outdoor setting near the sea; its touching vignettes, such as the caging in steel of the mourning Ophelia, her happiness at last when she is mad; its workaday Fortinbras, who, as Kozintsev said, is a good common soldier, hardly one to usher in a new era (271). Its breathtaking fencing scene: Hamlet joyous in physical activity, the uninformed Gertrude rushing in to see what is happening, Hamlet and Horatio ready to leave, disgusted at Laertes's dishonorable blow with unbated sword, and the headlong dash of the dying Claudius past his smiling statue. The film comes so close to being a perfect Shakespearean adaptation that one can only wish that it had been even better, wish for the impossible—for the filmmaker to layer all possible interpretations onto one piece of film. Making choices inevitably means that other choices must be left out.

Notes

1. On the other hand, G. Wilson Knight felt that, once he understood the central core of a play, the director was free "to cut, adapt, even on rare occasions transpose" (43).

2. The text for this section is *The Norton Critical Edition*, the text I used to mark the lines used in the film's subtitles, which derive mainly from Shakespeare with a few added transitions (indicated in square brackets when I quote from the film) to seam together the patches.

3. Harold Jenkins, editor of the Arden *Hamlet*, also thinks that Hamlet avoids her, but he does not cite her lines in support (150).

4. Rowe (137) points out that the "participation of the populace [in *Hamlet*] is a Russian tradition dating back to Sumarokov's *Hamlet*" in 1748, the first in Russia.

5. Kelly (40) says that around 1600 the flat cap denoted the lower class.

6. Alec Guinness also taps a drum during this scene in his 1938 production, but "with sinister effect," a reviewer says. See Babula, number 119.

Part II

Setting in Television Productions

From the undifferentiated space of Shakespeare's stage as we understand it today, to the illusionistic proscenium arch stages of the eighteenth and nineteenth centuries, to open, bare stages with both differentiated and undifferentiated areas, each age has used space to express its understanding of what constitutes the ideal setting for Shakespeare. Film and television settings exemplify the choices of every period, from empty to spare to filled, from undifferentiated to coded— and combinations of these. The issue is realism.[1] Interestingly, some of the most mannered stage acting was at home on some of the most elaborately realistic settings, while some of the most natural has been performed in the barest spaces. Film and television have gone overlapping but essentially separate ways in style of sets, a sign of their inherent difference.[2] The new medium of the fifties, television tried for the *mise en scène* of film or of stage, but gradually found the particular settings that best suited its low-resolution picture and small frame-size.[3] To discuss setting is to discuss camera distance and movement, for through these means an audience is made aware of setting. Both camera and setting shape interpretations.

Notes

1. Bazin makes the connection between space and realism, 1:112. See his important discussion of space, 1: 108–15.
2. The difference, Hawkes claims (1972, 233), is that film is all-absorbing, while the outside world always claims some of our attention when we watch TV—just as, I might add, it does when we watch a play.
3. The low-resolution picture and small screen-size are variables that will change with improved technology. Picture resolution will probably equal that of 16mm film by 2,000— the technology, in fact, is already available. The size of some home TV screens now approaches that of screens in some multicinemas.

5

Maurice Evans's *Hamlet* (1953)

In the heyday of live television, Joyce C. Hall, daring President of the Hallmark Card Company, sponsor of the Hallmark Hall of Fame, agreed to an innovative experiment: live Shakespeare in a two-hour production, not only the first "complete" Shakespeare on American television, but also the first dramatic production of that length in the medium (*TV Guide*, 203–5). To accommodate the experiment, NBC delayed other scheduled broadcasts. It was 1953, and one of the principal Shakespearean actors was Maurice Evans, who, only a few years before, had produced and acted in the successful GI *Hamlet*, performed in the Pacific theater for American soldiers during World War II, with George Schaefer, a young sergeant, as director. The soldiers had responded to a Hamlet living in a state of siege, where every man wore a uniform, where the sense of imminent disaster was palpable. It was all familiar to them. This *Hamlet*, produced on Broadway shortly after the war, in 1946, was the basis for the Hallmark production, broadcast on 26 April 1953.

Reviewers, hopeful about what the experiment boded, were ecstatic.[1] As late as 1975, Cecil Smith, columnist for the Los Angeles *Times*, said that the two-hour *Hamlet* "made Hallmark a television standard for the rest of the industry" (22 October 1975, 4:20).

The opening shot of King Hamlet's tombstone (1830–90) tells us that it is the nineteenth century. In a dissolve, the scene shifts to a long shot of a large castle and then to a fussy interior for the first court scene (1.2). Nothing could be further from Olivier's moody set in his 1948 filmed *Hamlet* than this Victorian clutter (deplored by Rosenberg 1954, 169; admired by Griffin, 333).[2] Having once settled on a definite time, however, the producers were committed to a specific kind of space. In drawing rooms and sitting rooms are urns, crystal, candlesticks, statues,

117

The Evans *Hamlet*. Hamlet rails at the portrait of Claudius before the portrait of King Hamlet. *(Still courtesy George Schaefer.)*

The Michael Todd production of the GI *Hamlet* on Broadway. *(Still courtesy George Schaefer.)*

couches, portraits, china, inkstands, cushions, chests, pilasters, clocks, bric-a-brac of all kinds, all over. These environmental trivia not only distract but also contrast ironically with the elemental passions of the play—either that or they swamp any passions entirely. The setting opposes the atmosphere that the uniforms were to help create; the setting for the Evans/Schaefer stage production was much simpler.

The producers seemed to be aiming for the measure of illusion movie sets afford. But the television setting, not large enough to represent convincingly a castle interior, inevitably clashes with the solid weight of so many objects. The spatial relations of one part of the set to another are studiolike, that is, unrealistically close to each other, while, in any one shot, realism dominates the frame. This combination is similar to Olivier's successful design for *Richard III* (1955), a film partly financed by arrangements to show it on television coincident with its theatrical release and thus filmed with television in mind. But its set was much larger and more sparsely furnished. Another difference may be that the time of *Richard III* allows for a medieval-Renaissance grandeur while the time of Evans's *Hamlet* diminishes mystery with distance as it places us in our Victorian grandmothers' living rooms. In any case, the set designer's mix of artifice (in connections between parts of the set representing different areas of the castle) and reality (within each part) is not quite right, though it is difficult to pinpoint the specific errors of judgment and taste. That such a mix can work is clear not only from Olivier's nearly contem-

The Evans *Hamlet*. **The play-within-a-play, the players from the audience's perspective.** *(Still courtesy George Schaefer.)*

porary work but also from the more recent BBC-TV Shakespeare Plays, such as *Measure for Measure* and *All's Well That Ends Well.*

The several creative settings suggest what the whole production might have achieved. The nunnery and prayer scenes take place in the set's most believable section, which has few distracting objects. A wrought-iron doorway allows for some attractive shots, especially of Hamlet peering through it at the praying Claudius. Also workable is "The Mousetrap" setting, which, like the nunnery setting, provides opportunities for scenes in mid- to long-shot with at least two planes of action. Perhaps the use of such long shots derives from illustrations of *Hamlet,* where long shots can vary with closeups, as W. G. Simmonds's illustrations do; perhaps from film models, such as Olivier's *Hamlet.* The "To be" soliloquy precedes the play-within-a-play. Its setting, as we soon see, is the players' backdrop showing the orchard scenery for their play. It begins with an overhead closeup of Hamlet's reflection in a birdbath, then widens out to include the painted scenery behind him. This artificial setting is more congenial to the verse than the "realistic" settings of other segments.

Even when some of the cluttered areas of the set are used, creative camera work sometimes minimizes the oppressive effect. When Horatio, for example, confronts Hamlet for the first time (1.2.159), the camera shoots from outside a window looking in on Hamlet, who is framed by the window. Though something of a movie cliché, the shot has its

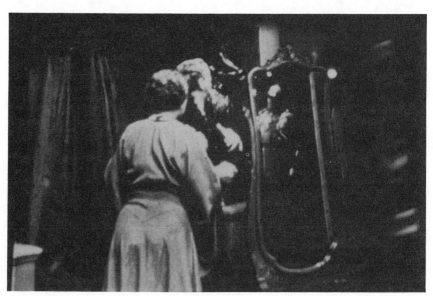

The Evans *Hamlet.* The ghost, in the mirror, is visible only to Hamlet. *(Still courtesy George Schaefer.)*

usefulness here. Since the resolution of the television picture is not sharp enough to present scenes with much depth of field, Horatio, behind Hamlet, is almost a blur. In effect, Hamlet, isolated, concentrates our attention. The director also controls response with tight shots. Camera work throughout is varied, with high-angle, low-angle, close- and long-shots. In the closet scene, mirror shots are effective, first for views of Hamlet and Gertrude at her dressing table—a traditional view now in moving images—and then for a representation of the ghost's appearance to Hamlet only. While effective shots do compensate for the set for a time, inevitably it intrudes again.

This is not to say that had the *mise en scène* been different, Evans's *Hamlet* would have succeeded. Several funny bloopers interfere with the audience's attempt to set aside its understanding that the characters are not real.[3] The most amusing is the stagehand who tiptoes upstage across the set after Hamlet, downstage, says, "Now I am alone" (2.2.515); also distracting are microphone and wires in full view—in spite of the fact that Richard Sylbert, the set designer, had four towers built on the set to house mikes and booms to keep them off the set (Kliman 1983, 31). An unlucky shot catches (and he realizes it) a footman in the background of the duel taking place in the foreground (5.2).

For a second, before the footman froze, making me aware that his presence was a mistake, the sight of a person walking in the background, doing what seemed at first to have no relation to the plot in the fore-

The Evans *Hamlet*. Laertes gives Hamlet a foul hit, while in the background the page is caught carrying the poisoned cup. *(Still courtesy George Schaefer.)*

ground, was exactly the touch the TV production needed of the incidental and inconsequential to make the performance appear more like the
real thing. In "real life" all action does not concentrate on the main
event. Incidental events are not the obviously contrived happenings like
the strolling and chatting of supernumeraries on stage. They are like the
one film moment in *A Raisin in the Sun* (1961), a film otherwise cramped
by its dependency on stage conventions, the moment when beyond a
window in the apartment where most of the action takes place a woman
on a roof next door hangs wash on the line (*a* woman, *a* roof, *a* line—all
the indefinite article).[4] This woman never appears again, unlike supernumeraries in a stage production who reappear, performing other contrived actions that are supposed to give the illusion of a full life around
the plot. This accidental person in a moving image is equivalent to
Barthes's *punctum* in photographs, "a hidden, often unintentional, yet
highly revealing detail" (Petric, 205)—though Barthes did not recognize
the possibility of such incidental details for moving images. But this
footman in Evans's *Hamlet*, unfortunately no incidental background figure, was to have remained out of sight, for he is here functioning as a
stagehand carrying the poisoned cup from Gertrude's side around the
whole set to get to Claudius in time for Hamlet to make the king drink.
That he was walking with the cup not only occasions a blooper but also
exposes an error in concept. Why would a footman do anything with the
poison but remove it or leave it where it was? The realistic set invites
criticism of contrived action. Of course, many viewers probably did not
notice this footman in rear frame because in the foreframe Laertes is
giving Hamlet a foul hit, to which Hamlet responds vigorously. Soon,
indeed, the camera shifts to cut the footman out of the frame.

I reveal my bias when I say that the production seems to have no
informing intelligence desperate to communicate with a receptive yet
agonistic audience (to use George Steiner's formulation). With no overall
interpretation, it is "Let's run through *Hamlet*, Gang." Since Bernard
Grebanier found this to be true also of Evans's 1938 stage *Hamlet* directed by Margaret Webster (307), the fault in the TV version cannot be
laid to the medium or to a particular production concept. The
throughline that Frances Teague (75–77) perceives in Evans's 1938 performance—that is, Hamlet as a man of action—was not, for Grebanier,
enough to unify that full-text production. Even more for a modern
audience, who take that interpretation of the character for granted,
Hamlet's manliness is not enough to make a whole production coherent.
John Mills, in his study of stage Hamlets, speaks of Gielgud's and Burton's "shared belief that it was the actor's task to play each moment for its
own inherent value instead of trying to make successive speeches and
scenes illustrate some all-pervasive aspect of character or some control-
ling dramatic theme" (253). Schaefer and Evans belong to this same

school. Because our time—John Russell Brown and *Free Shakespeare* notwithstanding—stresses the director's shaping power over the raw material of the play, because we see the director as the one able to impose order on the chaotic clashes of actors' disparate interpretations, we are apt to see themeless productions like Evans's and Burton's as lacking in unity.

In Evans's production, much is uncertain. Is Claudius friendly or not? Gertrude will not let Claudius finish his hostile, pompous lecture on mourning (1.2.87–106), a tidy way to effect a needed cut, by the way, yet Claudius motions her to persuade Hamlet to stay at Elsinore (in the pause between lines 117 and 118). The courtiers do not react to the news that Hamlet is heir. Is it therefore an empty promise in this version? Or were the courtiers not rehearsed?

Some incidental interpretations are satisfying. Ophelia and Laertes exchange a knowing look—"Oh, no, not again"—when Polonius advises Laertes (1.3.58–81). A mistake, made by many productions, is to depict Polonius as a source of humor, not only to the king, queen, and Hamlet but also to his family. Ophelia and Laertes must respect as well as love their father, however he may appear to others, or their subsequent behavior may be inexplicable. For the sake of an easy laugh here, some productions rip the web of connections. Other productions, like the Evans, solve the problem that Polonius poses by conveying both ideas, fond amusement and respect. As in the later CBS versions, the Evans

The Evans *Hamlet*. Ophelia looks calculatingly at Laertes during Polonius's advice to him. *(Still courtesy George Schaefer.)*

Ophelia listens seriously to Polonius's last words of advice. Her glance at Laertes, however, questions whether he can be true to himself. This is an interesting interpretation, but soon the production returns to easy answers to problems of the text.

In the same scene, Ophelia shakes her head, objecting to Polonius's aspersions against Hamlet, but then she says "I shall obey" without being pressed (with much of Polonius's lecture cut). The two responses are at odds. Hamlet, in his scene with Ophelia, shows his love for her, making unintelligible Claudius's cruel declaration, "Love! His affections do not *that* way tend" (pointing to her). From behind the wrought-iron doors, Claudius and Polonius have presumably seen, since that is why they are there, that Hamlet becomes bitter only after Ophelia reveals the spying by looking towards them. There is no hint in this production that Claudius merely pretends that love is not the reason for Hamlet's distraction so that he can be rid of him (as in the Boston Shakespeare Company production). Since, also, in this production she realizes, with deep chagrin, that she has given herself away, her last speech of the scene, "Heavenly powers, restore him!" (3.1.138), is incongruous; she knows very well how to account for Hamlet's agitation.

Such inconsistencies continue throughout the production. The producers unfortunately place Ophelia's mad scene at her bed, with a doctor and nurse in attendance, making it difficult to understand how she gets away to drown herself, especially after Claudius urges the nurse to "give her good watch." There is no willow scene to tell how it happened. On the other hand, the rag doll Ophelia cradles in her arms is effective; it was a prop used also in the stage production. And since Laertes does not jump into the grave (there is none—the scene takes place inside at the altar where Claudius was praying and near the spot where Ophelia and Hamlet had their last "private" talk), Hamlet's passionate outburst seems unmotivated, because Laertes's outcry had not borne such an emphasis.

Other choices, while avoiding inconsistencies, put clarity before subtlety. Hamlet, for example, does not speak his "What a piece of work is a man" to Rosencrantz and Guildenstern but almost to himself as he turns away from them and looks out a window (2.2.292–97). Thus McCleery, who directed the television camera crews, loses the opportunity, grasped by some other productions, to show that Hamlet tests them with these lines, tentatively revealing some of his inner pain to them—but their callous response, laughter, persuades him they are no longer his friends.[5] Instead, as in Schaefer's stage production, Rosencrantz and Guildenstern early in the scene try to steal a letter from Hamlet's book when he turns away (Kliman, "Schaefer," 31).

These courtiers, both dark and dressed alike—not in uniform—are suitably sycophantic, but many of the actors are less than adequate or sadly miscast. Sarah Churchill is too forthright and steady a soul to go

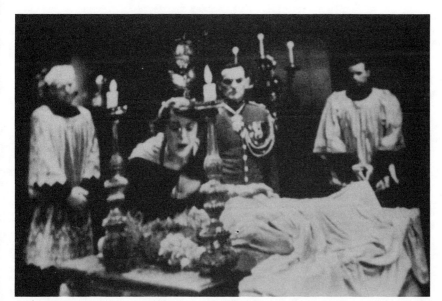

The Evans *Hamlet.* **Ophelia on a bier in the court.** *(Still courtesy George Schaefer.)*

The Evans *Hamlet.* **Hamlet asks his mother how she likes the play.** *(Still courtesy George Schaefer.)*

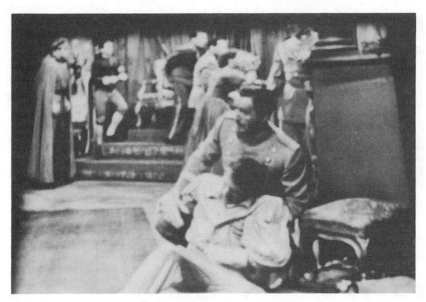

The Evans *Hamlet*. In rearframe, Gertrude is spirited off the set before she falls, the cup now is ready for Claudius near his throne, and Laertes lies dying in Osric's arms. *(Still courtesy George Schaefer.)*

The Evans *Hamlet*. Claudius and his crown. *(Still courtesy George Schaefer.)*

mad. In closeup, Evans, at fifty-two, seems old for the part, older than Claudius, played by Joseph Schildkraut, fifty-eight. Gertrude, perforce, has to be older than Hamlet, limiting her credibility as a sensuous woman, her low-cut gowns notwithstanding, and Ruth Chatterton, fifty-nine, who plays her, forgets some lines. Her smile is grotesque, a false-looking grimace that flashes on and off. Our last view of her is indeed strange. As she literally sings out the word "poisoned," those around her, in rear frame and under the cover of others blocking the view, spirit her off the set before she falls. Hamlet says no "adieu" to her. The director here returned to an earlier stage tradition, when Gertrudes presumably did not like falling onto the stage or pretending to be dead for dozens of lines (Sprague, 181).

Some viewers may have an aversion to Evans's mannered and declamatory style, with quaver in voice and quiver on lips, a somewhat exaggerated "Shakespearean" style of acting. His technique, however, illustrates the historical development of Shakespearean acting. Clearly, Evans's method was in fashion in the thirties, forties and even the fifties in a way it cannot be today. By 1959, John Neville's similar vocal delivery did not meet with approval. George Jean Nathan (1882–1958), in praising Evans's stage performance, cites particularly his naturalness, yet this is precisely the quality that modern audiences might miss in his television performance.[6] The sound track of the Mogubgub film "Enter Hamlet," a three-minute short, animates Evans's "To be or not to be," with his characteristic pauses and quavers. This mannered style is not necessarily typical of his work, for Evans does not act in this "Shakespearean" way in non-Shakespearean roles, for example in Hallmark's magnificent *Dial 'M' for Murder,* directed by Schaefer and aired on 25 April 1958. Evans was performing in this play on Broadway, presumably in naturalistic style, in 1953 while he was in rehearsal for *Hamlet* on TV. A contemporary reviewer says that Evans, whom he likes in the modern play, "often struts and 'tears a passion to tatters' when he comes to Avon" (*Saturday Review*, 16 May 1953, 33). In later Shakespearean roles on television, Evans adopted a more natural persona. This production gives a delightful foretaste of that naturalness with Hamlet's "Here they come" when he sees Rosencrantz and Guildenstern after stowing Polonius away. Evans's tone of voice as well as his grimace of distaste are winning. But as George Schaefer notes, Evans "primarily is a stage actor: his voice, his style, his personality thrived in the theater. . . . I think television was a . . . nice in-between for him because we could take advantage of the theatricality of the performance" (Kliman, "Schaefer," 31). Television is indeed something between stage and film, but it was some time before set designers addressed themselves to its particular attributes.

Though bloopers, failure of conception, downright poor acting by some of the supporting cast, and old-fashioned acting by Evans impede this production, the sets ultimately are what spoil it because, by imposing, with those artifacts, an aura of realism on the play, they highlight all the other defects, which in essence are failures of verisimilitude. *Marty*, the much-acclaimed TV drama about two aging ugly ducklings who find each other at a dancehall, was also aired in spring 1953. Its studio sets redolent of lower-middle-class life might have persuaded audiences of their reality then, though they would not today. Spaces are small; shots are tight. This was the standard of realism at the time—artificial realism, a standard that Evans's *Hamlet* meets or even exceeds. All representations of reality on stage or on film are illusions, of course—but it is easier to see the artifice from a distance. This is the same artificial realism found in the set of a thirties film, like *The Petrified Forest* with Leslie Howard, that was evidently meant to fool the eye. But it differs from the frankly artificial realism that stage sets have essayed for a long time, as film became more adept at the construction of sound sets and the use of location, and as theater sought its own ground. In *Twelve Angry Men* the yellowed woodwork was suitably marred with dirt and finger marks but the edge of the setting ended at the proscenium arch.[7] Or to cite a more contemporary example, in *Cat on a Hot Tin Roof* with Elizabeth Ashley (1974), the realistic set ended with a jagged edge before the proscenium arch, or in Jules Pfeifer's black comedy *Grown Ups* (1981), the kitchen setting did not fill the whole stage. Frank admission of illusion on stage contrasts with film's insistence on reality. With television's inability at present to achieve the illusion without resorting to televising films,[8] the most viable course could be that same frank admission. The Evans/ Schaefer pioneering *Hamlet* shows the way, not only through its successes—as in the nunnery scene and the play-within-a-play—but also through its errors—the cluttered setting and even the "accidental" footman. It also demonstrates, sometimes by negative examples, to a viewer what he or she values in productions—a natural and believable Hamlet, clarity without loss of subtlety, coherence and unity.

Notes

1. See, for example, Gould and Hamburger. In England, *Hamlet* had already been televised; in Mander and Mitchenson there's a photo from a London BBC-TV production of 1947, with Patrick McNee as Laertes (134, 220).

2. Hallmark's setting was lavish compared to those of some other television Shakespeare productions, such as Studio One's *Julius Caesar* (1 May 1949) and *Coriolanus* (1 June 1951).

3. For the effect of errors on an audience, see Goffman, 206, and 206 n. See also, "Alas Poor Stagehand, We Saw Him Well," *New York Journal American*, 27 April 1953.

4. Bazin (1 : 110) similarly discusses incidental sounds as having the power to make a film from a work otherwise stagy.

5. For example, the commentator in the Oxberry Edition (opposite 28) speaks of the way Kemble did this scene. "He was uttering an affecting description of his melancholy. . . .

They broke in on the delicacy of his feelings, by a jest out of place . . . he felt that he was not understood by them."

6. Nathan is quoted by Dent 1948, 65.

7. *Twelve Angry Men* came to the stage via television (1955) and film (1957).

8. When televised films are not specifically made for TV, they almost always have too many long shots that cannot be assimilated by audiences. To cite one example of many: *Night of the Shooting Stars* (1982).

6

Dupont Show of the Month
with John Neville (1959)

Continuing, like Olivier, the stage practice of issuing an acting edition, Michael Benthall, director of both the Old Vic stage and television versions of *Hamlet* in 1959, produced, with CBS Television prior to broadcast, a cut edition of *Hamlet* as performed on television, with directions marked in red. Though admittedly there were changes before the broadcast, a month after the book was released, it is an excellent record of the text of the production (and I quote from it for this chapter). The stage directions, however, are pale suggestions of the television production's rich business.

Like Olivier (and Evans), Benthall used Q1 order with the F1 text; for example, "To be, or not to be" precedes the arrival of the players, avoiding, he says in the introduction, the wrench of mood change we see in the folio, the shift from action with Hamlet's idea of the play to suicide in the very next scene. Benthall does not mention Olivier's film as a model, but it is a likely influence. Since Olivier chose to say "The play's the thing" with great energy and direction, and those words indeed mark a turning point in Hamlet's emotions in the film, following this by "to be" would certainly have been a mistake. But wrenching of mood, vacillation, is part of Hamlet's character in many productions, and thus a shift from joy to despair would not be out of place. Nor need the couplet express joy. Both Q1 and Olivier give a smoother shape to the drama, a simpler structure that might be suited to a television production like Benthall's, only seventy-eight minutes long.[1] He also used Q1 order, however, for the 195-minute contemporary American stage production at the Broadway Theater.

Other similarities demonstrate the influence of the early film on the

television (and to some extent the stage) production. Besides the transposition of the nunnery sequence and the arrival of the players, the Old
Vic production used another Olivier transposition: the Claudius/Laertes
plot follows rather than precedes the graveyard scene.[2] Naturally, with
such a shortened production, one finds the usual characters cut—Fortinbras, Rosencrantz and Guildenstern, Reynaldo, and others. Though
much longer, Olivier's film eliminated these same characters. Amazingly,
the Old Vic's smooth stitching avoids choppiness. Further similarities:
Hamlet's first soliloquy, like Olivier's a voiceover, has a few lines said
aloud. At the end of the first court scene, as Hamlet says "Would the
night were come," a bell tolls in both productions. As in the 1948
Hamlet, the camera zooms into an extreme closeup of Hamlet's head to
show the enactment of the poisoning in the garden as the ghost speaks of
it (though in the television production, Hamlet's forehead remains in
view the whole time).

The Old Vic television production has, however, its own excellences:
the setting by Bob Markell and the camera work, presumably the responsibility of network producer and director Ralph Nelson. Interestingly enough, these are excellences of the medium; the television
people were highly professional.

The camera reveals in a swift pan the expressionistic setting for the
first scene, with triangular crenelations, winter snow falling on battlements, a cylindrical towerlike structure at the rear, interesting curves,
arches, steps, levels, and finally, beyond a brazier with glowing coals, a
shadow and then a caped figure, Marcellus, whipped by howling wind
and snow, soon challenged by Bernardo and then joined by Horatio.
The ghost, a superimposed shadowy figure, in crown and ermines over
armor, walks from foreframe to the three men at the rear of the frame
huddled behind the brazier. Horatio runs towards the ghost, but it walks
by him towards the other two. Marcellus strikes at it, and then it is gone.
The three men leave to find Hamlet, but the ghost appears again between the brazier and the camera, walking toward us, closer and closer
to a bust-sized closeup, saying "Hamlet, Hamlet," several times in an
urgent, pleading tone, as titles appear on the screen. So begins this
production—suitably compact in text for its time limit but not at all
compressed in its acting space.

I believe this would have been a successful *Hamlet* and a model for
television abridgements if John Neville's acting had been more moving.
As it is, it is too easy to blame its failure on the cut text. Neville's
performance does not live up to the expectations aroused by the opening
sequence, with its eery sounds, expressionistic setting, and mournful
ghost. Kenneth Tynan may have exaggerated in saying that Neville's
stage Hamlet conveys no emotion, that he is cold and bloodless, but he is
not far wrong (1958, 52–55). No production value can compensate for

the flaw at the center of the drama—an inadequate Hamlet. He overacts, with exaggerated trilled *r*'s, with voice quavers, and with indications of emotion rather than felt emotion. Neville's skin-deep suffering cannot make me care about him. Leaving that aside for the moment, the achievements of the TV production—distinction of setting, camera work, and relationship of actors to the setting—are worth noting. The set designer was not afraid to move between relatively realistic and expressionistic space.

From the face of the ghost the camera dissolves to the pained face of Hamlet in closeup. Beyond him in long shot, the king holds a crown above his head as his queen stands by, smiling. A reverse shot from behind the king and queen reveals much of the set and in the distance Hamlet leaning on a pillar; quick cuts from one to the other give the effect of montage. In this black-and-white production, the set looks very white, avoiding busy shades of greys and blacks. The stage production had, in contrast, been dark, with pillars seen in silhouette, according to Kenneth Tynan (1958). Much as on stage, little furniture distracts the eye—here only the thrones under a canopy and candles on tall sticks. The shifting camera reveals through the scene architectural features such as a two-storied space with sweeping stairways on right and left, alcoves, arches, small-paned windows, pillars, and smooth marble floors—all giving this set a suitably elegant look. As in the stage production, the men wear Chocolate-Soldier uniforms, unobtrusively placing the production in the nineteenth century.[3]

Through economical maneuvers, the production cuts while maintaining a sense that what has been cut is still there.[4] After the king's announcement about having taken Gertrude to wife and after the court's approval, Hamlet's painful soliloquy ("O that this too too solid flesh") covers without completely obscuring the voices of Claudius and others continuing the court's business. The space allows us to see them in a blur beyond the closeup of Hamlet's face. When Hamlet, looking at a miniature on a chain around his neck, says, "So excellent a king," the camera cuts to a closeup of Claudius's smiling face, responding to the courtiers' clapping; the camera thus points up the comparison that Hamlet is making. Again, just before Hamlet says aloud, "Frailty, thy name is woman!" the camera shows us a closeup of his mother. Describing it thus makes it seem more unsubtle than it is, but the expressionistic sets allow for expressionistic cuts, Eisensteinian montage. The soliloquy ends as Claudius says, with a sound of completion, "Thus much the business is," turning to Laertes, not noticing Hamlet until Gertrude urges the king to turn.

For the dance among Hamlet, Claudius, and Gertrude, the camera shoots a variety of straight-on and high-angle shots. Taking advantage of one of television's strengths, the director has his characters engage in

The Neville *Hamlet*. Claudius speaks quietly to Hamlet.

private conferences where stage convention demands open audiences. Gertrude, moving to him in foreframe, speaks her first lines to Hamlet alone, while in the frame beyond them Claudius and Polonius confer. A closeup concentrates our attention on Hamlet for his response "Seems, madam? Nay, it *is*." Claudius's smiling intrusion between them composes a three-shot and then a two-shot, without Gertrude, as Claudius usurps her place. After his public announcement, for which the frame enlarges in a high-angle shot to show the court, Claudius whispers harshly to Hamlet, telling him not to go to Wittenberg; a television audience can hear the softest whisper knowing that no one is hearing it who should not. The camera shows in the two-shot Claudius's eyes on Hamlet, Hamlet's eyes turned inward. His mother whispers her request too, and, since she thus focuses on him alone and Hamlet answers her similarly, there is no insult to Claudius in "I shall in all my best obey you, madam." This is, however, a three-shot, with both Claudius's and Gertrude's hands on Hamlet's chest: they physically overwhelm him. When Claudius says "come," she immediately moves off frame with him. A soldier carrying the crown stops in left frame as Claudius, almost off frame left, acknowledges the accolades of the court. Because the television camera brings us so close, because it selects so carefully what we *can* see, we notice Hamlet unobtrusively looking at the crown.

The director chose to have Ophelia present at the first court scene. One shot shows the whole family, with Ophelia holding Laertes's hand—

blocking that emphasizes their familial closeness. Though Claudius's flattery of Polonius is cut, Polonius *looks* flattered by the notice Laertes gets and the king shows his regard by putting his arm around Polonius's shoulder. In the next scene, blocking establishes Ophelia's precise relationship to her brother and father. When her brother sits to advise her, she kneels, placing herself lower than he is; she gives no counteradvice. For Polonius's argument with Ophelia about Hamlet after he has accidentally overheard Laertes's last whispered caution, the camera in a high angle shot catches both on the stairs, with Polonius going up, Ophelia following him. This setting works well for this scene because it puts Ophelia at a disadvantage (behind and below Polonius) that she cannot overcome. He begins quietly, becoming satiric as he belittles her judgment. As she continues to resist his arguments, he gets angry, looking back at her sternly, finally asserting all the force of his authority over her. Then he stops, slips back into affection, and looks back at her for her acquiescence. With a gulp, she assents. Finally, eyes down, she must say, "I shall obey, my lord."

Their relationship had already been established during the court scene and was reinforced as Polonius gave his advice. Both son and daughter have heard these words often and smile at the iteration. Distracted by the advice about clothing, "not express'd in fancy," Laertes and Ophelia stop listening (in rear frame) while Polonius continues the advice in closeup (in the foreframe), rounding the words with palpable

The Neville *Hamlet*. The expressionistic setting reflects Ophelia's fright.

The Neville *Hamlet*. Ophelia is present as Polonius reads Hamlet's letter to her.

self-satisfaction. Laertes protests silently to Ophelia and she examines his clothes. But when Polonius notices they are not following and gathers them in again, they both listen solemnly and respectfully to the last lines, "This above all, to thine own self be true, and it must follow, as the night the day, thou canst not then be false to any man." They recognize the difference between trite and true. This is a complex, fully realized relationship that prepares us for Ophelia's mourning of her father in the mad scene.

For Ophelia's harried entrance to tell Polonius about Hamlet's visit to her closet (2.1), a more expressionistic set again echoes her state of mind; a group of triangular arches make a kind of tunnel through which she runs. Though she is completely sane at the beginning of the nunnery scene, in retrospect the setting provides a kind of foreshadowing of her madness. Polonius and Ophelia go to the library, one of the alcoves beyond the big public room of the court scene, with tables, chairs, three steps, an arch where Polonius and Claudius can hide, a shield with swords decorating a wall. Ophelia stops at the door, as Polonius breathlessly begins his explanation. Comprising a fine four-shot are, at far left, the king in foreframe, moody, looking down; behind him at the door, Ophelia, embarrassed at the reading of her letter; to the right rear Polonius, standing with the letter; Gertrude, closer to camera, to right of Polonius, looking more interested than she had when Polonius began his obscure recital. The size of the frame shows all the characters in relation to each other yet separated from one another, each lost in his or her own concerns. Claudius and Polonius hatch the spying plot as Hamlet appears, before Gertrude or Ophelia has time to protest, though Ophelia does try to say no. She runs off before Hamlet can see her.

Hamlet takes a dagger-shaped paper-cutter from the table to cut a leaf of his book and then is drawn to consideration of the knife itself: the prop calls forth his soul's anguish. "To be, or not to be—that is the question." He sits at the table facing the fireplace; the camera moves until he is in profile shot so that the door through which Ophelia will re-enter appears beyond him. As he puts the knife down after "fly to others that we know not of" and turns to the left, he sees Ophelia. Closeups show his concern for her. After a quiet "Get thee to a nunnery," he becomes angry only when, as he is leaving, he sees the shadows of Polonius and Claudius. She, facing the camera, does not see, making her last speech credible—that is, her shock and surprise at his behavior. His word "mad" ("It hath made me mad") or his mad behavior hurls *her* into madness, the beginnings of which appear here. Thus in this production, the severed connection to Hamlet—which began in her closet—is a more powerful force against her sanity than Polonius's death, which simply completes her disintegration.

Barbara Jefford is a remarkable Ophelia, whose every speech un-

The Neville *Hamlet.* Ophelia's sore distraction begins at the end of the nunnery scene.

covers fresh nuances of the character's feelings. Her mad scene is a model of what is possible for Ophelias. At "thoughts" she throws the flower away in disgust; she *hates* thoughts. She shifts believably from tenderness to passion to a kind of crazy sense, to joy, to defeat, and finally, for a moment, to reality, when she recognizes Laertes. What she then knows is too painful to live with, and she runs off in tears, crying "No, no." The serenity of this lovely room, with statues, tapestry, altar, and cross on the floor, contrasts touchingly with the pain she feels.

The chapel is of course where Claudius prays after the play, which had truly moved him to the brink of penitence. In this space the idea of Claudius's successful repentance becomes believable, and thus the space affects our response to Hamlet's refusal to kill him here. Claudius's contrition inspires pity, which makes Hamlet's words seem unbearably bloodthirsty. In a more neutral space, with a Claudius less sincere in his effort to pray, Hamlet's words do not seem as violent and irreligious. As in the 1934 *Hamlet* with Gielgud (Mills, 215), Hamlet comes into the chapel unarmed and picks up the king's sword. The king, missing it, knows that Hamlet is a present danger to him—yet must wonder why Hamlet has not acted.

Because this setting and others appear several times, the areas of the castle become familiar. Others are worth mentioning. The queen's bedroom displays Gertrude's sensuality, with its grotesque, highly figured wallpaper, a sharp contrast to the clean whiteness of the other sets, with,

The Neville *Hamlet*. The Yorick scene.

as a low-angle shot shows, its elaborately filigreed ceiling border pattern, and with its bed, dressing table, and other furniture, making this a more cluttered space than any other. In this room, it is not surprising, though still a shock, that Gertrude responds to Hamlet's filial kiss passionately, with mouth open, making him draw back in horror. The director settled on a seductive Gertrude to convey an Oedipal conflict. The graveyard presumably is studio-shot, but looks very realistic, with snow, bare trees, and wide grey sky. In a typical gesture from many *Hamlet*s, Hamlet holds the skull before his face, a macabre foreshadowing. There is ample room for at least eighteen followers in Ophelia's procession, following the closed casket. The cavern where the ghost speaks to Hamlet is suitably strange and otherworldly. Through a kind of special-effects meta-morphosis, the ghost itself evolves from otherworldly to domestic.

Because of the attractive television values in setting and camera work, it is just possible that the television production was superior to the generally panned stage production with the same cast. The producers employed film techniques—that is, a large unit setting, with a wide range of camera distances and angles. Perhaps they were not thinking in terms of television's usual problems—the small screen and the shallow depth of field—but in any case, in ignoring the problems, they seemed to have found at least one solution: combining the long shots of films with sets more bare than those usually in films but more spacious than those usually on television.

Notes

1. In his introduction to the show, Fredric March implies that the stage and television productions are alike, that viewers will see what they would have seen had they attended a performance during the Old Vic's ·coast-to-coast tour. No mention is made either of television's superiority or inferiority to stage productions—or of the substantial cuts.

2. Not that Olivier was the originator of the transposition. With much of act 4 cut in productions, it was natural to place Laertes's and Claudius's plot in act 5, just before the duel.

3. The uniforms may have been inspired by the Maurice Evans GI production in 1946. But notes on *Hamlet* in the text accompanying the recording by Burton (*Hamlet 1964*, 16) mention that a Tyrone Guthrie Old Vic production with John Gielgud used Rumanian uniforms. Gielgud is a likely influence on the 1959 Old Vic production as well. Uniforms, however, are not uncommon. According to a reference in these same notes to Mander and Mitchenson, a Japanese production of 1891 dressed in the military and court costume of the day.

4. Overlap is another economy: the gravedigger sings as Hamlet and Horatio enter the frame and begin talking.

7

Peter Wirth's Production with Maximilian Schell (1960)

Peter Wirth for his 1960 version chose yet another solution for the setting, a nonillusionistic dark world. Not as open as the Old Vic production, nor as claustrophobic as the McKellen, which was to be taped eleven years later, the Wirth production favored close shots that make it difficult at times to get the whole view. The production begins with the voice of Maximilian Schell speaking Rosencrantz's lines on the "cease of Majestie" (F1: 3.3.11–23), with two steel thrones on view against a black background punctuated by distant light sources. Inspired perhaps to include a prologue by Olivier's example, Wirth selected, however, words that express the theme of danger, violence to all who challenge the king. Showing the thrones as the initial image (rather than the tombstone, Elsinore, or any other prologue choice) emphasizes politics, the struggle for power that Wirth sees as a central theme of *Hamlet*. Taken out of their context, Rosencrantz's flattery of Claudius applies equally well to Claudius and to Hamlet: Claudius has brought a king down and is doomed to plunge with that massy wheel (of fortune); Hamlet will bring down a king and so will fall too. The extremely pessimistic view accords with the darkness of the setting, blackness that conveys the dark night of the soul. Harsh, metallic-sounding, mechanical, militaristic music reinforces the set's imagery.

As it tracks around to the rear to discover the sentry, the camera shows a simple, dark, metallic setting of catwalks, steps, ramps, and columns. The set demands a flexible shooting style. In addition to straight-on shots, three-shots of Marcellus, Bernardo, and Horatio from the point of view of the ghost below them alternate with high-angle shots of the ghost from the men's point of view. High- and low-angle shots extend the limited space: the guards' catwalk barely tops the burnished metal thrones; we can see them later (in 1.4) a short distance away. No wide-angle shots of the whole set reveal its dimensions, which must be inferred from bits assembled piecemeal. Except for this framing, the set is remarkably like many symbolic stage sets of the period (Styan 1981, 196).

For "Ile cross it, though it blast me," Horatio takes out his sword, goes down to the ghost with the sword pointed at it, while the ghost simply backs up and leaves. The space does not allow for much dramatic movement; so instead the production substitutes a kind of deliberate intensity.

Wirth uses the tight style to make points about relationships. After the sentry scene, the camera cuts to the court, where men and women engage in a rigid dance to the same mechanical and militaristic music. Closeups and medium shots show that Ophelia is there and that Hamlet is looking at her, she at him. The camera (Hamlet) looks from Ophelia to Gertrude and back again, making the connection. Claudius's public announcement at the opening of the scene begins with the camera providing the only view of the whole court in a wide image. As the camera moves in for a medium closeup and then a closeup of Claudius and Gertrude, as Claudius becomes more passionate and whispers possessively, the scene becomes less and less public. No wider shots show the whole court during Claudius's first speech to allow a view of their

The Schell *Hamlet*. Gertrude and Claudius. *(Still courtesy Edward Dmytryk and Sam Weiler.)*

reaction, to convey Claudius's standing among this group. Only a brief glimpse of bent heads at the end bowing into the limited space that the camera gives Claudius indicates that the court is indeed still attending. The conversations between Polonius and Laertes, Gertrude and Claudius are private. Claudius whispers "let the world take note," not at all letting the world take note. Hamlet need not stress the *you* of "Obey you Madam," because he says it only to Gertrude. The frame shows Claudius alone or Claudius and Gertrude or Hamlet alone, smiling sardonically at the proceedings, but no one else until the end of the scene when all the courtiers walk out in a procession, close to Hamlet.

As they file by, he soliloquizes in voiceover. Ophelia when she passes tries to get his attention, but though he had shared glances with her before Claudius spoke, now, deep in thought, he ignores her.[1] Aloud he says "not so much; not two," then catches himself and darts a swift glance to see that no one has heard. As he walks from the crowd, he continues aloud. This is a court of exclusions, of private intrigues, where outsiders do not even have the illusion that they are among the elect.

For the next scene on the battlements, a long, low-angle shot of the three watchers establishes the whole space before it inevitably becomes a medium closeup three-shot. When Hamlet speaks of Claudius the camera crosscuts to a closeup of the drunken crowd, whose heavy-headed riot is accompanied by the discordant music. A montage of shots gives a sense of the whole, though the whole is not shown: men, women, fool, all laughing. The camera can thus clarify and objectify: what may seem in the text to be Hamlet's prudishness about drinking becomes our view too as we see the riotous crowd. The camera thus removes an area for perhaps fruitful ambiguity. (Kosintzev was to use this same technique four years later.)

The return to the battlements shows Horatio, blurred in the shot, behind Hamlet, not listening to the "one defect" speech but looking intently at something off screen. The camera holds shots a long time; Hamlet's entire speech is one take. Since film (and television too but perhaps not to so great an extent) normally holds shots only for moments, these long-held shots give us some of the focusing power of a stage speech that keeps our eyes riveted on the speaker. Here the audience has no choice; our eyes cannot stray elsewhere. This can work against the effect, for if the speech does not hold us, we will notice we are being held against our will. At home, watching television, this is when we get up for another beer. Since Schell, however, does indeed capture our rapt attention, we get the benefit of stage focusing without any of the pitfalls for television. That we *are* held is especially noteworthy in this shot because Horatio's not listening signals us not to listen also.

This time, the ghost is above the men, and Hamlet, who cannot in this small space make a great effort to free himself from the others' grasp (a

The Schell *Hamlet*. Polonius's advice; Laertes's amusement. *(Still courtesy Edward Dmytryk and Sam Weiler.)*

The Schell *Hamlet*. Hamlet sees the ghost. *(Still courtesy Edward Dmytryk and Sam Weiler.)*

constriction reminiscent of the 1907 silent film discussed in the next section), climbs the stairs to join the ghost. From this point, the thrones on the platform are visible. Hamlet cannot go far before he says "Ile go no further." The very lack of visual illusion forces us to accept the illusion of the words. A closeup of Hamlet's face shows his reactions to the ghost's revelations, but the frame excludes the ghost while it speaks. The closeup of Hamlet with his eyes closed, especially without a view of the ghost, seems to suggest that the ghost's words are all in his head, a suggestion avoided when the ghost is on screen for his speech or reinforced when the ghost's voice is the same as that of the actor playing Hamlet (as in Richardson's *Hamlet*). Here we cannot be sure because, though the ghost is not on screen, the voice, old and weak, is so different from Hamlet's.

The Polonius space is nowhere, an undifferentiated space marked only by a pillar or two. In the advice scene, Polonius runs to an open book when he forgets his lines, as for a 1937 Stratford-upon-Avon production (Babula, number 56). This business takes away Polonius's one opportunity to impress an audience—or at least his children—with his wisdom. Neither Laertes nor Ophelia is impressed. For Ophelia's closet scene, a nonverbal, added scene in pantomime, we first see a closeup of needlework, then hear danger music as Hamlet's shadow falls on her. When the frame widens somewhat, we see nothing marking this as a room. Seeing Hamlet, dirty and unbuttoned, we cannot doubt his

The Schell *Hamlet*. **Hamlet's distraction.** *(Still courtesy Edward Dmytryk and Sam Weiler.)*

madness, whether real or pretended. That is, we cannot infer that her interpretation is naive or mistaken. Without seeing him, hearing only her words, we could guess that the long look at her was his test of her, a test that she both fails and misunderstands. After he leaves, in long shot she runs along a colonnade to Polonius, where she says very little; the encounter between her and Hamlet (2.1) has been represented visually.

Ophelia is so soft, so modest and gentle with her brown hair and childlike face that she seems out of place in this metallic setting. Her costume, a simple long dress with puffed sleeves, contrasts sharply with Gertrude's futuristic dress, with winglike gauze collar flying up, with rigid hair style piled above, but Gertrude's fits this environment. Hamlet, too, wears softer, more "natural" clothes than the others, black shirt and slacks, in contrast to the curious windowpane-check tunics that Laertes and Polonius wear. Costumes complement the set, reflecting no time period, no place.

The director next adopts Dover Wilson's or Olivier's ploy of having Hamlet overhear the unloosing plot (2.2.159–68). In spite of the constricted setting, he can by using two levels make the point. As the conspirators scheme, the camera lifts to show Hamlet on the upper level, book in hand, unashamedly listening, a cynical smirk on his face. Olivier is the more likely inspiration because Wilson deplores the idea of Hamlet purposefully eavesdropping; it must all be accidental, Wilson thinks, or we will lose our high opinion of Hamlet. The sight of Hamlet eavesdropping in this setting does not discredit him, however; this is such a devious world that any defense is justifiable. The music that accompanied his arrival in Ophelia's space marks him as indeed "something dangerous," a man who would not hesitate to spy.

A production that chooses to have Hamlet overhear gives us and the director a problem in the nunnery scene, however, for, if Hamlet knows that Claudius is listening there, what Hamlet says to Ophelia should be directed at Claudius. Hamlet could either welcome the opportunity to prove he is mad, that is, if he acts mad as a cover for further action, as in Shakespeare's source, or he could act mad in spite of himself, though an actor might have a difficult time conveying this, or if he normally acts mad to confuse and worry Claudius, then maybe he would not act mad when being watched but would say things that would worry and confuse Claudius even more. Schell makes the latter choice.

Wirth solves the problem he sets himself by making the unloosing and nunnery segments contiguous.[2] A change in Hamlet's costume shows that some time has passed; that is, though (as in Q1) the nunnery scene immediately follows the unloosing plot, in this production (as in Q2 and F1) the nunnery scene is a new one. The queen, who had objected with head shakes to the spying, is not in sight. This breakup of scenes into a new configuration emphasizes Gertrude's objection or at least does not

The Schell *Hamlet*. **The nunnery scene; Polonius encourages Ophelia.** *(Still courtesy Edward Dmytryk and Sam Weiler.)*

make her a party to the spying. Through a transparent curtain, from Polonius's point of view, the camera shoots Ophelia kneeling at the altar, praying fervently. Cutting to this view several times during the scene, the camera calls attention to the spying. There is no doubt about what Polonius and Claudius see and hear because, when the camera frames Ophelia and Hamlet through the arras, it shows what the spies see. Ophelia faces the camera and Hamlet stands behind her, menacing, with music to match. Then the camera swings around to the other side of the curtain, from the Polonius-Claudius side to the Ophelia-Hamlet side, moving to a medium closeup.

As Hamlet turns away from her after the initial greeting, Polonius steps out from behind the curtain and motions her to follow Hamlet. Of course, realistically, Hamlet would catch this motion in his peripheral vision, but I think we can accept the convention of his not seeing in this nonillusionistic setting. Hamlet speaks to Ophelia as if he does not know the others are hiding until she looks back at the arras; he then smiles sardonically in recollection—the closeup can catch the subtle change in his demeanor. She had looked back when Hamlet had said "beleeve none of us." Perhaps her glance shows that she recognizes dimly that she should not believe Polonius, or perhaps she hears Hamlet's words as corroboration of Polonius's advice to her about Hamlet, whom she made no attempt to defend in the first scene with her father (1.3), Wirth having

The Schell *Hamlet.* **The nunnery scene; Hamlet gives her a chance to tell the truth.** *(Still courtesy Edward Dmytryk and Sam Weiler.)*

cut her few objections to Polonius's characterization of her lover. Hamlet, standing, raises her, whispers his question about Polonius, giving her an opportunity to side with him. She, lifting her hand to his shoulder, which he takes and holds next to his heart, opens her mouth to tell him the truth. As he holds her closer and closer, she lies, falteringly, "At home, my Lord," at which he starts away, throwing her down on the bench. Then he speaks angrily for the benefit of the auditors, but also partly out of real dismay. He treats Ophelia as if she were a prostitute, kissing her violently. Directly to the arras (again like Olivier) he speaks about the "all but one" who shall keep as they are, and (yet again like Olivier), he comes back to her and kisses her hair, unnoticed by her, as Tree also had done in his 1892 *Hamlet* (Sprague, 155).

From behind the arras the camera shows Ophelia as she says her last speech, "O what a Noble minde," gently beating her fist on the bench. Polonius, convinced Hamlet's behavior does come from love, speaks of the love he experienced as a youth (lines from 2.1). Claudius, disagreeing, comes close to Ophelia, who looks frightened by him; she rushes off. Her tone indicates that madness begins at the end of this scene. Polonius follows after Hamlet for the fishmonger scene.

After Polonius finally leaves him, Hamlet discards the emblem of his antic disposition, a daisy in his hair, as well as his scarf and book. He walks to the steps, where a reverse shot shows his eyes only between two

The Schell *Hamlet*. "To be or not to be." *(Still courtesy Edward Dmytryk and Sam Weiler.)*

steps as he begins his despairing question: "To be, or not to be." Hamlet between the steps is a visual metaphor: the machinations, the timidities of those around him squeeze him into a small space for maneuvering. At "To Dreame" he walks away from the steps, the camera showing his pained expression, tracking with him until he stops to lean against a pillar. The appearance of Rosencrantz and Guildenstern immediately after only confirms the visual metaphor: spies are all around, giving Hamlet very little room to move. Tight shots say this. A cut shows Rosencrantz and Guildenstern, alone, listening to him. When he becomes aware of them, he says "uh"—like "Oh these two." There is no friendship here. Schell varies a static three-shot by walking from the left of the two around them to the right. He is the one with mobility or restlessness; they stand pat. "What a piece of worke is a man," however, is a one-shot of Hamlet, with no reaction shots. That he says it alone, without their response, undercuts the speech as a plea to them for understanding—much as Evans had undercut it by saying it out of a window—making it instead a private declaration of belief. But after all, in Wirth's version Hamlet has been suspicious of them from the start, so an attempt to persuade them to side with him would have been inappropriate in any case. Since a note in the Oxberry edition (opposite 28) says that "Hamlet seems to immediately suspect Rosencrantz and Guildenstern," we may infer that Wirth is following a hallowed stage tradition—also found in Welles's radio broadcast, by the way—that calls in question Gertrude's "And sure I am, two men there are not living, / To whom he more adheres" (2.2.20–21).

We hear their laughter after "nor Woman neither," but when the camera finally shows them, they look serious. Rosencrantz has a hard time finding a reason for his laugh, suggesting that the laugh had indeed been at Hamlet's expense, that he had shown no understanding at all of the pain in "and yet to me, what is this Quintessence of Dust? Man delights not me . . ." (2.2.321–22). There is a moment of uncomfortable silence while he thinks of what to say. Guildenstern is palpably relieved by his partner's answer.

With Rosencrantz's response that the players are coming to serve Hamlet, the director cuts to a new scene, marked again by a fresh costume for Hamlet, this time with a cloak and with the locket he will need for the closet scene. First the players enter, with tumblers and jugglers somersaulting in, as Polonius tries to organize and restrain them. Then Hamlet enters after Rosencrantz and Guildenstern and others, including four court ladies, who listen. Closeups show that Hamlet approves of Hecuba, a queen who mourns her husband, and that Hamlet stares Rosencrantz and Guildenstern off when they try to hear what he says to the First Player.

"Oh what a Rogue and Pesant slave am I" (2.2.576) is meditative, not bitter, with one shot from the beginning to "Vengeance," which, shouted, echoes off the metallic set. Then Hamlet looks sheepish, self-satiric, and claps at his own ranting, as if he were a player who out-Herods Herod. After "Scullion" Hamlet walks, the camera following him, to sit on the steps and tap his fingers one after another while he hatches his plot. Depending on how Hamlet says it, those lines about not trusting the ghost can sound like a lame excuse for delay; here they do not because he does not stress the devil-ghost idea. In fact, the production gives no sense that Hamlet has delayed or is delaying now. This is true partly because, in spite of breaking the scenes into small units, the director gives the production sufficient momentum to rush events along. This scene ends with a fade and threatening music for the beginning of the play scene.

Throughout this scene, the camera provides the view we want to see; it never frustrates us or jolts us by withholding information. First showing us Polonius counting chairs and the court coming into the throne room, the camera swings around to reveal Hamlet behind the curtain watching the court, a neat reversal of the spying in the nunnery scene. And in yet another twist, Polonius is listening at the curtain to Hamlet. Horatio is with Hamlet behind the curtain. When Hamlet comes from behind the curtain, Claudius, not devoid of a sense of humor, leads applause. Hamlet sits on a chair next to Ophelia, who speaks like a zombie. She has

The Schell *Hamlet.* **Player king and queen.** *(Still courtesy Edward Dmytryk and Sam Weiler.)*

sunk further into madness. Claudius and Gertrude bill and coo. The camera reveals that Hamlet directs "As Womans love" at Gertrude rather than at Ophelia, while a two-shot of Rosencrantz and Guildenstern shows them bored, sardonic. Only Ophelia seems to respond to the romance of the player king's and queen's love. The camera also shows Gertrude's distressed response when the player queen, dressed and coiffed like Gertrude, begins to protest her perpetual loyalty to her husband, dressed like Claudius. With subtle pressures of his hand and by example, Claudius tries to encourage Gertrude to remain cool. After the player queen's departure, Hamlet leads the clapping, perhaps parodying Claudius. Since Hamlet stands behind the thrones for the second scene of *The Murder of Gonzago,* we see the faces of all three principals at once. To Claudius Hamlet says, "This is one Lucianus—uh—nephew to the king." (Nicol Williamson similarly says "brother—uh—*nephew* to the king.") These words do not disturb Claudius's surface calm until Hamlet calls Lucianus a murderer. Then the king's face changes. But earlier Claudius had taken his hand from Gertrude's when Lucianus came on, a sign of emotion. With the stage murder, Gertrude looks at Claudius in shock and dismay. She finally begins to suspect what her doting husband may have done to win her. When Hamlet says "gets the love of Gonzago's wife," Claudius, not with excessive emotion, gets up and calls for light. The close-in camera makes this effective. Schell's Hamlet, like Olivier's, grabs a torch, but he does not thrust it into Claudius's face.[3] He makes a threatening gesture with it first towards Claudius, stopping him for a bare moment, and then towards Gertrude. Ophelia, upset, leaves last. Although it seldom provides a very wide view, the camera focuses on those we wish to see at any time. This makes it unobtrusive.

Wirth uses the setting for the prayer scene well. The camera shoots Hamlet's approach to Claudius through a series of the burnished steel columns. Framed by steel so that he is seen as through a faraway aperture, further distanced by a diagonal steel slash (a ramp) across the space between the two, Claudius from Hamlet's point of view appears isolated yet protected. Then in a reverse shot, we see both men from in front of Claudius. Claudius's head is bent down so his face is not visible, his hands clasping a large cross on the altar in front of his head; behind him, framed by columns, the coiled-spring figure of Hamlet stands upstage. Then a closeup shows Hamlet while in voiceover he thinks of the time he *will* kill Claudius.

Props establish the conventional setting for the queen's closet, with bed, chair, and curtains, behind which Polonius hides. When Hamlet says "as kill a King," awareness, prepared by the suspicion she had felt during the play, after a moment of wide-eyed surprise, comes to Gertrude forcibly. She kneels at a cross as Hamlet responds to Polonius's death. As to the ghost, because we see nothing, we are left in doubt about its reality. Though the bed is there, this is no Freudian interpretation.

The Schell *Hamlet*. Gertrude realizes that Claudius killed her husband. *(Still courtesy Edward Dmytryk and Sam Weiler.)*

Gertrude at the beginning is tender and soft-spoken with her son ("Have you forgot me?") until he frightens her. Later they do not embrace but merely touch each other as a gesture of mutual understanding. As it turns out, Hamlet does persuade Gertrude; for this interpretation, the director could have gone to Olivier or perhaps back to Q1, which of course makes Gertrude's defection from Claudius explicit by giving her a conversation with Horatio in which she states her intention to side with Hamlet.

The next scene (4.3) shows Claudius in one of his few moments within a political structure. It begins with a closeup of three councillors, sober men who nod and agree with Claudius's "How dangerous is it that this man goes loose . . ." (4.3.2). When Rosencrantz and Guildenstern together with two guards bring Hamlet in, Claudius emphasizes his power by sitting on the throne, then by leaning over Hamlet, who is one step below him.

With the Fortinbras scene (4.4) eliminated, the cemetery scene is the only outdoor setting. A surreal space marked by a forest of metallic or stone crosses, it is large enough to show the conveyance of the body with a sizeable procession. Yet, of course, through closeups the space is also intimate enough to focus on Hamlet contemplating the skull, first in profile, then in three-quarter view with the skull towards the audience. Using the Olivier shift, the director has Claudius connive with Laertes after the confrontation with Hamlet at the grave.

The last scene, the duel (as in so many stage performances, 5.2 is divided into two scenes) begins with a wide image, a view of the court in the throne room bowing for what looks a very formal occasion. A closeup shows us Claudius dropping a pill into the cup along with the pearl (most productions settle for the pearl as the poison) and Gertrude's reaction. Wirth seems to have wanted to use Olivier's interpretation of Gertrude's behavior in this last scene (Wilds, 134) and of course the closeups can make that behavior clear to the audience. But in this case, Rotha's acting does not succeed in making it explicit: in other words, closeups alone cannot do the work; acting is needed as well. Marvin Rosenberg agrees that her behavior is ambiguous and that there is only a hint she knows the drink is poisoned (1979, 51–53). We can infer her feelings only from the fact that she never seems close to Claudius again (with 4.1 and the first half of 4.5 omitted, their interchanges are minimal in any case) and that she smiles as she says "the drinke, the drinke," perhaps to show her satisfaction with her act.

The camera indicates the others' feelings plainly, however. Laertes immediately regrets the hit he gives Hamlet (again, as in the Olivier film), while Claudius looks enigmatic when Laertes is hit in turn. The set also works to express the denouement: Claudius runs behind the throne to escape from Hamlet, but after Horatio stops him on the ramp,

The Schell *Hamlet*. Yorick. *(Still courtesy Edward Dmytryk and Sam Weiler.)*

Claudius turns around and walks confidently and sneeringly towards Hamlet—he means to outface him. (Patrick Stewart's Claudius in the BBC-TV version also attempts to outface Hamlet, but smilingly.) A reverse shot reveals Hamlet with his eyes shut as he almost accidently manages to hit Claudius slightly. Just as Hamlet does not see the hit itself, neither do we. When Hamlet opens his eyes, we see the result of the hit. Disdainfully, then, Claudius takes the cup from Hamlet and drinks voluntarily. A 1970 Claudius at Stratford-upon-Avon also willfully drinks the poison Hamlet gives him (Babula, number 156). Hamlet's pusillanimity is odd, because this version had never given the idea that Hamlet is a weakling, yet Claudius treats him without respect and Hamlet virtually caves in: this is not the clash of mighty opposites.

Like John Neville's, Schell's Hamlet is very satisfactory in looks, though in a different way. Neville has an aristocratic, lean, dark face. Intelligent, cynical rather than downcast, deeply observant and watchful, Schell is intense, handsome—with sharp nose, wide mouth, cleft chin, and quick smile. Gertrude is different from the matronly type we often see, but she too fits her part admirably. Middle-aged, slim and attractive, with a deep dimple when she smiles, she is sensuous, knowing. She controls Claudius with her eyes and with subtle gestures leads him, especially in the first court scene. She accepts his passion with satisfaction but remains relatively cool herself. Claudius, on the other hand, has just that appearance we could expect from Hamlet's description of him: swollen and dissipated, with bags under eyes, scruffy beard, a little fringe of hair showing below the flat sailor's hat he wears at times.[4] I have already mentioned Ophelia's looks, which are also ideal for the interpretation of innocence, passivity, and weakness. These characters' relation to the setting is instructive: Claudius and Gertrude seem at home, Ophelia uneasy. Hamlet, on the other hand, simply rises above his environment.

The performance is so severely limited by the inadequacy of the dubbing into English from German that evaluation is almost impossible, but, given the creative use of a television studio setting and Schell's fascinating Hamlet, it could have been excellent. As it is, it is only interesting. Within a limited space, however, Wirth creates some unforgettable images, such as the "To be" recited partly as Hamlet peers between two steps, closeup, or the head-high crosses in the graveyard scene, or the receding arches through which Hamlet sees Claudius at prayer, or the colonnade of pillars by which Ophelia runs when Hamlet frightens her in her closet, or the two burnished metal thrones that stand empty in almost every scene, a reminder to us of what Hamlet has lost.

Notes

1. Sprague (134) mentions that Tree also had Ophelia exit last, but his Hamlet does kiss her hand before he turns away.

2. Wirth uses the order of Q1 (in that the fishmonger scene follows the nunnery scene, which precedes the arrival of the players) and of Olivier (in that the "To be" follows rather than precedes the nunnery scene).

3. Stage Hamlets also used the torch prop, e.g., Sarah Bernhardt and Sothern, according to Rooker, 21.

4. Maurice Charney, in his ground-breaking essay on "*Hamlet* Without Words," objects to using Hamlet's description of Claudius for the king's portrayal (38), but obviously the option is there for a director or reader to choose.

8

Hamlet at Elsinore with Christopher Plummer (1964)

Inevitably, the one TV version to use a location setting is shot at Kronborg castle at Elsinore in Denmark.[1] While studio shooting suits television's limitations of size and depth of field, the lure of Elsinore was irresistible to the BBC, even without electricity, which BBC installed at a cost of £2,500 (Carthew). Starring the Canadian actor Christopher Plummer, co-produced by Danmarks Radio—which suggested the project—and shown in the United States in 1964, it certainly rivals the electronovision production of that same year directed by John Gielgud, a film of the stage performance starring Richard Burton, and invites comparison with the Kozintsev film, also shot on location and released in 1964.

Stage productions have foundered at Elsinore, battling poor acoustics and rain, but a television production can overcome these impediments with electronics and patience. For this production, an article in *Newsweek* tells us, technicians learned to shoot sequences between the twenty-four-second intervals of an incessant foghorn. But the possible is not always the advantageous, for the architectural drama of Elsinore does not necessarily enhance the drama of *Hamlet*.

Interestingly enough, perhaps because of the small size of the British and Danish home screen in 1963, the shooting style remains like that of the studio, emphasizing closeups, usually ignoring the setting. And indeed, sometimes the setting is not suitable. The problem is that of the artist in "The Real Thing" by Henry James; certainly Kozintsev's Russian substitute, shot on location, is more like the Elsinore of one's imagination than is the real thing. Even a made-up castle in the studio can have a more profound effect on the viewer's senses than Elsinore's elegant reality, which is both less and more than one wants.

The film tries to badger the viewer into seeing what the setting lacks: a title says, "On a Promontory on the Sound Leading to the Baltic Sea Stands a Fortified Palace Symbolic of the Power of the King of Denmark." The word "promontory" notwithstanding, there is no high point at the coast of Elsinore, a flat and unprepossessing shore. The filmmakers have to use some sleight of hand with the camera to give the effect they are seeking. Very low-angle shots of the surf look as if the camera has been dug into the sand to get a crab's-eye view of the beach. Even from this angle, with a little softening through out-of-focusing, with a cooperative surf, and with rugged wave sounds coupled with danger music, with light glowing on the foam in general darkness, the shore looks inviting rather than foreboding. For the third scene of the Plummer version, the camera shows a small boat at quayside, Laertes and Ophelia at the shore, with the castle in the background. This daylight shot reveals all too plainly how level the sea coast is. If the setting had been, like Kozintsev's, more dramatic in itself, the director would not have had to work so hard to create drama. Or, as in the Gielgud production, he could have used acting alone to suggest the danger and menace of Elsinore.

For the high promontory where Marcellus, Bernardo, and Horatio react to the ghost, a beach wall perhaps only inches high must do, but again, the extreme low angle of the shots, tilted upwards from ground level, tries to give an effect of height and distance to what is actually flat and close. These shots are coupled with overhead shots, as from the ghost's perspective, so that we never get an ordinary, straight-on shot of the three men, whom we see only one at a time. The film avoids giving a sense of the whole. Wind and surf sounds do not add as much as they might have if the setting had been more compelling. Perhaps because the setting is not satisfactory, the first scene is cut to a mere three lines, taking less than a minute of film time. We see the ghost neither here nor in the later scenes.

The director apparently meant to substitute the subsequent visual effect for the dialogue of scene one. A bridge between exterior and interior added to Shakespeare's script and entitled "Kronborg Castle" introduces a view of the castle. With the continued threatening music of both titles and first scene, a high-angle tilt shot through a row of columns shows a line of soldiers, marching across the courtyard below. A cut to the roof reveals another line of soldiers, partisans in their hands, standing guard. Seeing them, one wonders why the first scene did not take place on the roof, which might have felt dangerous. Perhaps it was thought that the proximity to the sea, with its wind-whipped sea-grass, gave the first scene more atmosphere. A cut to the inside and we see in a boot-level shot the soldiers marching through—as we finally see with a

low-angle shot—a low-ceilinged space with brass chandeliers. These soldiers should project the sense of danger that we ordinarily absorb from
the guards' talk in the first scene, from Francisco's uneasiness, and the
others' questions about Fortinbras. But this serene space—that is, the
little of it the camera allows a viewer to take in—holds no fear. The
white-washed walls, the large, multipaned windows flooding the room
with sunlight, the bare, polished floors—all these have the opposite
effect, one unlike that of the castle filled with ubiquitous soldiers in
Kozintsev's version. Maybe the difference is, again, that these Danish
soldiers are "the real thing," while the Russian soldiers are actors.[2]

Philip Saville has no additional techniques for the ghost vigil. For the
scene with the ghost, we see Hamlet in closeup, the sea, out of focus,
behind him, and we hear the ghost's hoarse whisper and then more
normal-sounding voice for the revelation. The shot remains in effect
virtually throughout the whole scene, varying only in distance from the
camera, from medium to extreme closeup—movement being provided
by the wind blowing Hamlet's cape, the waves behind him, and his
features. The use of the shot is unmistakable: the sea represents the
turmoil in Hamlet's heart—a facile image. But unlike Kozintsev's sea
reflecting Hamlet's mood, here there is no variation; that same shallow
surge persists throughout. The sea as symbol is redundant because
Plummer's face expresses better the many layers of emotion that Hamlet
feels.

The only other outdoor scenes are those with Fortinbras and his army,
well done in dim light with lots of trees and horses, and the graveyard
scene. Some shots in the former remind one of shots in Olivier's *Henry V,*
overhead shots through trees to riders below. One of these riders is
Hamlet, who dismounts to talk to the captain and then speaks his
soliloquy in closeup partly to the horse who shares the frame with him.
(Olivier had to cut out his soliloquy with a horse, he says, because the
horse stole the scene.) Though this additional touch of reality in
Plummer's scene is distracting, he pulls it off by the sheer intelligence
and sensitivity of his reading. Both this scene and the graveyard scene
benefit from the simple outdoor setting, the first large enough to accommodate an army, the second large enough to allow for a procession far
enough away from Hamlet and Horatio to realistically give them time to
hide. The sky is as featureless as a cyclorama, the setting unobtrusive
enough to give full play to Hamlet's newly achieved serenity.

Interior space has its own problems, with settings that may clash with
the play's locus. Evidently Saville felt that keenly, for he kept his camera
tightly focused on the actors. Only a few times does the interior setting
justify the location shooting—when Saville has the courage to pull away
from his actors and let the setting play some part. After Horatio and
Marcellus rejoin Hamlet, he runs into the castle, and they follow. Here

there is a truly beautiful shot, reminiscent of Josef von Sternberg's work with light and shadow. A huge arched gateway, one barred door open against the wall, the other filling half the doorframe, makes a pattern in bars of light in the gloom. The visual image may have little to do with the three men, who are dwarfed by the setting, but it is just this sort of grandeur that can give Elsinore as a location setting its potency. There is one other image in the film showing Hamlet in extreme long shot in a startling setting, heavy with light and darkness—in the midst of the "To be" soliloquy. If only Saville had had the courage to use more of these, the TV production might have been very special indeed. But to allow Hamlet's face to remain for long the size of a pea is too daring a departure from ordinary TV practice for most directors. These settings are successful because they do not have to bear the burden of at-mosphere that the ghost scenes require; rather, the atmosphere is gra-tuitous, surprising, and correct. They are unexpected flashes of visual pleasure.

All the interiors are indeed pleasing but Saville, through framing, allows us to see little of them. The squarish interior space where the king holds his council, like the hallway, is serene and empty except for a few rows of chairs, the two thrones facing the rows at some distance, a magnificent Gobelin tapestry before which Hamlet will first appear, and a table for Polonius and other councillors. Because of closeups we rarely get a sense of all the actors operating within a whole setting. That is one of the problems with the Gielgud production as well; though there are more long shots, we seldom see reactions as well as actions. A king, especially one as genial (if cold) as this Claudius (Robert Shaw), commu-nicates his power through his position in space. But the camera rarely affords us a view of him in his milieu; instead, it frames the others separately. The queen (June Tobin) sitting on her throne two feet or more from him appears tentative, uneasy—though young, attractive, and physically well-endowed. Business—glances exchanged, a pat by a courtier—tells us that Polonius (Alec Clunes) and his family are on the rise now with this king's ascension. Laertes (Dyson Lovell) sits in the first row of chairs facing the king, comes into the king's space to speak and does not hesitate to meet the king's eyes. In contrast, we see Hamlet, not part of the group seated, only seconds before the king notices him. Saville suggests separation: Hamlet avoids looking directly at the king or queen; Claudius crosses the space to stand behind Hamlet briefly; before exiting, Gertrude yearns towards Hamlet but Claudius keeps her from approaching.

When the others leave, Hamlet soliloquizes from his mother's chair, facing the chair once his father's, now Claudius's. Horatio, entering, indicates that Marcellus and Bernardo do not belong in this space by holding his hand up to stop them from following him too closely.

Though Hamlet is dark and Horatio (Michael Caine) is blond, the two standing in full-length facing profile seem an analogous pair in the cut of their garments—knickers and doublets—differentiating them from the soldiers with their gleaming armor. This Horatio also has a pleasing sardonic way about him that matches Hamlet's wit. Further indicating their relative equality, after Hamlet approaches and sits in one of the courtier's chairs, Horatio sits too, but Bernardo remains standing while Marcellus drops for a time into a crouch. Unfortunately, we rarely see both Hamlet and Horatio on frame at once to notice their similarities. As Horatio speaks, we see only Hamlet's face, his sad smile, hear his sad little laugh. All too briefly the camera gives us a four-shot for the guards' contribution. At the end, the camera is so close to Hamlet for his last lines that his nose is distorted.

This same space is the setting for the scene in which Rosencrantz and Guildenstern appear and Polonius discloses Ophelia's letter (2.2). Now the king is the administrator, pushing papers about. Ophelia enters this room with Polonius—obviously both are expected. Ophelia looks worried as she listens to her father and as she says a few words from 2.1 about refusing to see Hamlet. She does not belong in this space—the queen ignores her and the king, after a calculating look, questions her sternly—and Polonius eases her out before he speaks to both king and queen about spying on Hamlet. Indeed she does not seem to belong to any space. Because 2.1 is cut and no visualization is added to replace it, we never see Ophelia in a room of her own. In the undifferentiated space of a bare stage one would never note this absence.

The fishmonger scene follows with a cut to the bright hall we had seen before the first court scene—or one much like it. Now it is empty, except for Hamlet, holding a large book, dressed as Ophelia describes in 2.1, in lines that are cut in this production. This, the second attempt to substitute visuals for Shakespeare's words, is more successful than the first attempt, the soldiers that stand for the dialogue of the first scene. Still, one must question whether we are meant to see Hamlet in this disheveled condition. Perhaps this is a too literal reading of those lines. Perhaps Shakespeare describes Hamlet thus while he is offstage precisely so he will not have to show him to the audience with his stockings fallen down to his ankles. To add to the picture, Hamlet's movements are spastic. Since we do not see him from a neutral point of view we cannot tell if this antic disposition is put on. That is, we do not see him putting it on. Instead, the camera first shows Hamlet from the point of view of Polonius, king, and queen, who peer at him from the doorway to the king's audience chamber, then Polonius shooing them away and closing the door behind them to board Hamlet alone. Hamlet sits in one of the embrasures, the bright light behind him. Polonius pretends not to notice him until he has almost passed him, and then they speak, Hamlet gently, patting the sill to indicate Polonius is to sit beside him. Hamlet never becomes as impatient with Polonius as the king was in the previous segment. Hamlet and Polonius each mimic the gestures of the other, with a quietly comic effect. Hamlet has not overhead Polonius plot with the king against him, does not seem to be aware that Polonius has told his daughter to deny him access to her.

As Polonius scurries off, frightened by Hamlet's contortions when he says "except my life," Hamlet remains in the same space for "To be, or not to be," which here begins with a third "except my life," said to himself. Though the space is the same, the ambience has changed because the camera makes a disjuncture between the two segments by first skimming above the floor as we hear Polonius's footsteps receding, then gliding past the large multipaned windows looking across the courtyard to the other side of the castle, and finally zooming into a low-angle extreme close shot on a three-quarter profile of Christopher Plummer's ruggedly handsome face, the light from those windows glowing on his cheek. This sort of camera maneuver has to be frugally applied and must serve a purpose—as it does here—that justifies its intrusiveness.

Philip Saville has been criticized—unfairly, I think—for breaking up the words of the world's most famous soliloquy by placing it in three locations. But breaking up space is breaking up time: Saville gives us the sense of Hamlet brooding about the ideas he turns over and over in his mind in long, lonely sessions. Few Hamlets project the character's intel-

The Plummer *Hamlet*. "To be or not to be." *(Still courtesy Danmarks Radio.)*

lectuality as well as Plummer does in this sequence. No matter how close to the camera Hamlet is, his eyes never make contact with it. This is a Hamlet deep inside himself, not communicating to an audience. Except for the one beautiful extreme long shot of the medieval catacombs, a magnificent play of rough surfaced architecture, light, and shadow, Hamlet in this scene appears only in closeup or extreme closeup. Therefore, the settings and especially the changes in setting are unobtrusive yet quietly effective. Though the lobby is also where Hamlet first notices Rosencrantz and Guildenstern in the courtyard below, Saville, by moving about for "To be," does not—as do Olivier and several others—connect Hamlet to any particular space. Unlike Kozintsev's Hamlet, Saville's is not confined. There are other ramifications as well. For one thing, we are more aware of Hamlet always alone by this fragmentation of time and space: he does not appear with Horatio or Ophelia in all his roamings through the castle, never encounters Claudius or his mother. For another, because of the essential unity of the soliloquy, he gives the impression of deeply reasoning through a problem rather than delaying revenge. He turns ideas around in his mind. "To dye, [that is] to sleepe; No more [than that]." (This is Burton's interpretation of these lines also).

When Hamlet comes to "Thus Conscience does make Cowards of us all" (F1: 3.1.84), the camera shows a low-angle shot of Jesus and the two thieves at Golgotha, a wall sculpture in the sixteenth-century chapel. Appropriately, Hamlet looks at Jesus as he thinks of conscience, which he says with no self-disdain. In the reverse high-angle shot, we at last see Hamlet fully enough to notice that he no longer has the book—of course, because hours, days and perhaps weeks have gone by since Hamlet began thinking of "To be, or not to be," the same effect of timelessness that Kozintsev achieves through straight cuts alone.

As the last words end, the camera cuts to the wide doorway, open to the courtyard. Ophelia enters, walking past the camera, which turns to follow her, until she stops, caught in closeup, looking towards Hamlet, who is now above her in the lectern. When they begin to speak the camera shoots over his left shoulder down to her to include both of them, but as the scene proceeds, we see one or the other in closeup, mostly as each speaks, with few reaction shots. Joan Silber, in her doctoral dissertation, criticizes Saville for separating Ophelia and Hamlet in this scene, never putting them close together in the setting (195–97). But Saville needs this distance between them to keep Hamlet's focus on the thoughts of "To be, or not to be"; her presence does not much engage him. Played by Jo Maxwell Muller, eighteen, as a little girl, she does not make us believe that there has been anything serious between her and Hamlet, and indeed, the omission of her closet scene suggests that any relationship ended with the ghost's revelation.

Hamlet's very lack of anger, his position above her in the pulpit, his soft, brotherly tone—he reminds one, in fact, of Laertes giving advice to his sister—suggest that his feelings for her are affectionate rather than passionate. Saville heeds the stage direction implicit in Claudius's line: "Love? His affections do not that way tend" (170). Even at her graveside, when he says "fortie thousand Brothers / Could not (with all there quantitie of Love) / Make up my summe," one senses that he speaks of a difference in intensity rather than in kind between his love and Laertes's for Ophelia.

The only flaw in the nunnery scene for me is the sudden inclusion of a large block of the setting so that we can see the shadows of Polonius and Claudius behind a magnificent window. Changes of frame size must seem inevitable, not merely motivated by the director's need to include more characters in the frame. A credible way to include them, given the style this film establishes, would have been to have Hamlet notice them, then look off frame toward the window, and then a shot showing where he is looking. Also annoying is the fact that their spying, sure to be noticed, seems impossibly inept. When he sees them and they scurry under cover, Hamlet becomes angry, but his anger is not directed towards Ophelia particularly. He descends to her, stands behind her as she sinks to a kneeling position, and continues to speak softly after a brief harangue. Since Ophelia had not heard about the plot and since the production cuts the opening lines of 3.1, we cannot implicate her in the spying. Nor does he. His tone, however, is sufficiently bitter and sarcastic to make her think him quite mad, since she has not noticed the spies. Business at the end tells us indeed that she is shocked and horrified to learn that her father and especially that Claudius have eavesdropped. Hamlet does give her head a rough push at the end to motivate her last lines, which unfortunately the young actress is not up to delivering. Her mad scene is much better, with its combination of sheer lunacy, sensuality, and slyness.

Stills of the chapel setting (as for example accompanying Carthew's review in the *New York Times* or in "The Timeless Tragedy" in *Life Magazine*) show much more of the architecture than the television frame affords. It is as if Saville is afraid that the magnificence of the setting could swamp the scene, and perhaps he is right. The truth is that the scene does not need the Kronborg chapel and that a scrap of setting reproduced in the studio would have served the purpose as well if not better. But in effect Saville creates just such a studio ambience by selecting very carefully the bit of setting he wants to show. He resists the temptation to make this "Hamlet at ELSINORE."

When Polonius and Claudius enter the scene, walls or pillars that border the frames they are in constrain them. There is little or nothing chapellike in their shots. Far from being Claudius's sycophant, Polonius here is utterly shattered by the pain he has seen his child undergo and virtually dismisses Claudius's concern over Hamlet, walking off on the line "My Lord, do as you please," omitting the further spying plan and those treacherous words: "Or confine him where / Your wisedome best shall thinke." Later, at the play within a play, he wants to berate Hamlet for his bawdy teasing of Ophelia but Claudius restrains him. A Polonius with little comic buffoonery, he is a loving father to both children. With Polonius gone, Claudius's last line in the nunnery scene is said to himself, the camera shooting close up: "Madnesse in great Ones, must not unwatch'd go."

Claudius's prayer scene is also set in the chapel. This time the frame is large enough to show Hamlet looking down at Claudius from above, not close enough to get to him easily. Because of the distance, we do not necessarily see this as a real opportunity. In closeup, we see the joy Hamlet feels when he says he can now kill Claudius. The joy holds as he says "and so he goes to Heaven, / And so am I reveng'd. . . ." Then, as if he has suddenly realized the import of what he has just said, his tone changes for the next lines:

> that would be scann'd,
> A Villaine killes my Father, and for that
> I his soule Sonne, do this same Villaine send
> To heaven.
>
> (3.3.76–79)

Earlier, in a nineteenth-century manner, as he stood before a fireplace in the great banquet hall, Hamlet had expressed his ability to drink hot blood. The histrionic tone must affect the viewer's perception of the words: Are they sincere? Is he trying to convince himself of what he does not feel? Is he trying on an actor's mask as he did for "bloody, bawdy villaine" (Q2) in the "rogue" soliloquy? His self-persuasion in the prayer scene rings true, perhaps because in contrast to the "hot blood" soliloquy it is spontaneous and reflective. In the earlier instance words and feelings are at variance.

As Claudius rises and walks out, we become aware, perhaps for the first time, of his robe, open to reveal a bare chest, the nakedness reminding us of his sensuality (the device used in the Kozintsev film). Surprisingly then, Gertrude's closet has the same austere ascetic beauty as the other rooms. As usual, no establishing shot gives us a sense of the whole room; instead, the camera reveals pieces of it as they are needed. The bed is the dominant feature, and Hamlet of course flings his mother on it. There he almost wins her over with his comparison of the two kings, her locket and his, but as soon as he speaks of avoiding her husband, he loses her. The production presents the next scene as a continuation, as it should be, of the closet scene (3.4), and not as a new scene. Claudius here shows no trace of the drunkenness that had disarmed him in the play scene. He exits to find Rosencrantz and Guildenstern outside the room and sends them off, then re-enters to give and receive a fervent embrace. After Ophelia's exit from the first mad scene, the camera cuts to Gertrude's room where king and queen lie in the bed, his chest bare, she in the kind of garment that in the sixties substituted for nudity, as he engages in pillow talk—lines from 4.5: "Oh Gertrude, Gertrude, / When sorrowes comes, they come not single spies, / But in Battaliaes," etc. Ophelia's second mad scene is cut, as is Laertes's entrance, to allow for this spatial transposition, an unsubtle pointing of the fact that Gertrude remains attached to her husband. Given the severity of the cuts, Saville's interpretation of Gertrude had to be simple.

The camera had afforded glimpses of the courtyard exterior with its cobbled stones and wide expanses through many windows. From the open door leading from the courtyard Ophelia had entered the chapel. And the courtyard serves for the meeting between Rosencrantz and Guildenstern and for the entrance of the players, transposed to follow the nunnery scene. Less overpoweringly than the chapel, the courtyard can be shot in long shot to frame more than one character at a time. But the apparent inclusiveness of long shots is limited, for the camera shows Hamlet and the players in shots that exclude Rosencrantz and Guildenstern. Further, closeups still predominate—though relieved by a few group shots—more like the shooting style for the Gielgud stage version than in other parts of the film. The freer openness of the frame corresponds with Hamlet's renewed buoyancy upon seeing the players, but because so many rooms were sunlit, the brightly lit courtyard is not so much a contrast from the other settings as it is in Kozintsev's film.

Just as Saville kept space between Hamlet and Ophelia, so does he between Hamlet and Rosencrantz and Guildenstern; in contrast, Hamlet shares space with Horatio and the First Player. At first, Hamlet questions his former schoolfriends from a window above them. Though he had seemed happy to see them, the space tells more fully his true feelings. When he does descend to the courtyard he remains hugging the wall as they stand some feet away. He remains distant as he begins his explanation, full of self-irony and exaggerated self-pity. The camera shows no reaction shot of them but remains focused on Hamlet, who, with the words "foule and pestilent congregation of vapours," becomes serious and introspective, forgetting them until their chuckles bring him back to the present. He does not come close to them until his lines about welcome, and then his sardonic tone negates the effect of the physical closeness. After Polonius's entrance, Hamlet and his friends go into a well-practiced routine of bouncy, quick, high-stepping marches forwards and backwards, ending with Hamlet on their shoulders—all while Polonius tries to tell them about the players. The routine suggests school days together.

In contrast to the distance between Hamlet and Rosencrantz and Guildenstern, the director underscores the affinity of Claudius for them by showing them, just before the prayer scene (3.3), at his council table, sitting with the king in an intimate moment of self-revelation. They say virtually nothing, but the proximity says it all. We have no doubt that they know the king's plans. Thus, when Hamlet before his departure for England (4.3) looks at Guildenstern, the round-faced one, as he says "I see a Cherube that see's him" (Claudius or Claudius's plans, that is), we assent immediately to Hamlet's implicit accusation. Therefore, we accept without question Hamlet's declaration (5.2) that they are not near his conscience because they did make love to their employment.

The film departs from its usual manner for the scene between Claudius and Laertes, one of the more successful interiors in the production, but by its nature one not useful for other scenes. A high angle shot puts the camera in the position of judge. This is the only sequence shot entirely in long shot, giving it a disorienting, distancing effect. For once we see the whole room, cell-like, very narrow, though again white-walled and sunlit. Because the production cuts Laertes's entrance before Ophelia's second mad scene, Laertes never attempts to usurp the throne and kill Claudius but rather is decidedly in Claudius's control. As the triple plot unfolds Saville shoots from an angle that shows three receding doorways, a not-too-obvious visual metaphor.

Here and elsewhere the director allows actions that contradict the text he has kept. At the end of the scene, Claudius urges Gertrude to join him in following Laertes and then they go off in a direction different from Laertes's. Earlier, Polonius asks Hamlet if he'll walk out of the air. What on earth does this mean except that he and Hamlet have stepped outside? On Shakespeare's undifferentiated stage, it is easy to accept—and then forget—the setting indicated by the immediate dialogue. Where an actual setting is used, it should match these words, as in the BBC production with Derek Jacobi. At the very least, windows should be open. The most outrageous discrepancy is Gertrude's line "the Lady protests to much me thinkes" (3.2.240) when Saville presents only the dumb show and the Player Queen does not protest at all, even by mime. With so much cut, one wonders why Saville did not cut such lines.

The space for the scene of the play-within-a-play moves from the dim corridor with gothic arches where Hamlet speaks to Horatio (but the lines on why Hamlet admires Horatio are cut) to the interior banquet room where the play is to take place. The advice to the players is cut, an opportunity some directors take to show Horatio in quiet attendance with Hamlet, implying a further relationship between the lines (Boston Shakespeare Company, Olivier). This Hamlet is much more alone. The main visual point Saville makes is that Hamlet gets on stage and directs the action of the mimes from there. We see the play's action in long shot, from the point of view of Claudius and Gertrude, on a dais some distance away from the stage. From reaction shots, we learn that Gertrude knows nothing about the murder, that she cares deeply about Claudius's well-being, that Horatio believes Hamlet has demonstrated Claudius's guilt. When Claudius's drunkenness puts him off his guard sufficiently to reveal something of his guilt and he exits calling for light, Saville shoots a dark adjoining hallway punctuated by flames of torches. Inside, Hamlet exultantly gnaws on a leftover bone from the banquet table.

In this same space, the duel ends the drama, a space separate from that of the Osric scene, for which Hamlet is still garbed in his rough traveling costume. Because of the large number of courtiers and guards in the final scene, the large room can be shot from a distance without usurping the attention we must pay to the principals. Closeups, of course, reveal that Gertrude offers Hamlet the poisoned wine once she has drunk, that Laertes crosses himself as he takes the fatal rapier, that he gives Hamlet a foul blow after impatient urgings from Claudius, that the soldiers restrain Claudius after Laertes's revelation. Yet the setting allows enough space around the closeups for Laertes to make his first admission to Osric alone and for the supernumeraries to disappear while Horatio holds the dying Hamlet, the frame widening out for Fortinbras's stately entry. The film ends with the effect of his command— repeated boomings of the Elsinore cannons sound as credits appear on the screen—not with an image of Hamlet carried to the stage.

Most often Philip Saville avoids what he evidently saw as the pitfalls of the setting. But with so much restraint necessary to allow the play to play itself, is the slender margin of gain from a few apt settings—the outdoor setting for "How all occasions . . . ," the cell for Laertes's and Claudius's plot, the graveyard scene—worth the contortions necessary to reveal only enough of the other settings to convey pictures that whole settings would obscure? The actors are all remarkably comfortable in the setting, but the director's uneasiness shows in excessive closeups and poorly motivated high-angle shots. Long ago I told a friend who wanted to disguise the awkwardness of a long, narrow kitchen to pull out all the stops instead and paint stripes parallel to the long sides; rather than disguise the problem, embrace it, revel in it. He did not listen to me. Saville too, I think, should have reveled in the magnificence of Elsinore and had more faith that Shakespeare and these highly competent actors could have filled the volume. His model might have been Sven Gade's *Hamlet* offshoot (1920) with Asta Nielsen as Hamlet, where the architectural elements have full play. What Saville needed was a more judicious blending of all kinds of shots and more courage.

Notes

1. The BBC/Danmarks media production was not the first to use the setting at Kronborg castle, but it was the first to use the interiors as well as the exteriors. An advertisement in *The Moving Picture World* of 8 April 1911 (811) announces a production of *Hamlet* "Produced in the grounds of the original Castle at Cronenburg (Elsinore), Denmark" and claims that it "Surpasses any previous Shakespearean production in acting, natural scenery and ensemble." It also reassures the renter, "Although a classical subject, appeals forcibly to EVERY class of audience."

2. The producer, Peter Luke, was extremely proud it seems that his Danish soldiers *were* the real thing. "Actors are notoriously bad at playing soldiers," Garner quotes him as saying. On the contrary, his only soldierlike soldiers are Fortinbras (Donald Sutherland) and the Captain (Joby Blanshard), played by real actors.

9

Richardson's *Hamlet* with Nicol Williamson (1969)

Richardson's *Hamlet* confirms that setting and camera work are inextricably connected. The scene designer creates the set, but the camera determines what we see of it. The virtue of Richardson's television *Hamlet* is that it captures a vision creditable only on television: with attributes of all media overlapping, one longs at times for productions that exploit unique facets of the chosen medium. In the tightness of its shots, in its virtual exclusion of setting, this work is antithetical to the whole-set-encompassing settings of stage and to the wide-angle location shots familiar on film. Yet the production started life on stage, deriving its themes and interpretation from a theatrical conception of the play, and it was first released as a film. One remnant of its theatrical genesis is in the doubling of roles, with, for example, gravel-voiced Roger Livesey as both First Player and Gravedigger. The production's origin and subsequent development demonstrate again that, though directors have to rethink productions in media terms when they translate from stage to screen, the relationship between stage and moving images can be very close. Therefore, what can be noticed about the television film will enhance our understanding of other media as well.

For this television *Hamlet* one can imagine the director saying, "Yes, the frame is small; now what can we do about it?" His answer, the opposite of that of the production with John Neville (CBS, 1959), which attempted to make the setting appear as spacious as possible, was to shoot the play at the cavernous Roundhouse Theatre, but never to draw back far enough to give the viewer a sense of the whole space. Thus this is not a filmed play, but a new production, in spite of the mostly identical cast and even the setting. One reviewer of the stage production comments, for example, on the vast distances characters had to cross simply to enter and exit (Lambert, 18). He also says that the soliloquies were "reduced to pettish little chats with the audience," which, he says, he cannot see as "anything but a degradation of both Hamlet and the art of acting" (19, 20). On the small television screen, in contrast, these chats with the audience seem appropriate and indeed inevitable.

The filmmaker finds inventive ways to make the frame inspire solutions to its own problem—the need to use tight shots. The solutions affect the enactment of explicit and implicit stage directions; many that call for whole body movements must now be suggested, if at all, by face alone. Still, he avoids the claustrophobic effect of the McKellen production (1971) or the isolation of images of the Wirth production (1960) by filling many closeups with people.

Richardson brings a rich, textured life to tight shots by crowding lavishly dressed supernumeraries into all the court scenes. Often, six to nine people in mid-closeup fill a frame, with feathers, velvets, plumes, and bare shoulders capturing one's attention as courtiers gaze intently at the principals. Richardson packs frames with heads, sometimes on two levels vertically, sometimes in depth. In this, the laughing *Hamlet,* the faces crowding into the frame frequently show their hilarity. Thus, for the first view of Claudius, the stage direction in Hamlet's lines about Claudius determines his characterization:

The Williamson *Hamlet.* The frame is crowded with people. *(Still courtesy Columbia Pictures.)*

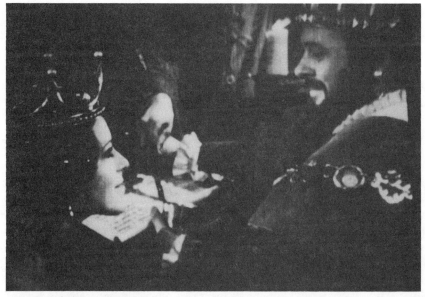

The Williamson *Hamlet*. A hand enters the frame with a document. *(Still courtesy Columbia Pictures.)*

> Oh Villaine, Villaine, smiling damned Villaine!
> My Tables, my Tables; meet it is I set it downe,
> That one may smile, and smile and be a Villaine. . . .
>   (F1: 1.5.107–9)

Obviously, productions can ignore this stage direction, as, for example, Olivier's (1948) does. Though Kozinstev (1964) uses it, his Claudius's mouth turns up in a false smile. Richardson's Claudius, played by Anthony Hopkins, is a genuinely jovial man. In the midst of all the richness and high spirits of Richardson's Elsinore, Nicol Williamson's Hamlet seems somber indeed.

Pushing against the limits of the tight shots, Richardson uses exclusions to imply that the frame could reveal more than it shows. The camera is not afraid to lop off whole bodies. By making the frame a keyhole, as it were, the filmmaker suggests a larger world beyond, a world we are eavesdropping on. As Claudius holds the scroll for Norway, a hand reaches into the frame to apply the wax into which Claudius presses his seal. Using Claudius's later line "For your intent / In going backe to Schoole in Wittenberg" (1.2.112–13) as a delayed stage direction, Richardson has Hamlet's hand reach into the frame at this point (line 38) with another scroll, a suit for Gertrude, but we do not realize it is he until the frame at last includes him. We have to grasp the narrative point in retrospect: Oh, that was Hamlet's request to leave for Wittenberg.

Often, when several characters are on frame, clever setting choices justify tight shots. Richardson's bedroom setting for the second court scene (2.2) is deservedly famous, comparable to the eating scene at the inn in his *Tom Jones.* Because the king and queen remain in bed, the frame need not widen but is filled by the plump poster bed, its two occupants surrounded by courtiers and ladies who wipe the hands of king and queen. The bed, covered with food, even sports two dogs. The sumptuousness of the *mise en scène* implies moral disorder (Litton), for their sensuality overcomes their scruples or worries. When Polonius says he knows the cause of Hamlet's madness, the king says, "Oh speake of that, that I do long to heare" (2.2.50) with a chuckle in his voice. Gertrude seems more concerned about the fruit she is biting into and sucking on than about Hamlet. She says "our o're-hasty Marriage" suggestively, leaning over Claudius for a kiss. When she says "It may be very like" (Q2), she is thinking of desire and of Claudius rather than of Hamlet. The king opens his mouth to receive the finger she puts on his lips. When this Hamlet speaks of honeying over the nasty sty, he speaks not out of neurosis but out of objective reality. In other words, Richardson uses Hamlet's lines in the closet scene as delayed stage directions.

Not surprisingly in this atmosphere the character of Ophelia (Mar-

The Williamson *Hamlet*. An intimate nunnery scene. (*Still courtesy Columbia Pictures.*)

The Williamson *Hamlet*. "What, frighted with false fire!" *(Still courtesy Columbia Pictures.)*

ianne Faithfull) seems drawn more from the stage direction implied by her Valentine's Day song than from that suggested by her brother's and father's watchfulness for her virtue. She is most innocent, in fact, when she is mad. Before that, she kisses her brother passionately, as passionately as she will later kiss Hamlet when she lies in a hammock for the nunnery scene, her breasts all but bare, the camera peering in closeup at her decolletage.[1]

Within these crowded closeups, setting is understated, virtually effaced. In the scene where Hamlet encounters Fortinbras's army (4.4), for example, six soldiers and a horse fill the frame all in medium close shot as a substitute for the wide spaces that film would seem to call for.[2] In noncrowd scenes, atmospheric elements contribute interest and variety to tight shots. The single head often occupies the frame with candles, thrones, and other props. The director's ability to create atmosphere within tight shots appears when candlelight punctuates a black background for Hamlet's "rogue and peasant slave" soliloquy (2.2) or when Horatio watches Claudius carefully from behind a high-flaming torch (3.2) or when a bit of brocade supplies an appropriately lush texture during the closet scene (3.4).

"Talking heads" is the frequent pejorative leveled at television, and that would seem to be more true for Richardson than for most, but he varies his heads in a number of ways. Two profiles at the edges of the frame face each other with the gulf of the empty frame between them or with other characters in the distance between them. Claudius and Hamlet face each other with a glowing torch between them after the play-within-a-play. Sometimes two characters face the camera, one a bit behind the other. Or, in a more typical television shot, one person in one-quarter profile faces another in three-quarter profile. When three heads fill the frame, Richardson sometimes varies the blocking, with one character, most often Hamlet, moving around or between the other two.

Small changes make for drama in a static frame when one face fills the frame. Because parts of the soliloquies are often in extreme closeups, with no intrusion of setting, the film concentrates attention on the landscape of the visage: tears in Hamlet's eyes, his fist grinding into his forehead; eyes focused straight ahead into the camera or tilted up or down. Pulled into the tight frame during the soliloquies, we share Hamlet's pain, self-irony, and bitterness.

But more daringly perhaps—because counter to the intimacy of the delivery—Richardson also has Polonius in closeup deliver his asides directly to the camera. Here, the intimacy only heightens the sense of Polonius's obtuse officiousness. Claudius's prayer-scene soliloquy also arouses an emotion counter to the usual pity we feel for him that should be heightened by the close, direct-to-the-camera delivery. Shakespeare has Claudius consider repentance just after the play-within-a-play, when the possibility still exists. Richardson has moved it to follow Hamlet's

The Williamson *Hamlet.* The ghost appears in the closet scene. *(Still courtesy Columbia Pictures.)*

The Williamson *Hamlet*. Gertrude dies horribly. *(Still courtesy Columbia Pictures.)*

The Williamson *Hamlet*. Fist grinds into forehead. *(Still courtesy Columbia Pictures.)*

The Williamson *Hamlet.* **Hamlet's first soliloquy, directed to us.** *(Still courtesy Columbia Pictures.)*

leavetaking (4.3), so that it reeks with hypocrisy: Claudius's efforts to repent cannot evoke pity when he has just delivered Hamlet over to be murdered. Claudius's final couplet—"My words flye up, my thoughts remain below, / Words without thoughts, never to Heaven go" (3.3.97–98)—follows immediately after he says "All may be well" (line 72), because Hamlet's speech is cut. Hamlet's absence allows Richardson to focus exclusively on Claudius in closeup; he need not widen the frame or cut to another character. But Richardson's placement of the prayer scene—as well as the speed of the reversal—remove all suspense; Claudius's weak effort is doomed from the first word.

Similarly pushing against the intimacy usually engendered by tight shots, Richardson uses Hamlet's half-revelations to Rosencrantz and Guildenstern to expose their shallowness (2.2.294–309). Richardson plays this confessional scene very differently from many productions by using a tight three-shot. This would suggest intimacy were it not for Hamlet's sarcastic greeting to them, his mistaking of Rosencrantz for Guildenstern, and his parodic turning of his head swiftly from side to side as he speaks to them. "Look you," he says to them as he describes "this Majesticall Roofe." Reluctantly, they follow his gaze upwards. Through the close shot Richardson shows us how poorly the supposed chums follow Hamlet's thoughts.

Richardson employs a combination of aural and visual effects to add

The Williamson *Hamlet*. Hamlet's attitude to Rosencrantz and Guildenstern may be read on his face. *(Still courtesy Columbia Pictures.)*

variety to the tight shots of the ghost scenes. General darkness with soft glows lights the sides of faces in settings with brick walls and bricked, sewerlike tunnels, soft-focus lights at the far ends. Mist, water dripping enhance their sewer atmosphere. The tunnels easily symbolize death. A tolling bell, taped and then played backwards, and an increase in light represent the ghost, whom we never actually see. We respond to the others' reaction to seeing it. When it speaks, we hear Nicol Williamson's voice, somewhat echoic but much more clearly his than, say, Olivier's slowed-down voice for his ghost sounds like Olivier's.

With no prologue beyond titles on bare bricks, Richardson begins with a shot of Francisco, and because he prefers to minimize the crosscutting that tight shots force when characters are not very close together, for the first lines Francisco is alone on frame. The opening lines of the play call, of course, for two sentinels—one, Bernardo, challenging the other when he should, according to the other, have waited to be challenged. The implicit reason seems to be an attack of nerves, for Bernardo knows what he has seen these last two nights and what he expects to see again: that which "bestil'd [him] / Almost to Jelly with the Act of feare" (1.2. 204–5). Richardson heeds this description by Horatio, considering it a delayed stage direction. He actualizes the stage directions of the opening lines by showing first, in closeup of course, Francisco's face as he bends his head down to blow on coals in a grate. Hearing something, he lifts his head and says firmly, dangerously, "Stand ho" (The words come from Q2, line 14. Q1, line 1, has the parallel figure, unnamed, say, "Stand: who is that?") We have also heard the off-frame sound that Francisco responds to, a redundancy that contributes to verisimilitude. From off frame, then, we hear Bernardo's fearful voice, "Who's there?" (the opening line in Q2 and F1). The dark setting realistically conveys the inability to see that his line implies. In accord with the relative sturdiness of Francisco compared to Bernardo, Richardson cuts Bernardo's lines that urge Francisco off ("get thee to bed Francisco" and "Well, goodnight"), since this soldierly Francisco hurries himself off. Richardson presents a straightforwardly phlegmatic version of Francisco.

Once Horatio, Bernardo, and Marcellus stand close together in closeup, Bernardo begins speaking. To keep them in this tight shot, the film cuts "Sit downe a-while" and "Well, sit we downe." Bernardo indicates by a slight turn of his head and upcast eyes where "yond same Starre" glows in the sky. Horatio's eyes follow Bernardo's, but Marcellus's fix on a point off frame right, for his "Looke where it comes againe." The film cuts the words "the Bell then beating one," in favor of a persistent and continuous tolling accompanying the ghost.

Since Richardson does not show the figure of the ghost, we do not see him stalk off (50), but he does fade, as the stage direction in the line calls for at the end of the second visitation (157)—that is, the light on Horatio's face and the bell tones fade. We do not, of course, see the

The Williamson *Hamlet*. Horatio sees the ghost. (*Still courtesy Columbia Pictures.*)

expression on the ghost's face, the description of which the film cuts, both here:

Hor.   So frown'd he once, when in an angry parle
         He smot the sledded Pollax on the Ice.

                                                        (62–63)

And later:

Ham.   What, lookt he frowningly?
Hor.   A countenance more in sorrow then in anger.

                                                    (1.2.231–32)

Richardson's ghost remains mysterious not only in being unseen but also in being undescribed.

For the second appearance of the ghost, Horatio says, "Ile cross it, though it blast me," but since Richardson does not relinquish the tight closeup on Horatio's face, Horatio means neither "to make the sign of the cross upon or over," (*OED v.*2), nor "to meet or face in one's way; esp. to meet adversely; to encounter" (*OED v.*11, which cites *Ham.* 1.1.127), nor "to cross the path of (anyone); to meet him in his way, to come in the way of; often implying obstruction or thwarting; also to pass across his path in front of him" (*OED, v.*12), as in most performances. In Richardson's version, the only interpretation for the stage direction contained in the line is "to thwart, oppose, go counter to" (*OED v.* 14 [fig.]), which opposition Horatio effects, apparently, merely by speaking to it. This ghost "would [not] be spoke too," for the line indicating that it would be willing to be spoken to is cut (1.1.45).

As one would expect, this production omits those lines that would require large movements or quick cutting from one character to another. Richardson has Marcellus say hesitantly, "Shall I Strike at [it] with my Partizan?" while standing quite still between Bernardo and Horatio. No large movement disturbs the tight frame. Richardson leaves out the abrupt cries of the men:

Barn. "Tis heere!"
Hor.   "Tis heere!"
Mar.   "Tis gone."

Sprague says the lines are often cut in acting texts (131), but I have usually heard them on stage as well as on screen. If it were not for Richardson's aim always to keep that tight little frame, he could certainly have managed the effect.

Without widening the frame when Horatio says "But looke, the Morne in Russet mantle clad," the camera directs our gaze beyond him to a blur of blinding light at the end of a tunnel. On stage, we would not expect to see the dawn (perhaps a change in lighting would suggest it), while in film, the failure to show it would strain verisimilitude. This film, by focusing on Horatio in medium shot and on the film's equivalent of dawn at the same time, is verisimilar (within its own conventions) without violating the frame size or the minimalist setting.

Richardson does sometimes begin a scene with a long shot, showing full figures in the frame. At the beginning of the vigil for the ghost (1.4), for example, Hamlet and the others enter the frame in mid-conversation and as they move stealthily into the tunnel, Hamlet seems to be peering into the shadows, as Henry Irving did almost one hundred years before (Sprague, 137). Typically, in nineteenth-century stage productions, Hamlet starts when Horatio announces the ghost's appearance (1.4). Indeed, his exclamation implies the start: "Angels and Ministers of Grace defend us" (1.4.39). Since the start requires a full-length shot, Richardson cuts that announcement and moves the start to the flourish that marks Claudius's drinking, so that later, when Hamlet is aware of the ghost, the camera can maintain the usual closeup to catch his response of awe and yearning love. Richardson's reinterpretation of the conventional business is persuasive, for Hamlet was, after all, expecting to see the ghost of his father but is caught off guard by the braying of the kettle-drum and the trumpet.

As Hamlet begins to speak to his father, though no implicit stage direction requires it, he moves into a one-shot, kneeling. The others enter the frame only when they speak. In another larger shot and using a special effect, Richardson has Hamlet rapidly following the ghost down an endless tunnel until he refuses to go any farther. After Hamlet has followed it, when the ghost begins his recitation, Hamlet kneels again, as Hamlets traditionally do. If Nicol Williamson does obey tradition in sinking to his knees when the ghost addresses him (Sprague, 138,140), the closeup here betrays only a minimum sense of movement because he and the frame descend together.

Richardson, on the other hand, flouts tradition in favor of the closeup for the sword business. If Hamlet were to take out the sword to threaten Marcellus and Horatio (following the implicit stage direction in the line "By Heav'n, Ile make a Ghost of him that lets me"), if he were to hold it before him or trail it after him when following the ghost as so many Hamlets do (Sprague, 140–41), the frame would have to widen out to show it. Hamlet does not, in fact, take out the sword until the moment when he asks the men to swear by his sword. And then we hear the swish of the blade, seeing only the hilt as he holds it up. Richardson also eliminates all the ghost's movements in the "swear" sequence. What remains is the ghost's last "Sweare," coming not from the cellarage but from close by. Because the frame shows only Hamlet's face, we cannot tell if the others hear or not. We are left in some doubt about the reality of the ghost's presence here.

Further examples from other scenes might be added to demonstrate that Richardson reads inherent stage directions in such a way as not to open up the frame. For example, when Polonius says, "And you are staid for there: my blessing with you," Laertes does not kneel, as conventionally he does on stage; instead, Polonius grasps him by the shoulders and kisses his cheek. Thus the camera can remain fixed in the closeup two-shot. Richardson similarly avoids large movement in the duel scene by having Hamlet say "Treacherie, seeke it out" quietly to Horatio who stands in closeup next to him. The louder a speech, the more space the frame would seem to require. Thus many lines one might expect to be shouted are whispered in this production, including the "Oh Vengeance!" of the "rogue and peasant slave" soliloquy. Even the duel never widens out to more than a medium shot; the intense movements so close up, with candles between the camera and the men, make this an exciting interchange, with every nuance of discovery subtly conveyed.

Certainly, Richardson knows what he is doing and he does it very well. As always, however, the actor who plays Hamlet determines the success of the production. The closeups give full play to Nicol Williamson's many moods, but finally, I think, his voice makes him the interesting Hamlet he is, as much for its nasalities, parodic whines, and mimicry of his enemies as for its expression of many emotions. Not everyone will love his performance, but the superb handling of the medium allows us to receive it unobstructed.[3] Much of Richardson's interpretation can be described as actualizations of stage directions: the king's and queen's sensuality, Ophelia's long-lost innocence, Polonius's officiousness. But Hamlet's character is so complex that no one line can define him; or, to put it another way, so many lines provide possible stage directions for his characterization that no one actor could encompass them all. Through activating stage directions in lines surrounding the character of Hamlet, Richardson creates the ambience within which the character of Hamlet unfolds.

Notes

1. This business was not, evidently, new. George Bernard Shaw, in a letter dated 22 February 1925 to John Barrymore about his *Hamlet* in England, criticizes the production for presenting brother and sister as lovers (Shaw 1961, 97).

2. See, for example, a preproduction script of Olivier's *Hamlet*, which calls for a vast army (Kliman, "Palimpsest").

3. For a very good analysis of Williamson's acting, see Mills, 267–80.

10

Richard Chamberlain for Hallmark (1970)

Like the John Neville Old Vic production, the Hallmark Hall of Fame version with Richard Chamberlain, directed by Peter Wood (1970), shows that expert camera work (Bill Brown) and flexible and attractive set design (Peter Roden) do not by themselves guarantee a successful *Hamlet*. Seeing this version both with and without the sound (sound tape in black and white and silent tape in color), noticing its many virtues that seemed especially prominent with the sound track absent, I became convinced that the difference between a magnificent television *Hamlet* and a humdrum one hinges on the actor's voice. Neither Chamberlain's voice nor his handsome face mirrors the multifaceted and fascinating Hamlet of one's mind, but with the voice absent (or rather perhaps with voice supplied by one's imagination), one could accept the actor's face as a reasonable facsimile. Since this version was also recorded, one can also listen to the voice alone to try to pin down its qualities: lack of variety, no hint of any but surface character. Visual attractiveness is not enough.

The production's main setting is a large room with a central stair at one end leading to a landing, breaking into right and left stairs up to a third gallery level. The camera focuses on the stairs alone or moves freely through the room, which at the end opposite the stairs has a display of weapons, and, variously placed, a fireplace, a doorway leading to the chapel and to the courtyard, and a stage area, all brought into view as occasion demands. The stair area offers variety within a reasonably small space; yet because the camera reveals its context at the start—that is, three of the room's four walls in a high-angle shot—it never seems confined or claustrophobic. For the first court scene, the king and queen proceed with suitable pomp across this large room and up the central stair, then separate at the landing to re-meet at the gallery level where

Claudius reads the proclamation. Gertrude's white gown, her veil, the priest and boys' choir leading the procession, all suggest that the marriage ceremony has just been concluded.

A closeup on Claudius's face supports the effect of his silky rhetoric: no sadness for his brother's death mars the happiness of this occasion for him. The set makes it easy for Claudius, descending again from the gallery to the landing, to talk privately to Polonius about Fortinbras—this is a king of secret corners—and then to stand above Laertes as the young man petitions the king from the foot of the stairs. Closeups mark every emotional shift. The stair set allows one character to be seen slightly below another in high-angle shots or above another in low-angle shots: thus, behind Hamlet at different moments, Laertes responds to Hamlet's pain; Polonius expresses concern at Hamlet's angry rejection of Claudius; Gertrude signals dismay. The stair set also allows characters to make decided movements without going far—Hamlet's abrupt ascent to leave after his first speech and his descent to avoid Claudius after the request that he "go not to Wittenberg." The stairs also provide a good background for the fishmonger scene and for Rosencrantz and Guildenstern's arrival; for Hamlet's hide-and-go-seek games of act 4; for Claudius's confrontation with Hamlet before sending him to England; of course for the *The Murder of Gonzago,* which takes place next to the stairs; and for the duel, when the focus widens to include the whole room.

In this varied room the camera can do exactly what one is led to want it to do; no unobtrusive technique is omitted: dolly shots move in and around characters at the correct angle, a zoom shot gives a closeup of Hamlet's reaction to Claudius and in an extreme long shot shows us the court's very different reaction. High-angle or low-angle point-of-view shots allow the viewer to identify with the characters, with reverse shots showing action and reaction: characters listening, characters talking. The camera work cannot be faulted, and clearly this free camera movement depends in part on the size and dimensions of the set.

Of three other notable indoor sets, two are related to the stair set by suggested proximity. One is the library, a room off the third-level gallery, something we discover when Hamlet exits from it and the matchcut shows him entering the gallery. In the library take place the letter scene (2.2), "To be" and the nunnery scene (3.1), both mad scenes (4.5), and, with Claudius alone, the segment when Claudius learns that Hamlet will return (4.7.47–53). Warmed by wooden bookcases, richly bound books, and a magnificent globe, unobtrusively decorated with a Madonna and child where Ophelia prays, the library seems the ideal place for Hamlet to meditate on the question "To be, or not to be"—that is, once one thinks of it as a library and not as Claudius's study.

When Hamlet enters for "To be," he does not see Ophelia because she is in a recess. The advantage of this blocking, as John Styan says, is that "the presence of her devout innocence, even though she is Polonius's decoy, adds a dimension of meaningful criticism of Hamlet's thoughts of sacrilegious suicide: she is the visible reminder of simplicity as he indulges in the complexity of his despair" (1967,106). More difficult to convey but effected through camera work and acting—Ophelia kneels praying all the while Hamlet meditates aloud (not voiceover); yet she does not hear Hamlet. The camera insists on this by repeatedly reminding us of her oblivious presence, catching her, unmoving, in the background of several shots; she cannot be too preoccupied to hear. Camera work here is interpretative, for if *she* does not hear, no one would imagine that Claudius and Polonius, hidden behind a movable panel, peering out through spy holes, could hear. Stoll points out that "when eavesdroppers are at hand for the purpose, soliloquies on the Elizabethan stage are overheard" (34). But if someone even closer cannot hear, then the usual convention would be overturned. Claudius must base his judgment of Hamlet's sanity on his behavior to Ophelia, visible from spy holes.

When he does notice her, Hamlet is uninterested in her at first—he almost leaves without speaking to her. When he does speak, his first words to her are sarcastic. Rough from the moment she returns his gifts, his actions escalate to fury when he notices the spying eyes through peep holes in the bookcase and when he hears her obvious lie. The camera tells us he has seen the eyes because, immediately after he looks towards the bookcase, a closeup shows us the eyes—the cinematic convention is that this closeup conveys what Hamlet sees. Claudius seems to be correct in judging that "Love? His affections do not that way tend" because this production shows very little interaction between Hamlet and Ophelia, eliminating even her report of his visit to her closet, so that his behavior at her graveside is totally unprepared for and unexpected.

The chapel is less obviously linked to the stair set, but a piece of the two sets appears to be the same, suggesting contiguity. A medieval room, with a heavy wooden gothic door, stone arched ceiling, wrought-iron candelabras, and a retable before a painted statue of Madonna and child, the chapel, though anachronistic in this production that costumes the characters in eighteenth-century garb, can be accepted because the courtyard scene reveals a gothic castle. Further, even the library, an updated setting with its French doors, eighteenth-century desks and fittings, has the medieval element of religious statuary. The chapel's long walls are slatted. Thus Hamlet easily can walk by to see the king at prayer, but at the same time the slats are a barrier between them, much as the wrought-iron gate is a barrier between Hamlet and Claudius in the earlier Hallmark production. There seems to be less opportunity for Hamlet to kill Claudius than closer proximity would suggest. Many Hamlets come within inches of Claudius. Again, set design affects inter-

The Chamberlain *Hamlet*. Hamlet determines not to kill Claudius at prayer. *(Still courtesy Chamberlain-LeMaire Ltd.)*

pretation. Ironically, it is in the chapel where Claudius could not achieve repentance through cleansing prayer that the king seeks Laertes, who is praying in his turn, to compound the plot against Hamlet. Gertrude—for once in a somber dress—comes through the gothic door to tell of Ophelia's death. After Laertes's last words the camera cuts away to the cemetery set, with no last speech by Claudius.

Linked through its medieval style to the chapel set, Gertrude's closet has a gothic door, stone walls, stone steps where the ghost appears, and pale draperies that will show Polonius's blood seeping down along Hamlet's sword. The room has, however, two nonmedieval mirrors: one at Gertrude's dressing table and one opposite it on the wall next to her bed. They afford interesting images—of the back of Gertrude's head towards the camera, her blond hair flowing down her back, and her worried face in the glass, and another of an infinite series of Hamlets when the camera lines up the two opposite mirrors with Hamlet caught by both. They also imply Gertrude's sensuality. The mirror next to the bed is particularly suggestive in the light of the "nasty Stye" that Hamlet sneers about. The way the camera first captures the bed and mirror, however, makes it look unlike a bed. We see only a surface, straight on, that Gertrude sits on. Only later, when the ghost arrives, do we see the bed at a sufficiently long distance and from a high enough angle to make out its "bed-ness"; nor is it sensuously decked with soft coverlets or

The Chamberlain *Hamlet*. The ghost of Hamlet's father in Gertrude's closet. *(Still courtesy Chamberlain-LeMaire Ltd.)*

draped with labial hangings (as in Olivier) that would emphasize its role in Gertrude's life. It has only one decorously tailored pillow roll. The Freudian aspect, therefore, is faint or absent; choice of props thus plays its role in interpretation. The avoidance of Freudian overtones with the bed, but nevertheless the bed's physical presence, with its adjacent mirror, captures the ambivalence of Gertrude herself in this scene, who, dressed in all her white wedding-night finery, nevertheless speaks as a mother to her son.

The ghost's appearance against the stone is apt. An eighteenth-century room like the library would have been wrong, one feels. Though the image fades towards the bottom, the ghost (played by John Gielgud) is solid enough and, unlike most ghosts, wears "his habite, as he lived"— not the costume of act 1, which was a white, officer's Napoleonic uniform, but a white robe (Q1's "night gowne?").

The outdoor sequences are equally effective, though only one of them appears to be an actual location shot. Misty backgrounds give the studio shots a realistic look. The first sequence, the appearance of the ghost to Horatio and the soldiers, takes place on what looks like a roof of a New York City tenement, with slanted section, skylights, chimneys, and pipes—a rather strange place for the visitation of a ghost, though suitably dark with corners for unexpected appearances.

In the vigil scene (1.4), the ghost exits through a doorway and Hamlet follows. A cut shows Hamlet in the cemetery, looking for the ghost, who walks through the wrought-iron gate closing the arched opening of a vault. Holding up his sword as a cross in front of him (like John Barrymore, like Olivier), Hamlet refuses to follow the ghost into the vault: "speak; Ile go no further"(1.5.1). It turns and stands within the arch as it speaks to Hamlet. After hearing that his uncle is a murderer, Hamlet sinks to the ground, and the camera presents low-angle, closeup shots of the ghost (from Hamlet's point of view) and high angle closeups of Hamlet (from the ghost's point of view). Exiting, the ghost walks into the recesses of the vault. Why the ghost's revelation should have taken place at the cemetery rather than at a more removed part of the platform where the men watched is not clear. Of course, the gravedigger scene and the burial of Ophelia take place in this same setting, though the camera focuses on another part of it; the echoing of settings allows an audience to recognize places and thus intensifies both the reality and the symbolic meaning of the setting. Again, for the burial the set is dark but moonlit, as so often in nineteenth-century productions of the play.

When the cemetery appears in 5.1, not only is it recognizable; it also reminds one of the ghost at a time when Hamlet by word and action seems to have forgotten the ghost's commands. Ophelia's fate is connected to the ghost's by setting. The same logic—that is, the desire to use familiar settings and perhaps to suggest ironic comparisons—probably dictated the repeated use of the stair set, and the double use of the courtyard—for Laertes's farewell and for the players' arrival. Similarly, in other scenes, glimpses of the fireplace again and again give a feeling of familiarity that reinforces verisimilitude. The only setting that makes only one appearance, in fact, is Gertrude's closet, and it, at least in architectural style, resembles the chapel.

Associated with positive forces, the courtyard is awash with sunlight in both scenes. Ophelia's blond beauty (her hair and her empire-style white garments connect her to Gertrude) glows in that bright light of day. Innocent yet sensual, modest in manner yet alluring without trying to be, Ophelia is strong-willed in her refusal to accept Polonius's advice about Hamlet. She steadfastly refuses to look at her father, a signal of her disagreement. Yet, at the end, she says, "I shall obey my Lord," a line that could have been omitted in this version, for Polonius does not force it from her or does so only by walking away from her. Our last view is of her anguished face. We see no reconcilement of daughter and father, as in many productions, probably because his urging has been rather more mild than authoritarian.

The courtyard also offers the one establishing shot during the play (there is also a long shot of a castle under the titles after the end). Works usually begin with establishing shots to place the characters in a larger setting. Withholding the establishing shot until the third scene contributes perhaps to audience unease; certainly that was Kozintsev's reason for withholding the establishing shot in his cinematic version.

The second scene in the courtyard setting is the arrival of the players. The bright daylight contrasts ironically with Hamlet's bitter self-reproach during the soliloquy but corresponds with his inspiration about the play. Ground becomes figure—that is, what was simply a background prop becomes a symbolic prop as Hamlet, sitting in the players' cart, caresses a pig's head and taps on the drum when he contemplates the results of "The Mousetrap." (The cart and the drum remind one of Kozintsev's *Hamlet.*) The courtyard scene connects to the stair set, also consistently well-lit, by the doorway through which Hamlet, Rosencrantz and Guildenstern, and Polonius exit to make their way to the players in the courtyard.

The stair set offers one of the few set fragments used symbolically. An early view of Hamlet shows him standing next to a shield-and-spear display (the spears radiating out around the circumference of the shield), fingering his own dagger as he watches the marriage procession. This conects to another at the end of "The Mousetrap" scene. At this shield, appropriately, he says, "Now could I drink hot blood." Recollections of the shield recur with the high-angle shot of Hamlet surrounded by bayonets in 4.3 and also with the high-angle shot of the four dead

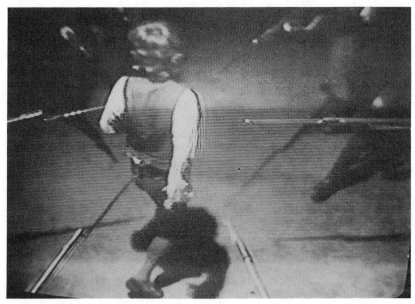

The Chamberlain *Hamlet.* Hamlet at sword points. *(Still courtesy Chamberlain-LeMaire Ltd.)*

The Chamberlain *Hamlet*. Hamlet just before his death. *(Still courtesy Chamberlain-LeMaire Ltd.)*

bodies at the end, configured as spokes of a wheel. Perhaps it is just as well that the producers did not try for other symbolic elements (such as Kozintsev's changeable fireplace and his crashing waves) because too many such elements would have weakened the realism for which the production aimed.

With so much restraint, so much cleverness, this *Hamlet* nevertheless does not work. It does not seize the imagination. Hamlet has no humor, lacks the sardonic wit we expect in the first court scene and in the disclosure scene. Nor is this a gracious Hamlet: he does not greet Marcellus and Bernardo; he does not say, "Nay, come let's goe together." Chamberlain makes an enigmatic Hamlet, but opaquely rather than luminously. Though interesting in themselves, all sorts of production values cannot compensate for the central failure of a bland Hamlet. The Ian McKellen *Hamlet* fails for the opposite reason.

11

Ian McKellen (1971)

Sometime before the Chamberlain production, George Schaefer, the distinguished director whose television career began with the Evans *Hamlet,* urged Hallmark to sponsor a second *Hamlet* for the Hallmark Hall of Fame. He wanted to direct a young English actor who had never yet played Hamlet—Ian McKellen. Hallmark refused, probably because it felt that McKellen, an unknown, would not draw (Kliman, "Schaefer"). Since time has proved Schaefer correct in his assessment of McKellen, it would have been interesting to see what this seasoned television director would have accomplished with the young actor. Instead Chamberlain was directed by Peter Wood for a second Hallmark *Hamlet,* and McKellen got his chance for English television after he had played Hamlet on stage. Aired by CBS cable on 12 June 1982, the Ian McKellen *Hamlet* was taped for television at England's Pinewood Lot over ten years earlier, late in 1971.

The production attracted little attention at the time and for good reason. It seems that a limited buget forced the director to avoid his less-than-adequate set by framing almost all shots in closeup. Though McKellen's acting cannot be faulted, the extreme closeups do not allow for anything beyond facial expression. Since McKellen moves so well, the camera cuts off much of a viewer's potential pleasure. These closeups go far beyond those for Richardson's *Hamlet,* with its crowded medium shots and richly varied closeups. Instead, for many speeches and for all soliloquies, the camera focuses on something less than full face and holds one shot for the entire sequence. The tape demonstrates the power of the closeup, but also shows that without relief the device palls. Since the direction of the actors by Robert Chetwyn was based on the London stage production, the television director, David Giles, the inventive director of the BBC Shakespeare Plays' first tetralogy, presumably can be held to account for camera choices.

The play unfolds in two basic locales, both unlike the mirrored setting for the stage production: the first is the unit setting, consisting of audience chamber, council chamber, Polonius's study, Gertrude's bedroom and a corridor leading to these, and the ramparts setting for the ghost scenes and for 4.4. The second setting, a typical carpenter's set, perhaps fifteen feet by three feet, mimics those nineteenth-century productions which played the first scene before a front cloth (Sprague, 127–28). Perhaps thinking the space was too small to contain both men and ghost, the director intercut shots of the men and shots of the ghost against a similar background. But the film does not provide a satisfying illusion for the dialogue between the men and the ghost because at no time do we see the ghost with anyone else in the same frame. Wirth made a better choice by including, through high-angle shots, ghost and men in the same frame in spite of the small size of the setting. While some viewers perhaps would not notice precisely what is wrong with Giles's version, the separation of ghost from auditors/speakers creates a distracting unreality. Though filmmakers often shoot speakers separately (Olivier complained that he rarely got to play with Elisabeth Bergner in the 1936 *As You Like It* because she was never around when his part of their dialogue was shot), the device works only because a few views of speakers together in the frame make the audience willing to fill in, to imagine the proximity of characters.

The extremely narrow space of the carpenter's set also affects acting style. Actors hug the walls. Though they try to extend the space by looking off afar, say, for the star or for the ghost or for the dawn, though wind blows through hair and heavy fur garments cover the shivering Hamlet and Horatio, though Hamlet tries to break free of the space to follow the ghost, we cannot easily accept the fiction that this is a vast outdoor space. On stage, of course, we are willing to accept imaginary extensions of small spaces by actors, but on television we expect to see what a character says he sees. Perhaps we can do without the dawn in russet mantle clad, but we do not want to make do without the evidence that both the ghost and the men exist in the same space. Because the space is so small, the production eliminates even the removal to different spaces during the "Sweare" sequence.

Instead of putting the ghost and Hamlet together, the tape shows Hamlet's face superimposed on another view of his face as it speaks. LSD images, with distortions of color, wavering visual images, and water-bubbling sound effects suggest that the ghost is not there at all. There is no visual inset of the poisoning scene, but an inset sound effect, the long death groan of the dying king.

Again, for Hamlet's meeting with Fortinbras's forces (4.4) the tape has two views intercut, with no demonstration that these occur together in the same space: Hamlet, the captain (why does he enter with Hamlet?), Rosencrantz and Guildenstern, and others enter the narrow

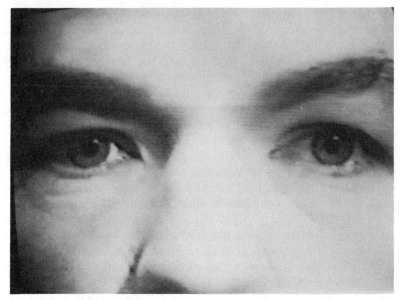

The McKellen *Hamlet*. The extreme closeup signals an interior monologue. *(Still courtesy Fremantle Corporation.)*

space and presumably see soldiers, represented by tops of heads walking from left to right across another frame in front of a dim back-projection of mountains. Fortinbras does not appear, the first lines of the scene being cut. For this scene's soliloquy, as for several others, the production employs a freeze-time technique. As Hamlet begins to think, extraneous sounds stop (here the drum beating for the soldiers' march), and Hamlet speaks the words (not voiceover). In a (probably unintentional) parody of Olivier's discovery that in soliloquies or in any kind of speech, as the emotion gets more intense the camera should move further away, the camera in this production starts with eyes-only closeups and extends to not quite full face. At the end of the soliloquy, the camera returns to the extreme closeup. Also at the end of this soliloquy we see (indirectly by the effect on his face) that Hamlet is nudged into attentiveness, that he starts, and that time has returned to normal, with the drum beating again.

By using this same freeze-time technique for Hamlet's soliloquy "Oh what a Rogue and Pesant slave am I," the production can transpose the soliloquy to the point before Hamlet speaks to the player about the play and about the speech to insert. Thus the consultation with the player comes as a result of the soliloquy. This transposition avoids, then, the question of why Hamlet seems to conceive of the play twice. Though the space for this scene is much larger than that for 4.4, the same extreme

The McKellen *Hamlet*. The slightly less than full face closeup is the shot for soliloquies. *(Still courtesy Fremantle Corporation.)*

closeups obtain. Whether the space is intimate or not, the actor never actually looks into the camera to make contact with the audience. His eyes focus on some spot inside his own head.

When, as it rarely does, the scene widens out, in the audience chamber of the unit set, we see a flexible set suggestive of rather than duplicating a castle. It is especially satisfying when the camera makes use of its two levels in the main area, as when Hamlet walks above and speaks down to Polonius below for the fishmonger scene (an Olivier reminder) or when the players listening to the Pyrrhus speech sit or stand on both levels. Pillars in this set provide spaces behind which the ever-present menacing figure of Osric can spy, behind which Claudius and Polonius can stand in the nunnery scene. The large setting is, of course, the site of the play-within-a-play and of the final duel.

The production also makes good use of a council chamber, off to one side of the large room, where Claudius receives the ambassadors (at the beginning of 2.2), and where Claudius's words to Laertes—"Now must your conscience my acquittance seal"—make sense, as they rarely do in productions, because they come at what appears to be the conclusion of a deliberation with the council. Very often, with 4.6 cut, productions ignore the fact that Claudius completes the winning over of Laertes, as the sentence implies, in action that takes place between the scenes. The connection between this space and the audience chamber becomes apparent in 2.2 when the queen sees Hamlet descending a stairway, reading. Instead of, as we would expect, Hamlet entering the council chamber, which Gertrude and Claudius have now vacated, Hamlet turns to his right and enters the audience chamber, where the "To be" soliloquy now takes place. Polonius enters the space after the soliloquy to begin the fishmonger scene, leading to the entrance of Rosencrantz and Guildenstern and then of the players. This means that Hamlet decides on "The Mousetrap" (2.2) after "To be" (3.1).

With its two sides open to other spaces, the council chamber, like Polonius's study, is unabashedly a stagelike setting, though the camera first makes us aware of that fact only when Laertes moves from the council chamber to his father's study. Before that, with tight shots on Ophelia and Laertes or on Polonius and Ophelia or on Reynaldo and Polonius, we are not particularly aware of the connections of this study-space with any other. It seems strange, indeed, that the camera should have let us in on this secret because everything in the production seems designed to keep from the audience by the subterfuge of closeups any hint that the various parts of the sets are related. It is almost as if by the last part the director had lost interest in that illusion.

The book-lined walls of the study-setting for Polonius may reflect what Polonius thinks he is—a scholar, a role that Polonius would like but that poorly suits him. In this production, he is something of a fool, not overly respected either by his children or by Claudius, who from the beginning seems to count more on Osric than on Polonius. When Gertrude staggers from this study in 4.7 to her bedroom in the midst of telling Claudius and Laertes about Ophelia's drowning, we see that her bedroom is also part of the unit set. During the scene with Hamlet, the bed is not much in evidence, except for a large post that Gertrude leans her cheek against. Appropriately in this production we do not see the bed, because Gertrude, though attractive, is not particularly seductive, especially with her son. Closeups of Hamlet and Gertrude earlier reveal that Hamlet feels passionately about her (he kisses her hand intensely as she leaves the first court scene) but that she feels nothing but maternal about him (she tousles his hair as if he were a small boy). In the bedroom scene, he would like to lay his head on her shoulder but she avoids him. Only after he browbeats her does she become distracted enough to allow him to put his chin on her shoulder. Played by Faith Brook as if she were the fishmonger's wife rather than the king's, given no space to act in, she must wrack her face with excessive sobbing, hysteria unbelievable in a queen. When she says he has cleft her heart in twain, he thrills—this is what he has wanted to hear. She further delights him by shaking her head "no," agreeing not to go to Claudius's bed. She does keep this promise, it seems, for she avoids Claudius from this scene on.

A wide-angle lens makes the pillared corridor connecting some of these spaces look rather deeper than it actually is. Only as we see how quickly the characters cover the distance do we realize that the depth is illusory. Within these small spaces, with the very tight camera, props assume a greater importance than in most sets. There are, for example, constant profferings of pieces of paper, including one that Hamlet tries to thrust first at Polonius (as intermediary), then at Claudius himself just when Claudius asks him not to go to Wittenberg—the paper is evidently his petition for leave to go, just as an earlier paper was Laertes's petition to go. Another recurring prop is flowers: Gertrude returns with a flower for Hamlet before she leaves the court (1.2); moments later, as Hamlet anguishes about her remarriage, he shreds it. Soon after, we see Ophelia, also with a flower, and when Laertes admonishes her about Hamlet, she nervously shreds it. Ophelia, through the flower, is, then, connected to Gertrude and to Hamlet. Later, of course, she distributes flowers in the typical way to Laertes, to the king, and to the queen, who, as demented as Ophelia, puts the flowers in her hair.

A third prop is wine. Gertrude puts down the wine flagon to accentuate her dislike of Polonius's description of her son as mad. But later, wine assumes an even greater importance, because this is the *Hamlet* with the alcoholic Gertrude. Interestingly enough, a Stratford, Canada, production of 1977, possibly independently, also features a drinking Gertrude (Babula, number 119). It is as if Giles had begun with the last scene and asked himself, "Now why would Gertrude drink after being asked not to?" then answered his question, "I know, she must be a drunk!" She drinks early in the play, but her dependency on wine escalates as her troubles increase. Her immediate response after Hamlet leaves her closet is to reach for the wine, and, when Claudius enters the room (4.1 is a continuation of 3.4), she clutches the cup to protect herself from Claudius's harsh questions. When Claudius tries to tell her his troubles just before Laertes's entrance (4.5), she will not let go of the cup of wine in her hand but puts him off with "Alas, looke heere my Lord," distracting him with Ophelia's entrance. The prop is interpretative.

Parallel gestures are also significant: Laertes, for example, kneels for his father's blessing and his father lays his hand on Laertes's head (1.3). Later, when Laertes says, "My Lord I will be rul'd" (Q2: 4.7.69), he kneels and Claudius lays his hand on Laertes's head.

Chetwyn, the stage director, said in a playbill article that Hamlet does not delay, that his own sense of his delay comes from his eagerness and would not be shared by the audience. In accord with this interpretation, the director changes Ophelia's words from "'tis twice two moneths, my Lord," in the play-within-a-play scene to "'Tis two months, my Lord," in other words only a matter of—at most—days since the ghost's revelation. (Kemble's edition of 1806 made the same change.) The closeups undercut Chetwyn's interpretation, however. Hamlet's self-lacerating criticisms are only too believable when we see that face in closeup. The television technique swamps the stage interpretation.

The question remains: who was this production for? At 210 minutes long, with the cuts mainly towards the end, this is one of the fullest Shakespeare productions in a visual medium. The fact that modernized idioms replace most unfamiliar words suggests, nevertheless, that the audience is not one used to sitting still for three-and-a-half hours of *Hamlet,* not one particularly familiar with the play. Yet this audience, most attuned to realistic settings that are totally illusionistic, is one liable to be disappointed by what may appear to be the visual poverty of the spare sets. This production stands as a document of McKellen's brilliant acting and of the proposition that even useful television techniques can be overdone.

12

Derek Jacobi in the BBC *Hamlet* (1980)

The producers of the BBC *Hamlet* (1980) found a solution to the specific problem of television frame and setting different from Richardson's or Wood's or Giles's. By choosing a relatively bare set, conceding only a few richly detailed movable panels and props to shape key locales, they pointed up the natural affinity between Shakespeare's stage and the undisguised sound set. This starkness of setting admits poetry, higher intensity than realistic sets, and "what not that's sweet and happy." Theirs was a more conservative solution than Richardson's but as creditable. More specifically adapted to the medium than Wood's, more able to turn television's deficits into gains than Giles's, the BBC production appeals most strongly to those who do not want to forget that *Hamlet* is a play.

The producers made a valid choice from the forms television had settled on by the eighties: (1) broadcast films, whether made for television or not, which exploit location settings, long shots, and all the clichés we associate with movies, including sudden shifts of time and space and full use of distance, from the most extreme long shots to "eyes only" closeups, but with the rack shot as the favorite; (2) studio-shot television drama with naturalistic settings, such as the hospital corridors and middle-class living rooms of sitcoms and soap operas, mostly in mid- to close-shots, often interspersed, to be sure, with a bit of stock footage of highways and skylines to establish a realistic environment, a style varying from a close representation of real action to frankly staged action, where canned laughter or even shadowy glimpses of the studio audience can heighten the staged effect; (3) bare space with little or no pretense that the activity being broadcast is not a televised event, perhaps with a glimpse of the television crew, certainly with our knowledge that it is nearby, as in news broadcasts, talk shows and some television drama. Because of its patently unrepresentational quality (that is, we accept what we see as what *is*, rather than as representing something else), this last type offers the most freedom in shooting style; camera work may, for example, be completely obtrusive because we already know that the characters in a television drama we see staged this way are being played by actors. The camera need not be restricted by the director's concept, as it was for Richardson and Giles, but can move freely as each separate image demands. To all three kinds of settings we bring particular expectations in response to their conventions. All are quite capable of gripping us, of seeming "real."

The last kind of television space has both advantages and pitfalls. It avoids, for example, the clash between realism and poetry, between the unity often expected in realistic media and the disunity and ambiguity of many of the plays, especially *Hamlet.* Closest of all television settings to the kind of stage Shakespeare wrote for, the bare television set can be stretched through creative camera work; such stretching is necessary to compensate for all that the stage has that television lacks. The closer the television performance tries to be to a stage performance, the more pronounced the deficiencies of television seem—*as stage drama;* whereas, when television pursues its own strengths instead, its deficiencies vis-à-vis stage do not come to mind. The producers of the BBC *Hamlet* did not want to forget the stage.

Freeing this *Hamlet* from location (used in the BBC *As You Like It*) and from realistic sets (used in *Measure for Measure*—however well those sets worked for that play) allows the play to be inconsistent, with, as Bernard Beckerman so brilliantly explains in *Shakespeare at the Globe* (54–55), a rising and falling action in each individual scene rather than through the course of the drama as a whole. It also allows for *acting*, the bravura kind that Derek Jacobi does so well.

Like the pointillism of impressionistic paintings gradually coalescing into a subtly textured portrait, Jacobi adds detail to detail to shape the character. If at first Jacobi's mannerisms suggesting madness seem excessive, gradually he wins our assent. Hamlet's aberrant behavior after the ghost scene fits traditional notions of his reaction, but Jacobi's rapid, hard blows to his forehead with the flat of his hand as he says "My tables" recall the desperation of Lear's cry: "O, let me not be mad, not mad, sweet heaven!" Though Gielgud had used this same gesture in 1936 (Mills, 218), I doubt that it was with such craziness. And soon after, following the last couplet of the scene, Hamlet, maniacally playful, widens his eyes and points, pretending to see the ghost again, then guffaws at Marcellus's fears. His laughter when alone, as while saying "The play's the thing / Wherein I'll catch the conscience of the King," unsettles us. More significantly, he breaks up his own "Mousetrap" by getting right into the play, destroying the distance between audience and stage (a very "real" raked proscenium-arch stage), spoiling it as a test, because Claudius has a right to be incensed at Hamlet's behavior. Of course, Hamlet does so because Claudius never gives himself away, an unusual and provocative but not unheard-of interpretation. Thus, Claudius can only have the court's sympathy as he calmly calls for light and uses it to examine Hamlet closely. Hamlet, in response, covers his face, then laughs.

Even Hamlet thinks himself mad. To Ophelia he says, as if the realization had suddenly struck him, "It *hath* [emphasis his] made me mad" (BBC text: 3.1.147). To his mother he stresses the word "essentially" in "I *essentially* am not in madness" (3.4.187). That is, in all essential matters he can be considered sane, though mad around the edges. This indeed turns out to be the explanation.

However doubtful about Hamlet's sanity Jacobi's acting leaves us, in this production the question does not have a bearing on the tragedy because in each scene on this nonrealistic set we seem to start anew, ready to let Hamlet's behavior reveal his mental state. Moreover, Hamlet's madness, when it surfaces, does not obscure his reason or sensibility. Rather, exacerbated reason and sensibility sometimes tip him into madness. This madness offers no excuse for action or delay but is simply part of the suffering Hamlet is heir to. This interpretation allows Hamlet to apologize to Laertes sincerely (5.2.220–36). His speech, uncut in this version, at the important verge between the prose that has preceded it and the poetry that sweeps to the end of the play, would be an embarrassment if Hamlet were only pretending madness, as in so many other performances. Yet if he *is* mad, how can he make those choices required if a figure is to be considered tragic? This production solves the problem by having it both ways; a few significant moments prove his "essential" sanity. Throughout "To be, or not to be," though he is infinitely sad, he reasons calmly. And no sign of madness surfaces as he coolly judges himself after the players leave (2.2.560–83).

Not madness but aloneness is the enduring impression this Hamlet gives, an aloneness emphasized by the emptiness of the sets, emphasized too by the soliloquies directed to the camera/audience.[1] He is isolated not only from the artifacts of existence (such as the tapestries, desks, and instruments of the Evans and Kozintsev *Hamlet*s), but also from people. Unlike other media Hamlets, he is visible from the beginning of the first court scene (1.2), emphasizing his aloneness among a multitude. In most media productions, with their ability to withhold part of the setting, Hamlet either makes an entrance only as Laertes leaves or sits inconspicuously or remains off frame. Here, he stands near the queen at some distance from Claudius. Shots encompass a whole group so that, as on stage, we see the actions and reactions of many at once. The king walks forward and takes Gertrude's arm, leading her to the seat next to his—ignoring Hamlet, who is left in the foreground. Claudius then conducts the business of court. The king disposes of both Fortinbras and Laertes before deigning to look at Hamlet, in clear sight all the while. To emphasize the slight, the director has Laertes far back in the crowd, surprised that Claudius calls out his name, having to push his way forward. The unmistakable message to all achieves the desired result, for indeed in exiting past the prince no one in the crowd speaks to Hamlet. Voltemand, Cornelius, and Laertes (and later some one or two others) nod very slightly as they exit. In a brilliant touch, Hamlet, turning to watch Laertes leave, has his back to Claudius when the king at last speaks to him. The frame thus captures both full face, isolated from each other.

A man who seems to choose solitude, Hamlet is all the more alone because of those around him. His chief friend, Horatio, as played by Robert Swann, is strangely passive. True, Horatio has few lines, particularly when he and Hamlet are together, but many directors give him feeling gestures that support Hamlet. The Olivier film's Horatio has presence enough to make him qualify as ruler of Denmark (in the absence of Fortinbras, omitted from that film). This is not conceivable for the BBC's Horatio. Occasionally he does put a comforting hand on Hamlet's arm, but for the most part he is phlegmatically opaque and unreadable. Does he think that Hamlet should listen to the ghost? Does he think that Claudius gives himself away at "The Mousetrap"? Who can tell? His passionate declaration of loyalty at the end, when he wants to take the poison, comes as a surprise. In the text, before "The Mousetrap," Hamlet calls out to Horatio, who immediately responds (3.2.50–51). In the BBC version, as the frame widens after the advice to the players and Hamlet's few words with Polonius, Rosencrantz, and Guildenstern, Hamlet moves downstage in the general lobby, approaching and speaking to Horatio, who is reading and whom Hamlet has to urge to look up and pay attention. At this moment, Hamlet praises him (3.2.52–72), as if for his very lack of attention! Hamlet's meaning in this context seems to be that Horatio does not fawn. But this interpretation for Hamlet's speech ("A man that Fortune's buffets and rewards / Hast ta'en with equal thanks") detracts from its profounder meaning for Hamlet's own growth of awareness. Yet the interaction depicted, with Horatio's lack of regard, certainly does reinforce the concept of Hamlet alone.

The point that Rodney Bennett, the director, has Hamlet make here would have been more telling if Rosencrantz and Guildenstern had previously acted as toadies towards the prince. But they have not behaved thus with Hamlet. From the beginning they decided who sits in the seat of power and they appear to have little interest in Hamlet. The shot that introduces them effectively reveals their nature—a long shot of king and queen approaching the camera, framed by Rosencrantz and Guildenstern in medium closeup. They nudge each other as they notice they are no longer alone; put on your mask, the nudge says. More subtle Rosencrantzes and Guildensterns in other productions descend into perfidy, presumably because Claudius brings about their moral disintegration. But this character development would not fit this production's Claudius. During their first interview with Hamlet, a low-angle shot of them standing puts Rosencrantz and Guildenstern in the position of judge over the seated Hamlet. They are cool in response to Hamlet's tearful, distraught cry, "I have bad dreams," and after "The Mousetrap" they cannot conceal their disdain. Hamlet, however, suffers no great loss of friendship in them because obviously his mother is wrong in believing that "two men there is not living / To whom he more adheres," for, in a neat reversal of the frequent stage joke, Hamlet (not Claudius) mistakes one for the other (as had Nicol Williamson's Hamlet). Hamlet's greeting to them is warm but not like his fervent embrace of Horatio.

Even the First Player, though the prince greets him with warmth and affection, is not a friend or a comfort to Hamlet. He treats Hamlet with impatience as a nuisance or humors him. The play scene (3.2) begins with a shot of hands making up the boy as queen, after, that is, a graceful allusion to Olivier's *Hamlet* with a shot of theatrical props. With the frame widening for the First Player's entrance, we see that those are Hamlet's hands; the player sighs wearily as he cleans Hamlet's hands, then listens with barely concealed condescension to Hamlet's advice.

Lalla Ward's Ophelia is too mousy and insignificant to be a friend to Hamlet. Laertes's and Polonius's advice to her rings true—what could a man like Hamlet see in this weak-chinned, insipid little girl? True, all Ophelias fail Hamlet, but not before leading him to expect a more spunky response. That can be the meaning of the long look at her that she reports to Polonius (2.1.75–100). Like many other directors, this one omits Ophelia's playful answer to Hamlet at "The Mousetrap": "Still better, and worse" (3.2.245). Hamlet's sarcastic "Soft you now! The fair Ophelia," lends credence to Claudius's analysis of the nunnery scene— "Love! His affections do not that way tend" (3.1.162)—an analysis that appears accurate because camera work makes clear that the king has overheard "To be, or not to be" as well as the encounter with Ophelia. While onstage characters normally cannot hear asides by other characters, one can overhear a soliloquy: Romeo, for example, overhears Juliet, and Autolycus is afraid the shepherds have overheard him. Because the camera frames not just Hamlet's face but the space behind him where Claudius and Polonius are hiding, we grasp that Claudius bases his later comment, "There's something in his soul / O'er which his melancholy sits on brood" (164–65), on his having heard Hamlet's soliloquy. This is a possibility that films often miss because with their spatial flexibility they can place Hamlet anywhere while he makes this speech.[2] Thus the very limitation of space on stage and in television studios can reinforce connections that Shakespeare may have intended.

The nature not only of his friends but also of his enemies tends to isolate him. Polonius, played by Eric Porter, is basically a good sort, well-meaning and affectionate with Ophelia. He hugs her sympathetically after she tells him about what happened as she was sewing in her closet, and he tenderly leads her away after the nunnery scene. The director diminishes Polonius's foolishness by having him read off the genres from the players' bill rather than having him invent them from his own too-hair-splitting brain.

Claudius, played by Patrick Stewart, is handsome, clear-eyed, seemingly guileless, a genial king whose repugnance for his misdeed expresses itself in such physical revulsion that he sobs out his remorse. Unfortunately, the American broadcast version omitted Rosencrantz and Guildenstern and Polonius from the beginning of the prayer scene (3.3.1–35), thus eliminating Claudius's "Thanks, dear my lord," which Claudius could barely articulate, because he almost retches out of self-loathing (as Olivier's Claudius does also). He is a good man sullied by one bad act. Since the production does not overemphasize the closeup, the extreme closeup of Claudius when he whispers his *first* admission of guilt (3.1.49–54) effectively emphasizes the shocking contradiction between demeanor and deed.

That Gertrude cleaves to Claudius is not surprising, once Hamlet has left. However, Claire Bloom's playing of Gertrude makes incredible the idea of shallow sensuality. Loving, self-possessed, she is almost too intelligent to play the queen. These enemies, good people all, do not give Hamlet sufficient resistance to push against.

Hamlet, then, is left to struggle against himself. One of the conflicts in this Hamlet results from his affinity, perhaps, more to the bureaucratic Claudius who handles war-scares with diplomacy and who sits at a desk while brooding over his sins than to the warlike King Hamlet who comes in full armor. Hamlet may admire Fortinbras but is himself more like the bookish Horatio. Through nuance of gesture, through body movement, through a face that is indeed a map of all emotions, Jacobi shapes a Hamlet who loves his father too much to disregard his command yet who cannot hate his step-father enough to attend to it. Because Jacobi conveys so fully Hamlet's aloneness and vulnerability, one could be struck, for the first time, by the ghost's silence about his son—the elder Hamlet makes no declaration of love, expresses no concern about his son's ascent to the throne. Hamlet is doomed, it seems, to care about those who consistently care more for themselves than for him.

All of this production's richness and suggestiveness was realized not only because Jacobi is a marvelous actor—as indeed he is—but also because within the set's spareness *that* acting, an acting style that transcends the "real," could unfold. This production's space tells us what is possible for television productions of Shakespeare as stage drama. The more bare the set, the more glowing the words, the more immediate our apprehension of the enacted emotion.

Notes

1. Mary Z. Maher points out that Hamlet, in his soliloquies, speaks almost always directly to the audience. Isolated from his fellows, he is forced to break the frame of the play to solace himself by communicating to his audience.

2. Hamlet in Kozintsev's version is watching water crash over rocks, and Olivier is on the ramparts of the castle (the speech transposed to follow the nunnery scene to boot).

13

A Swedish Television *Hamlet* (1984)

Made in 1984 for Swedish television and premiered in this country in February 1987 by WNYC-TV, this filmed *Hamlet* was directed by Ragnar Lyth, a young stage and television director trained in filmmaking. With its English subtitles barely reminiscent of Shakespeare's lines, language is not the central focus for an American viewer. Nor is it for the director, who cuts most of the lines in this production and concentrates instead on visual images—not to save time but to see the play in visual terms: in spite of cuts of more than 70 percent of the text, the production runs for a compelling two hours and forty minutes. Among sound filmmakers, Kurosawa has been the only one other than Lyth to capture a vision of Shakespeare through nonverbal means. Yet Lyth's *Hamlet* is much more connected to Shakespeare's text than are Kurosawa's films; like Kozintsev's *Hamlet*, Lyth's is a defensible interpretation of *Hamlet* rather than a brilliant offshoot.[1]

Reader-response critics—and audience-response critics—say that words, whether read or enacted, have no meaning until the perceiver supplies their meaning. The words on the page, or the spectacle and words spoken on the stage and on the screen, however different each from the others, must enter into the consciousness of the perceiver in order to achieve meaning. Once the play has been experienced (whether read or seen), it remains in the consciousness as another entity altogether, shaped by the recollected images of memorial construction. What I am affirming is that, after viewing Lyth's film, my memorial construction of the play is as rich and satisfying as any I can remember. This construction of mine does not displace any other view of the play; rather, it exists alongside the other interpretations, commenting on them and energizing them through the discovery of contrast.

The film exerts its subtle pressures on a viewer's mind not only through its difference from other versions but also through its internal differences—between the seemingly real and the obviously contrived, between one moral stance and another, and through characters not easily stereotyped who thus expose different facets from scene to scene. Through the disequilibrium that results from these contrasts, Lyth provides opportunities to look at *Hamlet* in new ways.

Realism and Artifice

Though I refer to acts, scenes, and segments of familiar productions in describing it, Lyth's production has a seamlessness and a verisimilitude that obviates scenic divisions. It alludes to the theater—in the cyclorama-like horizon at the gravesite, in the players' outdoor theater, in the indoor theater where Hamlet faces Polonius in the fishmonger scene, and in the fiction it maintains of the camera representing the equivalent of the fourth wall of the proscenium arch stage. Yet, nothing in the staging or in the acting hints that this work has been done before in human history, that it has been acted before by these particular players, that it has been rehearsed and previously formed.[2] Something spontaneous and apparently accidental in the realization of the play's creatures make it seem altogether new. Still, it is full of artful, even allusive details and editing that sculpt into artifice what may appear to be the raw material of life. The spaces—and the acting within the spaces— engage and persuade, wringing assent from the observer. The great contradictions in the film stem from the apparent realism of the acting (unlike Jacobi or Williamson, this Hamlet, Stellan Skarsgaard, never looks to us through the camera); the apparent, but contrived, realism of the settings; and the contrast of these with the straightforwardly artful camera manipulations.

Lyth, primarily influenced by the work of Peter Brook, aimed for the same spatial spareness he found in Brook's *Carmen* and *Lear*.[3] He wanted nearly empty rooms with clean, simple lines that would allow acting and lighting to concentrate audience attention without undo scenic attraction. The film equivalent of the bare, nonillusionistic stage is what both Brook and Lyth sought. Camera work is as diverse as the spaces it shows: Ophelia's intimate Vermeer-like room glimpsed from other Vermeer-like rooms (similar to but less finished than Jonathan Miller's spaces for the BBC series), ratty cellar, dim catacombs, musty attic, council chamber and antechamber, bedrooms and vast gymnasium, cribbed courtyard, muddy graveyard, snow-shrouded rock face, and restless seashore. But no view of the whole, no establishing shot, positions the space within a world—not at the beginning, not at the end, not at any time in between. The largest geographical elements we see appear briefly late in the play:

During the shooting of Ragnar Lyth's *Hamlet*. The setting is the 19th-century Nobel dynamite factory. Shown are the child who plays chess during most of the first court scene (until line 191), Dan Ekborg (Laertes, kneeling), Mona Malm (Gertrude), Frej Linquist (Claudius), and Sven Lindberg (Polonius). Photo by Bjoern Edergren. *(Publicity still courtesy Ragnar Lyth.)*

a vast, almost featureless snow plain that dissolves into a seascape against a narrow bluish horizon (4.5). The production concentrates on walled-in space, with wide-ranging variations in spaciousness.

Lyth's concern for space means concern for camera work. The production makes all of television's familiar close shots look new, melding them organically to long and medium shots by creative editing. This is far from the mechanical variations of distance employed by some video productions that are inspired by something less than intuitive or conscious artistry: Lyth appears to think through the implications of every camera view.[4] Large spaces lend themselves, of course, to the long shots that Lyth employs frequently and significantly—not only for the expected group views of the courtiers, the players, and the servants, but also for interpretive framing that forces understanding on the viewer. Many long shots, for example, feature Ophelia, alone or with one other person. Together with her words, her demeanor, and the sense of her being that the actress (Pernilla Walgren) gives her, long shots shape both her characterization and the audience response to her. The large space engulfs her when she stands with Polonius in the catacombs while he forcefully tells her not to see Hamlet again and also later when Polonius offers her to Hamlet (in the midst of Hamlet's conversation with his former friends, Rosencrantz and Guildenstern). After Hamlet refuses to approach her, looking right at her when he says, "O most true, she is a strumpet" (Arden, 2.2.235), and then turns away with Rosencrantz and Guildenstern, she stands forlorn, trying a brave smile. Moments before, standing alone in long shot, the object of Hamlet's hidden scrutiny, she had waited for her father to call her into the presence of royalty. Hamlet later snubs her because he had seen her enter the king's chamber. Later, at Polonius's further insistence, she waits, vulnerable and alone, for Hamlet to notice her, as she sits by the fireplace, her gown having been tastefully arranged by Polonius in folds around her. The false start, Polonius's attempt to unloose Ophelia twice (first in 2.2 and again in 3.1), contributes to the film's unexpected freshness. These views of Ophelia, distant and within large spaces, invite sympathy, contradicting the message of her complicity in entrapping Hamlet. Yet, if these long views were all Lyth showed of Ophelia, we might feel only detached pity for her; but closeups of her expressive face force us into her mind, and medium shots of her with Laertes or Polonius or her duenna or Hamlet enlarge our knowledge of her, as we watch her responding, trying to assert herself, excited by the interest the authorities take in her—thus showing a full range of reactions.

Montage, the combined effect of variations from shot to shot, is in its changes self-referential in the extreme; that is, it is noticeable and therefore artful. At its best, however, montage produces a whole more expressive than its parts, a more powerful sense of knowing the truth than more realistic methods might evoke. One feels that Eisenstein, had he lived, would have perfected the technique to the level of Lyth's practice, without the excesses that today make some of the Russian filmmaker's effects look dated. At times Lyth uses montage in a traditional way—to reflect the excitement of the arrival of the players, of their preparation before the play-within-a-play, and of Laertes's rebellion, with shots varying in distance and duration. But he can also use it for psychedelic, strained effects: as when Hamlet's father's face in closeup is superimposed over Hamlet's head (1.5); when Hamlet breaks up his room (after 2.1); when Rosencrantz's and Guildenstern's desperate search for Hamlet (4.2) is intercut with our first views of mad Ophelia and of Hamlet hurriedly digging a shallow grave for Polonius with his dagger and, his dagger breaking, with his bare hands. In the slow motion shots of the court exiting during Hamlet's first soliloquy, shots then followed by dizzying camera circles, the editing mirrors Hamlet's frame of mind. In several scenes, the camera *is* Hamlet, forcing us to understand his point of view by making us share it.[5] Similarly, changes in shots in the large gymnasium show first one group and then another engaged in courtly sports (a prologue to 1.2) in this court of genteel competition. Like a spectator at a play when the stage is filled with people, the camera looks nervously about the gymnasium, as if uncertain what should be the center of attention in this confusing action. Whatever the editing pace, from rapid montage to slow motion, the shot is the basic unit, as it is in films made for the big screen, and the rhythmic effects are musical. Lyth does not use the long takes that reflect theatrical rather than moving-image conventions—as many other television productions do. Although it is a film made for television, it aspires to the more varied life of a moving image on the large screen.[6] But because each shift in view, each cut from shot to shot, follows an inner, interpretative logic, the viewer subordinates each component to the total effect. Thus, more than usual, perhaps, to analyze the shots is to belie their summative power.

Both shots and spaces are one with the director's idiosyncratic inter-pretation. This Hamlet, played by Stellan Skarsgaard, is crazed, and the space is crazed; we are never sure what space the camera is going to show next, and the spaces are seldom in harmony with each other. Ophelia's Dutch-painting room has little to do with the monasterial bareness, the austerity of Hamlet's whitewashed and booklined room.[7] The rich, bur-gundy draperies of Gertrude's bedroom do not correspond with the ruined grandeur, the peeling paint and the spotty repairs of the hallway where Ophelia looks for the gracious majesty of Denmark (the court seems to rot before our eyes). Rich golden light glowing in the soft darkness of some spaces—the Dutch Masters' look—contrasts with the post-modernist light of other spaces. I am thinking in particular of the warm light on Hamlet as he kneels on the players' outdoor stage writing his additional speeches, intercut with the cool blue light on Claudius's and Polonius's faces who watch him from a window. Hence, incongruous spatial energies corresponding to contrasts in world-view are made avail-able for our consideration.

Genres

The editing style contributes to Lyth's playing with genres. Neither a romantic view of *Hamlet* like Kozintsev's, nor an absurdist view like Brook's, the film exploits elements from both. Within one segment, styles can clash. When Claudius speaks to Laertes about revenge, slow camera pans of a banquet table dissolve lovingly into further slow pans, alternating with long shots of the whole and with medium one-shots of Claudius eating eagerly, or of Laertes, or of the madrigal singer who is entertaining them (4.7). The fireplace behind the table reminds us of Ophelia, for she had sat before it waiting for Hamlet, and the fire behind her and Hamlet had reflected their passion. Lyth intercuts the banquet with the discovery of Ophelia's body: the camera focuses on a group of four kitchen helpers standing on rocks, staring at something below them. The youngest, a child with wooden spoons stuck in his head gear, stoops to pick up a pipe and tries to play it, and an older woman, perhaps the child's mother, snatches it away from him and tosses it aside abruptly. We hear a splash. Only then does the camera, following the sound, show us Ophelia, drowned, gently moving in the quiet water. The sound of the pipe and the splash, along with the editing and the space, helps Lyth convey his interpretation. The editing gives point to Claudius's seductiveness and the irony of all this prettiness: the persuasive power of Claudius's wealth and position (what one might call the political view); the visual beauty of Ophelia's death (in the romantic tradition); and the reactions of the servant bystanders to it (from a naturalistic tradition). The total effect is dissonant, as vectors from different genres collide: one might say that it adds up to a kind of theater of the absurd.

Repeated Motifs

At the same time that Lyth plays with these disparate genres, he also uses resonating elements for a reinforcing, cumulative effect. Music, while not as overbearing as Shostakovich's or Walton's, and other sounds continually guide audience responses. Especially noteworthy are the eerie whispers and wind noises of the ghost; the ratcheting grates of a large wheel associated with the ghost's revelation (heard again after Hamlet sees Ophelia being admitted to Claudius's room, in Gertrude's closet, and in the last scene when Laertes tells Hamlet "the King's to blame"); the sound of the deep bell tones that are related to the ghost's arrival (the men sense the association of the bell clapper with the ghost); the contrasting, foolish small tinkle of Claudius's scribe's bell; the discordant, whispering sounds of madness; the outdoor sounds of birds and sea, the sound of freedom; and the sound of Ophelia's pathetic pipe that

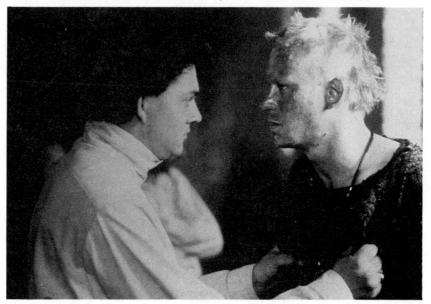

Laertes (Dan Ekborg) tells Hamlet (Stellan Skarsgaard) that the king's to blame. From the duel scene of Ragnar Lyth's *Hamlet*. Photo by Bertil S. Aaberg. *(Publicity still courtesy Ragnar Lyth.)*

she plays in her madness. Some of the repetitions of these sounds form yet another musical, rhythmic counterpoint to the more staccato rhythms of the editing.

Also noteworthy is visual repetition. Just as Ophelia's characterization is a function of her appearance within her frames, so do the flowers associated with her contribute to audience response. Her room is hung with delicate herbs she has collected and is drying, and Hamlet, in his room, shreds a dried chaplet of flowers that was hanging on his wall, evidently a memento from her. The little blue flower in the ribbon of the letter she hands Hamlet in the first court scene and the spray of tiny white flowers she gives to Laertes when he leaves suggest the delicacy of her sensibility, the care for detail that someone of Hamlet's intellectuality might appreciate. In contrast, the indistinguishable herbs she throws at the queen and hands to Laertes and the king in her second mad scene mark the disintegration of her personality. The clown mask that Hamlet wears through the events after the play-within-a-play (3.2, 3.3 and 3.4), which finally ends up on the floor in Hamlet's room, and which elicits a smile from the mad Ophelia, is another repeated motif. It points to the obvious: Hamlet plays a part; Hamlet is fool as well as scholar. But it does so with tact and finesse.

Another repeated image is a strange view of the dead king (in 1.1, 1.4

and 1.5). When the ghost is expected, Hamlet looks down the stairwell from the attic where he waits to the coffin several stories below. There the dead king is laid out, a telling evocation of time and decay, the death of the king kept perpetually in the present as a constant irritant to Hamlet. As his attention is drawn to the dead body, so the camera booms down closer and closer. The actual number of times any of these images repeats is small, but even one repetition of an unexpected image startles, just as even one repetition of an extraordinary word is riveting, while multiple repetitions of the most common words go by unnoticed.

The first image the film impresses on the viewer is Denmark as prison, an image repeated several times and in several ways. One evocation of imprisonment is surveillance, and Elsinore's spaces are made for spies. Frequently the frame shows a face sliced by a door or by a screen held in front of it, an eye peering out at someone. Doors and corners are spies' natural territory. People are constantly watching others. Hamlet, in the courtyard, is watched from windows by Claudius and others. Hamlet spies on Ophelia. Servants stare into the two doors of the room Hamlet enters with Rosencrantz and Guildenstern. Various servants have to be shooed away, and they leave scenes of impending action reluctantly. Even Claudius and Gertrude are listened to as they couple behind the bed curtains. Since the frame of moving images has the power to exclude, widening the frame can surprise the viewer with unexpected presence or absence. Kozintsev's camera discloses Hamlet's empty chair, Hamlet's absence from the first court scene just as Claudius first speaks to Hamlet. Lyth is more apt to reveal unexpected presence than absence: the sudden revelation of a spy, Laertes fencing in the first court scene, Ophelia there, too, gazing at Hamlet, Gertrude as much a spy as Polonius or Claudius during the nunnery segment, the listening child in the disclosure scene, and incidental people of all sorts. In fact, incidental presence is one of Lyth's primary devices of verisimilitude.

Even as the film opens, we see the spying that is a way of life at Elsinore. An eye in extreme closeup looks out, toward us but not at us. Someone is shrewdly assessing the situation at which he looks—a party from the sounds of it—from behind a partially opened door. As the frame widens, we see that the person is a chef or a maitre d' directing kitchen activities, overseeing the spectacular gustatory creations that are a part of royal entertainment. Seconds later, uncanny gusts of wind disturb the scene, frighten the kitchen help, and bewilder the chef. The wobbliness of a hand-held camera captures his hesitancy as he creeps toward the open door where Marcellus, his eyes wary, enters the weak circle of light from the kitchen to relight his torch: the wind has disturbed him also. This done, Marcellus recedes into the gloom, only the spot of light from his torch visible. As the camera fixes its attention on Marcellus, it leaves in doubt the chef's further response to the otherworldly wind that had disturbed him and his staff. Because the effect of its passage touches these incidental servants, the ghost's reality is never in question. Without this scene, its reality might be doubted, for the ghost appears only in the briefest of glimpses while he is speaking to Hamlet in the last scene of act 1, and is sensed rather than seen by the others.

When the camera, as if distracted, shifts from the chef to Marcellus, it partakes of the mystery and fullness of life; that is, art is unified, complete, while life is ragged-ended. The production is rich in such moments. Over Marcellus's torch, the film's titles appear on the screen. Soon Marcellus joins Horatio and the two approach Bernardo. They pass workers in the dim light, a couple of men busy at a forge, another couple moving a large wheel. Such diegetic images allow Lyth to cut many lines about the kingdom's preparations for Fortinbras's attack and allow him to expand the symbolic elements of the imagery, such as those that express the prison motif. A caged bird in the gymnasium is only the most obvious of these images. After the ghost's *adieu,* Hamlet's face is shadowed by iron spokes of a wheel suggesting the rack, the torture of life in Denmark. Most startlingly, when servants open a formidably heavy and ugly gate for Laertes, a color-bleaching shaft of brilliant light pierces the grey gloom of the castle. Laertes looks out with the wonder of one who knows that freedom lies in wait for him out there; Ophelia looks out with the wonder of one who knows that the freedom is not for her. (Rosencrantz and Guildenstern, in their search for Hamlet in 4.2, discover her sitting in darkness at the beginning of her madness, but she exits into just such a bright light after her second mad scene.) In contrast, the outdoor scenes connected to the castle are confined and narrow: the snow-filled courtyard for part of the first scene with Rosencrantz and Guildenstern and the arrival of the players; the garden party in weak sunlight for Ophelia's first mad scene. After Laertes's release, the door closes Ophelia in darkness again, without showing the viewer the freedom that both saw. As she and Polonius walk back through the cellar toward their apartment, shadows against a wall of the catacombs look like prison bars. When they return to her room—he arguing all the way, overcoming her with words and sheer force of will—he puts her under the control of a duenna, who latches her door (cp. The Classic Stage Co. *Hamlet,* 1984). Ophelia, as well as Hamlet, is a prisoner. The difference is that she is not sure that she has a right to object or even to yearn.

Antiromantic but not quite theater of cruelty, the work is nevertheless full of disturbing, even disgusting images. The text, of course, has images of putrefaction, smarmy lust, hidden pus, and other unpleasantnesses. Some productions concentrate on these images without any sense of the redemptive values in the play—the providential fall of the sparrow or the friend not passion's slave. The Swedish production balances the disparate motifs better than any other production, exposing what disgusts Hamlet without wallowing in it. Misleading as it is to clump together the revolting elements, doing so can demonstrate what the Swedish press—representative perhaps of any audience—found so disturbing about this *Hamlet*.[8] Sexual nausea is one of the centers of the film. Early on, we see the flirtatious coyness of a middle-aged matron in the first court scene. Claudius fondles Gertrude's breasts as he announces their marriage. For what in Shakespeare is the second court scene, medium shots show two male, then two female, attendants standing and waiting, listening with averted eyes and embarrassment to the grunts and heaves of active sexual congress, hiding their discomfiture, waiting for the climax so that they can get on with their business. The selectivity of the frame, the avoidance of redundancy in sound and sight, distinguishes the production. Polonius is there, and so is a ubiquitous scribe, as well as the body attendants, each set of two revealed in successive medium shots. Polonius peers at the closed bed curtains, an unlikely light brightening his face; then a quick cut to a reverse long shot shows the curtains of the bed, a lunge, and through suddenly parted curtains the queen, naked down to the waist, clutching the king. Quickly the king shuts the curtains again and the sounds continue. Once sated, they hop out, first the king in his nightshirt, then the queen, proud of herself, glossed with sweat, wrapped in a sheet. The rank sweat of an enseamed bed, indeed. The king allows a few drops of water to graze his hands, then repeats the sexual act by analogy, lunging with his sword at a mannequin. Later, Hamlet does not merely tell his mother what she has done and should not continue to do in bed (3.4); he searches out and finds the soiled spots on the sheet, thrusts it into her face, and then garrottes her with it, stopped only by the reappearance of the ghost. The mannequin—the sword still stuck in it—swings in the unearthly ghost-wind. Ophelia, searching for the queen (4.5), opens a door, allowing us to discover a servant on a divan on hands and knees, her skirts up, exposing her buttocks, being tupped by a fully clothed, bald-pated councillor (the priest). Lyth makes these images of aged sexuality seem repellant (no matter what our private feelings about aged sexuality might be). But he contrasts healthy and youthful eroticism in Ophelia lying on her bed with her skirts exposing her legs, reading Hamlet's letters, and in Hamlet, in his attraction to Ophelia.

Still, revolting images abound, most startlingly the spewing of Claudius's vomit—on Gertrude, on Polonius, on Rosencrantz and Guildenstern, and on us (the camera), as the king reacts to the play-within-a-play. In the prayer scene, vomit still soils his beard. Later, a closeup of a light-flooded windowsill shows a bizarre and distorted *un*still life with rotten fruit, fragments undulating and rocking with the motion of vermin. As the camera dollies out, we see mad Ophelia looking about in Hamlet's now empty room. Along with the visual and emotional ugliness, Lyth's Denmark is among those with the sickest body politic, from top to bottom. In the cellar, Ophelia, Laertes, and Polonius pass, without remark, a room where a cook with a stick beats a woman. Above, in the rooms of State, it is difficult to imagine a court more unpleasant than this at Elsinore, full of self-servers. The ending is most shocking: all the dead bodies are there on view, but when the formidable, bearded Fortinbras enters and takes charge decisively, the men and women begin to smile tentatively at him and are impatient with the efforts of Horatio to clear Hamlet's name, to hold up the tattered commission that will prove the king's conspiracy. They are not interested; no one cares about justice or right or wrong. Claudius is not the only one who can smile and smile and be a villain.

But just as Ophelia's innocent eroticism contrasts with the court's lasciviousness, just as the purity of the light at Hamlet's window contrasts with what is on the sill, so too do healthful images contrast with the sick ones. The androgynous servant who carries the buckets of slops to the pigs (overturned on the steps by Laertes, Polonius, and Ophelia; later, as Ophelia and Polonius return from seeing Laertes off, the servant scrubs the steps), is the same person who wonders at the fall of books from Hamlet's room and who delights in the players' impromptu performance for Hamlet upon their arrival. Both the captain (4.4) and the gravedigger (5.1) are honest and forthright men. Most significantly, children brighten what would otherwise be dark; they fill the screen as in no other media production of the play. Hamlet, realizing that Rosencrantz and Guildenstern have betrayed him, steps away from them, looking at children at play in the snow as he quietly says, "What a piece of work is man!" The open faces of the children, still innocent of duplicity, affirm that man indeed *is* a noble piece of work. The child whom Claudius lifts in his arms, the child at chess who overhears and is distressed by Horatio's revelations to Hamlet about the ghost, the crying baby of the player queen, the sweet-faced lad who stands by the king during the duel, watching with delight what he does not understand—all these suggest the possibility for healing and renewal at the same time that they deepen the irony of the diseased state: what would we care about Denmark if these innocents were absent? What may we not hope since they are present? A child, not "The Mousetrap" itself, undoes Claudius, and this undoing speaks for some spark of goodness in him. He watches the play unmoved as he sees the "brother . . . nay! nephew to the king," together with the player queen, murder the player king. But when the child enters upstage and points a finger at the murderer, the king is shattered. His tearful struggle for repentance is sincerely passionate, and thus his failure, his willingness to take on again the face of "the smyler with the knife," is all the more tragic. It is not inappropriate for *Hamlet* that the film be dark rather than light, that Denmark be sick rather than healthy. But Lyth, through the mediating force of healthful images, pays due attention to Shakespeare's balance and sanity.

The Characters

The motifs, the images, the spaces, the camera work—all serve Lyth's interpretative purposes, which revolve about the attractions and repulsions among all the characters. It is impossible, in fact, to talk about the stylistic choices without mentioning characterization. Because stylistic choices are subservient to interpretation, they are not, I think, what a viewer notices, particularly. For the viewer is caught up in the characters, imagined to be real people.

As much as he learns about feeling and tone from Kozintsev and Brook, Lyth's interpretative choices suggest that he has read the play without any preconceptions, without depending on traditional ideas. The players are one example of many. Upon their arrival, as a kind of advertisement, they spontaneously mime the dumb show from the play-within-a-play, amusing Polonius in spite of himself and giving Hamlet the idea for *The Murder of Gonzago*. The player is taken aback by Hamlet's request to add speeches, but he recovers his composure. In long shot, intercut with the second unloosing of Ophelia, we see Claudius looking down at Hamlet from a window, seeing him scribbling furiously on several sheets. Later, Hamlet hands these to the players, who are trying to practice and who, like the BBC's players, do not care to listen to his advice. One recalls the humanity of this crew: the lead player declaiming—at Hamlet's request—on Dido; his wife and another player looking concerned, wondering if this stuff is going to get them a job or not; their hug of relief when Hamlet says, " 'Tis well. I'll have thee speak out the rest soon"; and later the cries of their infant and the use of their young son as silent actor in the play—all these offer a rich fullness in their portrayal. Both Bill Cain and Joseph Papp (1982) in their stage productions took care to bring the players to life, but in most productions they are grounded rather than figured. In Lyth's view, the life they have *separates* them from Hamlet; their Bohemian existence, their dependency on patronage and their relation to him would not strike us were they not so fully developed. In a sense, this view of the players as a gritty troop of itinerants complements the view of the theater that Shakespeare provides through the much longer—and often cut—talk between Hamlet and Rosencrantz and Guildenstern.

The play of characters in the graveyard scene is one example of many in which Lyth reads the text as if new, distancing himself about as far as possible from the romantic tradition associated with the pathos of

Stellan Skarsgaard in the Yorick scene of Ragnar Lyth's *Hamlet.* **Photo by Bertil S. Aaberg.** (*Publicity still courtesy Ragnar Lyth.*)

Ophelia's burial. A small group in crude black costumes, seen in long shot, scurries hurriedly with a rough cart over the muddy ground to the grave. It had been pouring as the scene began, and though it has stopped now, the day remains grey. There is no dignity in the burial ritual. Two men remove the cover from the crude, raw pine coffin, the priest says a brief prayer, and Gertrude throws her flower in and hurries off. (Earlier, we recall, Ophelia had thrown herbs at the queen.) Hamlet need not say anything about maimed rites because we see them. His face averted from the scene, he asks Horatio who it is, but Horatio does not know. Not Horatio but Osric had been the gentleman set to watch Ophelia, and earlier, when Ophelia had been looking for Gertrude, Horatio, who was reading his book, had been irritated at her touch. It seems that he has not been intimate enough with Hamlet to know anything about Ophelia. Laertes asks the king, "What ceremony else?" and when he goes unanswered, he asks the priest, who speaks to him quietly enough. Laertes, however, spits in his face, an act that amuses the gravedigger, a man individualized by his responsiveness to others, as we see when he is featured in a closeup or backgrounded in a long shot. He had expressed interest in Hamlet when he heard him speak about Yorick, whose mud-encased skull is different from the smoothly polished skulls of other productions. Hamlet had reached for the dirty skull with a stick that he poked through the nose hole, and he drew the skull close without

touching it. He beckoned the skull with a crooked finger, bringing its
"ear" close to his mouth, and telling it to "get you to my lady's chamber."
Next he marched it forward on the stick, going too far, even for the
irreverent gravedigger, who turned away. As the funeral proceeds,
Laertes, without ranting, kneels next to the coffin. When Laertes fights
with Hamlet, the coffin slips lengthwise into the hole and Ophelia's body
falls, crumpled, into the grave. The horror of this desecration wipes out
any pretty image we may have had of the girl lying peacefully in the
water or in her coffin and comments ironically on Laertes's fighting on
her behalf.

Lyth's Ophelia is more childlike, less culpable, and more interesting
than most Ophelias: in love with Hamlet, she spends her time playing a
pipe, dreaming about her love, and clutching dozens of letters from him
to her bosom. She does not accept with good grace the warnings of her
sweet, shy brother about Hamlet, but hums and looks impatient. Her
counterwarning to him is sarcastic. She has a mind of her own, and
though her stern father does not give her much choice, she tries to be
independent. She is determined to approach the aloof Hamlet in the
first court scene, in the gymnasium. Among the crowds, aware of her
father's disapproval, she nevertheless makes her way to Hamlet, who
rebelliously stands by the window with his back to the proceedings. She
smiles when his hand closes on her letter. A visualization added for her
closet scene (2.1) shows Ophelia being corseted in steel, Hamlet pounding on the locked door, the duenna preventing Ophelia from going to
him, Hamlet then bursting his way in, thrusting the duenna out, poking
disbelievingly at Ophelia's steel corset, grabbing her, being smacked by
her. Confronted then by Polonius who steps between him and Ophelia,
Hamlet throws quills from Polonius's desk spitefully at Ophelia, tweaks
Polonius, who tries to protect her, on the nose, and finally leaves. All this
action is silent, spontaneous, human—far from the studied minuets of
many productions. And it is truer to the implications of the text than
many other versions. Since Polonius has warned her to deny Hamlet
access to her, it remains unclear in several productions that depict the
closet scene how Hamlet enters. Lyth avoids duplicating the text: there is
no miming of the exact words of Ophelia's story to Polonius. And
justifiably so, for to show Ophelia's story is to give it an objectivity it
does not have. After Hamlet runs out, Ophelia has only one line, given
like a lame excuse: "Alas! my lord, I have been so a-frighted!" From
outside her little room, the camera looking in shows Polonius picking up
the letters, which she has tried to hide. He has her take them to the king
and queen, and she, standing shyly by as he reads Hamlet's poem, stirs
with love and longing. Her presence at Polonius's revelation to the king
and queen is integrated into the interpretation—not merely an optional
choice as it is for the few productions that show her there. Hamlet sees

her waiting and then entering the chamber and thus, though he does not overhear the unloosing plot, he weeps with disappointment. He is disgusted but not, after a moment's reflection, surprised. He has a similar reaction when Laertes, in the duel scene, refuses to accept his apology. When Rosencrantz and Guildenstern similarly fail him, the blow is stronger because their defection is more unexpected. Recognizing Ophelia's weakness, he responds almost against his will to the sincerity of her anguished tears when he says "I loved you not." However much he may wish not to, he cannot help but answer with his own embrace. But when he hears the ghost sounds and is therefore prompted to ask her about her father, she cannot admit that he is there spying on them, and Hamlet thrusts her away. Earlier, it was his disappointment in her, mixed with the evident love they share—not an encounter with himself or with the demands of the ghost—that induced the self-destructive rage of the scene in his bedroom, as well as the despair of the "To be" speech (both after 2.1).

Hamlet's complicated persona is built upon many confrontations—those with Ophelia more evident in this production than in most others. After bursting into her room (2.1), in long shot we see him running through the darkened gymnasium. He rips apart his room, tears down books, throws them to the courtyard below (where the servant wonders at the rain of books), pulls down bookcases, and smashes the paintings of the king and queen. Before "To be," before turning the dagger on himself, Hamlet seems ready to use it for attack. Then Hamlet sits looking at his dagger, presses it to his jugular, while the camera dollies closer, like some obscene voyeur, to a closeup. He had stopped himself from violence directed outward, and he has no will to kill himself. He yawns and lies among his books, a high angle shot showing him almost in fetal position among the debris, one book with a cross on its cover. What do all these images mean, we wonder. Despite failure to act, however, Hamlet does not strike one as impotent. Rather, he is dangerous because we never know what he is going to do next; he surprises with every move. Stellan Skarsgaard is magnificent in the role, because he is a Hamlet of tantalizingly complex beauty of mind and soul. And he does it all with an awesome economy, the epitome of acting for the camera.

Because Hamlet is dangerous, his inability to act against Claudius is a shock. Time is not a factor: we are unaware of Hamlet moping about for months. Indeed, his very first opportunity occurs at the prayer scene. Several directors who have thought that Hamlet merely rationalizes his failure to kill Claudius, that he cannot kill Claudius, have somehow demonstrated that it is not a matter of Hamlet's choice. These directors have various schemes for treating Hamlet's blood-thirsty excuses. Lyth follows the advice of G. Wilson Knight, who, of course, proposes that once an interpreter of Shakespeare penetrates the center of a scene's meaning, then any molding of the text to put that interpretation into relief is allowable, indeed desirable. Having made his interpretative choice, Lyth clarifies it by eliminating the rationalization altogether and graphically presenting Hamlet's inability. Since within Hamlet's hearing Claudius says aloud his last lines about his prayers being useless, Hamlet cannot rationalize his failure by his belief that Claudius, killed then, would go immediately to heaven. Claudius sees Hamlet (wearing the clown mask) with dagger raised and more or less dares Hamlet to strike, bares his chest to him, so to speak, yet Hamlet does not do it. Moments later, Hamlet kills Polonius, but virtually by accident; he looks in surprise at the blood on his dagger and he "weeps for what is done." Again, when Hamlet says farewell to the king with his mother present, he draws a bystander's sword and could easily kill Claudius, though the king hides behind some others who are also cowering. Since almost everyone in the crowded room is intent on saving himself or herself, and because the two guards of Claudius lack nobility of bearing, it is obvious that Hamlet could easily kill the king with little interference. But he does not. Nevertheless, this Hamlet does not appear weak; as I have said, he is a dangerous man.

Hamlet's failure to kill Claudius during two opportunities is unexpected not only because this Hamlet does not appear weak, but because we cannot account for the failure by the usual means. The inscription for the first part of the production is drawn from Hamlet's rhyme in act 1: "The time is out of joint. O cursed spite, that ever I was born to set it right." While this declares a reluctance to act, it does not clarify why. There is nothing in his essential nature or condition to explain it. Lyth does not obviously draw upon the Freudian interpretation because nothing suggests that Hamlet identifies with Claudius or loves his mother excessively.[9] Hamlet is more defiant than melancholy. He is, however, mentally unstable, as the frequent sound effects of madness (in 2.2, 3.1, 3.4, and more) imply. Like the Jacobi Hamlet's madness, however, his is a madness that does not explain anything because it does not preclude action. What is certain is that he does love Ophelia, that his father's death and mother's remarriage have rocked his inner being, that he rejects the corrupt life of the court, that he is a man of keen intellect and sensibility, that he feels terribly alone—for Horatio is far from his equal in intellect or spirit—and that he is not willingly a violent man. Though this Hamlet is difficult to pin down—because Lyth does not pluck out the heart of his mystery and because any definition is inadequate due to his complexity—he is, I believe, a pacifist on principle, if not by nature.

Hamlet recognizes in himself the ungovernable rage and passions that in others lead to murder, and he chooses to wrench himself out of that groove. His speeches castigating himself for inaction are very much cut:

he says only a few lines from "O what a rogue and peasant slave am I" and even then he says them to the bewildered Horatio—not as a soul-baring soliloquy. His soliloquy after seeing Fortinbras's soldiers is drawn from the last six lines (4.4.60–66), and thus it is both a comment on the futility of violence as well as a pledge to revenge. (Finally, with the last lines of the soliloquy, he does promise himself that his thoughts will be bloody, and perhaps he has indeed convinced himself that he should avenge his father's death.) At the graveside, he kneels next to Laertes, not challenging him by action or verbal abuse, and then simply defends himself vigorously from Laertes's attack. Their verbal exchange occurs after they grapple. At the duel, after being stung by the unbated rapier on his posterior, which he had mockingly extended towards Laertes, in disgust he scratches Laertes's face with the point, obviously with no intention to kill him. Certainly, he has changed when he returns to the court, but what he intends is far from certain. By showing Claudius's treasonous commission, Hamlet exerts himself to justify to Horatio quitting Claudius "with this arm." And when Hamlet looks at Claudius in the last scene, cold danger shines from his eyes. With the drawn sword at the leavetaking (4.3), he had cut one of his locks of hair and dropped it on his mother's lap. When we next see him, his shaggy, unkempt hair has been hacked close to the scalp, his face is brown and rugged, and he is somehow older, more cynical, with psychic wounds less raw and open. He jokes now like a man who cannot see much humor in anything, but has no choice except to laugh. From sardonic rebelliousness, he has come not to serene but to sardonic acceptance.

But Hamlet's brutal killing of Claudius at the end takes us and the king by surprise; it is as if once Hamlet unleashes his rage and resentment, he cannot keep it in check at all. He cannot kill the king a little. Some of that fury had shown itself in the nunnery scene—when he barely restrains his violence against Ophelia and she subsides into passivity like a helpless rabbit in the mouth of a dog—and again in Gertrude's closet, when he almost throttles his mother. The actual killing of the king, the bloodiness, the relentless savagery of the attack confirms Hamlet's suppressed brutality. The overwhelmingly ugly images of blood also deny the audience any feeling of contentment at Claudius's death; we are prevented from feeling anything but revulsion. Lyth will not allow us to gloat at revenge. He thus sides with Hamlet against violence. But neither does he blame Hamlet for giving in, finally, because he makes Claudius's response grotesque. The king continues to smile and try to charm his adversary and his court, even when having obviously been dealt several mortal blows. The king smiles and smiles; a cough of blood sprays Hamlet's face, tainting him, just as Claudius's vomit had tainted Gertrude, Polonius, and Rosencrantz and Guildenstern. As before, the courtiers cringe against the wall, unable to muster enough conviction to support their king: cowardice is general and endemic. Hamlet does not exult in his deed; Horatio does not try to follow Hamlet; Hamlet does not sit on the throne; nor does he pass the throne on to Fortinbras; Horatio says no "Good night, sweet prince"; Hamlet, his head dangling close to the floor, is carried out unceremoniously by four men quick-marching, Horatio alone watching. The ending, then, is ignominious, antiromantic. Hamlet has not accomplished much by acting against his pacifist principles.

As in any production of the play, Hamlet's characterization is the centerpiece. But in a thoroughly seamless production like Lyth's, one in which every aspect contributes to the whole, many choices, from simple to grand, contribute to the overall effect.

Lyth is a master of properties and artifacts, several of them especially significant for the characterization of Gertrude and Claudius. The copulation scene begins with a view of mannequins, to symbolize empty vanity, as in Kozintsev's film. Before Polonius speaks to the king and queen about his daughter, closeups show them being dressed in the panoply of vanity: the queen's headpiece, her rings, the king's rings. Point-of-view closeups of both Claudius and Gertrude show their loving regard for their jewels. The closet scene is full of mirrors, distorted and true, whole and fragmented. Wavy mirrors in their room mean vanity and falşity, for the king and queen prepare their faces and bodies for the mirror view. Mirrors can expose as well as hide reality: after the play-within-a-play Hamlet thrusts a footlight into Claudius's face so that the king can see himself in its torch-lit, mirrored surface, and Hamlet holds a mirror over the supine Gertrude to show her what she really is (3.4). It is in this latter mirror that we see the killing of Polonius. Just after, the mirror falls and shatters, an apt symbol of the calamities that must follow this killing. Hamlet rips a strand of jewels from her neck and the headpiece from her head, exposing the unbeautiful truth. Hamlet himself cares nothing for surface appearance, as is evident from his monklike room. His sloppiness of dress and of hair has as much to do with an aversion to false show as to madness. At the end, for the duel, he wears the same tattered and filthy garments that he wears on his return to Elsinore: there has been no hiatus, no pause, from the beginning of the last act to the end. These garments serve an antiromantic naturalism. Costume is among Lyth's many convincingly manipulated, nonverbal signals in this work.

All his added visualizations are, like Kozintsev's, nonverbal; for example, Hamlet's confrontation with the duenna, Ophelia, and Polonius (equivalent to Ophelia's closet scene). But many Shakespearean scenes also include unexpected moments of silence. In the first court scene, Hamlet says nothing until his first soliloquy—and keeps his back to the camera, looking out of a window, away from Elsinore, until his mother speaks to him. There is very little dialogue as Rosencrantz and Guildenstern first enter before the king and queen, summoned by the scribe's bell. Laertes says nothing during or after the first mad scene. Polonius says almost nothing during the fishmonger scene, which begins with Hamlet eating a page of sheet music and ends with him playing a cello upside down. With no willow speech, Gertrude silently drops a soaked cloth before Laertes, who responds wordlessly. Silence is in itself a meaningful sign, first Hamlet's, but ultimately that of others as well. These nonverbal minutes are different, however, from the silence of Kurosawa's *Throne of Blood,* where characters are silent because words are not their best way to express themselves. In Lyth's work, characters, especially Hamlet, are capable of speaking but *choose* silence. Uncomfortable silences make one uneasy; Hamlet's silence certainly troubles Claudius.

So too these silences contribute to our anxiety as audience. While at times we can decipher the character's feelings without words—so sensitive are the acting, the sounds, the properties, the lighting, and the camera—silence can enhance ambiguity. The ghost's silence mystifies in the closet scene, for we do not understand its purpose. Silence deepens Gertrude's opacity, for we simply do not know what she is thinking. Only a few moments reveal the essential woman: she screams a real scream, a most unrestrained cry for help, when Hamlet threatens her on her bed. She drinks off the poison determinedly, pulling (in closeup) the cup from the king's hands, desperate, it seems, to win Hamlet back. For Hamlet, with cold, unforgiving stares, rejects her completely at the end, backing off from her extended handkerchief, not reacting at all when she kisses him and shaking his head. Her self-sacrificing gesture in drinking the wine is ineffectual, however, because he does not even approach her body after she dies. Her first concern had ever been appearances—that everything look all right. Putting on her gracious smile, she seemed as uneasy with Rosencrantz and Guildenstern as they were with her, a disarmingly human trait. Yet, she is capable of playing a part; duplicity is so much the nature of Elsinore that we cannot trust her. Thinking Hamlet loves Ophelia, Gertrude approaches her, all smiling condescension, and leads the girl away (2.2). Later, when Ophelia is positioned for Hamlet's discovery (3.1), we note that like Gertrude she is made up with rouge and scarlet lips. If Polonius is the pimp, then Gertrude is the madam, introducing a novice to the profession. Seeing Hamlet's subsequent reaction to Ophelia, and interpreting it as unloving, Gertrude turns her back on Ophelia. If Ophelia cannot be used as a tool, she is not a person at all. Ophelia, stung but proud, lifts her chin and hurries away. We follow the result of her indoctrination by Gertrude into the use of makeup: after being tossed about in a wild crowd, after her excitement at Hamlet's manic exuberance following the play-within-a-play, Ophelia runs laughing to her room. Her look changes when she sees herself in a mirror; she begins wiping the color from her lips—just as Hamlet in the nunnery scene had wiped away the color ("God hath given you one face and you make yourselves another"). Her madness is reflected in her continual effort to wipe away the color. Not Polonius's death at the hands of her lover, but her own alliance with her lover's enemies against him, however innocently and open-heartedly she allows herself to be used, contributes to her madness. Gertrude's use of her is the primary cause of Ophelia's madness and of our negative response to this complex queen.

Gertrude's mystery rests in part on her changeability and unreadability. When Hamlet accuses her with his words "as kill a king," she seems nervous rather than surprised. After Hamlet's burst of anger in the closet scene, he pulls the queen down on the floor and lays his head on her lap. Tentatively, she reaches her hand down to his head, then pulls it away: she cannot be affectionate with him. Moments later, Gertrude, disheveled but unconcerned about her strange appearance (this from a queen most concerned about appearances), seeks out the king, who is now fully recovered from his anguish after the play and, all smiles, flirts with a lady-in-waiting. Gertrude strokes his cheek: the hand that could not soothe Hamlet can soothe Claudius. But just then he rejects her, pushing her hand away abruptly. It is a moment of truth for her, and she never returns to him again, though he tries to draw her to him later, after Ophelia's mad scene and before Laertes's entrance. Still, she steps between him and Laertes, saying, "But not by him." Having recoiled from Claudius (4.1), she nevertheless does not turn immediately to Hamlet. When Hamlet enters just before he leaves for England (4.3), she barely looks at him, and in fact averts her head when he speaks to the king about the one flesh of man and wife. She is as frightened as anyone when he draws a sword out of a bystander's scabbard. In that public scene, she does not shrink from the king's purposeful touch as she will later when they are alone, but she opens her eyes wide in surprise.[10] Just as Olivier symbolizes the separation of king and queen by the divided stairway they ascend, Lyth has two paintings of the king and queen that had been hanging facing each other over the head of Hamlet's childlike, narrow bed. In his rage after Ophelia's betrayal, he had torn them down and smashed them. When Ophelia is in the room after Hamlet has left for England, a medium shot shows it emptied of all effects except the paintings on the wall, the two portraits now facing away from each other. A closeup reveals the repair to his mother's visage, the tear on the queen's forehead now crudely pasted together—the hidden blister on the fair forehead made apparent to all. But the queen is not totally evil; certainly her mystery precludes any single response to her.

Claudius is as much an enigma as she is, with his persistent smiling and his mood changes. He enjoys the children—whose they are being unclear. In the prayer scene, he asks with believable sincerity if one may "be pardon'd and retain the offence?" His tears then and also after Ophelia's first mad scene seem sincere. Yet moments later, when Laertes enters, he affects a calm that completely shatters Laertes's resolve. At the duel, he does not comport himself with sufficient aplomb: his eagerness to have Hamlet drink off the poisoned wine makes both Horatio and the queen suspicious. And his final effort to pretend that all is well is bewildering.

Gestures of impatience and irritation mark the behavior of both king and queen—a nonheroic motif in the production. Their spying having proved wrong Polonius's theory about Hamlet's madness, the king rudely pushes the old councillor. The king thrusts aside the herb Ophelia has given him and snatches Laertes's also, throwing it down. The queen, with a similar grimace of distaste, tries to push Ophelia away from her in the first mad scene. In the closet scene, the queen hits the hand of the lady trying to help her off with her jewels. Those who can afford to, reveal their pique; those who cannot, hide it. But these gestures simply remove these characters from the realm of archetypal evil; their defects of character seem totally trivial.

Like the king and queen, neither Polonius, nor Laertes, nor Rosencrantz and Guildenstern are altogether bad sorts. And neither is anyone totally a good sort. Polonius weeps on Laertes's chest when his son leaves; in his own way, he loves his family. Laertes is a beautiful young man; his youth and inexperience much excuse him. Besides, Lyth omits the details of the scheme against Hamlet (from 4.7), and though a closeup shows a hand wiping a substance on the unbated point of a rapier, and though we assume it is Laertes's, we cannot with certainty identify it. The two childhood friends of Hamlet are uncomfortable to the very end in their role as Claudius's helpers; in the last view of them, they reluctantly accept the scrolled commission from Claudius's hands (4.3). Their original nature is apparent in their relationship to Hamlet, who is joyful to see them; the actions of the three express familiarity and strong feeling. Hamlet, in an ironic manner, kisses Guildenstern on the lips when they lead him to Claudius (4.2), an allusion to their early and now lost friendship. Their alignment with Claudius stems from their poverty and their eagerness to please whoever can help them. Thus we cannot completely agree with Hamlet's description to Horatio of their love for their employment. In contrast to this initial response to Rosencrantz and Guildenstern, Hamlet is at first suspicious of Horatio. When Hamlet sees him, he asks "Horatio?" in the tone of one who vaguely recalls someone he has known slightly. He questions Horatio closely and suspiciously about his reasons for coming to Elsinore. Horatio, as he stands by faithfully, proves himself to Hamlet, winning Hamlet's praise about his nature. Still, he is one of the more ineffectual Horatios in moving images. Given by Hamlet, seconds before his death, the commission that proves Claudius's conspiracy with Rosencrantz and Guildenstern, Horatio is not able to make anyone listen to him. He jumps on a billiard table, he tries to speak to the unhearing—but the film ends with his face, wondering, chagrined, defeated. By ending with this everyday image, the face of a man who cannot make himself heard, Lyth puts a very human and nonromantic stamp on the production.

Lyth's *Hamlet* converts most of Shakespeare's language into persuasive images of the characters and their conflicts; through the artifice of frame manipulation (locale, scope, duration, juxtaposition), Lyth elicits the viewer's willing suspension of disbelief, the acceptance, in other words, of those images as representative of a compelling world that is neither romantic in spite of romantic elements, nor Brechtian in spite of cruel elements, but whole and complex. If he scants Shakespeare's verse, he does not ignore the poetry. Though the film's ending does not leave one exalted, it nevertheless sharpens one's sense of Hamlet's human potential—"in action how like an angel, in apprehension how like a god: the beauty of the world"—subverted by the events that overtake him. We are moved by the waste, the promise shattered. An artist can win assent to his or her world view, even if it contradicts the audience's view. That is, audiences can be led to cheer what they would in life deplore. However we as individuals feel about what Hamlet should or should not have done to reach the highest human state, Lyth makes us regret the alternative that his Hamlet set aside, the opportunity to abjure revenge. Lyth's *Hamlet* is both humane and tough.

The BBC production and the Swedish production mark the poles of television production—the one wedded to the studio set as analogue to stage set, the other committed to a more filmic approach. A hybrid of film and stage, television can accommodate itself to productions that concentrate on its verbal or visual elements. Viable reworkings of the play—for example, the Richardson, the BBC, and the Lyth—demonstrate that there need not be any one way for television. The tragedy and Hamlet's character can be served whether the director bows to television's imperative of the closeup and to its poor resolution, or ignores both and treats it essentially as a film medium. The success or failure of a production does not depend on the director's consenting to or rebelling against the perceived restrictions of the medium. Creative directors persistently use limitations to strengthen their art: each one becomes not a restriction but a challenge to genius. In a mere thirty years of television history, there have been one or two outstanding *Hamlet*s and three or four creditable versions. With such plenitude, it would be ungracious to scant one version in favor of another; we can be grateful we have all of them. None alone can exhaust the possibilities of *Hamlet;* all together they explore more of those possibilities than could be dreamt of in our philosophy.

Notes

1. Lyth, in a telephone conversation, said that he admired the Kozintsev film. He seems to use Kozintsev as a model for his style rather than for the Russian's interpretation, which was shaped by East European politics. Certainly, Kozintsev influenced Lyth's choice to cut speeches rather than characters. Reynaldo and the second gravedigger are the only important ones cut. Lyth includes, in some form, every one of *Hamlet*'s twenty scenes. For a comparison of Lyth's version with Kozintsev's, see *SFNL*, April 1987: 1. I wish to thank WNYC-TV for allowing me to screen the videotape.

2. A flawed moment in the film can illustrate what I mean. When two servants lift the cover of Ophelia's coffin and then wait there for Laertes to prevent them from covering her, they are actors "playing the result" rather than living persons who don't know what is going to happen next.

3. Lyth, in a telephone conversation, stressed this influence.

4. Lyth worked on the storyboard, the sketches of frames, with John Olsson, the photographer.

5. Though the camera frequently *is* Hamlet, two notable examples might be mentioned: in 1.2, after his heady conversation with Claudius, Laertes looks out with a smile toward the camera (Hamlet), and the smile fades. In the last scene, when Hamlet enters for the duel, the camera (Hamlet) approaches and brushes by the obsequious king.

6. Long takes are important in film too, however, especially in the work of Welles. See, for example, his kitchen scene in *The Magnificent Ambersons,* where long takes and deep focus photography are used to brilliant effect. Generalizations about the *nature* of film are overturned by artists who push against film's apparent restrictions. See Panofsky.

7. Both rooms, however, were found in the same seventeenth-century castle, north of Stockholm.

8. A press release from WNYC describes the Swedish press reaction in an article by Ana-Maria Narti from the magazine *L'Art Du Theatre,* no. 1 (1985), translated into English by Mimmi von Troil, STV 1.

9. I suppose the Freudian interpretation could be argued. After Hamlet pulls Gertrude down to the floor following the ghost's departure, he bangs his head into her lap. One could interpret this as a suppressed sex act. However, his gesture could also be interpreted as his anger about her sexuality.

10. Shrinking from Claudius is another repeated motif: first Hamlet (in 1.2), then Rosencrantz (in 4.2), and finally Gertrude (in 4.3) shrink from Claudius's touch.

Part III

Silent Films and Sound Recordings: "The eye of man hath not heard, the ear of man hath not seen"

The anachronistic turn to silent films in this section announces that I am not interested in these merely as historical documents. Though historical development and influence from silent to sound film are certain, the paths are not sharply etched from the 1913 *Hamlet* to the 1948 *Hamlet* but are traceable in many non-Shakespearean films that cannot be considered in this study. The turn here to sound recordings may be just as puzzling as the turn to silent films, for not many scholars think of these when they consider Shakespeare in performance; an exception is Bernard Beckerman, who, as director of the National Endowment for the Humanities Institute on Shakespeare in Performance at the Folger Shakespeare Library in 1982, compared several sound recordings to identify and study performance choices.

The two incomplete forms, sight without sound and sound without sight, belong together, and from each we can discern much that will enrich our perception of whole forms. Each has its conventions and devices to overcome the limitations of the medium, and whenever a production has to reach beyond its limits to present Shakespeare, something can be learned from the effort—about the medium and about Shakespeare performance. Furthermore, silent films and sound recordings sometimes preserve the artistry of important actors: Forbes Robertson, Orson Welles, John Barrymore, and Richard Burton—among many others. In addition, by providing examples of perform-

225

ances each with one very important factor missing—the voice, the person—silent films and sound recordings reveal what is important in full performances. Ultimately I include them because they demonstrate yet again the links among stage and media performances.[1]

Since silent films are unavailable for general viewing because only specialized archives have them, I describe three silent films in detail. Two fragments from the Museum of Modern Art (MOMA) begin the topic in chapter 13; in chapter 14, Forbes Robertson's 1913 film, as a good representation of film's early phase, concludes the discussion. It was made before D. W. Griffith revolutionized film practice with closeups and crosscuts, and especially with matchcuts—all the subtle transitions of *The Birth of a Nation* (1915). Since sound recordings are available in the form of discs and tapes at many sound archives and public libraries or even for purchase, after discussing general principles of audio performance in chapter 15, I limit my discussion, in chapter 16, to three particular Hamlets, rather than describe full productions.

Note

1. For a contrasting view of the value of silent film, see Jorgens, 1.

14

Early Silent Films

In some ways we can never revisit the territory of the silent film. We cannot go back to a state of innocence, of awe before the novelty, to naive appreciation of the moving shadows before us. We cannot see these films emotionally as they were seen in 1907, 1910, or 1913. Nor can we see them physically as they were seen. For the most part we see them alone, sitting before Steenbeck editors in cramped rooms of archival collections, without the all-important breathing audience around us to stimulate and authenticate our response. We also miss the music (often full orchestra music like, for example, sixty musicians for the Asta Nielsen *Hamlet*), music that tells us we are to feel pity for Ophelia, amusement at Polonius, sympathy for Gertrude, disdain for Rosencrantz and Guildenstern.[1] We seldom see the films at the speeds at which they were intended to be shown (faster speeds causing the well-known jumpiness of the silents), and we cannot see them in their crisp purity of sharp blacks and whites, with intact frames and accurately placed titles.

Since it is observably easier to make a short, silent *Hamlet* into a parody or farce than to create a serious work meriting serious concern, Robert Ball unsurprisingly lists many Shakespearean spoofs among the silent films he discusses. Yet a few silent films do produce credible Shakespeare. These are not wholly lacking in verbal elements, for most silent versions depended on an audience aware of and familiar with the words and able to anticipate at least the famous lines, offered by title or suggested by mime. Moreover, while we cannot *hear* the actors, we can see that they sometimes speak, sometimes remain silent just as they do in aural films. Still, silent films clarify actors' resources when they are stripped of what can be their chief ornament, the voice. Without voice, admittedly the lifeblood of the play, the serious performance releases for

227

our immediate perception the effects on interpretation of nonverbal elements. These films also urge us to supply what is missing, for truly *silent* films (as they are when we view them today without music) are the least passive of all entertainments.

They force us to discern meaning from actors' gestures, body language, and business, from costume and setting. The films preserve at least these nonverbal elements in the performances of actors who otherwise would be known only by the imperfect vocabularies of impressionistic adulation or criticism. By examining these performances *with* the words contemporaries used to describe the performances, we can see that our present conceptions of naturalness differ from former conceptions. We would not be likely to apply the term "natural" to Forbes Robertson or even to John Barrymore—as did their contemporaries. Silent films complete the history of visual representation of *Hamlet;* by looking at film versions spanning eighty years, by noting what is filmlike and what is theaterlike in early moving pictures, we can better grasp the relationship between these two media.

When I consider a play-length artifact, intuitively I recognize that not everything can be encompassed in an analysis. I choose, sometimes unconsciously, to make limited sense out of a whole too rich with meanings for complete discussion. When I come across a short work, however, I am tempted to think that its totality can somehow be understood, analyzed, and put to work for the study as a whole. When, however, it took me two hours to view a six-minute film—and then without absorbing everything—I realized with stunning force how selective I must be in talking about these works, with the inevitable distortions that arise from selection.

Also, to describe even some of the aspects of a particular image takes many times as long as for that image to flash by. This is not surprising, considering the number of pages that can be written about a still photograph or painting, but the difference between the moving and still image is that the latter sits there and thus remains as a test of the words. The moving picture image is, in contrast, falsified in some way by the discrepancy between the number of minutes needed to read the words about the image and the number of split seconds the image is actually in place before the retina. And it does not remain there for testing, but is put back into the can, back on the archive shelf. I feel that I am in Laurence Sterne's predicament in *Tristram Shandy* when I try to deal with this problem: trying to describe what each character is doing, what the setting looks like, where the camera is, I feel that I am caught in an excruciatingly slow-motion film, violating the pace that is film's essence.

Both silent *Hamlet*s under discussion rely on intertitles,[2] but they demonstrate the power of the camera (the cinematic CINES) and of the actor (the static LUX production) to transcend the limits of titles and of

CINES *Hamlet*. Hamlet enters reading as Ophelia sits with the king, queen, and Polonius.

film length. Very short, no more than five or six minutes long, these silent films offer someone's notion of an essential *Hamlet*.

To the title writer of the CINES *Hamlet* ("Amleto"), which may be the 1908 version described by a reviewer quoted by Robert Ball (97) or a CINES 1910 version, plot was primary because all three titles (in German) summarize content: "Ophelia's Madness," "Ophelia's Death," "The Challenge" ("*Der Wahnsinn der Ophelia*," "*Ophelia's [sic] Tod*," "*Die [H]erausforderung*"). As we would expect, then, the film stresses action more than psychology. The order establishes the interpretation. After a brief overture,[3] the film begins with the nunnery scene (where Hamlet's anger transmutes into love), continues with Horatio's disclosure and the ghost's revelation, introduces the players, followed by the play, then the closet scene with the murder of Polonius leading to the one mad scene and Ophelia's death, and ends with the graveside scene (the duel scene missing)—in all, nine "scenes" and fourteen settings. This is no vacillating Hamlet but one who as soon as possible tests the ghost by arranging for the play, who loves Ophelia, who tries to kill Claudius the first chance he gets (in his mother's closet) and again when he sees him at the graveside, who in fact has his sword drawn during the play scene, except that Claudius gets away in the crowd before Hamlet acts. This is not a dreamy, philosophic Hamlet, though he does spend a few moments shaking his head over the skull. Nor is he a witty Hamlet. He does, it seems to me, express Hamlet's power, for violence just below the surface can bubble up easily. He is a passionate Hamlet.

As befits this sturdy Hamlet, Claudius too can be a strong character. In the graveside scene, for example, Hamlet leaps into the grave, expressing his love for Ophelia, and jumps out again, not to fight Laertes, who had not leapt into the grave, but to get at Claudius. Blocking has the king dominate frame center as Hamlet is restrained on the right and Laertes, who had been moving towards Hamlet, is restrained on the left. The two men are taken off, but the king exits with dignity. Since this scene ends the fragment (the duel scene would evidently have shown Hamlet's killing of Claudius after both he and Laertes are mortally wounded), our last impression is of a strong Claudius. He and Hamlet are indeed mighty opposites.

Though, compared to the second MOMA silent *Hamlet,* most of the CINES' conversations are difficult to interpret through gestures, the film's grasp of camera technique is impressive, especially if it truly does come from 1908 or 1910, as seems likely—D. W. Griffith made his first film, about the same length as the CINES film, in 1908. In indoor locations the Italian director (possibly Mario Caserini, according to notes at MOMA) sometimes composed asymmetrical shots, a dynamic arrangement different from the static symmetrical compositions of most silent films of this period. Outdoors, where early film directors were always more free, his panning and tracking camera in the players' scene shows architectural features that imitate effectively the grandeur and expansiveness of a castle, and, most astonishing of all, two or more settings for a single scene.

The disclosure scene begins with Hamlet standing at a waterfall. Two friends come to tell him that they have just seen something (pointing off frame). Pushing them off when they try to stop him, Hamlet dashes in the direction they have pointed. Now, with a straight cut, the director shows us Hamlet, closely followed by the two friends, in a field. The high-angle shot at extreme long distance gives the setting its full dimension. His back to the camera, Hamlet waves the two away, forbidding them to follow, and as they hang back, the camera pans left to exclude them, with Hamlet approaching a stream. On the other side stands the transparent ghost, which beckons and moves off.[4] Hamlet crosses the stream to follow. Now an abrupt cut (probably caused by missing transitional frames, and curiously disjunctive in its effect) reveals in close long shot (that is, full-length figures fill the frame) the inset orchard scene of the murder of Hamlet's father, showing his mother's full complicity. A cut away from this shows the same scene in a long shot that now includes Hamlet in a rocky setting looking at the projected image of the poisoning, in which the king has fallen to the ground. Thus the two scenes— equivalent to 1.2.160–255, 1.4, and 1.5—use five settings, counting as

CINES *Hamlet.* **In long shot we see the vision and Hamlet watching it, as the ghost stands by.**

two the inset and the larger scene in which it appears. The use of painted scenery for the projected inset, unlike the natural setting of the exterior where Hamlet watches, suggests that the inset is the ghost's construct. It effectively raises a question about the inset's objective reality, just as in the text the ghost's narration could raise such a question.

The play-within-a-play repeats analogically the ghost's narration.[5] Through two camera distances, that is, close long shot and distant long shot, the CINES director points up the parallelism. The shot of the inner stage corresponds to the shot of the poisoning inset, and the whole view of the audience and players corresponds to the larger view of Hamlet's rapt attention to the poisoning scene. The setting for the poisoning inset is the same as the painted scenery for the play-within-a-play (no doubt an economy measure, but no matter: it has its effect regardless of the motive); costume and even King Hamlet's position match in the two scenes. (In contrast, the play-within-a-play in the Forbes Robertson film is as "real" in setting as the film itself, much as if the style of the Pyrrhus speech or of *The Murder of Gonzago* were the same as the style of the rest of the play.) These similarities are effective: they demonstrate how closely Hamlet followed the ghost's story in his attempt to shame Claudius and Gertrude. Yet differences in the enactments also express Hamlet's individual understanding of the event. In the ghost's vision, Gertrude smiles as she is embraced by Claudius, then leaves before he turns to the sleeping king. There is no doubt about her knowledge of

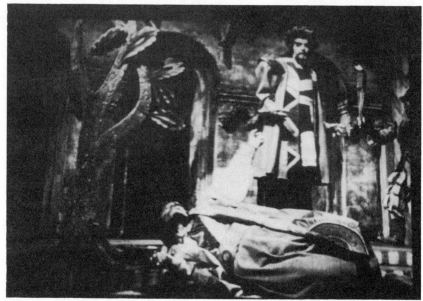

The Olivier *Hamlet*. Like the CINES version, the play-within-a-play mirrors the ghost's vision. The dying player king raises an accusatory finger, just as the king had in Hamlet's vision of the murder. *(Still courtesy Janus Films.)*

what Claudius intends, but she plays no active role. In the play-within-a-play, however, the Player Queen enters, makes sure that her husband is sleeping, motions the murderer to come on, then clasps his hand before he motions her to go off. This is presented in long shot so that we can see Hamlet unsheathing his sword as he watches. After a shift to a close long shot that excludes all but the players, Lucianus pours the poison into the king's ear, then grasps his lapels together, quite pleased, as if to say, "Well, that's done." The camera returns to extreme long shot. The play's structure, with extreme long shot, then close long shot, then extreme long shot again, is the mirror image of the inset's structure.

The filmmaker achieves powerful characterizations through the two views within one scene. At the center of the play, "The Mousetrap" often provides a crucial picture of Hamlet's character. In this scene in the CINES film, Hamlet's rapt attention (parallel to his attention to the poisoning scene), partially conveyed through the intensification of the image with the close long shot, shows that his own version of the murder of his father so mesmerizes him that he fails to do what his drawn sword suggests he intends to do to Claudius. When the camera cuts to an extreme long shot again after the close long shot, *we* see Claudius's reaction and Horatio's reaction to the king, but Hamlet's intent regard is on the stage. This Hamlet (like Fechter, Sullivan, Tree, and others) holds the manuscript of the play and (like Fechter) throws the sheets up in the air, a metaphor of failed action, as the king runs off followed by all the court.[6] The scene ends with one brief exultant gesture by Hamlet, fists held up to head level, then stretched out. This Hamlet knows what he wants to do but does not acknowledge the opportunity he has just missed.

This film also breaks free of silent film's self-imposed rule of one setting for each scene in another way. For the closet scene, the producer arranged two adjacent rooms, an arras separating them. Delicate gothic molding in the first contrasts with sturdier gothic molding in the second room, evidently Claudius's room. At first the film shows only the queen's closet, where the queen is praying, her back to the camera (a substitution for Claudius's prayer scene and an interpretation suggesting her guilt). Hamlet points to the portrait on the wall and then gestures towards the ghost, which appears at far left for a few seconds. Then the camera pans right to include a portion of the second room, showing Claudius urging Polonius to listen through the arras separating the two rooms, then exiting. Thus, though Gertrude shares the blame for King Hamlet's death, on Claudius rests the onus for Polonius's death. Hearing something, Hamlet stands poised, ready with his sword. After Hamlet kills Polonius, Hamlet and his mother enter the adjacent room through the arras, see whom Hamlet has killed, and then exit, thus ending the closet scene (3.4). After the camera pans right sufficiently to exclude the first

CINES *Hamlet*. **The mad scene.**

CINES *Hamlet*. An interpolated scene of Ophelia's madness.

CINES *Hamlet*. Hamlet with the skull of Yorick.

room, Ophelia enters from an upstage doorway for a newly visualized non-Shakespearean scene which might be called "the discovery of the body and the beginning of Ophelia's madness." The film thus uses a moving camera to introduce a changing setting for one scene and a related setting for its new scene, so that cause (Claudius's manipulations) and effect (Ophelia's madness) are neatly juxtaposed.

The next two scenes also use setting effectively, though the camera remains stationary. Ophelia's mad scene is an interior/exterior shot, a salon that leads into a garden. The king and queen and then Laertes cannot stop Ophelia from laughing and tossing flowers around. She is dressed now in a loose gown (like Gertrude Elliott in the Forbes Robertson film) and her long hair is free. As they exit forward out of the frame, she backs out of the open door, outside. Hamlet enters and sees her as she exits. Hamlet, who has not left Elsinore, blames Claudius for Ophelia's pitiable state, for he makes a gesture of defiance towards the king. He then muses with one hand on his elbow, the other on his chin, a gesture not completed before the next title appears. With a cut to the exterior, Ophelia's scene continues. She walks near a stream, happily strewing flowers on the ground, a futile action that well expresses her distraction. We do not see her fall into the water.

The graveside scene, in contrast to the other exterior shots, appears to be studio-shot—again with stationary camera. As was traditional in many stage productions, the setting is moonlit, the backdrop painted, and everything looks artificial—brick wall, monuments, crosses, and all. The setting indicates that the filmmaker still connected film and stage, regardless of how free he had been in the earlier scenes. The gravediggers, at the end, merely suggest the filling of the grave by moving dirt around a little. Interestingly, as in the disclosure scene, Horatio seems to be divided into two equal characters. This simplifies matters for the silent film because the two of them together can indicate their concern for Hamlet more easily than one character could. Having two Horatios, however, also diminishes him—though one does appear alone with Hamlet when Hamlet greets the players and also at the play-within-a-play. In fact, this inconsistency also diminishes the Horatio character and affects our perception of Hamlet; it is as if Hamlet has several friends rather than one—with all that implies.

Within these scenes, and in this clear, straighforward interpretation, many interesting things happen. The titles, not of course the original ones but titles for a German audience, tell us someone's view of the film, and for that person it seems that Ophelia was most important, for two of the three titles refer to her (her madness and her death), and the third introduces her burial. This view is justified to an extent by the film's structure, which begins with Ophelia (with Claudius, Gertrude and Polonius) just before the nunnery scene and ends with her burial. Of the nine scenes, she appears in five, while in contrast, in Shakespeare's text, she appears in six of twenty. (Interestingly enough, the reviewer quoted by Ball mentions her only once, briefly.)

With her dark, long, braided hair, denoting youth and innocence, and her white form-fitting dress, she is a beautiful Ophelia. She loves Hamlet. In their first scene, she has the strength to resist his angry passion, his rough embrace, pushing him away forcibly with her two hands on his shoulders. Why he is angry with her is not clear, except that her cozy fraternization with the king and queen just before Hamlet entered, reading, may have upset him. His mother had lowered her head in dismay at his strange behavior—a sign that he has before this behaved madly—before the ghost's disclosure. Since in this version they remain to greet him and then exit, Hamlet sees them and makes a deprecatory gesture. Ophelia hangs back to see him (this is her own idea: there is no spying). After his rough embrace, she is loving and forgiving when he apologizes, falling to his knees and kissing her hands. With some hesitation she gives him something pinned to her dress. She could be returning his gift to her, but his response seems to show that this is a gift from her to him, for he accepts it passionately, kissing it, kissing his hands to her as she leaves. She is dignified, with an erect, noble carriage and a soulful face. Only her depiction of her early madness leaves something to be desired. After discovering and weeping over the dead body of Polonius, she shakes her arms mechanically to suggest hysterical laughter. In her next mad scene, portraying madness as giggling joy, she has her body movement under better control. Kozintsev too views Ophelia as escaping through madness from her intolerable existence to happiness. Still, the CINES Ophelia's madness is one-dimensional. At her burial, however, semi-reclining in repose with hands folded, she is the proper object of the court's sorrow.

MOMA has two other short silent *Hamlet*s with imperfect identification, but it is certain that a three-minute version marked in the cardfile "Ruggeri Version" and another six-minute one, marked "Lux," directed by "Gerard Bourgeois?" are fragments of the same film.[7] There are no identifying marks on either film. The three-minute version starts with the arrival of the players (2.2) and continues with the immediate aftermath of the play-within-a-play. The longer one begins with the disclosure (1.2.160–255), continues with the vigil (1.4) and the ghost's revelation about the poisoning (1.5), interpolates a scene between Hamlet and Ophelia, leading into her scene with Polonius and Laertes (1.3). This action culminates in Polonius's betrayal of Ophelia by showing Hamlet's letter to the king and queen (2.2.86–158). They are interrupted by the entrance of Rosencrantz and Guildenstern (2.2.1–39) and, after the exit of the school chums, by the entrance of Hamlet. The fishmonger scene comes next (2.2.171ff), followed by the return of Rosencrantz and

Guildenstern and then by the arrival of the players. Then we see the same parts from 2.2 and 3.2 as in the shorter film. I shall call these two fragments "LUX"[8] and consider them as one film.

The Hamlet of this film is handsome, with a lithe body, which seems to exclude the possibility of Ruggeri, who was (in 1917, not 1910, it is true) forty-five and portly, according to Ball. But Ruggeri then becomes a possibility for the CINES film, whose Hamlet is a short, stocky man about forty. Though the LUX version uses intertitles to indicate settings and to refer to lines from Shakespeare (seldom quoted accurately), it chiefly relies on the actors' aptitude for conveying language through action. It demonstrates clearly the ability of the actors to suggest not only language but even thought without words, and, at the same time, underscores the affinity of the film with stage traditions.

In the first scene, introduced by the place title, "CORRIDOR IN THE CASTLE," Horatio anxiously waits with Marcellus and Bernardo for Hamlet's arrival so they can tell him what they have seen. This scene takes only a few seconds and is shot in what appears to be a fragment of a room, showing only about a three-foot width along one wall, with a doorway to the outdoors from which a shaft of light falls into the narrow space. This is, turned sideways, a carpenter's set, which on stage is, of course, the shallow playing area in front of the curtain. Nevertheless, within that small space and time, the film differentiates between Marcellus and Bernardo through the near disappearance of the latter in the

LUX *Hamlet*. **After the disclosure.**

shadows and offers a suitable introduction to Hamlet. The prince enters through the door and later motions Horatio to precede him through it. Before Hamlet exits, he stops to reveal a good profile in the light and to make a passionate gesture with one hand at his chest and the other stretched out to the diagonal. This gesture precisely fits our notion of the nineteenth-century Hamlet on stage; one thinks also of Barrymore, with that magnificent profile to the audience. We recognize the convention; the gesture tells us that the LUX Hamlet is noble, suffering. He exits with his face tilted upwards, followed by the two soldiers.

For 1.4, titled "THE RAMPARTS," this film offers the usual stage convention, for this scene, of the carpenter's set, with a perspective painting of castle crenelations, water, and so forth, as backdrop. (A treetop showing over the low railing at the back seems to be waved by hand to represent a tossing wind.) A turret, through which the ghost will enter and from behind which the four others enter first, and a stairway for the ghost to go up and for Hamlet to use in following him give the tiny set a little flexibility. As Hamlet enters with Horatio, he gestures expansively, then nods, crosses his arms across his chest, and looks off pensively. The gesture communicates an idea we usually grasp of Hamlet through many interchanges and soliloquies: the philosophic Hamlet. Marcellus, hearing something behind him, turns and attracts Horatio's and Hamlet's attention. Again, Bernardo almost disappears in the shadows. Both Hamlet and Horatio press themselves against the stones for support as they await the ghost's appearance—an appropriate equivalent for the hair-raising effects of 1.1, which this fragment omits. A fade out and fade in prepare for the ghost's entrance. It walks slowly and with very short steps (to maximize the space) from the turret entrance to the stairway while the four men regroup near the turret entrance. Here Hamlet throws off the others as they try to hold him back. Hamlet makes again that favorite gesture—one hand at his chest, the other outstretched, then both hands at his chest—to delay his move forward or he would be right on top of the ghost, so tight is the space. Before he follows the ghost up the stairs, he makes a pleading gesture, his two hands pressed together in front of him. Because the whole space is visible throughout, since the set is small and the camera remains static, each actor's contribution is important, as on stage. Horatio watches Hamlet tensely while the two others watch the ghost. Thus, the friend is distinguished from the sentries by action as well as by costume. As Hamlet leaves, Horatio and Marcellus confer, while Bernardo remains apart.

Again in the next scene, gestures suggest language, approximating speech, but titles relate specific facts. With a cut, without an intervening title, the film shows a new space for the next scene, the ghost's revelation (1.5). The ghost, a truncheon in his hand, is just appearing in an arch as the scene begins. Hamlet steps through after him, his hat still on, his cloak draped over his arm. After a brief title, "I am thy father's spirit," Hamlet, his arms out wide, loose, seems to say,"What can I do for you?" Then he gestures as if to say, "I think I know." He begins to walk forward but the ghost waves him back to the entrance arch. As Hamlet turns back, the title flashes on: "The serpent that did sting thy father's life Now wears his crown. Look!" Then, on a fade in within the arch, an inset picture shows the poisoning in the garden. This seems to be accomplished by light rather than by a projected image. That is, within the dark space, a fade in of light shows the king and his murderer; then a fade out returns the arch to darkness. Thus the director quite comfortably uses film techniques (fade in and out) along with stage techniques (acting style, set design). Hamlet holds his hands to his head, then sinks on the steps below the arch as the picture fades. The ghost walks towards the camera, but Hamlet sits looking at the darkened arch with one hand raised towards it. Then he rises, his hands on his chest, and turns to the ghost. Suddenly, the ghost simply disappears; Hamlet runs to the spot, half-kneeling. When he realizes the ghost is gone, he strides from left to right, hands at his head, after pointing again to the arch. Now the title: "My uncle! Haste me, that I with wings—As swift as meditation—May sweep to my revenge." He vows to himself rather than to the ghost as in the text. A series of gestures reinforces his vow: he half-kneels, then ends with his hands in prayer position, as he looks up and *begins* to rise.

LUX *Hamlet*. Hamlet kisses Ophelia as Polonius enters unseen by them.

As in a modern film, the action remains incomplete as the next scene opens.

The place title sets the next scene, "OPHELIA'S HOME," but the acting conveys the emotional and even verbal information, including additions to Shakespeare's text. The production establishes Ophelia's love for Hamlet and his for her through this added scene of them together. It opens with Ophelia seated, Hamlet standing next to her, holding her hand. Raising her, he kisses her forehead, with two hands on her head, just as her father, unnoticed, comes in, sees them, and looks displeased. Hamlet gives her a letter and both of them look at it, but then a movement by Polonius—who is as on stage depicted as an old, white-bearded man with staff of office—attracts their attention. She hides the letter behind her while Hamlet steps away from her and, with one hand at his chest, bows graciously to Polonius, who returns the bow, with a short forward tilt of the head. Hamlet takes Ophelia's left hand and kisses it fervently. His arm raised in farewell, he walks out keeping his eyes on her—a reminiscence of Ophelia's lines in another scene (not included in this film):

> And with his head over his shoulders turn'd
> He seem'd to finde his way without his eyes,
> For out adores he went without their helpe:
> And to the last, bended their light on me.
> (F1 2.1.97–100)

The silent film can more easily show Hamlet's wooing of Ophelia than refer to it in titles through the conversations of 1.3. The result is a loss of ambiguity. Because we see his behavior towards Ophelia, Hamlet's feelings are much clearer than they can be when the text is followed and Hamlet and Ophelia are alone together only for the nunnery scene.

The nuances of the family relationships in 1.3 are not beyond the resources of this little film, which, however, depends on titles here more than it has to in other scenes. Moving forward, Polonius snatches the letter from behind her back and moves right with it. She follows, pleading. The title has Polonius's warning: "Ophelia, do not believe Lord Hamlet's vows." Laertes, who now comes on, seems to grasp the situation immediately, perhaps because he has seen Hamlet leaving (he enters the same way). Pointing towards where Hamlet has exited, he warns, by title: "If he says he loves you, fear it, Ophelia, my dear sister." He points a finger at her warningly. Polonius responds to Laertes's request for a blessing with a smack to Laertes's head; in one gesture we get a comic vision that can remind us of Polonius's obvious lack of respect for Laertes in Shakespeare's Reynaldo scene. It also places Polonius in a stage tradition that made him a buffoon (see Bell, opposite 18). LUX's Ophelia is more complex than many Ophelias seen in full-length sound films. To her father's anger in the Laertes farewell scene, she responds with sorrow rather than submission; there is no scene of her complicity with the others in spying on Hamlet, nor a scene of her madness, since the fragment ends after the play-within-a-play. After her brother leaves, Polonius comes to her, reading the letter. She sinks down in the chair, her head down, her body bent almost double, a gesture not of acquiescence but of pain, as Polonius walks out with her letter.

Even the subtleties of the second court scene are not beyond the film's capabilities. Again, a title indicates place: "A ROOM IN THE CASTLE." The scene opens in medias res with Claudius reading the letter, Polonius standing in rear midframe with hands lifted, the queen turned away from the camera to look on with the king. As a courtier enters, left, to announce the arrival of Rosencrantz and Guildenstern, the king folds the letter and puts it away. Rosencrantz and Guildenstern now enter, left, and soon exit rear. As if the king and queen glimpse someone off frame, they quickly rise and move forward, off, leaving Polonius there. The variety of exits effectively lends the tiny, cramped set an aura of spaciousness by implying that there is more to be seen than what is on frame. Dressed typically in black tights and doublet with a white shirt showing at the neck, Hamlet comes in from the left, his hand on his chin, his eyes cast down at his book. He sits on his mother's throne and with a quick gesture smooths down his hair, ignoring Polonius. Polonius turns to him. A title: "Do you know me, my lord?" Hamlet briefly looks up, then back at the book resting on the arm of the chair away from Polonius, then back at Polonius; title: "Excellent well, you are a fishmonger." Polonius raises his arms in consternation. As Hamlet flips through the pages of his book, Polonius leans forward to see. Now Rosencrantz and Guildenstern return. Hamlet puts his hand to his chest and swings it out—a welcoming gesture. While Hamlet greets them, Polonius retreats behind the thrones. The playing space is so small that not many people can be centered at once. The three men make gestures and quick movements of the head as if they are quipping. We gather the kind of playful, witty relationship they have with each other. Pointing to the door, the two former friends tell Hamlet that "The actors are come hither, my lord." As the actors come in, Rosencrantz and Guildenstern move to the rear and Polonius comes around the queen's throne to the extreme right foreframe, so that Hamlet and the players—especially the First Player—can remain at the center.

Immediately after Hamlet greets them, a title announces Hamlet's idea: "Can you play the murder of Gonzago.—We'll have it tomorrow night." (This is where the three-minute fragment begins.) The brilliant little segment communicates the germination of the idea of the play-within-a-play, making redundant most titles. We see Hamlet's delight

LUX *Hamlet*. Rosencrantz and Guildenstern try to eavesdrop.

with the First Player's script, drawn out of a commodious pocket jammed with scripts.[9] Hamlet's gesture says, "Ah, the very thing." Keeping the script, Hamlet signals to Polonius to lead the players off. Hamlet graciously stops a player girl to speak to her for a moment. In a bit of burlesque humor, Rosencrantz and Guildenstern sneak up behind Hamlet, with ears comically bent towards him, to overhear his directions about the inserted speech. Hamlet's gestures indicate where the speech should go. Then, having noticed Rosencrantz and Guildenstern conferring, Hamlet sneaks up on them to mimic their spying. When they notice him and respond with chagrin, he simply smiles as if to say, "I'm only joking; please be at ease." He bows them off graciously, all good humor, seemingly enjoying his little joke. He does not take these clowns seriously. Alone, Hamlet looks at the script, hits it, gestures up, looking serious and intense; then the redundant title: "The play's the thing—O Vengeance!—I'll catch the conscience of the king."

For the advice to the players, titles provide the general idea: "Suit the action to the word, the word to the action. Go make you ready." But action rather than titles furthers the plot, as Hamlet demonstrates for them the pouring gesture he expects them to use, and his actions betray his frenetic excitement (in contrast to the more deliberate and cerebral actions of the CINES Hamlet in his scene with the players). Hamlet makes the connection between the dead king and the Player King by

CINES *Hamlet*. With the players, in a dramatic architectural setting. Hamlet has sent for them.

providing the costume—the white cloak, white helmet, and long beard—that duplicates the ghost's appearance. (The Forbes Robertson ghost also wears white cloak and helmet.)

Action continues to replace language. After the players retreat behind the curtained area, Hamlet shows Horatio where to stand. When Polonius enters, Hamlet bows extravagantly just before dashing behind the curtain with his speech. From various entryways, the court appears, many dressed in Viking costumes, wearing helmets with horns. Hamlet, reappearing from behind the curtain, still with the paper in his hand, looks towards Ophelia, who modestly keeps her head down. The title introduces the play: "We'll call the play the Mousetrap." At a motion from Hamlet, the curtain is drawn. Hamlet lies down on Ophelia's gown (the CINES Hamlet had spread his cloak at her feet to lie down), while onstage the villain walks across and off the set, followed on by the Player King, who takes off his headpiece and lies down. Then the villain returns and poisons the king. There is no Player Queen in sight. While the brief scene is being enacted, Hamlet crawls across the floor towards the king (a favorite piece of stage business begun by Kean and done by Irving also [Sprague, 158]), who, moved by the scene, rises and exits with the others. Even more than sound films, silent films demonstrate the unbroken line of business connecting stage and film productions—because silent films privilege "business." Hamlet, jubilant, almost sits on the

CINES *Hamlet*. The camera pans with the players and Hamlet.

throne, then jumps up to speak to Horatio, who looks pleased too. Beyond them the players, having descended from the stage to question Hamlet, express bewilderment. With extravagant gestures of his arm, Hamlet waves all of them off, making it clear that he wants Horatio to take the players away; Horatio urges them off with gentle pressure on their shoulders.

Alone, Hamlet unsheathes a dagger and strikes with it again and again at Claudius's side of the throne. No image, I think, could so forcefully illustrate impotent rage as this unavailing action. Other Hamlets have used this gesture but during the "rogue and peasant slave" soliloquy (Sprague, 149) rather than here. Soon Hamlet drops the dagger ,and, with his hand on his head, sinks down, head on throne. Polonius's entrance shows the depths of Hamlet's character, his feeling for correctness, his need to wear the courtier's mask; Hamlet rises to greet the councillor courteously. When Polonius leaves, Hamlet picks up the dagger. He shakes his head "no" and, walking toward the camera, goes off, left, slowly, hand on head. We have no confidence that this Hamlet will be able to bring Claudius to justice. (The film here blacks out with no further titles.)

The actors, through gesture, body language, and expression, convey, in a rapid shorthand, gradations of meaning altogether more subtle than the rough titling. The production minimizes the role of Gertrude by having her always act the role of adjunct, looking on as Claudius reads

Hamlet's letter, her gestures echoing Claudius's in the play scene, where she is obscured by Polonius. She plays no role in the poisoning inset, nor does a Player Queen appear in "The Mousetrap." The film also communicates perfectly Hamlet's reluctance to act, partly by its structure, partly by the able actor who plays the role. In structure, we see that Hamlet woos Ophelia after the ghost has revealed the murder and after Hamlet has vowed revenge. This figures forth well enough, I think, his inability to concentrate on revenge. In Shakespeare's *Hamlet* it is far more likely that Hamlet does not continue to woo Ophelia after the ghost's revelation. Contrast the CINES *Hamlet,* where the nunnery scene is gotten out of the way before the ghost scene, giving Hamlet an opportunity to show his single-minded attention to his vow. Also, in the CINES version, it seems that Hamlet has sent purposely for the players rather than that they have happened by: they appear waiting in the courtyard for Hamlet, who comes to greet them enthusiastically but without surprise and strolls with them casually. More importantly, the aftermath of "The Mousetrap" shows the LUX Hamlet's lack of will. Exuberant over what Claudius has revealed—an exuberance seconded by Horatio—Hamlet expends his energy uselessly. Nevertheless, his great personal charm also comes through in the few minutes of film time: his graciousness towards all, his wit in teasing Rosencrantz and Guildenstern by mimicking their spying. Even in the last few seconds of the film, after he has collapsed before the throne, when Polonius enters, Hamlet rouses himself to respond to the old man with a gesture of acquiescence. All this in six minutes of film time.

While this film offers very little of cinematic interest, with its cramped sets (supposedly built like a nest of Russian dolls and removed one at a time as each scene was shot, according to *Hamlet Revisited*),[10] stationary camera, and symmetrical blocking, we can admire its integrity of vision and its clarity, achieved through its acting—even if some of the gestures seem dated today. Is it only a coincidence that the more cinematic film fails to convey Shakespeare's language where the more stagelike film succeeds? Perhaps this question cannot and need not be answered. Both films do communicate not only the plot but also the emotional and psychological states of the characters. Gestures, body language, facial expressions—the visual aspect of the actor's art—shine out in these early silent films.

Notes

1. Asta Nielsen's 1920 film, while within range of film's greatest power as a silent medium, is so far from Shakespeare's *Hamlet* that I consider it separately, in a forthcoming study of offshoots.

2. Though titles offer a possible clue to the producers' ideas about *Hamlet,* they must be

relied on with reservations, for often the titles we see now are not the originals.

3. The "overture" actually consists of four outtakes from the film, scraps that were spliced onto the beginning of the film rather than where they belong. To be comprehensible, the film must be considered as if those scraps were in their proper place. I discuss the order of events as if they were so placed. The outtakes are as follows: Hamlet's greeting of the players, a fragment from the nunnery scene, Ophelia's entrance and Hamlet's introduction of the play to the king in 3.2, and Ophelia's entrance for her one mad scene. Within the body of the film, there are a few other misplaced frames, which one must mentally place in their correct positions.

4. The ghost, at first, floats *over* the stream—a not unusual problem with superimpositions.

5. For a general discussion of the presence and effect of analogical scenes in Shakespeare, see Hartwig, 3–15. She provides a method for analyzing Shakespeare's plays, including *Hamlet*, through such analogical scenes. See also Rothwell 1980, 240–57.

6. On Fechter, see Field, 567. A 1787 text of *Hamlet* shows a picture of Kemble tossing a book away; this could be the play scene but more likely is the nunnery or fishmonger scene. Buell, 97 says that Tommaso Salvini, who chewed on the ms. during the play, also threw the sheets in the air.

7. Ball describes the longer fragment (106–7) but cannot identify it; he suggests it might be ca.1908–10, Milano or Cines. *Hamlet Revisited*, which excerpts a segment, refers to it as a 1907 film. MOMA appears to have withdrawn the shorter fragment from circulation after I told them its provenance.

8. I consider Lux a good bet in spite of the fact that a contemporary review of the Lux film did not like the acting, while the MOMA fragment, in my opinion, is well acted. See "Comment on the Films," *The Moving Picture World*, 12 February 1910, 217. The next week, three other Lux films were accorded the highest praise "for photographic excellence, stagecraft and action," 245, which implies that Lux was indeed capable of good work.

9. Their legs cross-gartered, the players are in cloaks to indicate their recent arrival. Sprague says that both Forbes Robertson and Sarah Bernhardt obtained a promptbook from the First Player (149). The contemporary critic William Winter, Sprague notes, said sarcastically that the "First actor must, 'conveniently,' have 'carried his whole repertory in his belt.'" LUX makes that seem credible.

10. Ball (77) refers to a Barker *Hamlet* of 1910, the first English *Hamlet*, for which the set was so built. Ball, however, in a telephone communication with me, said that he did not think that the so-called LUX film could be identified as the Barker film—though he thought that such nested sets were a rarity.

15

Sir Johnston Forbes Robertson's Hamlet "The Glass of Fashion and the Mould of Form"

Cinematically, the Forbes Robertson film (Great Britain 1913), directed by E. Hay Plumb and produced by Gaumont-Hepworth, but with the main responsibility evidently in the hands of Cecil Hepworth,[1] falls somewhere between the CINES and the LUX films in setting, camera flexibility and extratextual visualizations. Like CINES, the Forbes Robertson film uses location and studio settings, the latter more complex than LUX's studio sets, but without the monumentality of some of CINES'. Camera shifts, more timid than CINES', introduce structures from film to supplement those of the stage: changes in camera angle (shifts in point of view), variations in distance of subject from camera (two closeups and some medium shots approaching closeups) and deviation from the stationary camera (panning and tracking) are the three main cinematic devices—used, however, so discreetly that noticing them requires concentration. Filmmakers thought that a fixed camera with a limited setting was best to catch the audience's experience of a staged performance. All three films introduce extra scenes, again with the Hepworth film falling between LUX and CINES. Though Forbes Robertson finally agreed to the depiction of scenes not in the play (Ball, 190), he took some convincing because he saw the film as a record of the stage production. The filmmaker, on the other hand, said that the film required "all sorts of visualizations"—but Ophelia's willow scene and Claudius's and Laertes's plot were the only ones he added. Precariously balanced between the imperative of the film medium and the aim to reproduce a stage play, Hepworth's *Hamlet* clarifies both the connections

The Forbes Robertson *Hamlet*. The first court scene; Laertes asks permission to leave.

between film and stage and the limitations of film that is merely dependent on the sister medium.

Given Hepworth's and the Gaumont company's background in film innovation, it would have been surprising if they had not attempted something beyond a static stage production. Hepworth, according to Georges Sadoul, first inserted a closeup in a 1901 film and continued to use the device regularly—including closeups of people as well as of things, the more common use. Hepworth was also one of those who developed the pursuit film, which used tracking, panning and crosscutting; Alfred Collins, of Gaumont, made the first tracking story film in 1903. Collins also used panoramic shots and metonymy, showing part for whole.[2] Though ostensibly their purpose was to reproduce a stage play, Gaumont-Hepworth worked some of these innovative techniques into their film.

Probably with a freer hand, the filmmakers would have produced a better film, but their limited vision of what film could do hampered them also. If Hepworth did have some notion of the possibilities inherent in camera variations, he did not have the vision of a D. W. Griffith in regard to that other powerful tool—editing. The first requirement for the moving image is movement. In both film and stage, actors move, an important area of overlap between the two media. But for film, camera movement and editing specifically create cinematic movement. Griffith used camera movement only rarely, an occasional pan perhaps. Instead, editing, the juxtaposition of short takes, creates the sense of movement. In particular, Griffith had by 1909 in *The Lonely Villa* perfected the matchcut, a device artfully executed in *The Lonedale Operator*, 1911. Cutting from one shot to another is so natural that few in the audience are aware of it: a girl walks to a door; with a cut to a new shot we now see her coming through that door into a new setting. Because the new shot is precisely what the audience wants to see, it does not notice any disjunction. In spite of cramped sets and a stationary camera, Griffith was thus able to achieve fluidity and a masterful linking of one indoor setting to another and of indoor to outdoor settings. The same may be said for the closeup: when a closeup comes at precisely the moment an audience wants to see something close and lasts only as long as it should, the audience has little sense that one shot has been cut into another. Griffith's advances seem beyond the Gaumont-Hepworth team. Averse to straight cuts, because he felt them always to be wrenching (Hepworth, 139), Hepworth did not see that in matchcuts and in cuts to closeups there was no dislocation. Avoiding the straight cut, a necessity of matchcuts and of most cinematic editing, Hepworth had to rely on much slower fades and panning to create cinematic movement.[3]

While Hepworth may not have rushed into the future, as did Griffith, he did stand at the forefront of the main ranks. Rachel Low points out that, as late as 1919, "in Elvey's *Nelson* . . .the polar landscape was even represented by the use of slightly creased backdrop" (4:243), a case of film merely imitating a paltry stage device. Hepworth's scenes never betray such amateurishness. If we compare his *Hamlet* with the contemporary *Queen Elizabeth* with Sarah Bernhardt, we see that of the two Hepworth's film is the more cinematic. The Bernhardt vehicle aims to do what the stage could do but to an extent impossible on stage, that is, to provide many three-dimensional settings, often a new one for each scene. To a degree, this was Hepworth's aim also. Henry Irving's turn-of-the-century *Hamlet* on stage took over five hours in spite of drastic cuts because of the scene changes; film could change settings better and faster. A review in *The Moving Picture World* of the Forbes Robertson film says, "the picture gives the backgrounds as no stage could" (10 July 1915, 317–18), meaning three-dimensionality rather than scale. Satisfying as such films may have been at the time, they now seem far removed from the nature of film. Nor were they close to the nature of the stage, which at that time took what many consider a mistaken step towards realism with such elaborate scenic displays. Just as painting and sculpture have retreated from realism as photography advanced, so too has theater.

It was easy enough for filmmakers to absorb stage conventions into film because they recognized the kinship—if not identity—between the two media. They repeatedly use terms from theater to described their work, such as "downstage," "stage setting," etc. It took a long time for them to free themselves from the three-sided stage set. The Hepworth vigil scene (1.4), as in LUX and as was so common for stage performances, features a carpenter's set,[4] a narrow playing area with painted backdrop of distant cliff and sea—though in this case the backdrop is real, offering a true panoramic shot that connects to the beach scene for the ghost's revelation. The film takes its inspiration from the stage but then, by exploiting the location at Lulworth Cove, goes the backdrop one better.

Because the actors are all so far downstage (that is, in foreframe), they occupy only one plane of action. This is true for most scenes, with a few notable exceptions.[5] Horatio and Hamlet enter (from the same arch with portcullis we had seen in 1.1) to discover Marcellus, and then the camera tracks with them until the frame reveals a tower. After an intertitle, the ghost appears suddenly in the frame. A superimposed, transparent image, the ghost wears a helmet and a white cloak clutched close with arms held akimbo. After Hamlet throws the others off with his bare hands (without the sword he took out on stage), he moves, right, after the ghost. The camera pans left to exclude Hamlet, then pans right after Hamlet, catching his heels in the frame, then left again to the others. One can only speculate that the intention might have been *not* to catch him, to indicate thereby that he had already gone on. Since Hepworth never looked at rushes and never re-shot, indeed never edited out "bad" frames—because with his planning he never expected any (see Hepworth 136–38)—it is likely that the intention to follow but avoid Hamlet was foiled by a faulty panning shot.

Coincidentally, Alan Dent used this technique to show that Ophelia had gone on beyond the camera in the Olivier *Hamlet.* At the end of the second mad scene, she seems to think of the idea of suicide and walks down the corridor toward her room and the outdoors. The camera follows belatedly but does not catch her.[6] A number of other correspondences between the Olivier and Forbes Robertson films bring out the Fluellen in one.[7] Like Forbes Robertson, Olivier sits brooding at the end of the court scene (1.2.159), and a transposed scene is then interposed— in Forbes Robertson the first scene; in Olivier the third scene. In both cases the purpose seems to be to put similar plot strands together. Forbes Robertson did not transpose or interpolate 1.1 on stage, but the transposition in the film makes for the shorter segments common in moving images. When the camera returns to Hamlet in both films, he is still sitting, brooding (1.2.160). Interestingly, the 1913 film conveys the idea of repeated habitual action by having Hamlet sit in a second chair for the second segment; we sense that time has passed.[8] Like Forbes Robertson, Olivier falls back into Horatio's arms upon the arrival of the ghost and faints as the ghost leaves. For the nunnery scene in both productions, a

The Forbes Robertson *Hamlet*. Hamlet's other chair.

The Forbes Robertson *Hamlet*. The ghost on the ramparts.

The Forbes Robertson *Hamlet*. The nunnery scene; Hamlet touches Ophelia's hair.

The Olivier *Hamlet.* **Hamlet kisses a lock of Ophelia's hair.** *(Still courtesy Janus Films.)*

curtain simply appears between the pillars in a setting that had no such curtain before. Both Hamlets touch Ophelia's hair in the nunnery scene, Forbes Robertson before he discovers the king, Olivier as he leaves; both speak tenderly to the dead Polonius; neither leaps into the grave. Forbes Robertson's stage and film productions bridged scenes with music—as does Olivier's *Hamlet.* Both Hamlets die on the throne. These similarities speak for the continuity of performances in general, both on stage and on film.

In the location setting of Hepworth's revelation scene (1.5)—a brightly lit, rocky seacoast—the camera pans to find Horatio and Marcellus. As usual, it never varies its distance from the scene to take in more or less of the action at once. And even here, where the setting is not restricted by inherent shallowness, one plane of action obtains, with actors remaining in the foreframe. But once, as Hamlet removes himself from the ghost, he steps into the mid distance, changing a close long shot to a long shot.[10]

The seacoast setting evidently comes not, as one would think, from the inspiration of cinematic location shooting, but from the stage production: George Bernard Shaw, in a *Saturday Review* article (2 October 1897, 364–65) ends his favorable review with this advice: "And that nice wooden beach on which the ghost walks would be the better for a seaweedy looking cloth on it, with a handful of shrimps and a pennorth

The Forbes Robertson *Hamlet*. The ghost on the beach.

of silver sand" (also in Shaw 1961, 92). Similarly, the addition of a scene dramatizing Gertrude's words about Ophelia's last moments seems an obvious film ploy, but Shaw, for one, thought of creating such a stream for a stage production with Ellen Terry. He proposes "a trout stream of the streamiest and ripplingest to drown yourself in" (Shaw 1961, 84, from a letter to Ellen Terry, 27 July 1897). In other words, like the book illustrators and moving image makers, he also wants to show the scene rather than to summarize it.

Back indoors, Hepworth's camera pans less conspicuously.[11] For the scene of the arrival of the players, the camera pans slightly to include Polonius in the frame when he is needed. In the duel scene also, the camera moves a bit to keep actors on frame. Perhaps the director thought he could get away with such "natural" camera movements. Even *The Great Train Robbery* (1903) could risk such minimal movement. In most scenes, however, the camera is stationary, with the important exception of the interpolated scene of Ophelia at the waterside, in which the camera tracks with her through a woodland setting. Indoor settings in effect constrict the action; outdoor settings allow for more freedom. For the graveyard a wooden Norman church was supposedly built, but it is not much in evidence. I detect only a scrap of arch in what appears to be a location setting. The encounter with Osric, as in so many productions, is a separate scene, making three in act 5 rather than two. Like 1.1 this scene combines location setting with a studio feeling, here with plenty of ferns and lots of real trees, but with the playing space limited to the equivalent of a small platform. As usual all the action takes place in a very constricted space in the foreframe.

Contrary to the practice of the earlier silent films, for which a straight cut was a possibility, the camera for the Forbes Robertson film moves to a new setup almost always under cover of a title.[12] The filmmaker would not cut from one camera position to another during a sequence because of decorum, that is, the need to keep within the proper bounds of what he thought an audience could accept. The title between the nunnery scene and "The Mousetrap" scene, for example, allows the camera to move from an oblique to a straight-on position, so that the rear of the set, where *The Murder of Gonzago* will be enacted, is visible and centered.

An apparent freedom of cutting (shifting camera point of view) in several scenes results from flaws in titling position in a particular print.[13] This fact makes all the more interesting the few cuts that cannot be accounted for by such misplacement. No nearby title belongs between the king's and queen's departure in 2.2 and Hamlet's arrival, when the angle of view changes with a fade. Another cut comes later in this scene, while Hamlet speaks to Rosencrantz and Guildenstern. Still another is the fade out and in to show a shift in view from a two-shot of Polonius and Hamlet to another of Hamlet and Gertrude (3.4). The film needed more of these variations in camera position because kineticism on film depends less on the actors than on the camera. The film contains only two closeups—of the point of the unbated foil and of the cup. After a foil is drawn across the frame, a finely molded hand reaches into the frame, touches the point, withdraws and re-enters holding a vial and pours the liquid onto the point. After foil and hand are withdrawn a heavy, bejeweled hand with a cup enters the frame and another pours a liquid into it. The shot effectively conveys the dual complicity of Laertes and Claudius. Yet its style is very different from that of the rest of the film. Such disembodied closeups, detached from a film sequence, while an example of film metonymy, nevertheless look very old-fashioned today. To understand the convention, it is necessary to look at the practice in contemporary films. A better, but still "stop action", closeup occurs in Griffith's *Lonedale Operator,* when the brave operator shows that she has held the tramps at bay with a wrench. In Griffith's *Judith of Bethulia* (1913) in contrast, the closeup of Lillian Gish's baby comes exactly when one would want it and for approximately the right length of time, smoothly fitting into the particular sequence. Or to mention a more current example, Olivier cuts the closeup of the foils, showing one unbated, into the dueling sequence. The difference between Hepworth's closeup and all these others is that his is not connected to a larger narrative point but is complete in itself. Hepworth's closeup, then, is mainly interesting as an example of a detached visualization of Shake-

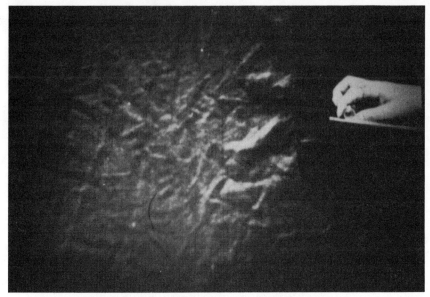

The Forbes Robertson *Hamlet*. The point envenomed.

speare's words, rather than as an example of film technique, with its dynamic range of camera distances.

Closeups in photography and portraiture were by then a commonplace but did not inspire film closeups, perhaps because filmmakers saw their art as theatrical rather than pictoral. In the souvenir text for the stage production, two pictures—of Forbes Robertson, hand in bosom, right profile highlighted, and of Mrs. Patrick Campbell as Ophelia in the mad scene, with chaplet of flowers, holding daisies—appear in closeup (bust size). The film has the corresponding two prologue shots, of Forbes Robertson and of his wife, Gertrude Elliott, who played Ophelia in the film, but in medium shot (head to thigh). Hepworth does not choose the closeup.

Like the Forbes Robertson film, several moving pictures begin with prologues. And stage productions sometimes have such prologues too: Papp's 1964 (Babula, number 142) and 1982 productions featured a funeral scene for King Hamlet, the first with Gertrude and Claudius present; Jacobi's London *Hamlet* had a procession (Trewin, 1978, 220.) Olivier's film, of course, supplies the establishing shot of both locale and of psyche—that is, the high angle model shot of the castle by the sea and the segment on "one defect" that supposedly explains Hamlet's difficulties. Wirth begins his production by having Schell (Hamlet) recite Rosencrantz's "cease of Majestie" speech from 3.3.15–23, which, taken out of its context, explains as fated the general destruction following the deaths of King Hamlet and King Claudius. By beginning with a view of his father's tombstone, with Hamlet alone kneeling by it, Evans's production not only establishes the time and determines the *mise en scène*, but also reifies Hamlet's reverential attitude to his father. In Kozintsev's complicated vision of sea, stone, fire, and iron, the announcement of the death, the ride along the beach, the greeting of Hamlet and his mother—all become powerful icons that will reverberate throughout the production. Forbes Robertson's image, Hamlet setting down the words in his notebook, show him as the intellectual, distant here from his emotions, in fact rather unlike his demeanor during the scene itself. Gertrude Elliott's flower-bedecked beauty offers the pathetic Ophelia whom audiences expected. All the prologues, with the exception of Kozintsev's, seem to say, "Don't worry, we are offering you something familiar, something you can grasp, something that won't upset your preconceptions too much." Each prologue offers a visual as well as a thematic foreshadowing of the remainder of the film. Not surprisingly, the Forbes Robertson produces the most conservative view, not even daring, it seems, to use the closeups of the photographs. Yet, perhaps inadvertently, the camera does something filmic with the Gertrude Elliott picture. When Ophelia stretches her hand out shyly towards the camera with a flower spray, the camera has become an actor, or, to put this another way, the film audience is invited to identify with the camera. This is a different depiction from the passive photograph in the text, but this filmic use of the camera does not occur in the body of the film.

Just as the prologue photos were inspired by the souvenir book, Hepworth modeled the settings where possible on Hawes Craven's drawings for the book (Ball, 190). Critics extol the virtues of Orson Welles's films for at last in 1940 showing ceilings—partly a matter of large-scale sets—but illustrators had shown ceilings for years, a case in point being Craven's illustration for the closet scene (3.4) in the Forbes Robertson text. The chief difference between the three Hawes Craven illustrations and the sets in the film is scale. The orchard setting in the film for the mad scene corresponds approximately to one-sixteenth portion of the Craven set. With a stationary camera, a large set made no sense.

View expanded only gradually from the single-mount stationary camera, though illustrations could have shown the way. Filmmakers could or would not absorb liberating conventions from media other than the stage. Christy has an overhead view of the dead Hamlet in an 1897 text, but quite a few years pass before overhead shots appear regularly in films.[14] Similarly with crosscuts. Gilbert, in mid-nineteenth century, shows Polonius and the king from a view behind the arras spying on Hamlet, a view we can not get in the play but which seems natural to film. Perhaps Gilbert did not show the corresponding view from the other side of the arras, but no matter; he broke out of theater with that

H. C. Christy (1897). An overhead view of Hamlet. *(Photograph courtesy the Folger Shakespeare Library.)*

John Gilbert (ca. 1864). Claudius and Polonius behind the arras, spying on Hamlet and Ophelia. *(Photograph courtesy the Folger Shakespeare Library.)*

view. You could say he gives us something from life, yet who is the observer? Something not present in life: the artist's eye, the equivalent of the camera. In 1910, the Simmonds *Hamlet* illustrations show a shift in point of view, from behind the king and queen looking to the stage for the play-within-a-play and from the stage looking at the king and queen. Again, the point is not so much that such illustrations are taken from life rather than from the fixed focus of the theater as that the view takes on the role of narrator, as in fiction. In spite of these visual precedents, the corresponding, now commonplace, film device of the reverse shot entered the grammar of films with difficulty. Griffith used it first in *The Lonely Villa,* but Mast considers *Birth of a Nation* (1915) and *Intolerance* (1916) the first important uses of the reverse shot.

Within the conservative Gaumont-Hepworth production, the crosscuts in the fourth act are an anomaly. There is nothing so cinematic, so visually interesting elsewhere in the film. Once Forbes Robertson agreed to include the extratextual scene of Ophelia walking in the woods, the director took the opportunity to insert it as he pleased, using the intercutting for which Griffith was to become famous. The added segments are interlaced with the plotting sequence (4.7), which takes place in the same orchard where Ophelia's textual mad scene was played out. The scene shifts from one to the other six times. The effect, in fact, is of even more shifts because four of the six shots are interrupted by titles. There are, then, ten shots. In the last Ophelia segment, the shot shows Gertrude looking at something in the stream. She had been in the orchard scene with Ophelia, Laertes, and Claudius for the mad scene itself, and while we had not seen her exit (not called for in Shakespeare's text but very common in stage versions) a fade and the shift to another setting had effectively masked her disappearance so that her absence in the segment with Laertes and Claudius is not marked. Now she comes running into the orchard into Claudius's arms, goes to Laertes to tell him, then returns to the king's arms again. Immediately, as in the stage version, two bearers bring Ophelia's body into the orchard (also in the Sothern 1900 *Acting Version* and, according to Sprague [173], earlier in Booth).[15] As on stage, too, the scene ends in a fade on a static tableau, with Laertes kneeling over the body and Claudius observing. The segments comfortably blend stage and film techniques.

The film's relation to theater may have made Forbes Robertson believe that the film was as close as possible to his stage production. Perhaps that is why he fails to mention the film in his autobiography. For those who had seen him it would be a souvenir (like the souvenir text); for those who had not, it would substitute for the "real thing." In accord with this aim, the film's intertitles seem directed to an audience familiar with *Hamlet.* Their very infrequency supports this view. The whole

W. G. Simmonds (ca. 1910). Two views of the play-within-a-play. *(Photographs courtesy the Furness Memorial Library, University of Pennsylvania.)*

"Mousetrap" scene, for example, has only one title, and that one—"The play's the thing Wherein I'll catch the conscience of the King"—comes from 2.2, serving thus to remind the audience of the purpose of the play-

within-the-play. Hepworth, avoiding the excesses in titling of the Thanhouser *Lear* (1916), which cut up that film into disjointed vignettes, does not use titles merely to introduce characters.[16] The style of the titles varies according to their function: to indicate on-film speech, to advance plot through summary (something Hepworth liked to avoid, 124), or to interpret.

The Forbes Robertson *Hamlet*. Gertrude sees Ophelia in the stream.

Most commonly, titles indicate speech: "Let not thy mother lose her prayer, Hamlet / I pray thee stay with us" appears just before we see her mime her appeal, with arm stretched out towards Hamlet. "Get thee to a nunnery" comes immediately after Hamlet discovers the king and returns to Ophelia, just before he says the words. Audiences easily integrate these intertitles into the viewing experience—much as speech subtitles are integrated in foreign sound films, with little loss of forward impetus.

Though some titles derive from dialogue, their purpose is to introduce a plot segment, to alert an audience already familiar with the plot. The title before the closet scene is a curious example:

Let his Queen mother all alone entreat him
And I'll be placed, so please you, in the ear of all their conference.

It has no place in the film, for Polonius, cut from the prayer scene, never says this to Claudius. Such titles come from the world of the text rather than from the world of the film characters. Separated as these titles are from speech and speaker, they wrench one out of continuity. Brook in his *Lear* aimed for exactly that disorienting effect with whiteouts and strange angles that called attention to his film as artifact. Though Hepworth probably had no such goal, that is the effect of these titles. They bring us close to Tom Stoppard's world in "Dogg's *Hamlet,*" where Shakespeare is reduced to famous lines.

Titles that interpret are the most problematic. As in all versions where someone has to make choices based on inferences, some titles offer surprising assumptions or declare as factual something that the audience might infer from acting. Though the film shows that Hamlet sees someone, a title during the nunnery scene informs us that "Hamlet discovers the king behind the curtain." What the title implies, then is that Hamlet does not discover *Polonius*. This is an interpretative choice that affects the way Hamlet responds to Ophelia. The title in the closet scene informing us that "Hamlet believes the king is behind the arras" intrudes on the audience's right to interpret capable acting. These titles point to valid interpretations, but film whenever possible should show rather than tell, unless the filmmaker wants to pull us out of the story and distance us. The telling with the showing gives us two views that cannot always be reconciled. Gertrude seems stung to remorse in the closet scene; yet why is she so moved by Hamlet's words if, as a title tells us, she considers him mad? The answer to the double view we get may be the film's need to justify her continuing relation with Claudius.

A silent production's particular interpretation may benefit from information withheld. Many nineteenth-century versions of *Hamlet* eliminate most of act 4; Forbes Robertson's film, based on his 1897 stage performance, his debut as Hamlet at age forty-four, is no exception. It cuts all but the second mad scene and the plot between Laertes and Claudius. Yet no title tells us that Hamlet has been sent away, so, as far as we are concerned, he need not have left. Forbes Robertson leaves the matter ambiguous. He compresses time.

Acting often makes silent film titles unnecessary. The LUX and even the CINES film, which contained only three plot-pointing titles, certainly conveyed emotional content. The CINES Hamlet, as he stands at the waterfall after the nunnery scene, before his friends arrive to disclose what they have seen, expresses the melancholy of "Oh that this too too solid Flesh, would melt" with a hand held to forehead. With subtle head, body, and arm movements after the play scene, the LUX Hamlet expresses the self-loathing of "Oh what a Rogue and Pesant slave am I," caused by his inability to revenge his father's death. In the two short silent films the main emotions do come across: the despondency, the intensity, the determination or lack of it. Not surprisingly, then, the 1913 film also says a good deal even without language. Forbes Robertson's acting is, in fact, the chief value of the film.

A master of the art of expressing melancholy, sorrow, inexplicable vacillation, intellectualizing, and the other emotions of the soliloquies as he interprets them, Forbes Robertson constructs a coherent, satisfyingly complex Hamlet. And when he acts with others, he is superb, because the film then conveys meaning through both action and reaction. The length of the 1913 film (sixty-three minutes in the somewhat cut version at the Folger) allows him the scope he needs to express the complexity of his Hamlet. The short silent films flash the dominant emotion of a soliloquy in seconds. Forbes Robertson, in contrast, marks all the beats. In many sections, his brilliant acting recalls whole segments of dialogue to one familiar with the play.

Like the LUX Hamlet, Forbes Robertson is the epitome of gallantry, never imposing his suffering on others. Entering last in the first court scene, Hamlet bows graciously to individuals ranged about the room before taking his place beside the king and queen. He betrays no disgust with Claudius and Gertrude but rather a despondency he cannot mask. This is not Hamlet the rebel. After the king gives Laertes permission to leave, Hamlet rouses himself to salute Laertes, who kisses his hand. Later, Horatio and the First Player will also kiss his hand. Hamlet accepts these marks of deference without pride, with unstudied ease. In the duel scene the royal character of Hamlet is underlined when he removes his cloak and sword, letting them drop into the hands he knows will be there, hands that reach into the frame—another rare example of metonymy.[17] The respect shown to Hamlet by all amplifies his princeliness, expressed by his perfect courtesy. The reviewers of his day commented on this as one of his outstanding attributes. The *London Graffic,* 29 March 1913, calls Forbes Robertson's the most "princely, gracious Hamlet seen in our day—a thing of perfect beauty." The *London News,* 29 March 1913, exclaims, "Never in our time has there been so courteous, so gracious, so princely a Hamlet."

Forbes Robertson's Hamlet has none of today's Hamlets' taciturnity. In the first court scene he speaks almost before he is urged to, and then not angrily but earnestly, feelingly. The film avoids the implication of such baiting lines as "Not so my Lord, I am too much i'th'Sun" (1.2.67). Even at the end of the sequence, when Hamlet has swallowed the public announcement of the marriage and after he has reluctantly agreed not to return to Wittenberg, he bows to all who leave, most especially to Laertes. When Horatio, Marcellus, and Bernardo enter (1.2.160), Hamlet is still sitting with head and eyes down, and when they hail him, he reluctantly pulls himself out of his thoughts. But then his greeting to Horatio is spontaneous and warm. Putting his two hands on his friend's shoulders, he expresses his happiness in seeing Horatio, but he speaks politely to the others as well. A reviewer remarks with precision that "discipline, not inborn affability, is the source of his courtesy."

Through his expressive acting Forbes Robertson makes us see the emotion of Hamlet's words, "My father, me thinkes I see my father," and the startled reaction of the others reinforces our understanding. Brought to the present by Horatio's disclosure, Hamlet has one hand at his mouth, the other stretched out, then clasps both hands. Though they may seem extreme to us today, these gestures are differentiated from the more rhetorical style of the First Player's gestures for the declamatory

Pyrrhus speech, when the player places his forearm across his chest and then flings it out. Like all great Hamlets, Forbes Robertson is described as "natural," "colloquial" (see, for example, *New York Sun,* 3 October 1913). What this seems to mean is that he inspires belief—not that his actions are those we expect to see around us in everyday life.

The chief constituent of his believability is variety that springs from the realization of each turn of the text. His reactions to the ghost's revelation range from holding his ears with both hands, to kneeling and stretching out his arms, to bending his head over his clasped hands, to fainting after the ghost's disappearance. Unlike some other Hamlets, he does not drop his cloak nor follow the ghost sword in hand.[18] All the feeling comes from his inner being to his face and body—rather than from external business. He takes out his sword for the first time to swear his oath by kissing the hilt, after writing in his notebook, during which he laughs and makes wry grimaces. This is neither madness nor an antic disposition but the dislocation of the exquisitely sensitive soul. The critic who states that Forbes Robertson makes Hamlet absolutely sane is correct (Darnton). In fact, on stage he left out the lines about madness in his apology to Laertes (5.2.224–35).[19] As he speaks to Marcellus and Horatio, Hamlet's face conveys seriousness, wit, anguish. When they move away from the ghost's voice, Hamlet takes Horatio's hand for support, leaning heavily on Horatio for the third remove, betraying his weakness. After the final remove, Hamlet lays the sword horizontally across their hands and bends their heads forward to complete the vow.

In the fishmonger segment, Hamlet for the first time lets his feelings show through the veneer of polite behavior. Hamlet walks in, reading, looks up when he is aware someone is there, then looks quickly down again to show his dislike of seeing Polonius. In his demeanor and satirical gestures, he betrays impatience with Polonius, tries to ignore him, even turns his back on him, attempting to read. Intent on seeing Polonius out, Hamlet gets up and bows eagerly. Polonius, exiting rear, directs Rosencrantz and Guildenstern to Hamlet, who has walked forward, his handsome, ascetic profile lit. He does not welcome Rosencrantz and Guildenstern as he had Horatio. While these two avoid the burlesque excesses of the LUX pair, they do confer very often behind Hamlet's back; inevitably he notices. Perhaps the director thought this mannerism was necessary without the oily insinuation of their toadying voices to give them away. (The promptbook does not indicate if the stage production had this business.) Each time Hamlet catches them, he bows to them and they to him, this device being a metaphor for the wit and playfulness with which Forbes Robertson acted this scene on stage—an interpretation that delighted Shaw.

The film creatively solves a crux in this scene. Some find that Hamlet twice conceives of "The Mousetrap," first while the player is on and again at the end of the soliloquy. The usual solution is to indicate that the idea comes for the first time at the end of the soliloquy. This leaves the problem of why Hamlet would know beforehand which play to request if he had no plan or why he would want to insert lines in it. In the film, after the initial conversation with the players, Hamlet almost leaves without communicating with the First Player. Reaching the second pillar, he stops, ruminates. Doubtful at first, his face lights up with the idea. Thus he clearly conceives of "The Mousetrap" at this point. Calling the player back, he comes forward again to speak to him. Before leaving, the First Player hands Hamlet a script, and Hamlet asks him about inserting a speech. Then Hamlet soliloquizes, giving utterance to a distress even unto despair. Sinking down on a chair, his hands stretched out on the table, his head down, he vents his tortured emotions. Then he *recollects* his plan for "The Mousetrap," snatches at the thought as at a lifeline, and grasping the script, expresses a fevered joy. The Folio supports this reading, for after "About my brain," it has no "hmm," as does the second Quarto, to suggest that he is thinking of the idea for the first time (2.2.617). This phrase without the "hmm" simply means "Turn away from this self-laceration back to the idea you had before" or "brain, get about your business."

For "To be," more an intellectual than an emotional deliberation, Forbes Robertson conveys the beats of the speech before a title announces the soliloquy. Having stepped behind the curtain in place for the nonce, Claudius and Polonius are in a position to hear Hamlet's musings, and to remind us of this a hand remains in view, stretching the curtain taut. When Ophelia puts her head on her arms in response to his coldness, he almost touches her, resists, visibly thinking, "What should such Fellowes as I do, crawling between Heaven and Earth. We are errant Knaves all" (3.1.124–25). But then he relents and does touch her. The interpretation is much as Shaw describes it for the stage play: Hamlet rejects Ophelia because, too self-observant, he cannot lose himself in a lover's passion. After his shocked response to noticing the king, he dashes back to Ophelia, but raises her gently and tells her tenderly to "Get . . . to a nunnery."

"The Mousetrap" energizes Hamlet again. Playfully he peeks around a pillar to see who is coming, ducks behind another, walks around it, and pops out from another, demonstrating the wit that as Shaw says interpenetrates the play (Shaw 1961, 93). He hides from all except Ophelia. When she enters, he takes her hand and leads her to a seat, enthusiastically greets others, waves them in, hands high, manuscript in his hand. After all are in place—Ophelia seated at the left, king and queen at the right, everyone else standing along the sides—Hamlet reclines at Ophelia's feet, stretching into the middle of the frame because the space is so narrow. (Like the LUX sets, the Hepworth sets vary between deep, narrow spaces and shallow, wide ones.) Hamlet reacts much more strongly to the depiction on the stage than does Claudius. Just before the murder, the king turns away from the stage and toward the camera, stroking his beard reflectively. Gertrude's head is bowed. Since Claudius is looking away from the stage, Hamlet rises to a half-kneel to call his attention to it. Pointing to the manuscript he says something to the king and moves towards him. The queen, almost off frame, right, restrains the king from reacting. They both then quickly leave with everyone while the rear curtains unobtrusively close.

Hamlet, happy, confirms his impression with Horatio. His playfulness echoing Hamlet's, Horatio exits for the pipe at Hamlet's request. Hamlet sits down, takes the notebook out of his shirt again and writes—a recollection of the tables of the ghost scene. He barely notices Rosencrantz and Guildenstern upon their re-entrance, but continues writing for a few moments. Then he speaks mockingly about the pipe, which a player brings on, to Guildenstern, imploring him to play, leaning forward to say "it's easy," pointing to the stops. Then with an abrupt shift, he angrily accuses Guildenstern of playing with him. He returns again to mocking courtesy as Polonius enters. Guildenstern looks crestfallen; Hamlet's criticism has touched him. Hamlet, meanwhile, enjoys playing with Polonius about clouds, looking off frame toward the camera to find them.[20]

Forbes Robertson's Hamlet slides from certainty to hesitation. In the soliloquy after the cloud scene, Hamlet seems determined at first, one hand to chin, the other stretched out, expressing, "Now could I drink hot blood." Then thoughtfully, finger to mouth, he ruminates before coming to the conclusion already flashed on the screen, shaking his finger decisively:

> . . . Now to my mother
> I will speak daggers to her, but use none.

Just as in this scene and in the nunnery scene Hamlet had kept himself from acting by deliberating, so too in the prayer scene. Crossing the room in which Claudius prays after dismissing Rosencrantz and Guildenstern, Hamlet finally notices the king, ducks his head down to make sure who it is, makes a sudden move as if to use the sword he has quickly unsheathed, then stops, and, face tilted down, raises his other hand in a "consider this" gesture. He speaks, as if to Claudius. What would be the use, says his gesture, hands spread out to his sides, with a kind of shrug. He puts up the sword and exits. At the rear curtain he gestures as if to say, before he exits, "Don't worry, you'll get what's coming to you."

Hamlet does not threaten the queen; that would be far from Forbes Robertson's style. Nor would that fit her persona; she is a lovely and

modest woman, with covered head and an unrevealing gown, a conde-
scending queen who embraces Ophelia lovingly during the mad scene.
In the first court scene, Gertrude does not, as in the stage version, move
to Hamlet and take his hand as she speaks to him. Perhaps this is
because, without words, the interactions are briefer, not allowing time
for movement. The effect is to distance Hamlet and his mother, making
her less important to him than in the stage version. This is, however,
altogether a pre-Freudian *Hamlet.* Though he does not menace her in
the closet scene, his sword held negligently at the back of his neck
unsettles her. Nor is it more reassuring that he puts it down on the table.
As she tries to move away from him, he looks wild. Gertrude flings
herself down on the table when Hamlet strikes and kills Polonius. In
response to her cry he grimaces as if saying, "almost as bad, good
Mother, / As kill a King and marrie with his Brother," though the title
itself does not appear until later in the scene, when Hamlet admonishes
her. Hamlet lifts the curtain to reveal Polonius, then kneels and tenderly
touches him. Returning to her, Hamlet speaks gently to her, turning her
head, perhaps to see the portrait on the wall.[21] Hawes Craven in the set
design has two full-length portraits on the walls, but the film print I saw
shows no portrait at all, possibly because of missing frames.

The ghost materializes between Gertrude, frame right at the table,
and Hamlet, frame left. Her hands are on her face in response to
Hamlet's strange behavior; she then extends them towards him, but in
such a way that she seems—unawares—to be touching the ghost, which,
however, has eyes only for Hamlet, watching him and turning to follow
him with his eyes, before exiting. The Hawes Craven drawing shows
much greater distance between Hamlet and ghost and mother, obviating
any contact between Gertrude and the ghost, but the relative positions of
the characters are the same. The similarities between the stage and film
versions point up the emotional effect, perhaps accidental, of the film's
tighter space. Hamlet turns for a moment to the prayer desk, then to his
mother, taking her hand, concerned about her, but his words to her are
not sweet. Large gestures warn her, and his stern look criticizes her.
With a salute of the hand, his mouth twisted in anger, he leaves, as she
sinks to her knees in front of the table. Returning to her, Hamlet lifts
her, hugs her, and guides her, her head bowed, to the exit.

Again Hamlet displays a wide range of emotions in the graveyard
scene. Genuinely interested in the gravedigger, Hamlet asks for the skull
with some urgency. Entering the funeral, his reactions are flamboyant,
prompting his mother to restrain him and to beg Laertes to be forbear-
ing with him, which he is. Otherwise, neither Claudius nor Gertrude is
much in evidence until the end of the scene.[22] Hamlet defiantly points at
himself, expressing the question, "What wilt thou do . . . ?" and then pats
himself emphatically. When he leaves, after kneeling at the grave briefly,

The Forbes Robertson *Hamlet*. Hamlet and Yorick's skull.

he raises his arms to signify sore distraction. The others kneel at the grave to complete the scene—including Claudius and Laertes after conferring briefly.

Hamlet and Horatio enter arm in arm for the next scene, followed very quickly by Osric. Hamlet is ever so slightly sarcastic with Osric, who manages to suggest his self-importance and superciliousness in a scene that does not last more than one minute. There is even time for Hamlet to express his misgivings by scrunching up his body and crossing his arms across his chest, then placing his hand over his face. Horatio tries to get him to give up the contest, but with a shrug and toss of his head, Hamlet persists. His eye turned upward, his hand, very slightly, imitates the fall of the sparrow.

For the duel, an eager Hamlet asks Laertes's forgiveness, taking the hand held by the king. Laertes's reaction, because his back is to the camera, is enigmatic. But as he turns away from Hamlet towards the camera, his arms akimbo, we see that he is unyielding. Hamlet makes playful remarks as he removes his sword to prepare for taking a foil from Osric. He fights with verve and enthusiasm, joyfully. After the first touch, Claudius rises and calls for the cup, which a page brings to Hamlet from off frame. By the tilt of his body and the wave of his hand, Hamlet graciously indicates that the page should put it by awhile. The supers in the back seem to be talking about the second hit, as both Hamlet and Laertes face towards the king and queen for the judgment.

After a quick fade, a new shot shows Gertrude standing, extending her handkerchief to Hamlet, off frame. The page stands beside her. Hamlet enters the frame and accepts the handkerchief from Gertrude, wiping his own brow. This gives her the opportunity to raise the cup with arms held straight in front of her, then to drink, while the king turns towards her quickly. Gertrude smiles indulgently at him and gently persists, continuing the upward sweep of the cup to her lips as she speaks. The king's hand goes to his mouth. Hamlet refuses Gertrude's offer of the cup, but kisses her hand, as the king turns to Laertes. Many nineteenth-century productions exculpate Claudius for his failure to stop her by changing her response to his request that she not drink to "I *have,* my lord, I pray you pardon me." He can hardly stop her if she has already drunk the wine. In this film, Claudius is close enough to stop her before she drinks.

Rarely does the film give us a sense that someone has composed the shots with a view to artistic effect, but here there is a nice four-shot or double two-shot: to the left, Claudius and Laertes stand; to the right, the queen stands and Hamlet kneels next to her after kissing her hand. A similar composition appears just before "To be," when Polonius lectures Ophelia in left frame, while Claudius asks Gertrude to leave in right frame.

A fade to the second camera angle shows the continuation of the fight. Laertes imparts the idea of "'tis almost 'gainst my conscience" by looking off frame with a faraway look in his eyes and clutching his hand to his bosom. After squelching his reluctance, he fights eagerly. There is no foul hit; Hamlet simply feels the point when Laertes strikes him. Hamlet, nonplussed, turns to someone off frame (toward Horatio?), a horrified look on his face. Briefly glancing at the blood on his hand, he purposely exchanges the rapiers, very quickly hitting Laertes what looks like a death blow in the chest. (Unlike Olivier's Hamlet who merely returns Laertes's scratch.) Gertrude stands in distress; Hamlet notices, dashes to her, and she puts a hand on his shoulder. Running to the rear, Hamlet silently shouts "Treacherie, seeke it out," while Gertrude falls surrounded by her women, who remain at her side, mourning her death until the end, hardly noticing anything else. As he shouted, a whole group had run out, right. Now as Laertes speaks, the king, running towards the arch where Hamlet is standing, is quickly killed there by Hamlet, and then is spirited off by still another large contingent. This leaves only a few necessary people on frame. Hamlet rushes foreframe as Laertes raises himself to a kneeling position. In many productions Laertes dies before Hamlet's forgiveness, but here Hamlet holds him tenderly at the last. Hamlet now reaches his mother's side but then quickly steps between Horatio and the poisoned drink, struggling intensely for a moment. A soldier, Marcellus it seems, enters with a cloak

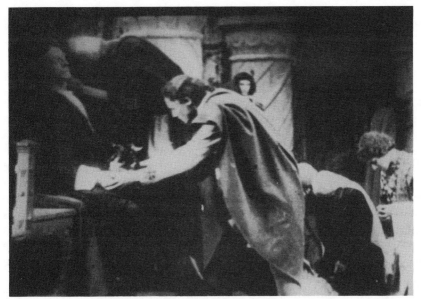

The Forbes Robertson *Hamlet*. Hamlet's death.

for Hamlet and, with Horatio, helps Hamlet to the throne, where he takes the scepter before he dies. Horatio puts the crown in his hands and kneels as Osric enters and kneels respectfully. At the rear, someone shows his grief by turning his face away and pressing his forehead against a pillar. Marcellus is leaning against Hamlet's shoulder in sorrow. The director showed excellent control over the supernumeraries who contribute significantly—evidently an improvement over the stage production. Shaw had criticized the supers in October 1897 for not playing the part of courtiers listening to a king. The film presumably ended with the entrance of Fortinbras, missing from the Folger print.[23]

Though camera work and setting leave something to be desired, the film, inserting now and again what might be called a cinematic moment, concentrates on bringing out Forbes Robertson's acting ability. Describing the stage version, Shaw, in a letter to Alfred Cruikshank, said, "Forbes Robertson's gallant, alert Hamlet, thoughtful but not in the least sentimental, is *the* Hamlet of to-day" (Shaw 1961, 82). This description holds for the film version as well. He is sublime, gentle and gentlemanly, even with Claudius. It is easy to sum him up in a few words, and yet there are depths beneath the surface courtliness: the outbreak of an unexpected sarcasm with Polonius and Osric, the playfulness and wit, the tenderness for Ophelia—nuances of sensibility. This is an aristocratic Hamlet, one that is every inch a prince. No wonder Forbes Robertson's contemporaries raved about his performance, a Hamlet in the tradition of Edwin Booth.[24] While Forbes Robertson does not uncover some of the more menacing or tortured aspects of Hamlet's character, his is one of the best of its kind.

Ironically, the long takes that allow this acting to unfold also run counter to cinematic imperatives, which make the shot rather than the scene the basic unit of film grammar.[25] Rachel Low blames Forbes Robertson for the long takes, finding the failure of the film inevitable "when . . . a famous veteran of the stage, accustomed to knowing best, . . . insisted on speaking every single line and only reluctantly agreed to certain cuts when the results were finally seen" (188). On the other hand, since Hepworth uses the word "scene" in defining the shot (122–23), the long takes are as much his responsibility. Part of the reason the film is so long compared to the other silent films is that it allows close-to-real time for speech instead of conveying the salient emotion more quickly, as mime could. With body, gesture, and expression, Forbes Robertson communicates Shakespeare's language—especially to one who knows the play well—from the mocking tones of "the Funeral bakt-meats" to the resigned yet sad notes of "O I dye Horatio."[26]

Early silent films like Hepworth's show strong relationships to the theater in setting, in business, in interpretation. Both the Forbes Robertson and the LUX *Hamlet* use a carpenter's set for the vigil scene: this was a stage tradition. The painted backdrop is also a feature of stage productions of that period as well as of the films. The crawling of Hamlet towards Claudius in the play scene, the use of a script, the loose dress for Ophelia when she is mad—these are just some of the correspondences in *Hamlet* business between stage and screen versions. In interpretation, we can see the same dichotomous ideas about Hamlet as on stage. Forbes Robertson and LUX present the Castiglione/Werther kind of hero, CINES the more energetic, nondilatory Hamlet with few psychological nuances in characterization. The silents not only show the inadequacy for film of the stage scheme of things; they also show film's strength in concentrating attention on the actor—something film theorists occasionally deny. In film we know characters as much by their body stance, costume, and presence as by their words, for a silent Hamlet can nevertheless appear to be articulate, witty, and rational. In recorded sound versions, the voice virtually alone must characterize.

Notes

1. Producers in the early days of film seem to have been responsible for everything. See Talbot, 153. It's clear in any case from Hepworth's autobiography, *Came the Dawn*, that he was the prime creative force in his company. Plumb was an actor. Unfortunately, Hepworth has very little specifically to say about his *Hamlet*—except that it was one of his first important films. Looking back over a lifetime of stage Hamlets, E. Martin Browne in

the 1956 volume of *Shakespeare Survey* declared that Forbes Robertson's was the best of all. Forbes Robertson was Browne's first Hamlet; perhaps firsts are always best.

2. Georges Sadoul 1948. Leon Gaumont was the first to produce a sound film, in 1902 (Talbot, 184–85).

3. Rachel Low says that "Hepworth . . . excelled above all in pictorial composition and photographic work rather than in the pace of the film. In any case, reviewers and, so far as can be ascertained, film makers themselves seem to have been guided by the conventions of pictorial beauty which applied to static art" (3:222). See also Krakauer, who claims photography is the art form most closely related to film (ix).

4. A picture of the set in *The Literary Digest*, 2 August 1913, 173, interestingly enough shows a very deep platform set, but the camera captures only the back ten feet or so, because it remains sixty feet away from the subject for the long shot. On the carpenter's set for 1.1, see Sprague, 127–28.

5. Ophelia in the family scene (1.3) and Gertrude in the unloosing scene (2.2) drop upstage (rear frame) while others are talking, a not unusual stage blocking. The play-within-a-play, as expected, takes place in rear frame. More aptly for film, the interaction between Rosencrantz and Guildenstern and Polonius in left rear as Hamlet, foreframe center, talks to the First Player sets up two planes of action, not impossible for stage but not likely to be used because on stage it might be too distracting; in silent film, the audience can easily grasp the two separate groupings and subordinate the less important one. Because there are two centers of interest this grouping is different from the blocking with relatively passive supernumeraries in the background to be found on stage and in film in court scenes.

6. Dent knew the Forbes Robertson film because he writes about it in "The World of the Cinema: Speculations and Regrets," *London News*, 14 May 1960, when the film was revived at the National Film Theater, but if, as seems likely, he had not seen it before working on the Olivier script, any similarity is fortuitous.

7. Richard Levin (209–11) describes "Fluellenism" as the comparison of two unrelated things, as Fluellen compares King Henry to Alexander in *Henry V*.

8. An advertisement for the film in *The Moving Picture World*, 10 July 1915, 329, shows the two chairs with a more generous slice of the set than the moving picture affords.

9. Ball (191) cites the *Kinematograph and Lantern Weekly* as crediting the arrangements from Tchaikovsky to Henry Gibson; Hamilton Clark had done the music for the stage production, much to Bernard Shaw's displeasure (see Shaw 1961, 92).

10. This variation occurs whenever a character moves from front to rear frame, as in "To be" and the nunnery scene. Sometimes also the placement of characters at variable distances from the camera produces a variety of effects. For example, in the letter scene (2.2), Claudius sits in near closeup, left frame, Gertrude in medium shot in center frame, while Polonius stands in long shot in right frame.

11. Hepworth says that he liked to use a panning camera but "we were informed by America—then our biggest customer—that Americans would not stand these movements and we must keep our camera stationary" (75–6).

12. Not surprisingly, at that time editing and titling were considered the same function. See Woods.

13. Such misplaced titles are not infrequent in the Folger Library print. A typical example is the abrupt appearance during the disclosure scene (1.2.160–255) of the title for the beginning of the family scene (1.3). Another is the title for the prayer scene, "Now might I do it pat, now he is praying," cut in a few frames before the end of the recorder scene. Still another is the title "The treacherous instrument. . . . Unbated and envenomed. . . . The poisoned cup," which should appear between the Osric scene and the duel but instead appears before the end of the Osric scene. Finally, in the duel scene where the director shifts between two camera setups, twice under cover of a title but twice with only a fade, two misplaced titles could be the cause. If, for example, the title "They bleed on

both sides" had come—as logically it should have—after the rest period rather than during it, the camera shift would have, as usual, been masked by the title.

14. In 1914, the exceptional film *Spiritisten* features constant changes in point of view, including a high angle (overhead) shot of the seance table. See the photograph of three views opposite 167 in Georges Sadoul's *Histoire Generale.*

15. A modern production, which used the Forbes Robertson promptbook, had Ophelia brought in on the bier with her blonde hair dripping—a particularly poignant touch, the reviewer thought. See Horobetz, 409–10.

16. Robert Ball says that this film "does not rank with Forbes-Robertson's *Hamlet* because Warde [Lear] was not as great an actor as Forbes-Robertson." But the too frequent titles are another important reason for its inadequacy. Ball provides a full summary (241–44).

17. The commentator in the Oxberry Edition notes that "Mr. Kemble—when he took off his sword and gave it to Horatio's care, his gesture was all elegance" (opposite 81).

18. Many book illustrations show Hamlet with sword up, forward or down, e.g., 1779, 1782, and 1806. Cp. Barrymore, with sword held like a cross (1933 "Test Shots for *Hamlet*"), business followed by Olivier, 1948, and begun, according to Sprague (141), by Booth.

19. His idea about Hamlet's sanity derives, as he says, from George Mac Donald, for whose study of the Folio he wrote a one-page introduction.

20. See the photo in *The Literary Digest,* 18 October 1913, 683.

21. The Rowe edition shows two portraits on the wall; an 1801 edition shows two miniatures. Except for the few productions that use imaginary pictures (e.g., Burton 1964), most have one or the other. Olivier in 1948 has miniatures, one that Hamlet wears, one that Gertrude wears. Evans (1953) uses portraits early on as well as miniatures in the closet scene. Cain (Boston Shakespeare Co.) has Hamlet take the miniature of Claudius from Gertrude during the play scene. Papp (1982) has Hamlet take the miniature from Rosencrantz.

22. Surprisingly, there is no "sweets to the sweet" by mime or by title. One of the court ladies, rather than the queen, holds a basket of flowers, and the Priest signals her to toss the blooms in the grave.

23. *Motion Picture World,* 10 July 1915, 317–18, mentions Fortinbras's entrance.

24. On Booth, see both Shattuck 1960 and Clarke.

25. In 1915 and 1916, Griffith, through his monumental films, persuaded filmmakers that the essential unit of film is the shot. This was so much accepted that by 1917 a film critic (Epes, 369–70) was saying that excellence is not to be measured merely by the number of shots.

26. A contemporary reviewer says he could not always make out the language ("Forbes Robertson on Two Continents," 683), but his criticism indicates that he expected to.

16

Sound Recordings

That recordings exist for such performers as Sir Johnston Forbes Robertson and Edwin Booth seems almost a miracle.[1] Nearer our own time, recordings of John Barrymore, John Gielgud, Orson Welles, and other Hamlets open doors that would otherwise be forever closed. Their photographs reveal something of their physical interpretation, but their voices, often, are the reason for their renown. Other recordings preserve in readily accessible form the soundtrack of moving-picture performances. Olivier, Chamberlain, and Burton are among those who have recorded part or all of their *Hamlet* productions. A Maurice Evans recording of six excerpts from *Hamlet* and three excerpts from *Richard II* (Columbia RL3107) does not reveal its origin but, since the original music by Roger Adams sounds the same as that for the Hallmark Hall of Fame production in 1953, the recording probably derives from the television programs. Still other recordings feature radio broadcasts or original productions.

As well as preserving vocal performances, the recordings measure the possibilities of the aural media.[2] Because so much of sighted people's information comes through visual perception, sound recordings may appear even more limiting than silent films. But, just as silent films communicate sounds through sight, so do recordings through sound imply setting and evoke an image of costume. Wind sound, crowd noises, music of a particular period, the sound of the metal rings of a curtain sliding along a metal pole, the rustle of gowns, the clatter of armor—all help the audience to visualize the production.

Space, surprisingly, is perhaps the easiest of the visual qualities to suggest aurally: technical sound effects, such as echo chambers, physical actions, and voice qualities contribute to the evocation of space. In the script of Gielgud's 1948 broadcast, directions call for physical movement to help sound projection give the illusion of space—for example, when Horatio upon the entrance of the ghost spreads his arms; the physical act helps the actor to produce the voice effect that creates the illusion of space between him and the ghost. Complementary voice signals, including shouting from close to and far from the microphone, effectively suggest large distances. A 1971 broadcast script has the direction "pitching" to show that Claudius throws his voice to Polonius, some distance away, and then the direction "approach" for Polonius. Varying distances from the microphone is the most common means to denote space through sound.

John Carey, in an unpublished paper on "Framing Mechanisms in Radio Drama," cited by Erving Goffman in *Frame Analysis* (145–49), analyzes conventions that impart through sound what would be known by sight. He mentions reduction of sound volume to signal the termination of a scene, that is, an aural "fade out," with the parallel "fade in"; music both between scenes to foretell what is to happen and during a scene to act as a kind of subtitle for the listener (besides background music that the characters can hear); verbal information to identify sounds for listeners; the volume of the voice, the angle and distance of the speaker from the microphone. One can detect these and more among the *Hamlet* sound recordings.

Like silent films, sound-only dramatizations have their limitations, of course. Obviously, the only spectacle that obtains is that within each listener's mind. Further, on stage, as Erving Goffman asserts, we focus on one character though other characters are witnessed simultaneously. Films sometimes prevent us from this simultaneity by tight shots and closeups, but at least it is theoretically possible to observe the cynosure and the bystanders. Since our capacity to single out sounds does not match our ability to single out individuals visually (209), most sound recordings have to focus on one person at a time. Such instances preclude simultaneity: when one person is the focus of attention, others may be forgotten. The productions try to overcome this limitation in various ways, sometimes, as films do, finding solutions that make the limitation an asset. For example, in the Welles radio broadcast, Claudius in the prayer scene does not say "Bow, stubborn knees" until after Hamlet has arrived, seen him and begun to speak (3.3). By interweaving the speeches rather than having them follow one another serially, the script approaches simultaneity. In addition, Claudius's prayer in Latin is faintly audible as Hamlet speaks. Later in the Welles version, Horatio moans as Hamlet, trying to wrench the cup away, says to Horatio, "If thou did'st ever hold me in thy heart. . . ." In the Micheál MacLiammóir and the Paul Scofield *Hamlet*s, Hamlet's "Mother, mother, mother" overlaps the voices of Polonius and Gertrude. These doubling sounds, with one person's voice dominant, the other's recessive, are equivalent to television's rack shot, which attempts to overcome limited depth of field by first focusing on one character while another in a different plane is out of focus and then switching focus.

Productions, like Gielgud's Old Vic recording, that do not provide some aural indication of presence, seem deeply flawed. In the nunnery scene, for example, Ophelia (Yvonne Mitchell) makes not a sound after her final speech, not even in response to Polonius's perfunctory words of comfort. On the other hand, extraneous sounds originally meant to accompany visual elements that are absent from the recording, as in the Chamberlain sound track recording of his *Hamlet* on television, mystify rather than compensate for these missing visual elements. Productions, like Scofield's, designed specifically with the sound medium in mind, are much better—that is, if one wants to get the sense that one is listening to a performance rather than a recording of a performance.

Though, as John Russell Taylor asserts, radio and audio recordings are "best calculated to swallow Shakespeare whole without indigestion" (100), cutting of the text, when it occurs, is, as on silent film, apt to be more drastic than usual on stage or in feature-length sound films. Barrymore's *Hamlet,* for example, eliminates Ophelia; Welles's "To be or not to be." Even the shortest of the silents included both, but other omissions are traditional: often no ambassadors, no prayer scene, no Fortinbras, just as on stage or on film. Early in this century, producers had the idea that an audience's attention span was not very long; probably audiences had similar notions. The feature film did not become popular until after 1913, and two-hour and longer films were not common until the fifties. Radio broadcasts vary from one-hour condensations to "uncut" versions, seldom fully uncut. Even the very full Scofield version cuts a line here and there from its composite Q2 and F1 text. Some of the early broadcasts were presented as short miniseries, one installment per evening. But later broadcasts (after 1945) become longer, corresponding with the development of length in films. The BBC's 1948 version with Gielgud ran for three hours and forty-four minutes, for example, while the Barrymore versions of various Shakespeare plays, the 1937 Streamlined Shakespeare series, including *Hamlet,* each lasted only one hour. A *New York Times* reviewer of Barrymore's radio *Hamlet* is certain that an hour is the longest that radio could hold a mass audience. Phonograph discs and tapes vary similarly because many are simply sound tracks of stage, television, or film productions—though some (like the Burgess Meredith production of 1937) are original sound productions.

Ophelia, of course, is a favorite character for line trimming. In the Welles production the narrator mentions Ophelia for the first time before the play-within-a-play begins. Hamlet's sexual teasing, however, is cut. There had been no nunnery scene. Her minimal role is thus virtually erased; she is included only to play the expected and awaited mad scene. The cuts in her role are extreme but in accord with many productions' depictions of Ophelia. Cuts, however, sometimes defy logic—for example, the Player Queen in this production says "confound the rest" before her husband begins.

Because of cuts, transitions between scenes may be needed, but even full-length productions make use of them. To bridge scenes, sound recordings supply sound equivalents of the fade in, fade out and dissolve. In doing so, audio recordings, inadvertently perhaps, come close to Elizabethan practice; Maurice Charney says that sound on the Elizabethan stage, rather than light as on our modern stage, represented the passing of time (1969, 181). However innocent and pragmatic any transition may be, it often has an interpretative effect. A direction at the head of the first court scene calls for subdued chatter underlying the narrative bridge; we are to imagine that the characters are entering. Before the narrator concludes, another direction calls for "chatter down." The sound is of a relaxed crowd—an interpretative choice. Other sounds are more neutral, but even neutral sounds have their emotional effect, distancing us, as it were, from the action. The Welles broadcast uses a wide range of sounds, including a gong as a kind of scene punctuation. For Barrymore's production, drum rolls mark the transitions between most of the scenes, but, to mark the juncture between 1.4 and 1.5, storm sounds rise, then drop.[3] Such sounds can of course be used on stage as well. A review of Papp's *Hamlet* with Sam Waterston (1975) refers to the "ominous drum rolls between scenes" (Babula, number 161).

Music, sometimes extradramatic—like those drum rolls or like the falling, on stage, of a curtain with a painted picture that has nothing to do with the drama—may indicate changing acts, as it does for the Barrymore production. The Armed Forces broadcasts surround productions with curiously inappropriate swing music. Radio often uses the same music for a whole series, and thus it has no particular relevance for *Hamlet.*

Sometimes, however, specific music introduces persons or places, thus acting as a subtitle. The discords of the Chamberlain recording for the choir procession of the first court scene imply that this marriage between Claudius and Gertrude upsets what should be harmonious. Harp notes in a minor key in this production after Polonius's order to Ophelia to stop seeing Hamlet foreshadow later events. Music with a big, symphonic sound, with an emphasis on violins, is fairly constant in this production, giving it a sentimental, slightly overblown sound.

Just as in visual media, particularly silent films, music in sound media can add important atmospheric elements both between scenes and within scenes. To distinguish the ghost, sound recordings must combine techniques. Few productions, however, take advantage of the full possibilities of the medium and the natural prominence of sound effects in the absence of visual effects. Some have the ghost speak into a grand piano to produce an otherworldly effect. Barrymore's ghost-sounds raise the hackles: a high soprano moan from the spirit world as irritating as a scratch on a blackboard. Scofield, more subtly (perhaps too subtly), has low, almost inaudible tones behind the ghost. Other productions content themselves with wind sound, but Welles's adds moans for a trite effect. The Marlowe Society Recording uses horns in notes not unlike those for scene breaks. The sound does not harrow one with fear and wonder. But sounds can be even more eerie, even more evocative of the fear of ghosts than visual devices.

Like music, a narrator's voice can bridge scenes or comment within a scene. In many of the sound recordings, we note first the narrator's voice, announcing characters when we cannot see who has entered. Narrators sometimes supply information cut from the script and are apt to be particularly important when commercials interrupt continuity. But more often the narrator is an interpreter or explicator who voices the production's choices. A summary on the jacket may provide for the phonograph what the narrator does for the radio audience. Like the silent film's title writer, the script writer often draws inferences, putting them into narrative bridges, undermining the audience's opportunity for discovery, making overt what the audience would indeed perhaps overlook.

A case in point is the bridge between act 1 and act 2, in which some narrators state that two months have passed. Though the audience may indeed infer that some time has passed when it hears Polonius sending Laertes money through Reynaldo (when that scene is included, as it rarely is), they do not know precisely how much time until Ophelia in act 3 says, "Nay, 'tis twice two moneths," in response to Hamlet's: "my Father dyed within's two Houres" (3.2.134–35)—that is, they will know then that two months have passed since Hamlet has spoken to the ghost if they remember that Hamlet had said in the first act that it has been a scant two months since his father died. Shakespeare, I think, had a reason for withholding the exact length of time for so long, for underplaying it by placing it within a conversation where many miss it, and for requiring an arithmetical computation to arrive at the correct time. As act 2 proceeds, we know only that Hamlet has put on the antic disposition he had thought of at the end of act 1; nothing indicates any untoward delay until his own self-castigation at the end of act 2.[4] Without the narrator's comment, recordings would have to rely on Hamlet's acting to express delay.

The narrator or the blurb may supply information that is not in the text itself. Though any stage or moving-image performance shapes audience perception through setting, costume, and blocking, audio media must be even more direct. In the Welles production, the narrator explains Claudius's departure from the play-within-a-play as motivated by the realization that his crime has been enacted before the whole court. The narrator also informs us that Claudius arranges for Hamlet's death before he falls to prayer. Shakespeare neither tells us why Claudius leaves nor fixes the point of decision for murder. In the text, at the beginning of the prayer scene, speaking to Rosencrantz and Guildenstern, Claudius says, "I your Commission will forthwith dispatch." This could mean that he will have the commission drawn up soon. In that case, he may not have decided to murder Hamlet until his attempt to pray failed. These choices affect an audience's perception of both Claudius and Hamlet. It is not so much that the broadcast's interpretations are not possible on stage or moving image as that the narrator divulges what the acting could imply. In contrast, in the BBC 1948 broadcast, the narrative link before the prayer scene says simply that

> The King, fully alive to his danger, on the ground that Hamlet is mad, immediately arranges that a commission headed by Rosencrantz and Guildenstern should take him to england [sic]—they depart, and the conscience stricken King is left alone—

In the Welles production, after Ophelia plays out her one mad scene before her brother, the narrator informs us that she drifts away to die. This version skips the first part of 4.5 and 4.6, leaving mysterious the fate of Rosencrantz and Guildenstern and Hamlet's escape, and 4.7, which is taken care of by the narrator who says that Laertes, determined to seek revenge, finds in Claudius a helper. This puts Laertes in control, although Shakespeare has Claudius manipulate Laertes into the dishonorable scheme.

Barrymore, acting as narrator in his radio production, explains that ghosts are not so believable, that Hamlet wants by his own actions to have the proof, that he feigns madness seeking to observe his uncle. He presents all of these problematical issues as if nothing could be simpler. He tells us that Hamlet has been visited by two school friends when Polonius enters to tell him the players have arrived. After Barrymore as Hamlet demonstrates Hamlet's dislike for Polonius and his warmth and good humor with his old friends the players, Barrymore the narrator again steps in, in modern dress he says, to bridge the action: he tells us that "The Mousetrap" has come off satisfactorily, that Claudius "proclaimed his malefactions in the most satisfactory manner, leaving no doubt in Hamlet's mind but that his ghostly instructions were absolutely correct." Again, Barrymore suggests that the text makes everything definite, but of course it does not. He then introduces the closet scene, which begins with Polonius's hurriedly whispered words, "He will come straight."

The narrator of the 1948 Gielgud production tells us between scenes 1 and 2 that Polonius heads the group of councillors, that Laertes is one of the courtiers, and that Hamlet's "claim to the throne has been overridden and he is not a member of the Council." This same narration, as near as I can tell, is used for another Gielgud production, the Old Vic Company's *Hamlet* recorded in 1957 (on RCA Victor LM 6404).[5] In the text, in contrast, we do not learn until the interview in his mother's closet that Claudius "Popt in betweene th'election and [Hamlet's] hopes" (5.2.66; 3.4.99–101), and we never learn that Hamlet had actually made a claim to the throne. Nor do we know that he is not a member of the Council, for Shakespeare does not mention one. Claudius's invitation to Hamlet to remain at court, in fact, implies that he is to be close to the king:

> we beseech you, bend you to remaine
> Heere in the cheere and comfort of our eye,
> Our cheefest Courtier Cosin, and our Sonne.
> (1.2.115–17)

John Gielgud recorded *Hamlet* several times, once in a ninety-minute version broadcast on NBC, 4 March 1951, with Horatio as the narrator. This version presents *Hamlet* as a flashback, beginning with Hamlet's request that Horatio tell his story. Perhaps the idea came from Olivier's 1948 film, which begins with dead Hamlet. Since the radio production is cut drastically, Horatio fills in several narrative gaps, as when he briefly explains the plot that Claudius and Laertes devise. Horatio also makes interpretive statements: that Hamlet had "dearly loved" Ophelia, that Gertrude "dotes" on Hamlet, and that Hamlet suspected the king of treachery. These additions hardly seem necessary.

Just as silent films might have redundant titles, so too many sound recordings add unnecessary narrative links: the narrator of the 1948 broadcast announces that the king has sent for Rosencrantz and Guildenstern, a fact revealed in the first four lines of the scene (2.2), and the narrator says that Gertrude is talking about Ophelia with Horatio and a Gentleman, again soon revealed in the scene (4.5). If for this first mad scene the producers had used F1 instead of Q2, there would have been no Gentleman to distinguish from Horatio. The fact that many radio scripts, even those cut severely (for example, a version broadcast by the BBC in October 1971), do not use a narrative bridge between scenes demonstrates that they are not necessary, particularly when the voices of all characters are distinctive, as they must be. Why then is the narrator so frequently used? What does that reveal about what the audience expected? The narrator may be the equivalent of the many explanatory prologues found in films, or of the explanatory passages found in playbills—a guide who can lead an unsophisticated audience through a Shakespearean play, by expectation "hard." Though narrative links smooth and soothe, they often shift emphasis or distort motivation or oversimplify.

In addition to the narrator's words to help us remember others' presence and to suggest interpretations, recordings add words to the text itself to clarify the action, just as silent films add their visualizations. For example, the 1971 broadcast frequently has listeners say an acquiescent "my lord," to indicate that they are listening. Polonius says "my daughter" after "Oh ho, do you marke that" (3.2.118) to indicate what he means; in visual media his glance would do it. When a character walks on, an added introductory word or two introduces him: "What says Polonius, our Lord Chamberlain," is one such addition, for Welles's production (2.2). In the 1951 Gielgud production Polonius calls out "well spoken" after Claudius asks Hamlet to consider him a father.

The duel scene particularly demands interpretative comments if the subtext is to be clear to a listening audience. In the 1951 Gielgud production, after Hamlet is hurt someone calls out that Laertes's sword is unbated and someone else yells that "Hamlet has seized the poisoned sword!" Without these added words, Laertes's death would impress one as accidental, unless, as in some productions, the narrator were to tell us otherwise. In the Welles production, during the fencing, voices from the crowd give us needed information: "A touch for Laertes"; "Look, they have changed rapiers." The last implies that Hamlet does not purposely exchange rapiers and thus that he never realizes Laertes's sword was unbated. In films, added visual scenes are apt to be more extensive than such verbal additions, being dramatizations of Shakespeare's summaries of action; in sound media, added words, auralizations of what we would see at a glance, tend to be brief. In the Barrymore production, the duel scene could have been confusing, but with a few deft interjections and sound effects is surprisingly lucid. We do not know precisely how Hamlet came to be wounded nor how Laertes received his death blow. We do not know the reactions of the bystanders. But we do hear the insouciant resolve of the queen to drink, Hamlet's workmanlike refusal to drink as yet, sounds of the exciting combat, the effete voice of Osric, Claudius's effort to outface all, and his death groans.

Like silent film, recordings also find it necessary to emphasize one trait of each of the subsidiary characters. Polonius's voice almost invariably creaks—he is an old man; the Scofield Polonius snuffs in after every line and utters many inarticulate hmms and ahs. Ophelia's voice is usually sweet and her style pathetic; Claudius and Gertrude vary from recording to recording but within each production they can usually be summed up with one or two words. In Welles's radio production, the flatness of Claudius's voice reveals the mediocre quality of the man. Gertrude's wheedling tone for her "go not to Wittenberg" indicates a woman used to manipulating men through her femininity. In that same production, Polonius's voice is very distinctive, possibly Welsh. Guildenstern also has a distinctive voice, making it possible for once to distinguish him from Rosencrantz, something visual media do not always do, usually purposely. Gertrude in the Gielgud Old Vic production conveys the Oedipal interpretation through her voice: arch, teasing, not maternal when she asks Hamlet to "Let not thy Mother lose her Prayers."

When the subtext *between* the lines dominates, recordings may not be able to indicate, without additions, the meaning of, for example, pregnant silences; but when the words convey the subtext, actors can interpret. Challenging Laertes, Welles's tone expresses Hamlet's anger. An actress playing Gertrude, however, is unable to use body language, gaze, and gesture to show, as she might on film, that she drinks the poison to protect Hamlet. Thus Gertrude in the Welles production instead sounds jolly, patently drinking the poison inadvertently. Since Horatio has no opportunity to embrace, kiss, or look tenderly at Hamlet, Horatio's last words, "Now cracks a Noble heart: / Goodnight sweet Prince, / And flights of Angels sing thee to thy rest," said very softly, must carry all the emotion.

Visual media can provide quick images to tell us Hamlet knows that Polonius and the king are spying, thus accounting for Hamlet's behavior to Ophelia in the remainder of the nunnery scene: usually, both Hamlet and the film or stage audience glimpse one or the other of the spies. Recordings usually must rely on superb acting to supply the reason for any sudden shift in Hamlet's behavior towards Ophelia. Micheál MacLiammóir, a magnificent, melancholy Hamlet, does it with a catch in his voice after a very tender "Goe thy wayes to a Nunnery," followed by a steely-voiced "Where's your Father?" and then a shouting, harsh, sarcastic, and finally choked tirade after her unsatisfactory answer. Though Gielgud's 1951 version allows us to hear, in the distance, Polonius saying something to the king, the acting itself has a greater impact. Immediately, Hamlet asks "Where's your father?" Since the answer is obviously a lie, he becomes angry, tearful, the intrinsic loudness of his voice sometimes diminished by movement away from the microphone as he paces about. In the 1957 production, nothing actually tells us that Hamlet sees the spies. Indeed, we see how possible it is to play the scene without the revelation. Hamlet (Gielgud) begins with a sharp edge in his voice (after a tender "Soft you now, / The faire Ophelia?" said to himself), which gets harder and louder as he describes himself. With a sudden shift in tone, he asks "Where's your father?" We do not need to see or hear the spies because her answer sounds like a lie. Hamlet's voice is so harsh that physical violence would not be surprising. When he says "all but one shall live," his voice sounds as if he has gone to the back of the room to say it directly to the arras behind which Polonius and the king are hiding.

Silent films suggest the stage through setting, business, and acting style—visual means. Sound recordings go further, standing in for stage productions through aural means and especially through their fore-grounding of the actor. This seems to be true regardless of the presence or absence of a physical stage, whether the recording is made in a studio, in an empty or occupied theater.[6] This appears to be true even when the sound recording is derived from a moving-image version. Many theater people protest the encroachments of moving images in their Shake-speare territory. Since Shakespeare, their argument goes, wrote for the stage and only for the stage, no moving-image production can be in any way a valid production of Shakespeare—however much, the kinder ones might say, it might be something quite good in itself.[7] Seldom, if ever, has anyone raised any such objection to Shakespeare on sound record-ings, though at first it would seem that the audio-only production must be more unlike Shakespeare's play than a moving-image production with sound would be. What makes the sound recording acceptable to the filmophobic dramaphile is the primacy of the voice and thus the primacy of the actor.

Notes

1.   Ball has a reference to a recording of Forbes Robertson, and Dan Watermeier, lecturing at the Columbia Shakespeare Seminar in May 1983, referred to an Edison recording of Booth's "To be," now lost, and of his speech by Othello to the Venetian Senate, still extant. Both extant fragments can be found at Harvard.

2.   Radio broadcasting must be distinguished from consumer-available sound record-ings because it places different demands on an audience, but for purposes of the discussion here, I am grouping them all under the heading "sound recordings" (even though I know some of the radio broadcasts only from the scripts). Radio broadcasts sometimes become available as sound recordings, as did the Barrymore broadcast of 1937 and the Gielgud broadcast of 1951 for CBS.

For important discussions of sound in films, see Altman.

3.   Excerpts are available on an Audio Rarities recording, including some of Bar-rymore's narrative, parts of Hamlet's encounter with the ghost (1.4 and 1.5), the instruc-tions to the players (3.2), "Oh what a Rogue and Pesant slave am I" (the end of 2.2), "To be, or not to be" (3.1), the introduction of the players (2.2), the closet scene (3.4) and the duel (5.2); the complete recording is at the Library of Congress (RU36–4, 3B).

4.   This is not to say that every production must explore delay. David Bevington says that "in the light of [Hamlet's actions in many scenes], Hamlet's self-accusations are signs of burning impatience in one who would surely act if he could" (6).

5.   The narrative of the 1948 broadcast was lifted not only for another Gielgud produc-tion but also for an entirely different 1966 version, also on BBC. It is difficult to imagine the appurtenances of any 1948 film or stage version reused for a production twenty years later—unless for a purposeful revival. That it was possible for a radio broadcast suggests that the medium is different in some fundamental way from stage and film.

6.   Bernard Beckerman made the distinctions in setting in a talk at the Modern Lan-guage Association in 1983 in a panel on *Othello.*

7.   See Homan on five ways of seeing Shakespeare translations in visual media (207–19).

Three Great Hamlets in Recorded Sound

The raison d' être of sound recordings of *Hamlet* is to highlight the voice, the actor's most important instrument—above all, Hamlet's voice. Three great audio Hamlets—Welles, Barrymore and Burton—demonstrate the vocal variety required of a sound-only recording. Barrymore, in his stage production of 1922, perfected a wildly energetic, Freudian Hamlet that influenced virtually all the productions that followed, with Olivier, who saw his production in London, as a conduit to the fifties and beyond (Teague, 66–68). Though Barrymore comes second in the chronological sequence of audio recordings, clearly his notions of the character affected not only Burton's but also Welles's interpretations.

The version starring, arranged by, and directed by Orson Welles in 1936, when the actor was only nineteen years old, was a CBS production. Without the visual effects, we can be even more aware of his voice as a remarkable instrument, evoking visualizations as well as clarifying interpretative choices. His whispered asides suggest interiority or complicity with the audience. By his distracted words over sounds of the entrance, Welles communicates his failure to notice the arrival of Horatio and the others. He reacts quickly to their disclosure, immediately intense. This Hamlet is suspicious of Rosencrantz and Guildenstern from the beginning, an effect perhaps easier to communicate than a gradual, awakening suspicion. Welles demonstrates the suspicion through his grudging, hesitant speech and then through his mimicking, mocking tone, used with Polonius as well. Hamlet is not very warm with the players; he knows them but they are not bosom friends. This allows Hamlet, not Polonius, to say impatiently, "Come to Hecuba." Earlier, in "Oh that this too too solid Flesh, would melt," his voice ranged from sorrow to anger to incredulity. "Oh what a Rogue and Pesant slave am I" gives him greater scope: pacing and pitch, musicality, harshness, loudness, tears, disgust, anger, regret, sorrow, and warning mark the beats of the soliloquy. Hamlet's advice to the players is low-keyed, conversational; he makes them laugh at his joke about nature's journeymen. Similarly, in the graveyard scene, Hamlet is in good humor, laughing quietly at the gravedigger's jokes. During such moments, we get a sense of the "normal" Hamlet, the man he would be if his world had not sundered. In act 3, quietly at first but increasing to a shout as he says what will make Claudius blench, Hamlet explains the play while the murderer continues to speak, the player's voice distanced, as if he performs at the rear of a room. Tone of voice expresses interpretations better than do narrators' explanations. In this production, when Hamlet tells Gertrude she has murdered a king, she sounds very surprised, and when Hamlet sees he has killed Polonius, he sounds amazed. Her rapid repetition of his words telegraphs her shock, while his gasp upon drawing the arras aside reveals his. Thus actors' voices can develop the subtext, and certainly Welles's voice is capable of anything.[1]

The closet scene gives both Welles and the actress playing Gertrude an opportunity to show their full range. As Hamlet describes his father, his mother cries softly. He says "Have you eyes?" very harshly. He lengthens or shortens syllables for their emotional effect, as does she; for example, for "cleft my heart in twaine" she separates each of the five syllables, scaling down in pitch. He says "go not to mine Uncles bed" very softly; "when you are desirous to be blest / Ile blessing begge of you" even lower. Though Gertrude assures him she will not give him away, she sounds sick rather than loving. The narrator confirms what we might expect, that Hamlet has not persuaded his mother. Thus later she says "But not by him" to Laertes, wholeheartedly protecting Claudius.

A year later, Barrymore's radio *Hamlet* was broadcast, enabling one to compare the older man and the younger one. In many ways the two actors, Welles and Barrymore, are similar in the sort of variety with which they wield their instruments. Welles's voice, however, is rich, mellow, fine wine; Barrymore's is a bit raspy, dry, unlovely compared to Welles's. Though the particular broadcast production does not use all of radio's resources to best advantage and though Barrymore is not at his peak, there are moments that give a listener a sense of what this great actor could do. He offers not only variety but intelligent interpretative choices. Just as in the soundtrack of the "Test Shots for *Hamlet*," Barrymore's voice rises to an emotional climax on "father": "I'll call thee Hamlet, / King, Father. . . ," a famous and still moving interpretation. While Hamlet sounds intense but fearless, the two distinctive voices of Marcellus and Horatio quaver, increasing our sense of Hamlet's bravery. Though they urge Hamlet not to follow the ghost, we hear no physical struggle or sword business, which could have been managed through

The Barrymore *Hamlet*. Test shots for Hamlet, 1933.

scuffling sounds and the metallic sweep of steel from scabbard, as we hear later when Hamlet kills Polonius. At the end of the ghost's words— "remember me" fading—Hamlet says "adieu" as if to the ghost (though it has evidently left) and then, his voice dropping, to himself he says, with quiet determination, "Remember me: I have sworn't." A drum roll then marks the end of the scene, followed, on the recording, by Hamlet's advice to the players, a few of Barrymore's words somewhat slurred and muffled. The famous naturalness is quite evident, however. Here especially he sounds colloquial, at ease, a contrast to the high emotional pitch of the ghost scene. When he says "and the verie Age and Bodie of the Time, its [sic] forme and pressure" (3.2.27–29), his voice betrays the pain he feels in this Claudius-dominated time of speedy remarriages.

The self-castigating "what a Rogue and Pesant slave am I" follows immediately with words low-pitched, harsh, out-thrust. Speaking of the player, Hamlet's voice, edged with sarcasm, rises. "Hecuba" is spat out, a steely sound. With "What would he doe / Had he the Motive and the Cue for passion / That I have," Barrymore's voice modulates to the warmth of the recollection of his father. On describing what the player would do, his voice imitates the histrionics of a player on stage. But when he describes himself, his manner, though varying from harsh condemnation to bewilderment, shades into colloquialism, at least up to "No, not for a King, / Upon whose property and most deere life, / A damn'd defeat was made" (2.2.564–66). A pause leads to "Am I a Coward?" asked most matter-of-factly. In his response he marks two beats: first his tone implies that no one dares call him villain, break his pate, pluck off his beard, and so on, but then, after a pause, and more of an "arghh" than a "Ha!", he admits angrily that he *would* take it. His emphatically enunci-ated verbal abuse of Claudius climaxes in a high-pitched exclamation (from F1) "Oh [actually more like "Oah," that is, a cry rather than an interjection] Vengeance!" (None of the recorded sound versions I have heard left out these words, which may indeed be an actor's interpolation in F1, but which obviously work. Even the seven-minute LUX version retains the words, in an intertitle.) A few more groans and Hamlet turns to his plan to use the players. From the first words, his tone reveals his pleasure: the plan does not gradually unfold in his mind; his words describe what is fully in place in his mind already, whether it had taken shape during the short pause or had already suggested itself to him when he spoke to the players. The words about the ghost being a devil are retained. In the last line, Hamlet whispers "The play" once, then shouts it out exultantly. With the last words, "Wherein Ile catch the Conscience of the King," his tone returns to a steely near monopitch. In the soliloquy, when background sound is not necessary, Barrymore's artistry can shine.

The recording continues with "To be," which begins low, close to the mike, expressive of the interiority of the speech. With the word "flesh," Barrymore's tone again becomes taunting, sarcastic, as it did when he spoke of "forme and pressure." Much of the soliloquy is colloquial. Barrymore lengthens the word "dream" in "perchance to Dreame." Then a pause. When he repeats the word "dreams" it reflects all the terror of the dreams in death. Venom infuses the words "sicklied o'er, with the pale cast of Thought . . . Action."

Since the shortness of the closet scene does not allow for much emo-tional variation, anger and contempt pervade most of it. Hamlet's first words to his mother are guarded, a bit cold. She responds without excessive emotion, the dignified matron not making a scene. He quickly becomes more emotional, as he says, "Mother (a wheeze here), *you* have my Father much offended." His choice is to avoid emphasizing the "my," instead emphasizing "you," which implies he will not even recognize her designation of Claudius as his father. She, on the other hand, remains cool, neutral. Her first gasp comes as Hamlet says, "You go not till I set you up a glasse"; he has grabbed her, shattering her facade of control. The distance from the microphone realistically represents Polonius be-hind the arras. The swish of steel as Hamlet speaks, "How now, a Rat?" marks the speed of his reaction. He says "a Rat" with real joy, and Polonius's death groans come with Hamlet's glad words, "dead for a Ducate, dead." Though "is it the King?" sounds merely hopeful, "I tooke thee for thy Better" sounds scornfully certain. With his mother, he more than adequately fulfills the stage direction implied in her words "In noise so rude against me." The scene is cut short by the curious keening sound that signals the ghost's arrival.

One hears in Barrymore's voice the range—in tone, from melodious to abrasive; in pitch, from gratingly low to artificially high; in volume, from whispered to nearly shouted—that characterizes all the great Hamlets of the twentieth century. The naturalness so often remarked upon by his contemporary critics is certainly in evidence here, but only fleetingly, only as contrast to more emotionally charged moments. What makes his voice and the intelligence that supports it special is the quality of gentlemanliness without weakness. Barrymore strikes one as hesitant to act without certainty but not as incapable of action.

The modern actor closest in gifts to John Barrymore is Richard Burton, whose mood shifts and voice range are perhaps even more varied. Part of the excitement generated by Richard Burton's Hamlet as directed by John Gielgud in 1964 stemmed from the reputation of these two giants in their field. In addition, Gielgud assembled a sterling cast to support the eccentric Burton, including Eileen Herlie to play Gertrude again as she had for Laurence Olivier's filmed version eighteen years before, in 1964 a more believable forty-five, and Hume Cronyn to play Polonius. Like the Chamberlain production, the Burton production has two recorded manifestations, one as a filmed stage play, the other as a sound recording. During three performances at the Lunt-Fontanne theater in New York, the production was filmed, edited and shaped into a film, and screened, though for only two performances, in 976 theaters all over the country. Then the film was to be destroyed (Crowther). The producers, true to their word, have never rereleased the film for general viewing. They also made a sound recording of the production, which remains available.

Not surprisingly, the film does not meet minimal criteria for cinematic excellence. Essentially, the document can give a viewer some notion of the stage production, but without the immediacy of the live experience. Even when a filmmaker strives to capture the ambience of the stage, he or she does better to build a stagelike set, as, according to Roger Manvell (118), director Stuart Burge did for Olivier's *Othello* (1965, based on the stage production directed by John Dexter), and direct the actors for specific camera positions. The producers of the Burton *Hamlet* instead appear to have arbitrarily chosen shots—closeups, medium shots, reverse shots—that make the play look like a film. The technique of using multiple cameras focused on live performances has worked well for opera on television, but does not work here. In the Burton production, large audience spaces that swallow sounds, few satisfactory camera maneuvers, long fuzzy shots that dwarf the actors, theatrical lighting in a very dark setting, closeups that block out necessary reactions and actions elsewhere on stage—all make this a less than satisfying production. It is different when the acting and the camera positioning and movement are all planned to coincide, as for example in the American Conservatory Theatre *Taming of the Shrew* (1976). For *Hamlet,* Gielgud planned the staging for the audience at the Lunt-Fontanne, who could grasp the whole stage setting at once, not for the film audience. The acting style, always geared to the long shot, with voice always directed at the back of the balcony, the small number of supernumeraries, the bare two-platform stage with few props, all appropriate to a stage production of 1964, make this a disappointing film. The darkness, while it may be appropriate for a stage production, is not for film. The CBS production of 1959 did better in moving a stage production to film, by changing the lighting from dark to light. The Gielgud production suffers especially in comparison to Kozintsev's *Hamlet,* which was screened in New York City at virtually the same time. (The Russian film previewed in April 1964 and opened the New York Film Festival on 15 September; the Burton film opened on 23 September 1964.)

For all these reasons, listening to the recording made for Columbia Masterworks is in some ways more satisfying than viewing the film. The recording, evidently made at the theater without an audience, allows one to concentrate on the voice qualities that made Burton an actor that other actors watch, study, and emulate. This is not to say that one will not miss a great deal knowing the audio recording alone. One of the features that made this a talked-about production escapes one when listening to the recording: Gielgud conceived it as a rehearsal, with actors wearing rehearsal clothes (Hannan). Though this aspect was not universally approved, Gielgud capitalized on the conception of a play-in-progress, an unfinished work, not yet ready to be judged, a conception the recording cannot express (the information is on the jacket, however). Therefore, the recording has to achieve a level of perfection not demanded, theoretically, by the staged "rehearsal."

More importantly, Burton moves superbly and relays much through body language and pace of gestures. Sometimes, however, his movements can (no doubt purposely) obliterate the meaning of the lines. When for example he says "What a piece of worke is a man," he gets up on a chair, bounces, then gets on the table, then puts one leg on the table, one on the chair. He himself laughs before he says "Man delights not me"; Rosencrantz and Guildenstern's laugh is the sycophants' response, for they can hardly pay attention to what he says while watching what he does—any more than can the audience. This is the antic disposition exaggerated. Various productions bring to the surface (figure) parts of *Hamlet* that are normally recessed (ground), recess parts that are normally at the surface. Burton's onstage treatment of "What a worke is a man" recesses meaning.

The audience of the recording will miss much of this physical play, for, in this instance, Burton, on the recording, reverses the effect of the staging and plays it straight. In fact, the chief feature of the recording is its sobriety, the absence of the outrageousness that makes the filmed version sometimes compelling, sometimes sheer camp. Purely visual business had to be cut for the recording, as, for example, the long look by Hamlet at Polonius when Polonius says "mobled queen is good";[2] the recording omits this long pause, which raised a laugh in the audience.

The listening audience may thus miss the outstanding feature of the production: its high comedy. On stage, Burton and Cronyn exposed the humor so important in the play, Hamlet's wry wit and sardonic high jinks and Polonius's inadvertent self-exposing buffoonery. This is a production that George Bernard Shaw would have liked, for when he reviewed Forbes Robertson's 1897 stage production for the second time, he said: "Hamlet is a very long play; and it only seems a short one when the high-mettled comedy with which it is interpenetrated from beginning to end leaps out with all the lightness and spring of its wonderful loftiness of temper" (Shaw 1961, 93). Shaw found that the lightness early in the production's run had hardened into lead after many weeks. The Burton recording captures fine actors at the top of their form; nevertheless, one misses much of the humor and the audience's response to the humor, not only in itself but also as it affected the actors. Burton's performance is much less expansive on the sound recording, much less punctuated by Hamlet's laughter—for example, before and after he forces Rosencrantz and Guildenstern out with his oddly voiced "I so, God buy'ye" (2.2.573), with each word separately spat out. The recording makes a good case, by negative example, for the communication of audiences with actors. On the other hand, Burton had so trained the theater audience to laugh that when he speaks sincerely to praise Horatio (3.2.54–74), some in the audience guffaw.

The modest number of laughs that remain in Burton's repertory in the recording do add a dimension to Hamlet's character: sardonic wit. Not unexpectedly perhaps, he chuckles as he responds to the ghost's voice from the cellerage. With laughter Hamlet belittles Ophelia's seriousness; he laughs when he says, "I never gave you ought," and again when she describes the gifts as rich. He laughs during the serious moment of "The Mousetrap" before he says the first "Wormwood," a word that many Hamlets say bitterly. More significantly, he laughs before he says "The rest is silence." This reminds me again of Shaw's review of Forbes Robertson's performance in 1897, in which he says that the actor plays this line as a "touchingly humorous apology for not being able to finish his business" (Shaw 1961, 88).

One of the distinctions of Burton's delivery is onomatopoeia. When Hamlet says, "Hast me to know it, That [I] . . . May sweepe to my

Revenge," he says "sweepe" with a swoop of voice. Speaking to Rosencrantz and Guildenstern, he lengthens the syllable "in" in "infinite" to match the meaning. Later, again to Rosencrantz and Guildenstern, he makes a swallowing noise on saying "last swallowed" (4.2.20). In the same speech, accusing Rosencrantz of being a sponge, Hamlet's voice sounds like a squeegee, rushing upward to a squeek, a sound perhaps more insulting to Rosencrantz than the word itself.

Another distinctive feature of his delivery is the separation of syllables, already mentioned above in Hamlet's dismissal of Rosencrantz and Guildenstern. To himself, describing the player's emotion, he castigates himself with the pronunciation of "Hecuba" as three harsh, separate syllables. For "bloody, bawdy villain," he pounds in each word like a pike. With the repetition of the word "wormwood," Hamlet, suffering, separates the two syllables.

Related to syllable separation is the pause with which Burton signals mood and sometimes mood change, as after Polonius's commentary on "mobled queen" in the film. Another significant pause occurs between "say" and "nothing," when Hamlet says "Yet I . . . can say nothing" (2.2.592–95); "nothing" is spat out. For "Oh Vengeance," though there is his customary pause between the first and second words, Burton does it differently from most: "Oh" is a long drawn-out syllable, from high to low pitch and from loud to soft, followed by a soft, tearful "Vengeance!" Most Hamlets rise on "Vengeance" (see Davison, 57–58). Burton's delivery emphasizes pathos at this key moment before intellect reasserts itself in Hamlet's idea of "The Mousetrap."

Mood change is Burton's strong and weak point: strong in that it mirrors Hamlet's antic humor, his famous mercurial, silvery changeability; weak in that it can tend towards excess—on film if not on the recording. For his first soliloquy, he begins with soft intensity, tears close to the surface. The voice speeds up and gets louder on "fie." He gives "hang," of "why she would hang on him," sarcastic emphasis. He says "woman" bitterly, returns to sorrow, and then on "beast" his anger bursts out. For "O most wicked speed," his voice doubles, a main line with harmonics, a harsh and metallic sound. For the last line he returns to soft melancholy.

When he speaks to the ghost, phrasing emphasizes the incantatory nature of the lines "Be thou a Spirit of health, or Goblin damn'd . . . Heaven . . . or . . . Hell . . . wicked or charitable . . ." (1.4.40–42). Like Barrymore's, Burton's voice rises to a crescendo on "Hamlet, King, Father, Royall Dane." Quiet desperation infuses his question, "what should we doe?" Responding to the ghost, his cry, "Murder!" is full of pain. His soliloquy after the ghost exits quickly rises to a high pitch, softens only to rise to a climax again on "Remember thee," descends to rise yet again for the second "Remember thee," speeds to "Yes, by

The Burton *Hamlet*. Two of Hamlet's many moods. *(Stills courtesy Varian Inc.)*

Heaven," then stops. Tears surface upon recollecting his mother— "woman!" is hurled out—but his voice is bitter about Claudius. Mocking sarcasm for "My tables" yields to soft sarcasm on "At least I am sure it may be so in Denmarke," then finally to quiet determination for his vow.

Vocal complexity, variety, and energy are the common features of these three great Hamlets on sound recording. By isolating the one supreme gift of the actor—the voice—sound recordings help us to realize that the voice binds all performance media. Whether the actor is on stage, on moving image, or on sound recording, the voice is the single most important means to communicate the richness and the mystery of Hamlet. The Hamlets of silent film, obviously lacking what is most significant, must suggest the emotional range of the role through gestures and body language—and through vocal qualities that they force us to imagine. The Hamlets of sound recording must make up by vocal energy what they lack in presence. On stage, perhaps, a Hamlet of great lassitude, a Werther-like man, might be compelling, but in sound recording, without the actor's presence, an actor's energy is necessary to rivet the attention. Scofield, whose Hamlet on stage (Babula, number 129) and on sound recording reminds one of the gentlemanly Forbes Robertson's, is no match for Barrymore or Burton, whose fire and thunder fill the gaps left by sound-only performances. Naturally, those media that enable an actor to use all his gifts are ultimately the most satisfying. But those media that isolate one or another attribute reveal precisely in what ways the full media *are* best.

Notes

1. Similarly, Micheál MacLiammóir stresses each word of "As kill a king," giving the listening audience time to grasp what he is accusing Gertrude of. Interestingly, Welles considered MacLiammóir the greatest Hamlet. MacLiammóir, who "discovered" Welles at age fifteen, played Iago to Welles's Othello in the 1952 film.

2. F1 has the Player and Hamlet say "inobled Queen," followed by Polonius's line: "That's good: Inobled Queene is good." Q2 has the Player and Hamlet say "mobled Queene," which Polonius does not repeat; his line is "That's good." Editors have conflated the two texts, choosing the troublesome "mobled" over the sensible "inobled."

Part IV

The Spiral of Influence

All modes of textual realization, whether on stage, screen or sound speaker, depend not only on the makers' perception of the choices that texts afford but on one performance's influences on another. While it is true that moving-image productions are different from stage productions, interdependence speaks for the unity of the play itself and the unity of its performance history. I am reminded of the magic of looking at a park in Mamaroneck, New York, through the openings in a tunnellike patch of road. These framed vistas look otherworldly; they are so beautiful. This is the magic of apertures. Yet when I actually stand in the park and can see the whole scene unframed, the image disintegrates into ordinariness. The glamor of the moving image comes from the frame, the exclusion and specialness it gives to the chosen image. The excitement of the stage comes from the physical presence of the actors before one, whether one is seeing them from the second balcony or from the second row, whether there is an audience-excluding proscenium arch or an audience-including thrust stage. Silent film offers the opportunity for total absorption in the actor's persona, sound recordings in the actor's voice. Each medium of expression has its own very distinct excellences. What I have tried to demonstrate is how much all the media share in traditional business, in cuts, and in interpretation. The conscious efforts of makers in one medium to remind us of other media argue both for the essential differences (for no reminders would be needed were they the same) and yet for the energies that each kind of presentation derives from the others. The diverse strands of *Hamlet* interpretation are designs in the whole cloth. These are the points I have made in the preceding chapters. The epilogue looks at the partnership of scholarship and performance and returns to the film that began this study, Olivier's *Hamlet*.

Epilogue
The Scholars and the Director

J. L. Styan, in *The Shakespeare Revolution,* describes the vast changes in stagecraft brought about by the interest of actors and directors in modern Shakespearean scholarship. A similar interaction between artists and academics has also shaped the development of moving images. At least since Swen Gade's *Hamlet* (1920) drew on Edward P. Vining's theory that Hamlet was a woman, and since Cornell professor Will Strunk, Jr., went to Hollywood to help with Cukor's *Romeo and Juliet* (1936),[1] some films have found their inspiration and perhaps their legitimacy in scholarly research and criticism.

Modern theories of literary analysis lead us to expect this linkage of scholarship and performance. If we agree with Harold Bloom, who in his controversial works on influence suggests that a great poet's art arises from a critical act, that is, a reaction against and a purposeful misreading of his or her predecessors; and if we agree with another Yale scholar, Geoffrey Hartman, that criticism is a creative act rather than an unfolding of an implicit or explicit truth within a work of art, then critics, like poets, must also misread their predecessors. Furthermore, these two separate lines of influence, artist to artist and critic to critic, may also cross, the artist reacting to the critic and the critic reacting to the artist.

A Shakespeare performance, as an act of criticism and creation, is generated by the misreadings of prior criticism and prior performances and in turn generates its own misreadings in the critical and creative works of others. Irene Dash, in *Wooing, Wedding, and Power: Women in Shakespeare's Plays,* has demonstrated how Shakespeare performance has influenced criticism (82 and passim); Olivier's *Hamlet* shows further the interactive influence of criticism and performance. Dover Wilson, Ernest Jones, Laurence Olivier, and Peter Alexander, all artist-critics who recreate *Hamlet,* exemplify the line or perhaps more accurately the spiral of influence. All grapple with the "one defect" theory, making it a useful point of comparison.

Reacting to E. E. Stoll's opinion that Hamlet does not delay and partly drawing upon A. C. Bradley's concept of melancholy, Wilson formulated his "one defect" theory.[2] According to Wilson, Hamlet's manic-depressive behavior, his tragic flaw, prevents him from acting. Hamlet, who does not merely put on an antic disposition, has, Wilson says, "attacks" on seven occasions: in the cellarage scene (1.5), in Ophelia's closet (reported in 2.1), during the soliloquy, "O, what a rogue and peasant slave am I" (Riverside, 2.2), in the nunnery scene (3.1), after "The Mousetrap" (3.2), in his mother's closet before the ghost comes and again just as Hamlet is leaving (3.4), and in the funeral scene (5.1). His behavior ranges from severe depression through unthinking exuberance to excessive violence and rage. Melancholy alternates with frenzy (213–15).

Hamlet's infirmity does not, nevertheless, excuse him, according to Wilson; he is still responsible for his behavior. Wilson (220) quotes Robert Bridges's lines from *The Testament of Beauty* about

> The artful balance whereby
> Shakespeare so gingerly put [Hamlet's] sanity in doubt
> Without the while confounding his Reason.

Although according to Wilson Hamlet is a man totally unlike those he admires—that is, he is one for whom Fortune *does* sound the stops (215)—his noble mind is not "o'erthrown": "We realize that the mind is impaired, but we do not doubt for a moment that its nobility remains untouched" (219). "Though . . . he often yields to moods of excitement or despondency, on the stage we never see him in a condition of unmistakable insanity" (221), and therefore, "despite his sore distraction, Hamlet retains moral responsibility for his actions" (224). "Hamlet struggles against his weakness. . . . But though he struggles in vain, and is in the end brought to disaster, a disaster largely of his own making . . . we are never allowed to feel that his spirit is vanquished until 'the potent poison quite o'ercrows' it" (218–19). "Shakespeare," says Wilson, "makes us *feel* that Hamlet is shirking a plain duty, and that he is blameworthy for this neglect. Yet at the same time he makes us realize that the procrastination is due to the distemper, is in fact part of it" (224).[3] The melancholy and the procrastination go together (226). Wilson sees Hamlet as "a genius suffering from a fatal weakness and battling against it, until in the end it involves him in the catastrophe which is at once his liberation and his atonement" (237).

Wilson's Aristotelean concept of tragedy clearly informs his analysis, though he mentions Aristotle only once, in an appendix (325–26). To Wilson, the "one defect" speech, from "So, oft it chances" to "his own scandal" (1.4.23–38), largely ignored by other critics (and frequently omitted in performances before Olivier), reveals an early clue to Hamlet's character flaw. He says that Hamlet's movement from general to specific shows that Shakespeare means us to apply the lesson to Hamlet, particularly the lines "By their o'ergrowth of some complexion / Oft breaking down the pales and forts of reason" (Wilson 207). Such hints as these lines give us an illusion of consistency, and the audience recalls them later, though Shakespeare begins to insist on delay only at the end of "The Mousetrap." Before that, because we are occupied with other things, we do not, says Wilson, notice any delay (204), particularly if—as is often the case—the director cuts the Reynaldo scene (2.1), which shows that time has passed.

Wilson refuses to ascribe a cause for the "one defect." We cannot, he says, pluck out the heart of Hamlet's mystery. In fact, "that it has a heart is an illusion; the mystery itself is an illusion; Hamlet is an illusion" (229). Jones, on the other hand, argues that "no dramatic criticism of the personae in a play is possible except under the pretense that they are living people, and surely one is well aware of this pretense" (18).[4] In support, he quotes Wilson as saying, "To spectators in the theatre he is more convincingly life-like than any other character in literature" [*sic*] (Jones, 22; Wilson, 219). Jones also approvingly quotes the same lines from Bridges that Wilson quotes, beginning, however, with these: "Hamlet himself would never have been aught to us, or we / To Hamlet, wer't not for the artful balance," and so on. Jones enlists the support of Wilson to do what Wilson said cannot be done: pluck out the heart of Hamlet's mystery. Wilson, however, accuses Jones of misreading him:

And when [Jones] gathered (p. 43) from these pages that I believed "personality" in *Hamlet* to be "consistent" I realized that my chapter VI had been written in vain, as far as he was concerned, and that we must go our several ways each convinced he is being misunderstood by the other. (vii)

Wilson argued against Jones, saying, "We are not . . . at liberty to go outside the frame of the play and seek remoter origins in [Hamlet's] past history" (218), and "to abstract one figure from an elaborate dramatic composition and study it as a case in the psychoanalytic clinic is to attempt something at once wrong in method and futile in aim" (vii). Jones, however he may disagree with Wilson's premise, makes use of him where it suits him, for example in his description of Hamlet's defect, which Jones labels "psychoneurosis" (69).

According to Jones's well-known thesis, the incestuous marriage of Gertrude stimulates Hamlet's long-repressed sexual desire for her, the desire to usurp his father's place and possess her, a desire that, because it has been repressed, fills him with loathing. Before her marriage, he had "weaned himself" sufficiently from her erotic pull to fall in love with Ophelia, but even here Jones finds evidence that he is using Ophelia in an unconscious desire to play her off against his mother, just as a jilted lover would rebound into another's arms. But after Gertrude's marriage, the mental energy that Hamlet must expend to repress again the renewed sexual desire for his mother reduces him "to the deplorable mental state he himself so vividly depicts" (80–82).

His behavior to Ophelia, says Jones, can be explained by the intense sexual revulsion that the clear view of his mother's sexuality causes in him, a sexuality made manifest by her marriage to Claudius. Hamlet's "infantile unconscious" has split his mother/woman into two separate images: one the untouchable Madonna, the other the slut. Jones says that in instances of sexual repression, as with Hamlet, "both types . . . are felt to be hostile [*sic*: Jones appears to mean "arouse hostility" but projects, or perhaps suggests that the victim projects, the feeling onto the object, for he goes on], the pure one out of resentment at her repulses, the sexual one out of the temptation she offers to plunge into guiltiness. Misogyny, as in the play, is the inevitable result" (86).

Sick to death already, Hamlet reels from the ghost's disclosure that Claudius gained Gertrude through murder, for he too had wished to replace the late king as her lover. Hamlet can hardly denounce Claudius for doing what he himself wished to do. If he lets his rage at his uncle have full play, "he stimulate[s] to activity his own unconscious and 'repressed' complexes" (88). Jones further states that Hamlet's "uncle incorporates the deepest and most buried part of his own personality, so that he cannot kill him without also killing himself" (88). For this reason, he cannot kill Claudius until he knows he himself is dying.

Only because of his sterling qualities, his breadth of vision, his deep sensitivity, his philosophical curiosity, his warmth, his wit, does Hamlet escape the contemptuous pity that would seem to be an audience's proper response to the psychological cripple both Wilson and Jones depict.

In his 1948 film, Olivier makes use of both Wilson and Jones, but without making Hamlet the pathetic figure they delineate. Wilson especially supplied the filmmaker with a number of ideas: the early entry for Hamlet in 2.2 so that he can overhear the "loosing" plot; the court's reaction to the *Gonzago* play; the management of the duel, with Laertes's foul hit; and finally, the "one defect" idea, which Olivier transmits by using the "So oft it chances" passage (1.4.23–38), which Wilson had emphasized, as a prologue. Since, according to Wilson (207), Hamlet is thinking of himself, it is appropriate that Olivier, in voiceover, recite it, ending with the non-Shakespearean statement, "This is the tragedy of a man who could not make up his mind." A preproduction script reveals, however, that at first the meaning of the "one defect" speech remained vague; the script calls for only a short line of explanation to be inserted (Kliman, 249). The film's explanation—indecisiveness—is akin to the procrastination that Wilson says is a corollary of Hamlet's mental state, but which he describes as effect, not cause. He can act, says Wilson, but only impulsively, never upon deliberation (225).

The absence of the explanation from the script suggests that, until the film had actually been made, the precise nature of the "one defect" eluded Olivier. He does not, in any case, demonstrate much faith in his own explanation, which the film disregards. Seemingly, the prologue and explanation are there to reassure the audience that they will understand this classic play. Foster Hirsch in *Laurence Olivier* says that "Olivier felt . . . that it was necessary to give the story an immediate focus for the popular audience." He also says that the prologue is misleading because Olivier's interpretation "is more complex than the simplistic 'This is the story [*sic*] of a man who could not make up his mind' would indicate" (88).

Neither does Olivier use Wilson's manic-depressive diagnosis. (For that we had to wait for Derek Jacobi's BBC-TV Hamlet.) Instead, in the early part of the film especially, we see him as depressed, not manic. In none of the scenes that Wilson lists does Hamlet's behavior seem even slightly abnormal. Olivier consistently cuts lines that could be so construed: for example, most of the cellarage scene, all of "what a rogue and peasant slave am I," most of the scene after "The Mousetrap," and much of the closet scene. One or two wide-eyed stares do not denote psychoneurosis. In the Ophelia/closet scene, which the film inserts, Hamlet is sad rather than manic, and in the nunnery scene, as Wilson himself explains it, Hamlet's anger springs from his knowlege that Ophelia is in collusion with his enemies. Only the funeral scene shows his behavior to be questionable, but there it clearly derives from his shock at Ophelia's death. Olivier does not seem to view Hamlet's emotion as excessive given the circumstances. Gertrude's insensitivity, Claudius's brutishness, Polonius's pompous subservience, his father's death and then revelation of murder, Ophelia's treachery—along with on the other hand Horatio's sympathy—help us to empathize with Hamlet. At no time do we feel that his response exceeds the cause. Still, when Hamlet apologizes to Laertes, we are bound to believe him, as Wilson asserts (216–17). His great suffering mimics madness too well to make us question his sincerity.

In the first part of the film, Olivier emphasizes Hamlet's melancholy by repeatedly showing him sitting on his chair in a black funk: from our first view of him (1.2.64) until he says "God, God" (line 132); again from line 159 through all of 1.3, inserted between lines 159 and 160; and again before the players arrive, when he is sitting alone in total blackness. Though his melancholy in effect never leaves him, his inaction

The Olivier *Hamlet*. Hamlet apologizes to Laertes. *(Still courtesy Janus Films.)*

ends after the players' arrival gives a plan—just at the point that Wilson says we are becoming aware of delay.

Although Olivier thus significantly modifies Wilson's description of Hamlet's mental state, he relies upon Jones to approach the cause of the delay: the oedipal conflict. As Olivier says in an interview, Hamlet "could safely be a man of action under the auspices of that particular idea" (Tynan, 19). Obviously, then, indecisiveness does not have much to do with Olivier's concept of Hamlet. The question, aside from the debatable worth of Jones's thesis, is, can a film express such deeply unconscious feelings as Jones describes? The best Olivier can do is present a set laden with Freudian symbolism and a Gertrude who leans sensuously toward Claudius, whose gowns fully reveal her sumptuously curved body, who kisses Hamlet with an ardor that we in our post-Freudian age consider too intense to be merely maternal. Olivier does not convey the subconscious identification with Claudius or the rigidly repressed sexual response to his mother. To "know" these things about Hamlet, the audience must bring the Freudian structure to the play. It defies staging or screening precisely because it does lie buried in the unconscious. Though Hirsch seems to think that Olivier succeeds in conveying Jones's Freudian interpretation (91), Cottrell in *Laurence Olivier* (120) and Trewin in *Shakespeare on the English Stage, 1900–1964* (164) say that most of even the sophisticated audience of Olivier's 1937 stage production missed the Freudian interpretation in spite of the fact that the stage

The Olivier *Hamlet*. Hamlet in the graveyard scene: we admire him rather than pity him. *(Still courtesy Janus Films.)*

production insisted upon the idea even more than did the film. Olivier could only assume that the viewers of the film would see something "funny" between Hamlet and his mother.

While his "misreading" vitiates Jones's theory significantly, the energy Olivier derives from it helps him shape the first half of the film, through the closet scene, when Hamlet and his mother are finally reconciled. By connecting Gertrude and Ophelia, Olivier makes us see both as betrayers. Once the "woman" theme has served to explain Hamlet's inaction, Olivier drops it. As soon as the players come, Hamlet hits upon the plan that transforms him. No further soliloquies (Olivier cuts not only "O, what a rogue and peasant slave am I" but also "How all occasions do inform against me"), no further views of Hamlet sitting alone in his chair, support the image of an ineffectual Hamlet. Olivier, giving his natural forcefulness free rein, becomes the athletic and dynamic Hamlet congenial to his native acting style. Wilson's Hamlet is a man of action stifled by his mental condition; Jones's Hamlet seems effete only because he is under the toils of his repression. Olivier agrees and goes one step further by making the sloughing off of his inaction the climax of the play. His own chemistry as an actor causes his "misreading" of Wilson and Jones and produces a *Hamlet* that another critic, Peter Alexander, would have approved of, had his own misreading of the film not interfered.

In his *Hamlet, Father and Son,* Alexander early remarks that Olivier's

Hamlet makes a convenient and useful point of departure because most have seen it (18). Although he proposes "to comment at some length on the film," he makes it in fact the staging area for launching his particular thesis. He objects to Ophelia's behavior in the nunnery scene and at length to the opening explanation, the "one defect" speech. He uses the film as a means to his true end: to show that neither Bradley, whom he takes to be Olivier's ultimate source for the theme (he does not mention Wilson), nor Aristotle, nor Sophocles meant the concept of *hamartia,* or tragic flaw, to be the foundation of tragedy (42 and throughout). K. R. Eissler in his psychoanalytic study concurs; he sees belief in it as "an attempt to free the gods from guilt, and at the same time to find protection against inner despair" (349). Alexander concludes, after a wide-ranging argument that only twice lights on the film (77, 113), that the effect of *catharsis* "does not rest on the faults but on the virtues of men" (113). He does not speculate why Olivier, who lopped off whole chunks from the play, not only left in the "one defect" speech but used it twice, as prologue and in its proper spot in 1.4, though actually, as we have already seen, the film ignores the prologue. It is, then, almost as if Alexander argues against a statement made in the film's advertising campaign when he argues against the prologue. It is a handy springboard; he is not really paying attention to the film.

Yet, without realizing it, he does in fact describe the film, for, just as Alexander would have it, we react to Olivier's Hamlet with admiration for his nobility and with sorrow for his suffering rather than with pity for his infirmities. He is no failure, as Wilson claims (268). The film leaves us, as Alexander says the play does, "with a faith in life that rises superior to the accidents of our lot" (83). For example, in discussing the prayer scene, Alexander suggests that Hamlet's refusal to stab Claudius in the back while he is at prayer may not be a cowardly or infirm act, as Bradley (and Wilson and Jones) declares, but a noble one, born of praiseworthy scruples (144–47).

Olivier's filming of the prayer scene (3.3) certainly leaves room for justifying Hamlet's refusal to kill Claudius, if perhaps on somewhat different grounds. By the use of an image of Jesus, a two-foot-high statue above the altar, Olivier implies heavenly approval for Hamlet's delay.[5] Not visible in the darkness while Polonius and Claudius speak or even as Claudius walks over to the altar and kneels, the statue dominates as Hamlet stops at the chapel entrance. A high-angle shot from the back of the figure catches Hamlet right after he decides "And now I'll do't." Keeping the image in the frame, the camera, after Hamlet walks the few steps to Claudius's back and as he lifts his sword, moves forward so that the figure of Jesus in left closeup and Hamlet in right mid-shot fill the frame. The music rises to a crescendo and stops as Hamlet focuses on the image. Deliberating (in voiceover), he looks up at it several times,

The Olivier *Hamlet*. Hamlet stops to look at the statue of Jesus. *(Still courtesy Janus Films.)*

particularly when referring to heaven. After he walks away, the camera position changes to show Hamlet in the foreground with the image, well-lit in a heavily shadowed space, strikingly visible in the background. Darkness conceals Claudius. The music, which had resumed, toys with the sensuous Gertrude motif, mirroring Hamlet's words: "in th' incestuous pleasure of his bed" (line 90). Hamlet looks back at the image again as he says:

> no relish of salvation in't—
> Then trip him, that his heels may kick at heaven,
> And that his soul may be as damn'd and black
> As hell, whereto it goes.
>
> (92–95)

After he slips away, the frame shows a profiled two-shot of the impassive image and Claudius's head looking up at it in despair. We see that Hamlet is right; this reprieve will but prolong Claudius's sickly days. The scene ends with a view of Claudius alone, crumpled against the altar, the frame cutting him off from the image of Jesus. The filming of the scene explains Hamlet's delay on religious grounds. The retribution that heaven (represented by the statue) approves calls for it. Alexander, who should have admired the film because it negates Bradley (and Wilson and Jones), does not refer to the production in his discussion of this scene.

He might even have made a strong case that the image of Jesus functions both as the embodiment and the cause of Hamlet's scruples, because the powerful visual image virtually masks the words.

Without mentioning Wilson, with whom he disagrees, Alexander asserts that the antic disposition *is* put on (177–85). Shakespeare retains Hamlet's pretense, though the antic disposition is not necessary for Hamlet's preservation as it was in the sources, so that Hamlet can make Claudius squirm—to prepare the king for the ultimate confrontation. "Hamlet will not come on his victim silently and suddenly from behind; the final encounter must be face to face. All this is in keeping with his holding his hand against the villain at prayer. The antic behaviour is all of a piece with his conduct throughout" (180). Though Alexander ignores the film, this describes its effect very well. Olivier, like Alexander, rejects Wilson's theory of the antic disposition. Alexander states that melancholy is no bar to action; the film demonstrates that. His discussion of the film starts and ends with a "misreading" of Olivier's prologue, which nevertheless precipitates his own valid, creative conclusions.

The matrix of connections neither begins with Wilson nor ends with Alexander. Other scholars, other directors continue the spiral of influence. Mack, Lyth, Kozintsev, Wirth, Richardson, Jorgens, Calderwood and many others, through their "misreadings," challenge us to shape our own creative revision of the play.

Notes

1.   Gade's *Hamlet,* starring Asta Nielsen, had a credit to Edward P. Vining of Yale. Vining's book suggested that, if Hamlet were a woman, his/her delay would be explained. Only a woman could be as passive as Shakespeare's Hamlet. Thus, Hamlet's inaction can be explained if Hamlet is a woman. "May not Shakespeare have at least entertained the thought that Hamlet might be a woman?" He admits that this was not Shakespeare's "original conception of the character" but asserts that he "certainly dallied with it" (59–60) and that the residue of that dalliance left its mark on Hamlet's character.

On Will Strunk's year in Hollywood, see "An Epilogue to 'Romeo.'" For the contrasting view, that academics and professionals are ultimately separate, see Wells.

2.   Terence Hawkes, using a new historicist approach, in "Telmah" analyzes the chain of associations that led Wilson to his theory.

3.   For a different, brilliantly persuasive view that does not find Hamlet blameworthy for this neglect, see Calderwood, especially 109–110, 146, 167–68.

4.   Because both Jones's and Wilson's work went through several editions with revisions, and because Jones refers to Wilson in the 1949 text, I found it useful to put Jones after Wilson, though in strict chronology Jones's work precedes Wilson's. Jones's essay on *Hamlet,* first written in 1900 and based on a note by Freud, received wide currency as the first chapter of his book *Essays in Applied Psycho-Analysis,* 1923, according to the "Preface" of *Hamlet and Oedipus,* 9. For a strong defence of treating Shakespeare's characters as real people, see Nuttall, 68–82.

5.   Peter Davison, in *Hamlet: Text and Performance* (53) objects to this scene because the image contradicts the text; he does not recognize that the filmmaker purposely overrides the text with the visual image. Instead, he considers it a mistake.

Appendix 1
Scenes/Segments in *Hamlet*

1.1 First ghost scene.
1.2 The first court scene; Claudius's proclamation: 1–39.*
Hamlet's first soliloquy, "too too solid flesh": 129–59.
The disclosure (Horatio and the sentries telling Hamlet what they've seen): 160–255.
1.3 The family scene. Ophelia advised by Laertes: 1–51; by Polonius: 88–136.
1.4 The second ghost vigil; "One defect" speech: 23–38.
1.5 The ghost's revelation; the cellarage scene: 144–81.
2.1 Reynaldo 1–74; Ophelia's closet (summary) 74–120.
2.2 Second court scene; the unloosing plot: 158–69.
Fishmonger scene: 170–215.
"What a piece of work is a man": 292–98.
The players: 302ff; the Pyrrhus recitation: 421–89.
Hamlet's soliloquy, "O, what a rogue and peasant slave am I" 526–72.
3.1 "To be, or not to be": 56–88.
The nunnery scene: 88–184.
3.2 Advice to players: 1–39.
Praise of Horatio: 43–66.
"The Mousetrap," *The Murder of Gonzago:* 124–250.
The pipe scene: 319–43.
Hamlet's soliloquy: "Now could I drink hot blood": 356–67.
3.3 The prayer scene.
3.4 The closet scene.
4.4 Hamlet's solilquy, "How all occasions do inform against me": 32–66.

4.5   Ophelia's first mad scene: 1–72; her second mad scene: 150–94.
4.7   Claudius's manipulation of Laertes; willow scene: 161–89.
5.1   Gravediggers' scene: 1–160; Yorick: 160–92.
5.2   Osric scene: 81–177.
      Hamlet's "There's a Providence": 192–203.
      Duel scene: 204–388.

---

*Line numbers from the Norton text.

Appendix 2
Film Terms

NUMBER OF PEOPLE IN SHOT: **one-shot, two-shot, three-shot;** this is usually meaningful only for **medium shots** or **closeups.**

POSITION OF CAMERA IN RELATION TO SUBJECTS: 1) distance: **long shot:** at least full figure, usually more, usually a good amount of setting will be visible also. **Medium shot:** approximately from the hips up. **close shot** or **closeup:** from the bust up. These shots can be further defined by terms such as **extreme** or **medium: medium closeup:** between medium shot and closeup.

2) camera angle: **high angle:** the camera tilted down from above the subject; that is, the **camera** is **high. Low angle:** the camera tilted up from below the subject; that is, the **camera** is **low. Straight shot:** the camera faces the subject at subject level. Since this is the usual position, this is mentioned only when needed for contrast or comparison to some other camera position.

MOVEMENT OF CAMERA IN RELATION TO SUBJECT: **pan:** the camera moves from right to left (so that the image moves across the screen from left to right) or from left to right or from top to bottom or bottom to top while the subject remains still. **Tilt** may also be used for the latter two (**tilt up** or **tilt down**). **Tracking:** the camera moves with the subject, keeping the subject in view. This can be done on a truck or on a track. **Boom:** the camera moves on a boom, allowing high angle shots as well as straight shots.

FRAME is what the camera shows us at any point.

SHOT is one distinct operation of the camera, from start to stop; during a shot, the camera may move or the subject may move or both. The shot ends when the camera stops or when the film is cut.

TRANSITIONS: the most frequent device to get from one shot to the next is the **cut** or **straight cut:** one shot is simply added on to the last one. Within any scene, there are many cuts, usually unnoticed because they are so natural: Someone looks to the left. Cut. We see the thing or person the someone was looking at. Cuts can also connect disparate scenes and they can lead to startling or energizing juxtapositions. A **crosscut** is a shot of an altogether different scene that usually has some relationship to the first scene. A series of crosscuts, back and forth between two scenes, can suggest parallel action occurring at the same time. **Montage** is a series of straight cuts in which the whole exceeds the sum of the parts. **Dissolve:** one image **fades out** while **superimposed** over it another image **fades in.** This can denote a passage of time or can also mean another action taking place at the same time. Usually it means the first unless context forces the second meaning. **Fade** or **fade out:** the scene slowly becomes black. This is often used with the **fade in,** in which a scene starts black and becomes light. It generally denotes a lapse of time. **Match cut:** used when a character exits from one space and enters another. The first shot might show, at right frame, a character going through a door. The next shot might show, at left frame, the character coming through the door. **Rack shot:** common on television where depth of field is shallow, the rack shot has a part of the frame (foreground or background) in focus while the rest is not; then with a quick switch, the out-of-focus portion springs into focus as the formerly in-focus portion becomes blurred. Also used in films.

TIME: one shot is also called a **take.** Normally a shot lasts for a few seconds, usually much less than a minute. If it's held longer, it can be called a **long take** or a **long-held shot.**

POINT OF VIEW: the frame is usually described from the camera's point of view; that is, **frame left** is the left side of the frame from the audience's perspective also; **frame right** is to the audience's right. This is of course directly the opposite of stage point of view, where **stage right** refers to the actor's right as he or she faces the audience. The camera can give us in effect the **point of view** of a character by pointing where that character is looking. If then the next cut shows the character who is looking, we have a **reverse shot. Shots** and **reverse shots** are frequently used in dialogue: first we see what one speaker sees, usually while that speaker is speaking so we can see the response of the other; then we see the other speaker from the perspective of the first speaker.

MOVING IMAGES: Following the lead of the American Film Institute, I am using the term to group together film, television, and video.

TAPE: refers to the reproducible television product, a videotape.

Appendix 3
Van Dam's Chart on Characters' Lines

CHARACTER	VERSE	PROSE	TOTAL
Hamlet	807	659	1466
Claudius	508	7	515
Polonius	275	61	336
Horatio	202	52	254
Laertes	174	—	174
Ophelia	117	52	169
Gertrude	128	—	128
First Gravedigger	14	93	107
Rosencrantz	34	65	99
Ghost	84	—	84
Marcellus	52	—	52
Guildenstern	14	36	50
Osric	3	46	49
Player King	40	7	47
Player Queen	31	—	31
Bernardo	25	—	25
Fortinbras	23	—	23
Voltemand	22	—	22
Second Gravedigger	—	19	19
Gentleman (4.5)	11	—	11
Doctor (Priest) (5.1)	11	—	11
Messenger (4.5)	10	—	10
Captain (4.4)	10	—	10
Lord (5.2)	—	10	10
Francisco	7	—	7
Lucianus (3.2)	6	—	6
Reynaldo	6	—	6
Ambassador (5.2)	5	—	5
Sailor (4.6)	—	5	5
Prologue (3.2)	3	—	3
Messenger (4.7)	3	—	3
Gentleman (4.6)	—	1	1
Cornelius	1	—	1
All (with Laertes)	1	—	1
Totals	2673	1113	3786

Van Dam says the figures are only approximately correct because, for example, there is no account of half-lines. Compare E. K. Chambers's count: 2589 verse, 1211 prose (408–25).

Appendix 4
Moving Image Credits: Full-Length Features

1913 *Hamlet,* supervised by Cecil Hepworth, directed by E. Hay Plumb, produced by Hepworth for Gaumont, interiors by Hawes Craven, exteriors at Lulworth Cove, Hartsbourne Manor, Halliford-on-Thames, and Walton-on-Thames, with Sir Johnston Forbes Robertson as Hamlet, Gertrude Elliott as Ophelia, Walter Ringham as Claudius, J.H. Barnes as Polonius, S. A. Cookson as Horatio, and Percy Rhodes as the ghost (Ball, 188–90). The print I saw, at the Folger Shakespeare Library, clearly has many frames missing. The credit frame (only one) ends with the word "and" but there are no further credits. The print appears to be in color, now much faded; one reviewer refers to the horrible color (*Literary Digest,* 683). This would have been hand-tinted.

1948 *Hamlet,* directed by Laurence Olivier; a Two Cities Film presented by the J. Arthur Rank Organization Ltd. Associate producer Reginald Beck; photographer, Desmond Dickinson; designer, Roger Furse; text editor, Alan Dent; art director, Carmen Dillon; editor, Helga Cranston. Music by William Walton, conducted by Muir Mathieson and played by the Philharmonia Orchestra. Laurence Olivier as Hamlet, Eileen Herlie as Gertrude, Basil Sydney as Claudius, Jean Simmons as Ophelia, Felix Aylmer as Polonius, Norman Wooland as Horatio, Terence Morgan as Laertes, Stanley Holloway as the gravedigger, Peter Cushing as Osric, Esmond Knight as Bernardo, Anthony Quayle as Marcellus, Harcourt Williams as chief player, John Laurie as Francisco, Niall Macginnis as sea captain, Patric Troughton as player king, and Tony Tarver as player queen. Widely available for rental on 16mm.

1953 *Hamlet,* an NBC presentation of Maurice Evans's production, on the Hallmark Hall of Fame, directed by executive producer Albert McCleery (camera) and George Schaefer (casting and actors). Maurice Evans as Hamlet, Joseph Schildkraut as Claudius, Ruth Chatterton as Gertrude, Sarah Churchill as Ophelia, Barry Jones as Polonius, William Smithers as Laertes, Wesley Addy as Horatio, Alan Shayne as Bernardo, Winston Ross as Marcellus, Ken Raymond as page, Rod Colbin and Charles Bellin as fencers, Chester Stratton as Rosencrantz, Francis Bethencourt as Guildenstern, Noel Leslie as player king, Neva Patterson as player queen, Malcolm Keene as the ghost, Norman Barrs as Lucianus, Tom Hughes as prologue. The University Film Study Center in Cambridge, Massachusetts, has an archival copy.

1959 *Hamlet,* produced by Michael Benthall (Old Vic) for Dupont Show of the Month (CBS, 24 February), directed by Ralph Nelson, adapted by Benthall and Nelson from the Old Vic stage production. Set design by Bob Markell. John Neville as Hamlet, Oliver Neville as Claudius, John Humphrey as Laertes, Barbara Jefford as Ophelia, Margaret Courtenay as Gertrude, Joseph O'Conor as Polonius, David Dodimead as Horatio, Job Stewart as Osric, Dudley Jones as gravedigger, Jon Ackland as Marcellus, Roy Patrick as Bernardo, Rich Wordsworth as player king, Barbara Leigh-Hunt as player queen, James Culliford as prologue, Robert Algar as Lucianus, and the Old Vic Company. Host Fredric March. A copy is at the Film Studies Division of the Library of Congress.

1960 *Hamlet,* produced by Hans Gottschalk, directed and adapted by Franz Peter Wirth, photographed by Kurt Gewissen, Herman Gruber, Rudolph Jacob and Boris Goriup. Music by Rolf Unkel. Maximilian Schell as Hamlet, Hans Caninenberg as Claudius, Wanda Rotha as Gertrude, Dunja Movar as Ophelia, Franz Schafheitlin as Polonius, Karl Michael Vogler as Horatio, Dieter Kirchlechner as Laertes, Eckard Dux as Rosencrantz, Herbert Botticher as Guildenstern, Karl Lieffen as Osric. Widely available for rental.

1964 *Hamlet,* directed by Grigori Kozintsev, screenplay by Grigori Kozintsev, from the translation into Russian by Boris Pasternak (subtitled into English), music by Dmitri Shostakovich, with Innokenti Smokhtunovski as Hamlet, Mikhail Nazvanov as Claudius, Elza Radzin-Szolkonis as Gertrude, Yuri Tolubeev as Polonius, Anatasia Vertinskaya as Ophelia, V. Erenberg as Horatio, C. Olesenko as Laertes, V. Medvedev as Guildenstern, I. Dmitriev as

Rosencrantz, A. Krevald as Fortinbras, V. Kolpakov as the grave-digger, and A. Chekaerski as the first actor. Available for rental from Corinth Films, 410 E. 62 Street, New York, New York 10021.

1964 *Hamlet at Elsinore,* a BBC Television/Danmarks Radio Production, directed by Philip Saville, produced by Peter Luke. Music by Richard Rodney Bennett. Decor by Paul Arnt Thomson. Costumes by Olive Harris and Tone Bonnen. Fights by William Hobbs. Mime by Margaret Rubel. Lighting by Robert Wright and Jorgen Moller Nielsen. Sound by Tage Krebs. Christopher Plummer as Hamlet, Robert Shaw as Claudius, Alec Clunes as Polonius, Michael Caine as Horatio, June Tobin as Gertrude, Jo Maxwell Muller as Ophelia, Roy Kinnear as gravedigger, Philip Locke as Osric, Dyson Lovell as Laertes, Peter Prowse as Marcellus, David Calderisi as Rosencrantz, Bill Wallis as Guildenstern, Charles Carson as Priest, David Swift as Player King, Lindsay Kemp as Player Queen, Steven Berkoff as Lucianus, Donald Sutherland as Fortinbras, Joby Blanshard as Captain, Michael Goldie as Bernardo, William Hobbs as Prologue. Tape screened courtesy Danmarks Radio.

1969 *Hamlet,* directed by Tony Richardson by special arrangement with Woodfall Ltd., for Filmways, Inc. Produced at the Roundhouse Theatre. Camera, Gerry Fisher; art direction, Jocelyn Herbert; editing, Charles Rees. Nicol Williamson as Hamlet, Judy Parfitt as Gertrude, Mark Dignam as Polonius, Gordon Jackson as Horatio, Roger Livesey as the first player and the gravedigger, Anthony Hopkins as Claudius, Michael Pennington as Laertes, Marianne Faithfull as Ophelia, Ben Aris as Rosencrantz, Clive Graham as Guildenstern, Peter Gale as Osric, John Carney as Marcellus and player king, John Trenaman as Bernardo, player, and sailor, Richard Everett as player queen, Roger Lloyd-Pack as Reynaldo, Michael Epphick as captain, Ian Collier as priest, Mark Griffith as messenger. Also Bill Jarvis, Jennifer Tudor, Angelica Huston. Widely available for rental.

1970 *Hamlet,* produced for Hallmark Hall of Fame. An NBC presentation; directed by Peter Wood; adapted for television by John Barton, Royal Shakespeare Company; music composed and conducted by John Addison. Executive producer, Cecil Clarke; fight arranger, John Barton; scenery, Peter Roden. Richard Chamberlain as Hamlet, Margaret Leighton as Gertrude, Michael Redgrave as Polonius, John Gielgud as the ghost, Richard Johnson as Claudius, Ciaran Madden as Ophelia, Martin Shaw as Horatio,

Alan Bennett as Osric, Nicholas Jones as Laertes, Robert Oates as Francisco, Godfrey James as Marcellus, Philip Brack as Bernardo, Nigel Stock as first player, James Laurenson as Rosencrantz, Desmond McNamara as Guildenstern, Norman Rossington as gravedigger, Robert Coleby as Fortinbras, Roger Green as captain, Donald Layne-Smith as priest. Available for rental on 16mm from Films, Inc., telephone 800 323 4222. Original cast album, RCA Red Seal Records.

1971 *Hamlet,* directed for television by David Giles based on the stage production directed by Robert Chetwyn; fight director, William Hobbs. Ian McKellen as Hamlet, John Woodvine as Claudius, Faith Brook as Gertrude, James Cairncross as Polonius and first gravedigger, Julian Curry as Horatio, Susan Fleetwood as Ophelia, Robert Grange as Marcellus, David Ashton as Francisco, Simon Prebble as Guildenstern, Colin Kaye as Cornelius, Eric Carte as Bernardo, Roy Montague as the ghost, Tim Pigott-Smith as Laertes, second gravedigger, and player king, Duncan Preston as Reynaldo, Terence Wilton as Rosencrantz, Alan Bennion as Voltemand, Stephen O'Rourke as Lucianus, Terence Wilton as Fortinbras, Brendan Barry as Osric. Screened at CBS.

1980 *Hamlet,* a BBC TV/Time-Life Production, produced by Cedric Messina, directed by Rodney Bennett. Script editor, Alan Shalcross; designer, Dom Homfray; lighting, Sam Barclay; sound, Chick Anthony, costume designer, Barbara Kronig; literary consultant, John Wilders; music, Dudley Simpson; fight arranger, B. H. Barry. Derek Jacobi as Hamlet, Claire Bloom as Gertrude, Eric Porter as Polonius, Patrick Stewart as Claudius, Patrick Allen as ghost, Emrys Jones as first player (player king), Lalla Ward as Ophelia, Robert Swann as Horatio, David Robb as Laertes, Christopher Baines as Francisco, Niall Padden as Bernardo, Paul Humpoletz as Marcellus, John Humphrey as Voltemand, John Sterland as Cornelius, Raymond Mason as Reynaldo, Jonathan Hyde as Rosencrantz, Geoffrey Bateman as Guildenstern, Jason Kemp as second player (queen), Geoffrey Beevers as third player (Lucianus), Bill Homewood as prologue and mime king, Peter Richards as mime queen, Terence McGinity as mime murderer, Peter Burroughs and Styart Fell as other players, Ian Charleson as Fortinbras, Dan Meaden as Norwegian captain, Iain Blair as sailor, Reginald Jessup as messenger, Tim Wylton as first gravedigger, Peter Benson as second gravedigger, Michael Poole as priest, Peter Gale as Osric, David Henry as English Ambassador. Available for rental from Iowa University.

1984 *Hamlet: den tragiska historien om Hamlet, prinz av Danmark,* a 16mm film made for SVT 1, Sweden, shown on WNYC-TV with English subtitles, 7 February 1987. Directed by Ragnar Lyth, produced by Bert Sundberg and Lasse Lundberg. Translation from English by Jan Mark, script by Ragnar Lyth and Leon Vitali, original music by Thomas Mera Gartz, editing by Lasse Lundberg, costumes by Kersti Vitali, Ann-Cartine Gustavsson, and Kim Aastroem. Art director, Bo-Ruben Hedwall; Photography, John Olsson and Bertil Rosengren; sound effects, Olli Soinio and Lasse Keso; lighting, Torbjorn Andersson and Ola Hjelm, with Stellan Skarsgaard as Hamlet, Mona Malm as Gertrud, Frej Lindquist as Claudius, Pernilla Wallgren as Ofelia, Sven Lindberg as Polonius, Dan Ekborg as Laertes, Per Eggers as Horatio, Tomas Bolme as Rosencrantz, Johannes Brost as Gyldenstern, Erik Appelgren, Kim Anderzon, Thomas Norstroem, Haakan Moeller, Thomas Mera Gartz as players, Ola Lindegren as Marcellus, Stefan Ekman as Bernardo, Tomas Laustiola as Valtemand, Dag Norgaard as Fortinbras, Aake Waestersjoe as Captain, Mikael Rundquist as Osric, Aake Fridell as gravedigger, Lenmart Tollen as Priest, Leon Vitali as seaman, Peter Holst as messenger.

Moving Image Credits: Short Versions

CINES? 1908? 1910? Italian film with German titles, ca. 5 minutes. Museum of Modern Art Film Archives.

LUX? 1907? 1908? 1910? British film? with English titles, ca. 6 minutes. Museum of Modern Art Film Archives.

1933 MGM "Test Shots for *Hamlet*" with John Barrymore, Reginald Denny and Donald Crisp. A 5-minute segment from 3.1 and 1.4. Widely available.

1970 *Hamlet Revisited.* Produced by Ron Hobin, National Educational Television. 56 minutes. Narrated by Sir John Gielgud with commentary by Brian Bedford, Richard Chamberlain, Tom Courtenay, Michael Kahn and Caspar Wrede. Excerpts from the Hamlet performances of Sarah Bernhardt, John Barrymore, Sir Johnston Forbes Robertson, Asta Nielson, Maximilian Schell, Laurence Olivier, Innokenti Smoktunovsky, Nicol Williamson, Sir John Gielgud, and others. Edited by Stuart Hersch, Angelo Perincone, Ken Werner, and Edward Deitch, Inc. Narration by Patrick Garland. Museum of Modern Art Film Archives.

1976 Celestino Coronado's *Hamlet*, a 67-minute film (1976), with Helen Mirren as both Gertrude and Ophelia and both David Meyer and Anthony Meyer as Hamlet.

1982 *Hamlet Act*, a 21-minute film with Dick Blau as Hamlet, Dave Fischer as Player, Bob Whitney as Polonius. B&W. Joseph Chang (screenplay) and Robert Nelson (direction). A Blau/Chang/Nelson production. Available from New York Filmmakers Coop and other distributors.

Appendix 5
Audio Credits

Orson Welles as Hamlet. Radio version. 19 September 1936. Edward Jerome, narrator; Alexander Scourby, king; Rosamond Pincho, queen; Edgerton Paul, Polonius; Sidney Smith, Horatio; Joseph Cotton, Laertes; Hiram Sherman, Bernardo. Women's parts were played by Shirley Olivier, Laura Straub, and Virginia Welles. Script at the Museum of Broadcasting, New York, and audio recording at ATAS/ UCLA Archives, Los Angeles.

John Barrymore as *Hamlet*. Radio Version. 21 June 1937. 60 minutes. *Streamlined Shakespeare*, a NBC series. Also recorded in Audio Rarities, 2280 and 2281, with Barrymore's readings from *Twelfth Night, Richard III, Macbeth* and *Hamlet* from *Streamlined Shakespeare*.

Burgess Meredith as Hamlet. Radio Version. 12 July 1937. 60 minutes. CBS series of eight plays. *Hamlet* adapted for radio by Brewster Morgan. Grace George as Gertrude, Walter Abel as Horatio, Montagu Love as Claudius, William A. Brady as Ghost, John Wray as Gravedigger, Margaret Perry as Ophelia, Ben Webster as Polonius, Morris Ankrum as Laertes, Victor Rodman as Bernardo, Priest, William Royal as Francisco, Stefan Schnabel as Marcellus, Player, Philip Terry as Guildenstern, Fritz Lieber, Jr., as Rosencrantz, Eric Snowdon as Player, Ethel Mantell as Player.

Micheál MacLiammóir as Hamlet. The Dublin Gate Theatre Production. Spoken Arts Recording 781. From production performed at the Castle of Elsinore, 1952, and in Athens. Directed by Hilton Edwards and Micheál MacLiammóir, with Patrick McLarnon as Narrator, James Neylis as Horatio, Michael Landor as Marcellus, Hilton Edwards as the

ghost and Claudius, Christopher Casson as Polonius and the First
Player, Genevieve Lyons as the Player Queen, Maureen Toal as
Ophelia, Patrick Bedford as Laertes.

John Gielgud as Hamlet. BBC radio production, entirety version, 3
hours and 44 minutes. 26 December 1948. Repeated several times to
1975. Text edited by M. R. Ridley. With Andrew Cruickshank as
Claudius, Leon Quartermaine as ghost, Sebastian Shaw as Horatio,
Stanley Groome as Francisco and Cornelius, Anthony Jacobs as Marcellus, Richard Williams as Bernardo, Baliol Holloway as Polonius,
Celia Johnson as Ophelia, High Burden as Laertes, High Danning as
Voltemand. Script examined at BBC archives. See Griffith, below,
which used the same narrative links.

John Gielgud as Hamlet. NBC broadcast of 4 March 1951. NCP
1705/1707; also LM6007, RCA Victor. Text showing cuts included
with recording. U.S. Armed Forces Radio Service. 90 minutes.
Gielgud, announcer; Horatio, narrator. Directed by Homer Thickett.
Dorothy McGuire as Ophelia, Pamela Brown as Gertrude.

Maurice Evans as Hamlet and Richard II. Columbia RL3107. This
appears to be excerpted from the Hallmark Hall of Fame television
broadcasts of 1953 and 1954.

Laurence Olivier as Hamlet and Henry V. RCA Victor LM1924. 1955.
Excerpts from the films.

John Gielgud as Hamlet. The Old Vic production of 1957. On RCA
Victor LM6404. Narrator, John Rye, with Derek Francis as Bernardo,
Edward Harvey as Francisco, Jack Gwillim as Horatio, Denis Holmes as
Marcellus, Paul Rogers as Claudius, Peter Coke as Laertes, Alan Webb
as Polonius, Coral Browne as Gertrude, Yvonne Mitchell as Ophelia,
Leon Quartermaine as Ghost, John Woodvine as Reynaldo, Derek New
as Rosencrantz, John Wood as Guildenstern, John Richmond as Volti-
mand, Richard Wordsworth as First Player, John Greenwood as Pro-
logue, Denise Bryer as Player Queen, Charles Gray as Fortinbras,
Ronald Allen as Captain, Dudley Jones as First Gravedigger, Job Stewart as Second Gravedigger, and Aubrey Morris as Osric. Also, English
Ambassadors, Priest, Gentleman, Lords, Ladies, Officers, Soldiers,
Sailors, Messengers and Attendants.

Marlowe Society recording of *Hamlet*. No credits listed. ©1960. London
OSA 1503.

Paul Scofield as Hamlet. Directed by Howard Sackler. Shakespeare Recording Society (SRS-M232).

Richard Burton as Hamlet. 1964. Directed by John Gielgud. Columbia Masterworks original Broadway cast album. Includes book with credits, photographs, biographies, and essays. Robert Burr as Bernardo, Michael Ebert as Francisco, Fortinbras, Barnard Hughes as Marcellus, Robert Milli as Horatio, Alfred Drake as Claudius, Philip Coolidge as Voltimand, Hugh Alexander as Cornelius, English Ambassador, Second Gravedigger, John Cullum as Laertes, Hume Cronyn as Polonius, Eileen Herlie as Gertrude, Linda Marsh as Ophelia, John Gielgud (voice only) as ghost, Dillon Evans as Reynaldo, Osric, Clement Fowler as Rosencrantz, William Redfield as Guildenstern, George Voskovec as Player King, John Hetherington as Player Prologue, Christopher Culkin as Player Queen, Geoff Garland as Lucianus, Michael Ebert as Fortinbras, Richard Sterne as a Gentleman, George Rose as First Gravedigger. Produced for records by Goddard Lieberson.

Kenneth Griffith as Hamlet. A BBC radio broadcast 18 September 1966. This has the same narrative links as the 1948 Gielgud radio production. Script examined at BBC archives.

Robert Vaughan as Hamlet: excerpts from the play (the soliloquies, nunnery, closet, and death scenes). MGM 4488. 1967. With music by jazz musician Buddy Collette.

Richard Chamberlain as Hamlet. 1970. Original cast album from TV production. RCA Red Seal Records. See moving-image listing for credits.

Ronald Pickup as Hamlet. BBC radio broadcast 31 October 1971. Produced by John Tydeman.

Appendix 6
Stage Credits

American Shakespeare Repertory 1984 *Hamlet,* directed by Janet Farrow with Douglas Overtoom as Hamlet, Timothy Flanagan as Claudius, Holly Booker as Ophelia and Gertrude, Anthony Rutledge as Polonius, John Noah Davis as Horatio, Jeffrey Logan as Laertes, John McDowell as Marcellus/First Player, Peter Lehrman as Bernardo/Osric.

American Shakespeare Theatre 1982 *Hamlet* directed by Peter Coe; settings and costumes by Davis Chapman; lighting by Marc B. Weiss; fights staged by B. H. Barry; music by Joe Griffiths. The American Shakespeare Theatre at Stratford, Connecticut, artistic director, Peter Coe. Dramatis Personae are divided into five groups: "The Royal Family of Denmark"; "From Wittenberg University" (Horatio, Rosencrantz and Guildenstern, and players); "The Lord Chamberlain's Family," including Osric, Polonius's servant (i.e., Reynaldo's part and Osric's); "The Military"; and "The Church." With Fred Gwynne as Claudius; Christopher Walken as Hamlet; Anne Baxter as Gertrude; Michael Allison as the Ghost and Player King; Stephen Lang as Horatio; Fritz Sperberg as Rosencrantz; Michael Guido as Guildenstern; Karen Trott as Player Queen; David Sabin as Prologue, Marcellus, and A Captain; Brian Rose as King Mime, Bernardo, and a Priest; Patrick Clear as Queen Mime and Fortinbras; Norman Allen as Lucianus and Second Gravedigger; Sophie Gilmartin as Harpist; Roy Dotrice as Polonius and First Gravedigger; Chris Sarandon as Laertes; Lisabeth Bartlett as Ophelia; Chet Carlin as Osric.

Boston Shakespeare Company 1981 *Hamlet* directed by Bill Cain; set designer Larry Sammons; costume designers Craig Sonnenberg and

Dru Minton Clark; lighting designer Marcus Dillard; fight master, Jerome Smith. The Boston Shakespeare Company production in repertory with *Rosencrantz and Guildenstern Are Dead,* artistic director Bill Cain. With David Fonteno as Claudius; Henry Woronicz as Hamlet; Richard Moses as Polonius; John Bower as Horatio; Sidney Atwood as Laertes; Kenneth Watt as Voltimand; Jack Clifford as Cornelius; Craig Calman as Rosencrantz; Mark S. Cartier as Guildenstern; William Betz as Osric; Michael Dorsey as Francisco, king's guard, and priest; William Hoverstein as king's guard; John Fionte as Marcellus and player; Jonathan Niles as Bernardo and player; Paul Santos as Reynaldo and player; Courtenay Bernard Vance as Player King; Andrew Sawler as player; Thomas Lyons as player and priest; Jack Clifford as Gravedigger; Kenneth Watt as A Captain; Sandra Shipley as Gertrude; Ursula Drabik as Ophelia; and Patrick English as Ghost.

Circle Rep 1979 *Hamlet* directed by Marshall W. Mason; sets by David Jenkins; costumes by Laura Crow; lights by Dennis Parichy; music by Norman L. Berman; duels staged by B. H. Barry; "Murder of Gonzago" staged by Geoff Schlaes. Circle Repertory, artistic director, Marshall W. Mason. With William M. Carr as Bernardo, Norwegian Captain and Sailor; Gary Berner as Francisco and Luciano [*sic*]; Timothy Shelton as Horatio; Robert Tenuta as Marcellus and Priest; Rob Thirkield as Ghost and Fortinbras; Douglass Watson as Claudius; Lindsey Ginter as Voltemand and English Ambassador; Michael Ayr as Laertes; Burke Pearson as Polonius; William Hurt as Hamlet; Beatrice Straight as Gertrude (28 Nov.–29 Dec.); Jacqueline Brookes as Gertrude (2 Jan.–3 Feb.); Lindsay Crouse as Ophelia; Charles Harper as Reynaldo; Roger Chapman as Rosencrantz, Ken Kliban as Guildenstern; Jack Davidson as Player King; Elizabeth Sturges as Player Queen; Bruce Gray as Osric; Jack Davidson as Gravedigger; Mollie Collison as Lady-in-Waiting; Greg Germann and Bruce McCarty as pages. Musicians: Frances Feldon, Greg Germann, Ron Leighty and Terry Pierce.

Classic Stage Company 1984 *Hamlet.* Christopher Martin, director/designer/text adaptor; Karen Sunde, associate director/dramaturg/text adaptor; Miriam Nieves, costume designer; Rick Butler, lighting designer; with Tom Spiller as first gravedigger, Thomas Lenz as second gravedigger, Noble Shropshire as Hamlet, John Camera as Claudius, Mary Eileen O'Donnell as Gertrude, Charles H. Patterson as ghost, Donn Youngstrom as Polonius, Gary Sloan as Laertes/fight director, Ginger Grace as Ophelia, Amy Warner as duenna.

Gielgud 1964 *Hamlet* directed by John Gielgud; designed by Ben Edwards; costumes by Jane Greenwood; lighting by Jean Rosenthal with Richard Burton as Hamlet; Hume Cronyn as Polonius; Alfred Drake as Claudius; Eileen Herlie as Gertrude; William Redfield as Guildenstern; George Rose as the First Gravedigger; George Voskovec as Player King; Linda Marsh as Ophelia; Frederick Young as Bernardo; Michael Ebert as Francisco and Fortinbras; Barnard Hughes as Marcellus and Priest; Robert Milli as Horatio; Hugh Alexander as Cornelius, Second Gravedigger, and English Ambassador; John Cullum as Laertes; John Gielgud as the voice of the Ghost; Dillon Evans as Reynaldo; Clement Fowler as Rosencrantz; John Hetherington as Player Prologue; Christopher Culkin as Player Queen; Geoff Garland as Lucianus; Michael Ebert as Fortinbras; Richard Sterne as A Gentleman; Alex Giannini as a Messenger; also, Claude Harz, Gerome Ragni, Linda Seff, and Carol Teitel.

McCarter 1982 *Hamlet* directed by Nagle Jackson; scenery by Daniel Boylen, costumes by Susan Rheaume; lighting by Richard Moorse. The McCarter Theatre Company, Princeton, artistic director Nagle Jackson. With Harry Hamlin as Hamlet; James S. Horton as Bernardo; Paul Donahoe as Francisco and Prologue; Darryl Croxton as Horatio; Francis P. Bilancio as Marcellus; Robin Chadwick as Ghost and Gravedigger; Neil Vipond as Claudius; Jill Tanner as Gertrude; Jay Doyle as Polonius; Gary Roberts as Laertes; Stacy Ray as Ophelia; Mark Kincaid as Osric; Greg Thorton as Rosencrantz, Gerald Lancaster as Guildenstern; Herb Foster as Player King; Penelope Reed as Player Queen; Jared Reed as Boy; Herbert McAnemy as Priest; Lesley Schisgall as Lady; Dale M. Ducko as Soldier.

Papp New York Shakespeare Festival 1975 *Hamlet* directed by Michael Rudman; setting by Santo Loquasto; costumes by Albert Wolsky; lighting by Martin Aronstein; fight sequences by Erick Fredrickson; percussion score by Herbert Harris; Danish anthem by Norman L. Berman. With Robert Burr as Claudius, Ghost; Ruby Dee as Gertrude; Sam Waterston as Hamlet; Larry Gates as Polonius, First Gravedigger; John Lithgow as Laertes, Player King; Andrea Marcovicci as Ophelia; Douglas Stender as Rosencrantz, Second Gravedigger; James Cahill as Horatio; James Gallery as Voltemand; John Heard as Guildenstern, Priest; Mark Metcalf as Marcellus; Richard Bresthoff as Francisco; Bruce McGill as Reynaldo; Franklin Seales as Fortinbras, Player Queen; Hannibal Penny Jr. as Captain; Vance Mizelle as Company Manager; Nancy Campbell as Apprentice Actor. At Delacorte Theater, Central Park.

Papp New York Shakespeare Festival 1982 *Hamlet* directed by Joseph

Papp; scenery by Robert Yodice; costumes by Theoni V. Aldredge; lighting by Ralph K. Holmes; music composed by Allen Shawn; fight sequences by B. H. Barry. A New York Shakespeare Festival production, at the Public Theater, Production by Joseph Papp. With Diane Venora as Hamlet; Bob Gunton as Claudius; Kathleen Widdoes as Gertrude; George Hall as Polonius and the Old Gravedigger; Robert Westenberg as Laertes; James Cromwell as Horatio; George Hamlin as the Ghost and Player King; Pippa Pearthree as Ophelia; Jamey Sheridan as Fortinbras and Bernardo; Stephen McNaughton as Francisco and Cornelius; Raphael Sbarge as Reynaldo, Player Queen, and Apprentice Gravedigger; J. T. Walsh as Marcellus, First Player/Lucianus, and English Ambassador; Ric Lavin as Voltemand and Priest; Rick Lieberman as Rosencrantz; Ralph Byers as Guildenstern; Brett Porter as Norwegian Captain; Jimmy Smits as Switzer and Messenger; Rocco Sisto as Osric; Annette Helde as Lady-in-Waiting and Player.

Bibliography

Alexander, Peter. *Hamlet Father and Son: The Lord Northcliffe Lectures, University College London, 1953*. Oxford: Clarendon Press, 1955.

Altman, Rick, ed. *Cinema/Sound*. Yale French Studies no. 60 (Spring 1980).

Auerbach, Erich. *Mimesis: The Representation of Reality in Western Literature*. Translated by Willard Trask. Garden City, N.Y.: Doubleday, 1953.

Babula, William. *Shakespeare in Production, 1935–1978*. New York: Garland, 1981.

Ball, Robert Hamilton. *Shakespeare on Silent Film: A Strange Eventful History*. London: George Allen and Unwin, 1968.

Barthes, Roland. *S/Z*. Translated by Richard Miller. New York: Hill and Wang, 1974.

Bazin, Andre. *What Is Cinema?* Edited and translated by Hugh Gray. 2 vols. Berkeley and Los Angeles: University of California Press, 1971.

Beckerman, Bernard. *Shakespeare at the Globe: 1599–1609*. New York: MacMillan, 1962.

———. *Dynamics of Drama: Theory and Method of Analysis*. New York: Drama Book Specialists, 1971.

———. "Sound Recordings of *Othello*." Modern Language Association Convention, 1983.

Berringer, Johannes H. "Rehearsing the Mousetrap: Robert Nelson's *Hamlet Act*." *Shakespeare on Film Newsletter* 9, no. 1 (December 1984): 1, 8.

Bevington, David. Introduction to *Twentieth Century Interpretations of Hamlet: A Collection of Critical Essays*. Edited by David Bevington. Englewood Cliffs, N.J.: Prentice-Hall, 1968.

Bloom, Harold. *The Anxiety of Influence: A Theory of Poetry*. London: Oxford University Press. 1973.

———. *A Map of Misreading*. London: Oxford University Press, 1975.

Brown, John Russell. *Free Shakespeare*. London: Heinemann, 1974.

Browne, E. Martin. "English Hamlets of the Twentieth Century." *Shakespeare Survey* 9 (1956): 16–23.

Brownlow, Kevin. "Josef Von Sternberg." In *The Parade's Gone By,* pp. 189–210. New York: Bonanza Books, 1968.

Buell, William Ackerman. *The Hamlets of the Theater.* New York: Astor-Honor, 1968.

Calderwood, James L. *To Be and Not to Be: Negation and Metadrama in Hamlet.* New York: Columbia University Press, 1983.

Carthew, Anthony. " 'Hamlet' Revisited: Elsinore Castle Gives the B.B.C. an Authentic Setting for Tragedy." *New York Times* 13 October 1963, 2:21.

Cary, Cecile Williamson, and Henry S. Limouze, ed. *Shakespeare and the Arts: A Collection of Essays from the Ohio Shakespeare Conference, 1981 Wright State University, Dayton, Ohio.* Washington: University Press of America, 1982.

Chambers, E. K. *William Shakespeare.* 2 vols. Oxford: Clarendon Press, 1930.

Charney, Maurice. *Style in Hamlet.* Princeton: Princeton University Press, 1969.

———. "*Hamlet* without Words." In *Shakespeare's "More Than Words Can Witness": Essays on Visual and Nonverbal Enactment in the Plays,* edited by Sidney Homan, pp. 23–42. Lewisburg: Bucknell University Press, 1980.

Clarke, Charles W. Manuscript description (108 pages) of Edwin Booth's performances of *Hamlet* in 1870. Shattuck, number 86.

Clay, James H. and Daniel Krempel. *The Theatrical Image.* New York: McGraw Hill, 1967.

Cottrell, John. *Laurence Olivier.* Englewood Cliffs, N.J.: Prentice-Hall, 1975.

Cross, Brenda, ed. *The Film Hamlet: A Record of Its Production.* London: The Saturn Press, 1948.

Crowther, Bosley. "The Screen: Stage 'Hamlet' with Richard Burton," *New York Times,* 24 September 1964, 46.

Darnton, Charles. *New York World,* 3 October 1913. Lincoln Center Theatre Library Scrapbook, 88.

Dash, Irene, G. *Wooing, Wedding, and Power: Women in Shakespeare's Plays.* New York: Columbia University Press, 1981.

Davison, Peter. *Hamlet: Text and Performance.* Atlantic Highlands, N.J.: Humanities Press, 1983.

Dent, Alan, ed. *Hamlet: The Film and the Play.* London: World Film, 1948.

———. "Hamlets—Modern and Ancient." in *The Film Hamlet,* edited by Brenda Cross, pp. 65–71.

———. "The World of Cinema: Speculations and Regrets." *London News,* 14 May 1960.

Dessen, Alan. Talk at the Ohio Shakespeare Conference, 1980.

Dillon, Carmen. "Building the Sets." In Cross, 43–48.

Duffy, Robert A. "Gade, Olivier, Richardson: Visual Strategy in *Hamlet* Adaptation." *Literature/Film Quarterly* 4, no. 2 (1976): 141–52.

Eissler, K. R. *Discourse on Hamlet and* Hamlet: *A Psychoanalytic Inquiry.* New York: International Universities Press, 1971.

Epes, Winthrop Sargeant. "What Is Photoplay?" *The Moving Picture World,* 21 July 1917, 369–70.

[Evans *Hamlet*]. "Alas, Poor Stagehand, We Saw Him Well." *New York Journal American,* 27 April 1953. Lincoln Center Performing Arts Library clipping file.

———. Jack Gould. "Television in Review." *New York Times,* 27 April 1953, 29.

———. Philip Hamburger. "The Dane." *The New Yorker,* 9 May 1953, 67–68.

———. *Saturday Review,* 16 May 1953, 33.

Field, Kate. "Fechter as Hamlet." *The Atlantic Monthly* 26 (November 1870): 558–70.

Forbes Robertson, Sir Johnston. *A Player under Three Reigns.* Boston: Little Brown, 1925.

[Forbes Robertson *Hamlet*]. *"Hamlet" by William Shakespeare: The Story of the Play Concisely Told, with 55 illustrations taken from the cinematograph film showing Sir J. Forbes-Robertson and Miss Gertrude Elliott and their company.* London: Stanley Paul, 1913. [A 64-page *Cinema Book.*]

———. "Great Plays in the 'Movies.'" *The Literary Digest,* 2 August 1913, 172–73.

———. Lincoln Center Theater Collection scrapbooks, clipping files, etc.

———. "Forbes Robertson on Two Continents." Illustrated. *The Literary Digest,* 18 October 1913, 683.

———. *The Moving Picture World,* 3 July 1915, 119; 10 July 1915, 173.

———. Hanford C. Judson. "Hamlet, with Forbes Robertson: the Knickerbocker Film Company Offers in Three Reels a Great Play with a Great Star and a Great Cast Supporting Him." Illustrated. *The Moving Picture World,* 10 July 1915, 317–18.

France, Anna Kay. "Boris Pasternak's Interpretation of *Hamlet.*" *Russian Literature Triquarterly* 7 (1974): 201–26.

Gardner, Paul. "The Bard's Play Is the Thing." *New York Times,* 15 November 1964, 2:17.

Geduld, Harry M. *Filmguide to Henry V.* Bloomington: Indiana University Press, 1973.

A Genuine Narrative of the Life and Theatrical Transactions of Mr. John Henderson. . . . Extra Illustrated. London: T. Evans, 1777.

[Gielgud's production of *Hamlet* with Richard Burton; text accompanying the audio recording] *Hamlet 1964.* New York: Dunetz & Lovett, 1964.

Goffman, Erving. *Frame Analysis: An Essay on the Organization of Experience.* Cambridge: Harvard University Press, 1974.

Gould. *See* Evans.

Granville-Barker, Harley. *Prefaces to Shakespeare.* 2 vols. Princeton: Princeton University Press, 1946, 1947.

Grebanier, Bernard. *The Heart of Hamlet: The Play Shakespeare Wrote, with the Text of the Play.* New York: Crowell, 1960.

Griffin, Alice Venesky. "Shakespeare through the Camera's Eye—*Julius Caesar* in Motion Pictures; *Hamlet* and *Othello* on Television." *Shakespeare Quarterly* 4(1953): 331–36.

Gross, Sheryl W. "Poetic Realism in Olivier's *Hamlet.*" *Hamlet Studies* 2, no. 2 (1980): 62–68.

Halio, Jay. "Zeffirelli's *Romeo and Juliet:* The Camera versus the Text." *Shakespeare on Film 3: Literature/Film Quarterly* 5, no. 4 (Fall 1977): 322–25.

Halstead. *See under* texts.

Hamburger. *See* Evans.

Hannan, Tom. "Costumes." In *Hamlet 1964: Notes on the Burton Hamlet.* New York: Dunetz and Lovett, 1964.

Hartman, Geoffrey. "Connoisseurs of Chaos." Lecture at the Andiron Club, New York City, 18 September 1981.

Hartwig, Joan. *Shakespeare's Analogical Scene: Parody as Structural Syntax.* Lincoln and London: University of Nebraska Press, 1984.

Hawkes, Terence. *Shakespeare's Talking Animals.* London: Arnolde, 1973.

———. *"Telmah."* Transcript of a paper presented at MLA in 1982, 32pp. Published in *Shakespeare and the Question of Theory,* edited by Geoffrey Hartman and Patricia Parker. London: Methuen, 1985. Also in *That Shakespeherian Rag,* a collection of Hawkes's works. London: Methuen, 1986.

Hepworth, Cecil. *Came the Dawn: Memories of a Film Pioneer.* Illustrated. London: Phoenix House, 1951.

Hirsch, Foster. *Laurence Olivier.* Boston: Twayne, 1979.

Hirsh, James E. *The Structure of Shakespearean Scenes.* New Haven and London: Yale University Press, 1981.

Homan, Sidney, with Neil Feineman. "The Filmed Shakespeare: From Verbal to Visual." In *Shakespeare's "More Than Words Can Witness": Essays on Visual and Nonverbal Enactment in the Plays,* edited by Sidney Homan, pp. 207–36. Lewisburg: Bucknell University Press, 1980.

Horobetz, Lynn K. "The Washington Shakespeare Summer Festival, 1967." *Shakespeare Quarterly* 18 (1967): 409–10.

Jenkins, Elizabeth. *Elizabeth the Great.* New York: Coward McCann, 1959.

Jenkins, Harold, ed. *Hamlet.* The Arden Edition of the Works of William Shakespeare. London: Methuen, 1981.

Jones, Ernest. *Hamlet and Oedipus.* New York: W. W. Norton, 1949.

Jorgens, Jack J. *Shakespeare on Film.* Bloomington: Indiana University Press, 1977.

Kael, Pauline. "Raising Kane." In *The Citizen Kane Book.* Boston: Little, Brown, 1971.

Kelly, F[rancis] M[ichael]. *Shakespearean Costume for Stage and Screen.*

Revised by Alan Mansfield. London: Adam & Charles Black, 1970.

Kliman, Bernice W. "'An Unseen Interpreter': Interview with George Schaefer." *Film Criticism* 7, no. 3 (Spring 1983): 29–37.

———. "A Palimpsest for Olivier's *Hamlet.*" *Comparative Drama* 17, no. 3 (Fall 1983): 243–53.

———. "Joseph Papp Presents *Hamlet.*" *Hamlet Studies* 6 (1984): 105–10.

———. "Opportunities Seized and Occasions Created: The Boston Shakespeare Company *Hamlet.*" *The Upstart Crow* 6 (1986): 94–104.

Knight, G. Wilson. *Shakespearean Production: With Especial Reference to the Tragedies.* Washington, D.C.: University Press of America, 1981.

Kott, Jan. *Shakespeare Our Contemporary.* Translated by Boleslaw-Taborski. Garden City, N.Y.: Doubleday, 1964.

———. [On Kozintsev's *Hamlet*]. *The Literary Review* 22, no. 4 (1979): 385–90.

Kozintsev, Grigori. *Shakespeare: Time and Conscience.* Translated by Joyce Vining. New York: Hill and Wang, 1966.

Krakauer, Siegfried. *A Theory of Film: The Redemption of Physical Reality.* London: Oxford University Press, 1960.

Lambert, J. W. "Plays in Performance: London." *DRAMA: The Quarterly Theatre Review* (Summer 1969): 18–20.

Lawrence, W. J. "'Hamlet' as Shakespeare Staged It." In *Pre-Restoration Stage Studies,* pp. 102–21. New York: Benjamin Blom, 1927.

Levin, Richard. *New Readings vs. Old Plays: Recent Trends in the Reinterpretation of English Renaissance Drama.* Chicago: University of Chicago Press, 1979.

Litton, Glenn. "Diseased Beauty in Richardson's *Hamlet.*" *Literature/Film Quarterly* 4, no. 2 (Spring 1976): 108–22.

Low, Rachel. *The History of British Film.* Vol. 2: 1906–1914. 1948. Reprint. New York: Bowker, 1973.

———. *The History of the British Film.* Vol. 3: 1914–1918. 1949. Reprint. New York: Bowker, 1973.

———. *The History of the British Film.* Vol. 4: 1918–1929. New York: Bowker, 1971.

[LUX]. "Comments on the Films." *The Moving Picture World,* 12 February 1910, 217; 19 February 1910, 245.

Mac Donald, George. *The Tragedy of Hamlet, Prince of Denmarke, a Study in the Text of the Folio of 1623.* Introduction by Sir Johnston Forbes Robertson. 1885. Reprint. 1924.

Mack, Maynard. "The World of Hamlet." *Yale Review* 41 (1952): 502–23.

Maher, Mary Z. "Hamlet's BBC Soliloquies." *Shakespeare Quarterly* 36 (Winter 1985): 417–26.

Mander, Raymond, and Joe Mitchenson, compilers. *Hamlet through the Ages: A Pictorial Record from 1709.* 2d ed. rev. Edited by Herbert Marshall. Freeport, N.Y.: Books for Libraries Press, 1971.

Manvell, Roger. *Shakespeare and the Film.* New York: Praeger, 1971.

Mast, Gerald. *A Short History of the Movies.* New York: Pegasus, 1971.

Mills, John A. *Hamlet on Stage: The Great Tradition.* Contributions in Drama and Theatre Studies, no. 15. Westport, Conn.: Greenwood Press, 1985.

Mullin, Michael. "Tony Richardson's *Hamlet:* Script and Screen." *Literature/Film Quarterly* 4 (1976): 123–33.

Nuttall, A. D. *A New Mimesis: Shakespeare and the Representation of Reality.* London: Methuen, 1983.

Olivier, Laurence. *Confessions of an Actor: An Autobiography.* New York: Simon and Schuster, 1982.

[OED]. *The Compact Edition of the Oxford English Dictionary: Complete Text Reproduced Micrographically.* 2 vols. Glasgow: Oxford University Press, 1971.

Panofsky, Erwin. "Style and Medium in Motion Pictures." Revised version of 1934 essay. Reprinted in *Film Theory and Criticism: Introductory Readings,* edited by Gerald Mast and Marshall Cohen, pp. 151–69. New York and London: Oxford University Press, 1974.

Petric, Vlada. "Barthes versus Cinema." *Sight and Sound,* Summer 1983, 205–7.

[Plummer's *Hamlet*]. "Hamlet at Elsinore." *Newsweek,* 14 October 1963, 78.

———. John Hyde Preston. "Hamlet's Castle." *Holiday,* January 1964, 24.

———. "The Timeless Tragedy of Prince Hamlet." In "Shakespeare at 400." *Life,* 24 April 1964, 78B–81.

Retzsch, Moritz. Drawings for *Hamlet.* University of Pennsylvania Library. Furness Collection C94.13.

Ripley, John. "Dialogic Performance Cues in *Coriolanus.*" Seminar paper, Shakespeare Association of America Conference. 1984.

Rooker, Henry Grady. *The Stage History of the Portrayal of Shakespeare's Character, Hamlet.* 35pp. Nashville, Tenn.: George Peabody College for Teachers, 1932.

Rosenberg, Marvin. "Shakespeare on TV: An Optimistic Survey." *Film Quarterly* 9 (1954): 166–74.

———. "The Stage and Hamlet." *Hamlet Studies* 1, no. 1 (1979): 51–53.

Rossi, Alfred. *Minneapolis Rehearsals: Tyrone Guthrie Directs Hamlet.* Berkeley and Los Angeles: University of California Press, 1970.

[Rothwell, Kenneth S.] "St Georges *Romeo and Juliet:* A Preview at the Folger Library," *Shakespeare on Film Newsletter* 1, no. 2 (April 1977): 1, 5.

Rothwell, Kenneth S. *A Mirror for Shakespeare: A Self-Study Guide for the Plays.* Burlington, Vt.: IDC Publications, 1980.

Rowe, Eleanor. *Hamlet: A Window on Russia.* New York: New York University Press, 1976.

Sadoul, Georges. *British Creators of Film Technique.* 10pp. London: The British Film Institute, 1948.

———. *Histoire générale Du Cinéma: Le Cinéma Devient un Art (1909–1920).* Vol. 1, *L'Avant-Guerre.* Illustrated. Paris: Denoël, 1951.

Shattuck, Charles H. *The Hamlet of Edwin Booth.* Urbana, Ill.: University of Illinois Press, 1960.

———. *The Shakespeare Promptbooks: A Descriptive Catalogue.* Urbana, Ill.: University of Illinois Press, 1965.

Shaw, George Bernard. "Hamlet." *Saturday Review,* 2 October 1897, 364–65; reprinted in Shaw 1961, 85–92.

———. "Hamlet Revisited." *Saturday Review,* 18 December 1897, 711–12; reprinted with omissions in Shaw 1961, 92–95.

———. *Shaw on Shakespeare: An Anthology of Bernard Shaw's Writings on the Plays and Productions of Shakespeare.* Edited by Edwin Wilson. New York: Dutton, 1961.

Silber, Joan Ellyn Frager. "Cinematic Techniques and Interpretations in Film and Television Adaptations of Shakespeare's 'Hamlet.'" A Ph.D. diss., University of Michigan, 1973.

Silviria, Dale. *Laurence Olivier and the Art of Film Making.* Rutherford, N.J.: Fairleigh Dickinson University Press, 1985.

Simmonds, W. G., illustrator. *Shakespeare's Tragedy of Hamlet.* London: Hodden and Stoughton, [1910].

Simmons, Jean. "An Exacting Role." In Cross, 55–56.

Slater, Ann Pasternak. *Shakespeare the Director.* Brighton: John Spiers, 1982.

Sprague, Arthur Colby. *Shakespeare and the Actors: The Stage Business in His Plays (1660–1905).* New York: Russell & Russell, 1963. On *Hamlet,* 127–84.

Stephens, John. *Essayes and Characters, Ironicall, and Instructive.* London, 1615. Reprinted in James O. Halliwell, ed., *Books of Characters, illustrating the Habits and Manners of Englishmen from the Reign of James I to the Restoration.* London: Adelard, 18——.

Stoll, E. E. *Hamlet: An Historical and Comparative Study.* New York: Gordian Press, 1968.

Stoppard, Tom. *Dogg's Hamlet, Cahoot's Macbeth.* London: Inter-Action Imprint, 1979.

[Strunk, Will: his year in Hollywood]. "An Epilogue to *Romeo.*" *New York Times,* 19 April 1936, 9:4.

Styan, J. L. *Shakespeare's Stagecraft.* Cambridge: Cambridge University Press, 1967.

———. *The Shakespeare Revolution: Criticism and Performance in the Twentieth Century.* Cambridge: Cambridge University Press, 1977.

———. *Modern Drama in Theory and Practice.* Vol. 2, *Symbolism, Surrealism and the Absurd.* Cambridge: Cambridge University Press, 1981.

Talbot, Frederick A. *Conquests of Science. Moving Pictures: How They Are Made and Work.* Illustrated. 1912. Reprint. The Literature of Cinema Reprint Series. Salem, N.H.: Ayer Co., 1970.

Taylor, John Russell. "Shakespeare in Film, Radio, and Television." In *Shakespeare: A Celebration, 1564–1964,* edited by T. J. B. Spencer. Baltimore: Penguin, 1964.

Teague, Frances. "Hamlet in the Thirties." *Theatre Survey* 26 (1985): 63–79.

Trewin, J. C. *Shakespeare on the English Stage, 1900–1964.* London: Borne and Rockcliff, 1964.

————. "Shakespeare in Britain: *Hamlet.*" *Shakespeare Quarterly* 29 (1978): 219–20.

TV Guide: The First 25 Years. Edited by Jay S. Harris, in association with the editors of *TV Guide* magazine. New York: Simon & Schuster, 1978.

Tynan, Kenneth. "New Vics for Old." *The New Yorker,* 27 December 1958, 52.

————. "Laurence Olivier." In *Great Acting,* edited by Hal Burton. New York: Bonanza Books, 1967.

Urkowitz, Steven. "*Hamlet* Revisions." Folger Shakespeare Institute, 1982.

Van Dam. *See under* texts.

Variorum. See under texts, Furness.

Vining, Edward P. *The Mystery of Hamlet: An Attempt to Solve an Old Problem.* Philadelphia: Lippincott, 1881.

Wells, Stanley. "The Academics and the Theatre." In *The Triple Bond: Plays, Mainly Shakespearean, in Performance,* edited by Joseph G. Price. University Park, Pa.: The Pennsylvania State University Press, 1975.

Wilders, John. Interview with author at Modern Language Association Meeting, December 1978. Reported in *Shakespeare on Film Newsletter* 4, no. 1 (December 1979): 3, 9.

Wilds, Lillian. "On Film: Maximilian Schell's Most Royal *Hamlet.*" *Literature/Film Quarterly* 4 (1976): 134–40.

Wilson, John Dover. *What Happens in Hamlet.* 1935. Reprint. Cambridge: Cambridge University Press, 1964.

Woods, Frank E. "Editing a Motion Picture." *The Moving Picture World,* 21 July 1917, 371–72.

Hamlet Texts

[BBC Text]. *The Shakespeare Plays: Hamlet.* Literary Consultant, John Wilders. The text of the *Works of Shakespeare,* edited by Peter Alexander. New York: Mayflower Books, 1980.

Bell's Edition. *Hamlet, by Will. Shakspere: Printed Complete from the Text of Sam. Johnson and Geo. Steevens, and revised from the last Editions.* Illustrated. London: Cawthorn, 1806.

Booth-Winter edition of *Hamlet,* 1879. Shattuck, number 104, at the University of Pennsylvania, Furness Collection: C59Sh1HP.

Craig, Hardin, and David Bevington, ed. *The Complete Works of Shakespeare.* Rev. ed. Glenview, Ill.: Scott, Foresman, 1973.

Dent, Alan, ed. *Hamlet, the Film and the Play* [complete text with cuts in Olivier's version marked in red]. 1948.

Furness, Horace Howard, ed. *A New Variorum Edition of Shakespeare: Hamlet.* 2 vols. 1877. Reprint. New York: American Scholar, 1965.

Halstead, William P. *Shakespeare As Spoken: A Collation of 5000 Acting Editions and Promptbooks of Shakespeare,* vol 11. Ann Arbor, MI: Published for the American Theatre Association by Univ. Microfilms International, 1977.

Hamlet, a Television Script. Adapted by Michael Benthall and Ralph Nelson for presentation on the CBS Television Network by the Old Vic Company on 24 February 1959 at 9:30 P.M. EST. N.p.: n.p., n.d. Lib. Cong. #PR2807 .A2842.

Hamlet, a Tragedy by William Shakespeare. E. H. Sothern Acting Version. Illustrated. New York: McClure, Philips, 1901.

Hamlet by William Shakespeare, as Arranged for the Stage by Forbes Robertson and Presented at the Lyceum Theatre on Saturday, September 11, 1897, with Illustrations by Hawes Craven. London: The Nassau Press, 1897.

Hamlet, Second Quarto 1604–5. Shakespeare Quartos in Collotype Facsimile, no. 4. London: The Shakespeare Association; Sidgwick and Jackson, 1940.

Hoy, Cyrus, ed. *William Shakespeare, Hamlet.* A Norton Critical Edition. New York: W. W. Norton, 1963.

Jenkins, Harold, ed. *Hamlet.* The Arden Edition of the Works of William Shakespeare. London: Methuen, 1981.

Kemble edition, 1806. Shattuck number 16. "With George Joseph Bell's commentaries on various stage performances, including notes on both the Keans in *Hamlet.*"

Knight's Pictorial Shakespeare: Hamlet. People's Edition. London: Virtue, n.d.

Maurice Evans' GI Production of Hamlet by William Shakespeare: Acting Edition, with a Preface by Maurice Evans. Garden City, N.Y.: Doubleday, 1947.

Oxberry's Edition. *Hamlet, a Tragedy by William Shakespeare. The only edition which is faithfully marked with the stage business, and stage directions, as it is performed at the Theatre Royal.* London: Simpkin and Marshall, et al., 1818. With extra manuscript leaves bound in and commentary in ink. At the Folger Library: PR2807 1818 Sh Col.

The Riverside Shakespeare. Edited by G. Blakemore Evans, et al. Boston: Houghton Mifflin, 1974.

Rowe, Nicholas. *The Works of Mr. William Shakespear.* Revised and Corrected by N[icholas] Rowe. Volume 5. 1709.

Shakespeare's Hamlet: The First Quarto 1603. Reproduced in facsimile from the copy in the Henry E. Huntington Library. Cambridge Mass.: Harvard University Press, 1931.

Shakespeare's Tragedy of Hamlet, Illustrated by W. G. Simmonds. London: Hodden and Stoughton, [1910].

Staunton, Howard, ed. *The Globe Illustrated Shakespeare.* Illustrations by Sir John Gilbert. 1864. Reprint. New York: Greenwich House (Crown), 1979.

Van Dam, B. A. P. *The Text of Shakespeare's Hamlet.* London: John Lane, 1924.

Vietor, Wilhelm, ed. *Hamlet: Parallel Texts of the First and Second Quartos and the First Folio.* Marburg: N. G. Elwertsche, 1891.

William Shakespeare: Hamlet, with Sixteen Lithographs by Eugene Delacroix.

London: Paddington Press, 1976.

William Shakespeare: Hamlet, The Text of the First Folio 1923. From the British Museum Folio shelf-mark C39.1.12. Menston, England: The Scolar Press, 1969.

William Shakespeare. *The Tragedy of Hamlet, Prince of Denmark.* With illustrations by Howard Chandler Christy. New York: Barse & Hopkins, 1897.

Index